Economy of Force

Retrieving the older but surprisingly neglected language of household governance, *Economy of Force* offers a radical new account of the historical rise of the social realm and distinctly social theory as modern forms of *oikonomikos* – the art and science of household rule. The techniques and domestic ideologies of household administration are highly portable and play a remarkably central role in international and imperial relations. In two late-colonial British 'emergencies' in Malaya and Kenya, and US counterinsurgencies in Vietnam, Afghanistan and Iraq, armed social work was the continuation of *oikonomia* – not politics – by other means. This is a provocative new history of counterinsurgency with major implications for social, political and international theory. Historically rich and theoretically innovative, this book will interest scholars and students across the humanities and social sciences, especially politics and international relations, history of social and political thought, history of war, social theory and sociology.

PATRICIA OWENS is Reader in International Relations at the University of Sussex. She is author of *Between War and Politics: International Relations and the Thought of Hannah Arendt* (2007) and co-edits the *European Journal of International Relations*. She has held research fellowships at Harvard, Princeton, UC-Berkeley, USC and Oxford.

CAMBRIDGE STUDIES IN INTERNATIONAL RELATIONS: 139

Economy of Force

Cambridge Studies in International Relations is a joint initiative of Cambridge University Press and the British International Studies Association (BISA). The series aims to publish the best new scholarship in international studies, irrespective of subject matter, methodological approach or theoretical perspective. The series seeks to bring the latest theoretical work in International Relations to bear on the most important problems and issues in global politics.

CAMBRIDGE STUDIES IN INTERNATIONAL RELATIONS

138 Ronald R. Krebs
Narrative and the making of US national security

137 Andrew Phillips and J. C. Sharman
International order in diversity
War, trade and rule in the Indian Ocean

136 Ole Jacob Sending, Vincent Pouliot and Iver B. Neumann
Diplomacy and the making of world politics

135 Barry Buzan and George Lawson
The global transformation
History, modernity and the making of international relations

134 Heather Elko McKibben
State strategies in international bargaining
Play by the rules or change them?

133 Janina Dill
Legitimate targets?
Social construction, international law, and US bombing

132 Nuno P. Monteiro
Theory of unipolar politics

131 Jonathan D. Caverley
Democratic militarism
Voting, wealth, and war

130 David Jason Karp
Responsibility for human rights
Transnational corporations in imperfect states

129 Friedrich Kratochwil
The status of law in world society
Meditations on the role and rule of law

128 Michael G. Findley, Daniel L. Nielson and J. C. Sharman
Global shell games
Experiments in transnational relations, crime, and terrorism

Series list continues after index

Economy of Force

Counterinsurgency and the Historical Rise of the Social

PATRICIA OWENS

CAMBRIDGE
UNIVERSITY PRESS

CAMBRIDGE
UNIVERSITY PRESS

University Printing House, Cambridge CB2 8BS, United Kingdom

Cambridge University Press is part of the University of Cambridge.

It furthers the University's mission by disseminating knowledge in the pursuit of education, learning and research at the highest international levels of excellence.

www.cambridge.org
Information on this title: www.cambridge.org/9781107545687

First published 2015
First paperback edition 2016

A catalogue record for this publication is available from the British Library

Library of Congress Cataloguing in Publication data
Owens, Patricia, 1975–
Economy of force : counterinsurgency and the historical rise of the social / Patricia Owens.
pages cm. – (Cambridge studies in international relations)
Includes bibliographical references and index.
ISBN 978-1-107-12194-2 (hardback)
1. Political sociology. 2. Households–Political aspects.
3. Counterinsurgency–Social aspects. 4. International relations.
I. Title.
JA76.085 2015
303.6′6–dc23 2015014243

ISBN 978-1-107-12194-2 Hardback
ISBN 978-1-107-54568-7 Paperback

For Bille

When it grew too hot for dreamless dozing, I picked up my tangle again, and went on ravelling it out, considering now the whole house of war in its structural aspect, which was strategy, in its arrangements, which were tactics, and in the sentiment of its inhabitants, which was psychology; for my personal duty was command, and the commander, like the master architect, was responsible for all.

T. E. Lawrence (1922/1991: 181)

Contents

Acknowledgements

Numerous individuals and institutions have supported the writing of this book. The first full draft was written as a Fellow of the Radcliffe Institute for Advanced Study at Harvard University, a very special place. I'm grateful to Dean Lizabeth Cohen and Associate Dean Judy Vichniac (our Radcliffe Major General), Rebecca Haley and Sharon Lim-Hing for creating utopia. Kim Hutchings, Andy Hurrell, Steve Smith, Justin Rosenberg and Benno Teschke helped to get me there. My Radcliffe Research Partners – Eliza Pan, Wendy Chen and Tyler Cusick – were diligent assistants. The project gained immeasurably from conversations with numerous fellow Fellows, especially David Engerman, Doug Rogers, Caroline Elkins, Katherine Ibbett, Tsitsi Jaji, Glenn Cohen, Jane Rhodes, Renée Poznanski, Ana Mariella Bacigalupo and Kristin Monroe. In the wider Harvard and Boston community, I'm indebted to the kindness and hospitality of David Armitage, Serena Parekh McGushin and James Bernauer.

I feared that returning to British higher education after the luxuries of the private American Ivy League might have negatively affected morale. I shouldn't have worried. The Department of International Relations at the University of Sussex is one of the most intellectually stimulating and collegial places I can imagine, providing a wonderful home for the completion of the book. For comments on the entire manuscript, I am grateful to my colleagues Paul Kirby and Anna Stavrianakis. For typically incisive questions and comments on smaller portions, I thank my colleagues Justin Rosenberg, Jan Selby, Lara Coleman, Kamran Matin, David Karp, Stefan Elbe, Louiza Odysseos, Beate Jahn, Zdenek Kavan and Earl Gammon. Other scholars and friends have generously given their time to read and comment on earlier drafts. I'm especially indebted to Michael Jago, Keith Stanski, Dustin Ells Howes and Helen Kinsella for comments on an entire draft. Tarak Barkawi, Huw Bennett, Catia Confortini, Andrew Davenport, Toby Dodge, Jean-François Drolet, Inanna Hamati-Ataya,

Lene Hansen, Lee Jones, Byran Mabee, Elspeth van Veeren and Ann Tickner commented on individual chapters or responded generously to requests for advice.

Some of the earliest ideas for the project were tried out while a Visiting Professor in the Department of Political Science at the University of California, Los Angeles, and while on sabbatical from the School of Politics and International Relations at Queen Mary, University of London, in the spring of 2010. I'm appreciative of Kirstie McClure, Joshua Foa Dienstag and Beltrán Undarraga at UCLA for their critical comments, Kirstie and Joshua for their hospitality, and Dana Villa and Ray Kiely for helping make the visit possible. I first started thinking about counterinsurgency at the Leverhulme Programme on the Changing Character of War at Oxford University, including during the darkest days of the Iraq occupation. I remain grateful to former colleagues and students at Oxford, above all Hew Strachan and Henry Shue, for my first real interdisciplinary experience concretely grounded in the study of war.

Some of the arguments in the book were first presented at various professional conferences and invited talks. I'm grateful for invitations to present, and questions/comments from discussants and participants at the International Studies Association Annual Conventions in San Francisco and Montreal; the Centre for Research in the Arts, Social Sciences and Humanities at the University of Cambridge; the School of Humanities at the University of Southampton; the Radcliffe Institute for Advanced Study at Harvard University; the Department of Political Science at the University of California, Los Angeles; the Center for Christian-Jewish Learning at Boston College; the School of Fine Arts at the University of Leeds; the Department of Humanities and Social Sciences at the Indian Institute of Technology; the Department of International Politics, Aberystwyth University; the Department of International Relations at the London School of Economics; the Department of War Studies at Kings College London; the School of Social Sciences at City University, London; the Department of Politics and International Relations at the University of Westminster; the School of Politics and International Relations at Queen Mary, University of London; and, of course, the Department of International Relations at Sussex University.

I am also grateful to John Haslam and Carrie Parkinson at Cambridge University Press, the series editors, Nicholas Wheeler and Christian Reus-Smith, and the anonymous reviewers of the manuscript.

A few paragraphs of the material are reprinted from Owens (2013), 'From Bismarck to Petraeus: The Question of the Social and the Social Question in Counterinsurgency', *European Journal of International Relations*, 19(1): 135–157.

1 *Introduction:* oikonomia *in the use of force*

> That each should in his house abide
> Therefore was the world so wide
> Thou shalt make thy house
> The temple of a nation's vows
>
> Ralph Waldo Emerson, 'Life' (fragment)

What does it mean to describe a relationship between people or form of rule as 'domestic'? In 1946, Hans J. Morgenthau claimed that debate regarding 'the application of domestic legal experience to international law is really the main stock and trade of modern international thought' (1946/1974: 113). To date, he argued, most international theories had been based on drawing analogies between the character of political and legal relations among individuals in the domestic sphere within the state and foreign relations among states. Perhaps the most controversial but influential analogy of this type is that international relations is similar to Thomas Hobbes' (1651/1968) state of nature where individuals live in constant fear for their survival. The validity of the domestic analogy hinges on whether and to what extent concepts used to theorise relations internal to a state can be applied to relations between them. However, of the numerous criticisms of the domestic analogy, such as the inherently weak reasoning of analogical thought, none of them centres on the meaning of 'domestic'. In the main stock and trade of international thought there is silence regarding the conceptual and political history of the dominant side of the analogy. If international theory depends on some form of distinction between domestic and foreign, then surely more must be said regarding *domesticity* itself. What is its meaning, its origins, its ontology?

Consider the etymology. The term derives from the Latin *domestic-us*, from *domus*, meaning house. The first recorded English usage from 1521 similarly indicates that domestic is to be of or in a household, an 'inmate of a house'. On the surface of things, perhaps this is obvious.

Etymology suggests that domestic, home and household are conjoined and this is reflected in everyday discourse (Rybczynski, 1986). Leaders talk of protecting the motherland or fatherland, of securing the homeland, of the problem of home-grown terrorism; distinctions are drawn between zones of war and the home front. That there is such a thing as 'domestic space' is fundamental to the enterprise of international studies as the study of relations between domesticated spaces. The distinction between domestic and foreign usually denotes a frontier, a boundary, which limits movement and influence. The earliest, clearest use of domestic in this sense is by Dutch jurist Hugo Grotius in 1665.[1] But merely pointing out that home is the dominant metaphor for the nation-state is a rather superficial level of analysis, albeit a politically powerful discourse. Like most if not all 'security' talk, analysis of home largely operates at the descriptive level, reproducing terminology while not penetrating very far into the basis of domesticity itself. As others have argued, 'house and home can be used as metaphors for almost anything one can imagine – a fact that points toward the all-pervading nature of the term and the importance of unravelling its multiple meanings in order to understand the past' (Barile and Brandon, 2004: 1–2). In fact, underlying the very idea of domestic politics is a more fundamental meaning of household space, from *oikos*, which is ancient Greek rather than Latin in origin. The more expansive concept of *oikos* captures what is really at stake for political and international thought in domesticity: its rootedness in household governance. International theory's focus on the 'domestic analogy' has obscured the theoretical and historical significance of this more fundamental form of household rule.

Household forms are historically and geographically variable. In ancient Greece, household governance, *oikonomia*, meant a form of rulership over those who resided within the household and, above all, was related to the fundamental human activity of managing basic life needs (Aristotle, 1962; Xenophon, 1923). Life processes are closely related to the biological and labouring activities of the human body. They are necessary, cyclical, and historically their administration has involved violent subordination in accordance with what has usually been conceived as natural hierarchies based on gender, age and degree

[1] 'That the contentions growing among Priests should be decided by Domestique Judges, and not at Rome' (Grotius, 1665: 859).

of civilisation/servility. Those living in the household were imagined to belong to and be of the household. In turn, the head of the household who managed its affairs was distinct from the household and its objects. The notion of a 'head' of a household is an adaptation of the Latin *paterfamiliās*, who in Roman law possessed absolute legal authority over members of the household. This rule may be more or less openly despotic – despot meaning 'master of the house' – but the *paterfamiliās* nonetheless had obligations towards the diversity of household members: women, slaves, children and animals. In fact, '*in order* to discharge these very duties,' writes Dubber, 'the householder enjoyed widespread authority to enforce submission and fidelity in return' (2005: 19, emphasis in original). This is significant for two reasons. First, even when despotic household rule was absolute in law, it was never so in practice. Resistance to despotism occurred inside and between households. Second, household language frequently indicates the continual need to maintain and administer the life of the household through domestic *oikonomia*, precisely in order to quell resistance to despotic rule. Nonetheless, it has been the most subordinated subjects – women, slaves and animals – that have tended to the needs of the household on the command of the household head. This captures the sense in which one belongs to and lives under the tutelage of the *paterfamiliās* and is subject to management; that is, one is *domesticated* in the space of the household. From this perspective, we might say that 'domestic' government occurs when the inhabitants of household space submit (are forced to submit through violence and other necessities) to the disciplinary authority of a household. After all, 'dominate' is by extension 'one of the derivatives of the Latin word *domus*' (Briganti and Mezei, 2012: 5).

Households are at the root of the language of modern economics and the traditional association of household rule with familial relations is the basis of leading theories of government, of management and control, of domination. We might even say that all traditions of political thought that assume rulership or sovereignty as the essence of government and politics find their origins in practices of household rule. The language of domesticity, rooted in household governance, has had a profound influence on political thought, including writing on the patriarchal and naturalist basis of authority; on the existence of hierarchy, of rulers and ruled; and on the obligations of rulers to attend to the welfare of the household as a whole. Although they have not received attention in international studies, there are literatures in the history of political and economic thought on households and their changing significance, as well as studies of different household formations in anthropology, archaeology and comparative politics.[2] There is a large body of scholarship in literary studies on domesticity, including its imperial and military forms; liberal empire was frequently and explicitly conceived as an efficiently and well-run household.[3] Unsurprisingly, there is a very large literature in gender studies on ideologies of domesticity and ongoing debate of whether home should be reclaimed by feminists as a site of empowerment or rejected as an ideal. Feminists have also written extensively on 'domestic' labour in private homes, or labour made domestic in spaces made private (Martin and Mohanty, 1986; Young, 1997; Elias, 2013). Given the breadth and sophistication of these literatures on households and domesticity, which in turn are based on the historical reality and rich theoretical traditions of household rule, why has analysis of household governance and terminology, as distinct from the use of terms such as 'homeland' and 'home front', been largely absent in modern international thought?[4]

[2] In political thought see Booth (1993); Shammas (2002); Nagle (2006); Faroqhi (2010); Mitropoulos (2012); in comparative politics see Hunter (1984); Mundy (1995); in archaeology see Allison (1999); D'Altroy and Hastorf (2002); Barile and Brandon (2004); in anthropology and ethnography see Bourdieu (1979); Netting et al. (1984); Trigg (2005). In the tradition of social anthropology, 'domestication' refers to the 'move from oral to literate culture; from collective life to individualism and private families; from myth to history; and from concrete to abstract thinking' (Bowlby, 1995: 75; see also Goody, 1977; Levi-Strauss, 1966). For a brief recent discussion of the metaphor of 'home' in international theory see Marks (2011: 45–47). There is a small literature developing the concept of 'domopolitics' to describe the state as being governed like a home (Walters, 2004; Hynek, 2012). There is also a very brief discussion of households at the beginning of Daly (2006).

[3] Pecora (1997); Smith (2003); on imperial domesticity see Hunt (1990); Comaroff and Comaroff (1992: 265–295); Hansen (1992); George, (1993/1994); McClintock (1995); Rafael (1995); Kaplan (1998); Wexler (2000); Raibmon (2003); Myers (2009); Wesling (2011); on military domesticity see Haytock (2003); Colomina (2007); Rachamimov (2012); Kramer (2006); on home and postcolonialism see Bhabha (1992); George (1996).

[4] This is not to imply an absence of discussion of the so-called 'domestic sources' of foreign policy or the significance of the 'home front' in studies of war. The best work on this undoes much in the distinction between the 'war front' and the 'home front' (Hagemann and Schüler-Springorum, 2002; Armstrong, 1983). For Quincy Wright, the classical international law terminology of 'domestic jurisdiction' is defined 'geographically as matters taking place within the territory of a state, personally as matters concerning individuals within

There are at least two explanations for this puzzling oversight, and both are associated with what is taken to be distinctive about liberalism. The first is the dominance of theories of contract, which are *explicitly* based on a rejection of patriarchal models of rule that, in turn, originate in household governance. For early modern theorists of natural law, writes Bobbio (1993: 2): 'The principle of legitimation of political society is consent; this is not true of any other type of natural society. In particular, it is not true of domestic society, that is, of the family/household.' On this account, liberal states are governed through contract; an arrangement defined as the antithesis of governance in non-contractual, patriarchal households. To be sure, liberal thinkers have recognised that familial modes of governance, such as between father and children, husband and wife, metropole and colony, may coexist alongside contractual arrangements between autonomous men. It is well known that forms of liberal despotism have been justified as a temporary means to the end of creating subjects able to enter freely into contracts (Mill, 1999: 14; cf. Pateman, 1998 and Elshtain, 1981). However, liberal individuals are only autonomous to the extent that they freely consent to be governed and engage in privately contracted commercial exchange. Despite its many variants, all liberal theories purport to account for the contractual relations between autonomous citizens able to manage their own conduct, and all are united in their rejection of classical patriarchal forms of rule over autonomous subjects. Although only liberal international theory is premised on the existence of contract societies, much of realist international theory's broader acceptance of liberal premises in the 'domestic' realm has hindered international theory's proper engagement with the history and ontology of domesticity and, in turn, the historical and contemporary significance of household forms of rule.

The second explanation for the absence of investigation into domesticity and households in international thought is that from the eighteenth century, household governance itself was transformed into a new structural form and understood through an entirely new language. Explicit investigation into the meaning of household governance

the jurisdiction of a state, functionally as matters which could be dealt with conveniently and efficiently by states individually, or politically as matters which could be dealt with by states individually without affecting the interests of others' (quoted in Vincent, 1974: 6).

declined with the historical rise of the *social realm* and distinctly social forms of governance and discourse: social regulation, social theory and sociology (Weber, 1978: 375–380). Consider when and why it became possible to conceive of specifically *social* relations requiring sociological explanations. It is surprisingly difficult to find an answer to this question in political and international theory. In fact, this form of social discourse is less than 200 years old. What changed? Relations of dependency previously rooted in – and understood to be rooted in – ancient and feudal households became a matter of public state regulation and administration in the core of the major European empires. With the rise and expansion of capitalist markets and imperial state bureaucracies through the eighteenth century, *oikonomia*, the activity of managing life processes, acquired its own public domain, the modern social realm (Arendt, 1958; Habermas, 1962/1991). This new social realm, initially conceived in the eighteenth century as bourgeois civil society, functioned as an intermediary between the newly distinguished activities of capitalist 'economics' and state/imperial government. By the nineteenth century, bourgeois civil society underwent a major structural transformation, with state and non-state 'social policy' interventions specifically targeted at populations in revolt, especially women, workers and colonial natives. However, this rise and transformation of liberal 'contract societies' did not destroy household governance; it only transformed it. Instead of the antithesis of the household, the nation-state is a distinctively modern and bureaucratic *social* form of household rule. Domestic terminology and iconography lingers. Yet, despite its fundamental significance to the history of modern political and international thought, the origins and real significance of household governance was concealed with the rise of social theory, sociology and social policy intervention. This is deeply ironic. As this book shall argue, the ontology of the social realm and distinctly social regulation are best understood in terms of household governance in which the life processes of populations are managed and domesticated.

There is a far deeper material and ideological significance of domesticity for international thought than is captured in debates about the domestic analogy (Suganami, 1989; Bottici, 2009). There is a *homology*, a correspondence in type and structure, not merely an analogy, between forms of distinctly social regulation at the national, imperial and international levels that is captured through historical and theoretical analysis of household governance. Homology is from the Latin *homologia* for sameness and Greek for agreement. The term is most commonly used to refer to organs that correspond to a fundamental type in another animal or plant, or to different organs in the same species. More broadly, we can say that there is a homology when there is a correspondence of type or structure – although not necessarily of function – between things. To make a claim of homology is obviously a much stronger argument than analogy, to claim a resemblance, a likeness in form or function, as in the domestic analogy. If to homologise is to claim a correspondence of type or structure, then what is the fundamental type of which social regulation at the national, imperial and international levels is an expression? The answer is that social regulation and government is the distinctly modern and capitalist form of household rule. The modern social realm is a distinctive form of household, one of the historically variable units of rule in which the life processes of members are reproduced and the collective unit of the household is maintained.

International and many political theorists are not used to thinking of households in this way. During the nineteenth century, and under the influence of liberalism, the meaning of the term was transformed to refer to the domestic space of the bourgeois family, making household synonymous with home, and obscuring the broader and earlier sense of a unit of rule in which a household head seeks to maximise the welfare of the whole through the art of household management (Spencer-Wood, 1999: 162–189). Even many feminists, who have insisted on the non-contractual nature of modern society, have not explicitly theorised the modern social realm as a form of household governance, instead primarily analysing the intimate domestic space of the small-scale family house as a 'patriarchal unit within a patriarchal whole' (Millett, 1969/1977: 33). Household rule is always gendered. And yet the history of households is not completely identical with the history of gendered and sexual relations (Hartman, 2004).[5] Moreover, households, houses and homes should not be treated as synonymous. Households can encompass more than one house in the sense of a shelter for specific persons, who may or may not be biologically related.

[5] But see Angela Mitropoulos' recent use of the term *oikos* 'to theorize the confluences of race, sex, class, sexuality, citizenship and gender … as oikonomic arrangements' (2012: 140).

Indeed, the notion of family as exclusively blood relations is relatively recent and parochial; in medieval households,'family' referred to those who lived in the household, whether or not they were kin. The most important thing about households, what is defining of household governance, is the nature of the relationships between people. They are not synonymous with the classical *oikos*, one very particular understanding of households in a relatively brief historical context. Household forms are historically variable. Yet what is common across all households is that they are organised around the administration of life necessities with activities arranged hierarchically according to the assumed biological and other status attributes of different members. As such, household rule is generally despotic, but again there is much variation. This despotism can be direct and centralised (as in a feudal manor or concentration camp) or indirect and decentralised (as in imperial strategies of 'indirect rule', of using local leaders to maintain order). This is important, especially in the history of international and imperial relations: *decentralised* household rule occurs through proxies, the financing and arming of local despots to govern, to domesticate, local resistance. Moreover, the hierarchical running of household affairs need not be a personalised despotism as in the model of the *oikos despot*, the Roman *paterfamiliās*, the village elder, the King's *mund* or royal household. The personalised despotism of the *paterfamiliās* is not a universal, ever-present and static form of domination separate from the system of organising life processes. Modern state administration is bureaucratic, anonymous and largely de-personalised household rule. Moreover, while households are always located in space this is not always fixed or strictly bounded space. The boundaries of households are fluid and porous. Households are mobile; techniques of household rule are highly portable and they play a surprisingly central role in the organisation of international and imperial relations. The absence of analysis of domesticity and forms of household rule in political and international theory is a serious omission.[6]

[6] The closest exception is Marxist-inspired world systems theorists who conceive the household as a basic unit of the capitalist world system that reproduces commodified labour. This literature is an important advance, drawing attention to household configurations that are not reducible to house/home or kinship. However, the household is theorised in the very modern sense of an 'income pooling unit', rather than in the much broader historical sense of a unit of rule whose functions include, but also go beyond, the pooling of income (Smith et al., 1984, 1992; Wallerstein, 1991b). In this view, there is related literature on global householding and transnational households (Peterson, 2010;

This book makes three claims. First, in contrast to most political and international theory, it is argued that the meanings of social and society can only be understood in the context of a specific historical constellation, which developed after – not automatically with – the rise of territorial states. There is an important story to be told of where, when and why social and society emerged as domains with specific patterns, norms and logics, through which human life could be intervened in and transformed. But this story needs to be told in terms of transformations in – and crises of – household forms of rule. Second, contra liberalism, there is strong historical and theoretical evidence to suggest that the modern social realm is a scaled-up and modified form of household governance. This is perhaps surprising, even for many non-liberals; all the major social theories of modern society – liberalism, political realism, Marxism and several critical theories – have explicitly claimed or implicitly accepted that the rise of modern capitalist states destroyed large-scale forms of household rule. More specifically, the household ontology of the social realm has been obscured, especially since the nineteenth century, by the dominance of distinctly social theories and political economy; that is, when *oikonomia* and political thought were demoted in favour of a new series of oppositions and distinctions that emerged with capitalist imperial states. In fact, the rise and transformation of the commercial and then capitalist empires reconstituted – rather than eliminated – the household governance of feudal and early modern forms of rule. Rather than the antithesis of household government, the nation-state itself is a distinctively modern and bureaucratic social form of household, governing populations both at 'home' and overseas through distinctly – but historically specific – social means.

Third, to illustrate the significance of attention to the rise and transformation of social forms of household rule, the book examines the history and theory of a military practice that has played a formative role in the dissemination of social governance, the overseas counterinsurgency wars conducted by liberal empires/states.[7] Since

Douglass, 2010). On the metaphorical uses of *oikonomia* beyond household administration see Leshem (2013).

[7] The language of 'counterinsurgency' emerged relatively late in the history of overseas wars of pacification, during the earliest stages of the US war in Vietnam. For clarity of argument, the Introduction and Conclusion to this book uses the terminology of overseas liberal counterinsurgency to refer to a number of specific military campaigns pursued by Britain, France and the United States

French army officer David Galula (1964: 62) claimed that in counterinsurgencies a soldier had to 'become a propagandist, a social worker, a civil engineer, a schoolteacher, a nurse, a boy scout', it has become cliché to talk of 'armed social work'. More recently, US military advisor David Kilcullen argued that armed social work encompasses 'community organizing, welfare, mediation, domestic assistance, economic support – under conditions of extreme threat requiring armed support' (2010: 43; see also Bacevich, 2009; Hodge, 2011: 152; Sitaraman, 2012: 37). There is now a body of literature debating the validity and meaning of armed social work, including analysis of earlier colonial pacification campaigns and so-called small wars (Porch, 1986; Finch, 2013; Callwell, 1896). However, historians and theorists of war are less prone to situate armed social work in the context of a proper history and theory of the social itself, its services and administration (from the Latin *ministrātiōn*, the act of ministering, tending or serving; rendering aid or care). While there is a large historical literature on relations between warfare and welfare, of how mobilisation for world wars contributed to the creation of social welfare states, few have used armed social work as a mirror to reflect on distinctly social forms of pacification in general, or theorise counterinsurgency rule as a distinctive type of government.[8] This omission is surprising. The history and theory of counterinsurgency is an excellent subject for exploring the rise of the social realm and therefore, more fundamentally, changing forms of household rule. The historical context for the development of distinctly social thought and intervention was precisely the problem of populations in revolt. Social theories, sociology and social policy all developed during the nineteenth century

from the mid-to late nineteenth century to the contemporary period. However, the detailed analysis of specific pacification campaigns avoids anachronism and adheres to the language used to describe and justify these wars in the specific context.

[8] In IR, explicit discussion of social work, a term first used in 1847, is not very common. It has been used as a derogatory term to criticise the Clinton administration's foreign policy of seeking (but failing) 'to put an end to suffering in Bosnia, Somalia, and Haiti' (Mandelbaum, 1996: 18). However, there is also a thriving field of international social work that applies social work methods to what is usually discussed in terms of human security and development in IR (Cox and Pawar, 2012). On the specific national contexts and international conditions for the rise of welfare states see Lindert (2004); Marwick (1974); McClymer, (1980); Skocpol (1992).

for very particular reasons, to explain and remedy various types of popular uprising. Galula even referred to pacification as 'the conduct of sociological warfare' (in Mathias, 2011: 37). At the same time, counterinsurgency has been described as 'domestic politics by other means' in which the value of domestic work is not necessarily disavowed (Kurac, 2011). Drawing and theorising these connections suggest that liberal counterinsurgency is not merely an intensive form of enlightened liberal despotism, John Stuart Mill even more militarised. The third major claim of this book is that the power and contradictions of this practice derive more specifically from their origins in sociocratic household rule, of *oikonomia* in the use of force. There is a correspondence in type and structure, a homology, between practices of social regulation as they emerged across European imperial states and liberal counterinsurgency rule. This argument is supported in the second part of the book through an examination of social regulation in colonial pacification campaigns and then full detailed case studies of two British late-colonial wars in Malaya (1948–1960) and Kenya (1952–1960); the United States counterinsurgency in Vietnam (1954–1975); and the US-led multinational campaigns in Afghanistan (2001–2014) and Iraq (2003–2011).

Bringing together these arguments, the overall purpose of the book is to analyse the household of the modern social realm as a concrete historical entity and form of government, as a category of political and international thought, and as an object of military strategy. Its main intellectual contributions include a new account of the importance of household governance and ideologies of domesticity in political and international/imperial history; correcting the ahistoricism of international theory in its use of social terminology and offering new grounds for interpreting specific theories, both mainstream and critical; attention to historical figures neglected in international studies that were significant in the imperial history of the social or in conceiving of sociocratic forms of government; and an original historical and theoretical interpretation of specific cases of counterinsurgency, as a form of *oikonomia* by other means.[9] The rest of this Introduction sets out the parameters of this project and offers more detail regarding the major claims of the book. The next section addresses the ahistoricism

[9] Cf. Clausewitz (1832/1976: 87), 'war is not a mere act of policy but a true political instrument, a continuation of political activity by other means'.

of political and international theory regarding the rise of the social and offers the beginnings of a new history and theory of the social realm in the transformation of household governance. The second part shows how the dominant theories of military counterinsurgency are variations on nineteenth-century paradigms of social regulation (*realpolitik*, liberal solidarism) or they rest on a false historical premise (biopolitics). The final section addresses methodological issues and provides a brief overview of the rest of the book.

A social question

In a very specific part of the world, in a relatively short space of time, the concepts and processes associated with 'society' and then 'the social' came to order forms of governance, modes of production and international/imperial relations. To the very limited extent that political and international theory tells a story about the origins of distinctly social concepts and processes, it is usually – although largely implicitly – described in terms of a methodological advance. At some point during the eighteenth century, the veils of religious authority and the dictates of sovereign power were finally revealed as inadequate to the task of understanding and regulating Europe's commercial and then industrial empires. 'Society' and underlying 'social forces' were discovered as the 'really real', the deep underlying causes of what merely appears in the world (Baker, 1994). But what if this narrative, which is shared by liberalism and its offshoots, some forms of realism and all Marxism, is wrong? What if 'society' and 'social' processes were not discovered during the French and Scottish Enlightenments (Collins and Makowsky, 1972; Greenwood, 1997), but were produced in a very specific context? As Eric R. Wolf (1988: 759) has written, 'the concept of Society has a history, a historical function within a determinate context, in a particular part of the world'. Without an historical account of this context, international studies is unable to even begin debating the real meaning and potential worth of distinctly social theories. Such an account might reveal that the rise of social government and thought was not primarily a methodological advance at all, but first and foremost an attack on political modes of action and thought.

Consider again how international theory, in particular, has under-theorised the social in its historical and geographical specificity. There is a profound ahistoricism in the recent social turn, including among critical theorists, in that it takes 'social' to be a timeless and universally applicable concept. Debate has centred on the degree to which international anarchy can be 'socialised', whether the international or the world is a particular kind of 'social system' and how social systems can be philosophically understood (Wendt, 1999; Wight, 2006; Joseph, 2012). Within liberal IR, Andrew Moravcsik may be right that 'in order to theorise rigorously about systemic social construction we *first* require a liberal theory' (1997: 540, emphasis in original). But he is wrong to assert that this is because a theory of 'domestic preference formation' is required to properly identify the 'socialising feedback effects' between 'domestic society' and the structure of the international system. Instead, it is because the very notion of 'socialisation', a term first used in 1840, was a product of a political and ideological crisis in liberal governance in the mid to late nineteenth century. Similarly, English School theorists have adopted an ahistorical functionalist definition of society, drawn more from Durkheim than Grotius, and anachronistically applied it to all periods and places. Even Marxists, historical sociologists and critical theorists in international studies – all more attentive to the historicity of language and ideology – reproduce terminology and ways of thought they might otherwise reject if they properly attended to the historicity of society and the social as well.[10] The point is not that all IR theory is ahistorical (Teschke, 2003; Nexon, 2009). Rather, that there have been no analyses of the historicity of social forms of practice and thought. For example, while constructivists have traced the history of a particular 'social norm', and even considered historical method, they have been silent on the historical conditions for the emergence of the very idea of a distinctly social norm to begin with (Barnett, 2002; Kratochwil, 2006; Reus-Smit, 2002, 2008).

It really is worth remembering how recently social discourse came to dominate political and legal thought.[11] The Greeks had no such concept. Human affairs were organised around a distinction between

[10] On the English School see Bull (1977); Watson (1992); Buzan (2004). For Marxist, historical sociological and critical international theory see, variously, Rosenberg (1994); Hobden and Hobson (2002); Jabri (2007); see also Neocleous (1995)

[11] On the historicity of social and society see Wolin (1960); Collini (1980); Corrigan and Sayer (1985); Singer (1986); Frisby and Sayer (1986); Wagner (1994, 2000, 2001); Heilbron (1995); Carrithers (1995); Heilbron et al. (1998); Walters (2000); Prakash (2002); Withington (2010). On the history of sociological thought by sociologists see Hawthorn (1977); Szacki (1979); Bottomore and Nisbet (1979); Swingewood (2000); Coser (2003).

polis and *oikos*, the public political realm and the privatised household. There was no mediating social realm or social explanations for politics or *oikonomia*. The linguistic origins of 'social' and 'society' are Latin. *Socialis* meant simply partner or friend, which is obviously much narrower than contemporary sociological use. The first substantial shift in the meaning of 'society' occurred by the end of the seventeenth century with the expansion of different forms of early modern corporatism leading to a new emphasis on sociability in theories of natural law (Pufendorf, 1682/1991; Hont, 2005). In opposition to absolutist state power, sociability increasingly came to refer to the underlying tie between members of Europe's commercial *sociétés*, forming the model for the earliest attempts to theorise an autonomous logic separate from state direction and control. As Withington (2010: 112) notes, '"household" and "family" figured much less frequently in the printed horizons of readers ... This contrasts with the increasing visibility in print of "society" and "company" and the concept of deliberate and purposeful association they invoked.' The crucial point is that the language of sociability and commerce were inextricably linked.

Still, into the eighteenth century, the only way of conceiving humans in their totality in European thought was religious or legal-political. There was no sense of an autonomous social logic separate from sovereign political will or social explanations for human affairs. It was only with the rise of Enlightenment theories of bourgeois 'civil society' that the terms 'society' and 'social' began to acquire a more general meaning as the ontological basis of all human organisation. With the Scottish and French Enlightenments, neither God nor sovereign power was the underlying basis of civilised order, but a 'social contract' between rational, self-regulating individuals. As Raymond Williams put it, the 'image of society ... changed first from the immediate "society of one's fellows" to the more general "system of common life", and changed later from reference to a particular system to abstraction of all such systems, the general state of "society"' (1961: 120). Humans were no longer defined as political animals, as Aristotle maintained. In fact, Aristotle's position was either explicitly attacked (by major Enlightenment figures) or anachronistically assimilated to sociological categories (by subsequent sociologists).[12] Either way, humans would henceforth be defined as fundamentally *social* beings.

12 For example, Outhwaite (2006: 1) argues that Aristotle's term *zoon politikon* 'can easily be translated as social'. It might be easy but that does not make it

This shift in discourse was a product of a fundamental change in the structures of organising and managing life processes; that is, a major transformation in household governance. In ancient Greece, *oikonomia* was the practice of maximising the welfare of the household to enable the despotic household head to participate in the political and military affairs of the *polis*. Under feudalism, there was no distinction between *polis* and *oikos*. The common land was organised as one household on which peasants laboured and over which lords paternalistically governed (Weber, 1978: 370–384). In the eighteenth century, however, commodity exchange 'burst out of the confines of the [feudal] household' (Habermas, 1962/1991: 28). The growth and expansion of capitalist markets created a new distinction between state-public administration and privatised economy. For the first time, activities and relations of dependency acquired their own public domain, the social realm (Arendt, 1958: 38–50). Increasingly, labour was exchanged for a wage in what was understood to be a 'private' contract. However, early modern imperial states were taking on public functions related to the regulation of commerce and labour. 'The "social",' writes Habermas (1962/1991: 127), 'could be constituted as its own sphere to the degree that on the one hand the reproduction of life took on private forms, while on the other hand the private realm as a whole assumed public relevance.' New distinctions between public and private, politics and economy, state, inter-state and imperial relations created the material and intellectual conditions for the rise of a new hybrid domain, the social realm. The social was not wholly political or economic, public or private, but a distinctly capitalist space of public regulation. As Jean-Jacques Rousseau observed in 1755, 'economy, a word derived from *oikos* meaning house ordinarily signified the wise and legitimate management of a household. The term has now been extended to mean the management of the larger family of the state.' Political economy was understood as the 'physiology of society' (Heilbron, 1995: 110),[13] acting in the interests of a new unified object,

accurate. Similarly, according to Jean Cohen and Andrew Arato (1992: 84), the 'first version of the concept of civil society appears in Aristotle under the heading of *politike koinonia*, political society/community'. More recently, Hallberg and Wittrock (2006) suggest that the 'conventional wisdom' 'posits Aristotle's *Politics* (c. 335–323 BC) as providing the early vocabulary of civil society theorizing'.

13 The language of *oikonomia* was replaced by the terminology of 'political economy'. 'Born within the classic concept of government of the *oikos*,' writes

national or imperial 'society as a whole'; the frequency of the evocation of wholeness in discussion of society is indicative of its origins in household rule (Myrdal, 1953; Polanyi, 1957/2001; Wood, 1994: 30).

Although the social realm first formed during the eighteenth century, the current meanings of social and society were forged during the revolutionary upheavals across European empires from the mid- to late nineteenth century (Steinmetz, 2013). Enlightenment ideas regarding the autonomy and civility of bourgeois society faced endless crises. Focusing first on Europe, new industrial working classes were subject to the vulnerability of economic convulsions to a degree never seen before and threatened a revolutionary overthrow of the entire system (Hobsbawm, 1962). The effects of the industrial and democratic revolutions, the contradictions between democracy and capitalism, increasingly bloody colonial revolts, all exposed the limits of bourgeois 'civil society'. Warring ideologies – conservative, socialist, anarchist, feminist and liberal – debated the famous Social Question that defined nineteenth-century European thought: was it possible to successfully manage the welfare of increasingly radicalised workers such that capitalism was not overthrown, and if so, how?[14] The broad centre of Europe's ideological spectrum answered in the affirmative. In exchange for revolution 'from below', there would be 'social' reform, largely – although not entirely – directed and administered 'from above'. The earliest focal point of contestation was the legitimacy and practicability of government legislation of labour relations and poor relief, then issues of housing, child labour, health and hygiene, morals, education and the stability of the working-class family unit (the newly

Maifreda (2012: 253), 'the conceptual model of *oikonomia*... came down to the Early Modern period and, as it did so, was transformed into the category of "economie" ... Through an elaborate system of infiltrations, interrelations and contaminations along fields of knowledge which include at least theology (especially Protestant theology), proto-physiology and, to some extent, biology, the structure of *oikonomia* as a systematic interrelation of cognitive, governmental and vital phenomena represented a much more powerful framework for thought than direct reference to Aristotelian precedent might suggest.'

[14] Since the middle of the nineteenth century, 'the social question has concerned politicians, scholars, social reformers, religious leaders, and cranks' (Senn, 2006: 240). On the Social Question in general and in different national contexts see Jacoby (1870); Peabody (1909); Arendt (1963); Beck (1995); Judt (1997); Aisenberg (1999); Pilbeam (2000); Moggach and Browne (2000); Castel (2003); Sage (2009).

constricted meaning of 'household'). Liberalism itself became 'socialised'; new forms of reformist social liberalism and modes of 'socialisation' were conceived and targeted directly at the problem of dangerous classes, populations not sufficiently domesticated inside the national or colonial household (Wolin, 1960: ch.9; Bellamy, 1992: ch. 3).[15]

Social policies emerged as both state and non-state interventions to pacify 'social problems' in an ameliorative manner, although always relying on more obviously violent means. Closely associated with liberal and 'progressive' ideas, social interventions and social work have been widely understood as non-repressive, although many influential thinkers have emphasised the extent to which they have always involved a whole array of disciplinary and other controls (Arendt, 1958; Piven and Cloward, 1971; Foucault, 1975/1995; Bourdieu, 1998).[16] As James Ferguson (1994: 253) has written: '"Government services" are never simply "services"; instead of conceiving this phrase as a reference simply to a "government" whose purpose is to serve, it may be at least as appropriate to think of "services" which serve to govern.' Significantly, alongside violent repression, tending to and administering the life processes and risks of populations in revolt was the other primary method for addressing their demands. Consider the concomitant rise of the language of humanitarianism towards the end of the nineteenth century. 'The more progressive and humanitarian the aspirations of politics and philanthropy,' notes Riley of this period, 'the more determinedly and exhaustively "the social" [was] shaped, wielded and scrutinised' (1988: 52). New sociological discourses would assist with the classification and analysis of populations based on their 'social' needs and condition, their class, gender, race, nationality, sexuality, health and disabilities. Given the pervasive gendering of household activities, it is no surprise that women became agents and objects of social reform at unprecedented levels.[17] Many of these

[15] In Stefan Collini's (1980: 227) words, 'an effective "ideology of social reform" was fashioned out of the older Liberal tradition ... by the infusion into that hitherto distinctively individualist body of thought of concepts of "community" and "the social"'.

[16] Together 'social' and 'work' encapsulate the dual concern with biological labour/life and fabrication/work. Work involves the fabrication of making something – or someone or some people – on the basis of an already determined blueprint (Arendt, 1958).

[17] Women's suffrage itself was justified in 'muncipal housekeeping' terms. 'As early as the 1850s,' notes Matthews, quoting Theodore Parkers, early feminists 'employed

interventions responded to, but also shaped and moulded, the aspirations and desires of the principle targets: populations most in danger of disaffiliation and threatening to the existing order, workers, women and landless peasants.

In the Empire, too, eighteenth-century notions of bourgeois civil society and utilitarian ideologies of liberal improvement met their limits with a wave of rebellions in the middle of the nineteenth century; the Indian Mutiny of 1857 was the most serious. The violent response to the Sepoy Revolt was swift and cruel (Metcalf, 1964). The distinctly social rejoinder was even more far-reaching. In particular, Sir Henry Sumner Maine, Legal Counsel in India, developed a 'social' (indeed, international historical sociological) explanation for native violence, advancing the notion of 'traditional society' to underpin a new form of imperial governance, indirect rule. The arrival of British-led modernity, he argued, had thrown into crisis the naturally stable and well-ordered social system of the Indian village. Village 'society' could not simply be replaced without causing a violent breakdown (Maine, 1876, 1878/1908). Importantly, on this account, the Sepoy Revolt required no political account of anti-colonial peasant agency because new, seemingly deeper social explanations were at hand. Moreover, rather than seek wholesale reform, as utilitarianism argued, Maine and other conservatives claimed it was Britain's duty to 'protect and preserve' India's ancient customary laws. In line with Maine's (1886) explicit theory of the patriarchal origin of all forms of government, Britain should return control over important village affairs to the local *paterfamiliās*, in exchange for maintaining order within. In other words, Britain's indirect rule in India was a form of decentralised household despotism.[18] Maine's successful revision and imperial expansion of older theories and forms of household governance is important to the new history and theory of counterinsurgency rule developed here.

The central point is that multiple crises of nineteenth-century order produced distinctly social theories; that is, explanations of and remedies for the increasingly violent demands of labour, natives and

the "government as housekeeping" analogy in a call for woman suffrage: "I know men say women cannot manage the great affairs of a nation. Very well. Government is political economy – national housekeeping. Does any respectable woman keep house so badly as the United States?"' (Matthews, 1987: 88).

[18] This is an adaptation of Mamdani's (1996: 39) term 'decentralized despotism'.

women. The social theories of Comte, Spencer, Tönnies, Maine, Marx, Durkheim and Weber make no sense outside this revolutionary Age of the Social. We might even say that distinctly social discourse initially developed to *counter* insurgencies. The one glaring and significant exception to this claim is Karl Marx's later theory of capitalism, which took inspiration from and, in turn, inspired worker uprisings. There is no doubt that of the canon of major nineteenth-century social thinkers, Marx did most to explain the new social forms of domination and provide resources for those seeking to politicise what others would depoliticise, especially those labouring activities traditionally relegated to the household. Hence, there are important, even fundamental, differences between the forms of social theory that emerged out of this revolutionary tradition. Marxists, socialists, progressives and others built on the new social language to resist capitalism, imperialism and new forms of patriarchy. However, by embracing and extending the Enlightenment notion of man as a 'social being', Marx and his followers carried with them the historical and theoretical baggage of social thought: a reliance on biological metaphors; a progressive historical teleology centring on 'deeper' social forces; a belief in the malleability and perfectibility of humans; a faith in technocratic administration; and, in the end, an inability to properly theorise politics as much more than an expression of violence. Marx's revolutionary analysis of capitalism is indispensable, not so his accompanying philosophical anthropology and historical teleology. The point is not to engage in a wholesale critique of Marx. Rather, with his very modern adoption of the social, Marx – and his followers – could not possibly have identified modern society as a scaled-up and transformed household. As a consequence, they have adopted an image of 'socialised mankind' as historically conditioned as that of bourgeois civil society or India's traditional society. In fact, society was not simply discovered as the real ontological ground of human existence, as if such a thing had always been there only to be revealed through the brilliance of Enlightenment thinkers. This claim is part of Enlightenment mythology. The rise of distinctly social thought among the earliest theorists of capitalism was less a methodological advance than part of a project of de-politicisation, a multilayered attack on political philosophy and, more importantly, political action, whether understood in terms of authoritarian states or the politics of the dispossessed in both metropole and colony.

Taking seriously the historical rise of the social realm as a transformation in household government, and distinctly social forms of thought as the modern form of *oikonomikos*, has important consequences for how we think about the main theories of politics and international relations in terms of their substantive theoretical claims and their place in the history of thought. Each of the main theories – again, liberalism and its many constructivist and English School offshoots, political realism and Marxism – are fragments of different answers to the Social Question.[19] Put differently, they all find their most important origin in eighteenth- and nineteenth-century shifts in perspective in the context of the rise and violent transformation of the social realm and seek to reproduce distinctive paradigms of social regulation at the international level. As George Steinmetz (1993: 41) has put it, paradigms of social regulation 'represent different ways of imagining the social realm and its fault lines, or trying to (re)organize it'.[20] Spanning the spectrum of modern political and international ideologies, these paradigms embody different assumptions about the nature

[19] Constructivism and the English School are offshoots of liberalism because the historical conditions of their emergence are wholly internal to the history of liberalism as the theory of *raison de la société* as outlined in Chapter 2. This is not contradicted by the fact that some scholars refer to themselves as 'constructivist realists' (Barkin, 2010). Perhaps the first thinker in this vein was one of the founders of sociology, Max Weber (1946, 1958, 1978). He adopted a realist position on the autonomy of the state, supported capitalism against its revolutionary overthrow and adopted a constructivist methodology in his science of politics. Perhaps this is why Agathangelou and Ling have been able to analogise the discipline of IR with a colonial household comprised of *Pater* (realism), *Mater* (liberalism), *Caretaking Daughters* (neoliberalism, liberal and standpoint feminism), *Bastard Heirs* (neorealism), *Rebel Sons* (Marxism, Gramscian IPE, postmodern IR and constructivism-pragmatism), *Fallen Daughters* (postmodern feminism and queer studies), *Native Informant Servants* (area studies and comparative politics experts), *Bastard Ward* (Asian capitalism) and *Bastard Twins* (peripheral and transitional economies). 'The House of IR,' they write, 'exhibits a similar politics of exclusion and violence. It clearly … stratifies who's "upstairs" and who's "downstairs". This hierarchical division of space reflects the house's participation in and complicity with material relations of production and its uneven distribution of social wealth' (Agathangelou and Ling, 2004: 23).

[20] Liberal international theory understands 'regulation' as the moderation of 'laissez faire libertarianism'; 'societal preferences concerning the nature and level of regulation impose legitimate limits on markets' (Moravcsik, 1997: 527; see also Drezner, 2007; Mattli and Woods, 2009). The approach to social regulation in this book diverges sharply from this neoliberal institutionalist literature.

and character of 'the social', including attempts at its forcible reconstruction. Almost all international theories purport to be objective theories of modern societies and their international/imperial relations. In fact, they actively seek to participate in the creation or destruction of distinctly social forms of rule, modern household governance. However, to counter this, this book does not begin with a new definition of social and society, as if the problem can be solved by further proliferation of their many meanings. Rather it is necessary to trace the historical specificity and relatively recent emergence of the social and its cognate terms, while drawing attention to their rootedness in the transformation of household governance. 'The social,' as Gary Wickham (2007: 254) has put it, 'is not a theoretical object at all, but a contingent object that needs to be historically retrieved.' Hence the use of the concepts 'social' and 'society' in this book departs considerably from how they are conventionally used; that is, as timeless and universally applicable. The book offers an alternative to sociocratic thought, developing the much older and powerful language associated with practices of household rule. To show concretely what is at stake in the historicity of the social, the second half of the book is devoted to an analysis of armed social work, placing it in a much longer history of the rise of the social as a form of government and object of military strategy.

From pacification to domestication: what kind of work is armed social work?

In the April 1965 issue of the United States *Naval War College Review*, French scholar and war correspondent Bernard B. Fall (1965) informed his American readers: 'When a country is being subverted it is not being outfought; it is being out-administered. Subversion is literally administration with a minus sign in front.' A month earlier, President Lyndon Johnson unleashed Operation Rolling Thunder, then the largest aerial bombardment in history, pummelling the people of Vietnam with six million tonnes of explosives, more than twice the number used by all sides in the entirety of World War II. This was not what Fall, a critic of the bombing, meant by 'administration'. In Vietnam, the effort to out-administer the enemy became known as the 'Other War', including the forcible relocation of eight million Vietnamese persons into camps and their former homesteads being burned down. Some peasants who had survived both the bombing and their forced migration were given rice and small plots of land, and materials to build new huts, schools and medical centres. That is, they were subject to *social* administration. Leading American social scientists agreed that the total physical control of surviving peasants was the only way to defeat communist insurgency. 'Quiet warriors', many of them former social workers with experience of first-generation immigrants to America, were given the 'chance', as one sceptic put it, 'to clear up the momentary misunderstanding created by those bombs' (McCarthy, 1967: 24)

There were several precedents for this kind of armed social work. The social reformist zeal of the late nineteenth century's Progressive Era strongly influenced the United States colonial occupation of the Philippines. From 1898, the forcible removal and concentration of populations was followed by 'policies of attraction', reform of labour, education, health and sanitation. These activities were often explicitly described as a kind of overseas housekeeping, a form of domestic engineering especially responsive to housewifery.[21] Then as now, women were viewed as natural improvers. 'If women's sphere was to be domestic,' a view shared by many Progressive men and women, 'then let the social world become a great arena for domesticated intervention, where the empathies supposedly peculiar to the sex might flourish on a broad and visible scale' (Riley, 1988: 46). In other words, liberal empire-building proved highly amenable to discourses of armed social work because they were really discourses about overseas housekeeping. During the nineteenth century, European empires defeated local rebellions through exemplary massacres and the co-optation of local leaders, who faced heavy financial and other penalties if they failed to contain popular revolts. Military commanders would then oversee various forms of 'liberal improvement' to facilitate the extraction of raw materials and the opening up of the territory to trade. Building roads and markets, canals and schools were viewed as the means to liberal improvement just as the labouring classes were being improved by various forms of social intervention back home. By the end of the nineteenth century, and echoing the language of the Age of the Social, French colonial military strategy, in particular, emphasised

[21] As Mary Pattison (1915: 248) claimed, homemaking 'could no longer be said to be a private undertaking. It is a public function, regulated and formulated by local and State authorities.'

the importance of the 'social environment' and the malleability of the local population if targeted by social administration (Galula, 1963/2006; 1964; Rabinow, 1989).

Now the most commonly cited template for successful 'armed social work' is Britain's 'hearts and minds' campaign during the Malaya emergency (1948–1960). According to Sir Harold Briggs, Director of Operations in Malaya, Britain was in a 'competition in government' with communist guerrillas, requiring the forcible relocation of 600,000 of the Chinese population into detention camps. Renamed 'New Villages', camps became permanent resettlements with shops, schools, medical centres and meeting halls. Dispersed and unadministered peasants would now be integrated into Malayan 'society' with the help of social welfare officers from Britain, New Zealand and Australia. In the near concurrent Mau Mau emergency in Kenya (1952–1960), Britain sought to constitute a governable Kikuyu population through all the activities widely (but mistakenly) claimed to have worked in Malaya, but with far less financial support and an even greater emphasis on racial vengeance and collective punishment. Depopulation and concentration, forced labour, systematic torture and starvation made a mockery of talk of rehabilitation, even for many of its liberal supporters.

These postwar occupations were unpopular and costly. The preferred method of defeating insurgencies was the creation of counterinsurgency client states, training and arming indigenous police and military forces to engage in decentralised national household rule. This changed with the US-led occupations of Afghanistan and Iraq. Displaced civilians were not usually administered directly by armed forces, but by UN agencies, non-governmental organisations and private contractors. Many civilians were usually not deliberately displaced, although some were. Instead, many Iraqi villages and eventually entire cities were encircled with concrete walls and checkpoints. Coalition forces were tasked with identifying and bribing 'local power holders', tribal elders, warlords and sectarian militia who participated in sectarian cleansing. In common with earlier military campaigns, the potential or actual civilian base of insurgencies was weakened with targeted social programmes and the selective delivery of humanitarian supplies.

What kind of work is armed social work? What common assumptions about populations inform this military strategy that recurs across historical and geographical contexts? If the conflict between insurgents and counterinsurgents is a 'competition in government', a form of 'applied political science' (Isaac, 2008: 347), and victory is achieved through social administration, then what is the nature of the government offered through counterinsurgency rule? In each of these cases – Malaya, Kenya, Vietnam, Afghanistan and Iraq – counterinsurgency was a form of distinctly sociocratic household rule. Military strategists drew on and innovated the organisational devices of direct and indirect household governance to create or shape units of rule in which populations were to be domesticated. They variously sought to achieve this aim through the selective delivery and withholding of humanitarian supplies and inside and through small-scale family homes, detention and concentration camps, depopulation and re-concentration in new villages and strategic hamlets, the creation or shaping of tribes and sectarian militia, and at the largest scale inside newly formed or reformed postcolonial and/or postwar national-states. In each of the campaigns, liberal counterinsurgents attempted, although never wholly succeeded, to negate the meaningful political agency of local people turning to old – as well as creating new – techniques of household rule.

Before setting out and defending this argument in more detail we must analyse the existing theories of counterinsurgency, and armed social work in particular. Very broadly, they can be categorised as political realism (most closely associated with Max Weber), liberal-solidarism (which originates in the structural functionalism of Émile Durkheim) and biopolitics (the genealogy of power associated with Michel Foucault and, more recently, Giorgio Agamben). These theories are analysed not simply to highlight their flaws or to demonstrate the superiority of the proposed alternative. Of even greater significance is the role played by political realism, solidarism and structural functionalism during specific military campaigns. Across each of the cases examined, armed social work activities undertaken for reasons of military necessity were reconceived and justified by advisors, scholars and propagandists in the distinctly sociological terms associated with variants of political realism and liberal solidarism. The argument is not that counterinsurgents somehow consciously put into practice some version of these social theories (with the partial exception of social modernisation theory, a form of structural functionalism, in Vietnam). Rather social theory and sociology were so amenable to counterinsurgency because they originate in and represent modern, social forms of *oikonomikos*, the science of household management. As already suggested, this is because they were forged in answer to the nineteenth-century Social Question posed by the increasingly radical and violent demands of workers, women and natives. Modern *realpolitik* and liberal solidarism can be situated within the history and theory of the modern rise and transformation of the social realm and, accordingly, must be understood as paradigms of social regulation instead of objective theories of modern 'society'.

Consider again the nature of the government offered through liberal counterinsurgency rule. For most counterinsurgents and much political science, the dominant position is a variation on Max Weber's writing on the history of European state-building. 'The state,' wrote Weber (1946: 78), 'is a relation of men dominating men, a relation supported by means of legitimate (that is, considered to be legitimate) violence. If the state is to exist, the dominated must obey the authority claimed by the powers that be.' In this context, counterinsurgents seek to create a state able to impose order through control of violence, and the provision or withholding of humanitarian supplies is the means to this end. Drawing explicitly on Weber, American military advisors McFate and Jackson (2006) write, 'counterinsurgents must be able to selectively provide security – or take it away ... [and] become the arbiter of economic well-being by providing goods, services, and income – or by taking them away'.[22] As Stathis Kalyvas (2008: 351) also writes, counterinsurgents must pursue 'a strategy of competitive state building combining targeted, selective violence and population control, on the one hand, with the dissemination of a credible mass ideology, the creation of modern state structures, the imposition of the rule of law, and the spurring of economic development' (see also Gregg, 2009). Although he is never explicitly mentioned in the United States' *Counterinsurgency Field Manual*, Max Weber's understanding of the 'absolute end' of the state – to control violence and then 'to regulate social relationships, extract resources and take actions in the public's name' informs its central premise (United States, 2007: 1–115; hereafter FM 3–24). Indeed, the *Manual* explicitly states that 'COIN [counterinsurgency] can be characterized as armed social work. It includes attempts to redress basic social and political problems while being shot at. This makes civil-military operations a central COIN

[22] McFate and Jackson (2006) open their article with the above quote from Max Weber.

activity ... one means of restructuring the environment to displace the enemy from it' (FM 3–24: A-7, A45; Kilcullen, 2009). Reviewing the *Manual* for *The Nation*, Tom Hayden (2007) observed that '[n]early half the Field Manual reads more like Max Weber than Karl von Clausewitz'.

Although counterinsurgents and even much political science rarely note the historical context for modern political realism, Weber himself was explicit about the role of social policy as a kind of *realpolitik* applied to internal populations. The historical context for this argument is well known in the geopolitical and *kolonialpolitik* history of *sozialpolitik* (Zimmerman, 2010; Grimmer-Solem, 2003a). During the 1880s, Otto von Bismarck founded the German administrative/welfare state to anesthetise radicalised and increasingly organised workers in competition with the more 'advanced societies' of Britain and France, combining social security with state militarism and the externalisation of the enemy with a policy of 'social imperialism'.[23] There is an obvious international dimension to the expansion of social regulation and social theory in nineteenth-century imperial Germany, the birthplace of modern political realism and its descendants. Bismarck's creation of the first comprehensive social insurance system became an extraordinarily powerful means for managing class conflict. This framework was subsequently adopted by colonial authorities and states and extended to numerous areas of life, including limited compensation for some civilian casualties of recent military interventions (Weizman, 2011). Crucially, for political realists, social insurance helped to transform identification with class to identification with the national collective, displacing antagonism into the international sphere. In establishing a political realism for the Age of the Social, Weber drew on and revised Bismarck's answer to the Social Question. Counterinsurgents ask a form of this question, whether it is possible – and if so how – to successfully create in the target territory a functioning social realm as a form of pacification, an entity that can be intervened in and regulated to counter the military and political authority of the enemies of the counterinsurgency state (Owens, 2013). Political realism is the preferred paradigm of social regulation for counterinsurgents because, from

[23] Semmel (1960); Wehler (1972); Steinmetz (1993); Grimmer-Solem (2003b); van Meerhaeghe (2006).

this perspective, the fundamentally political character of the regulation of the social is the creation of governable populations where they not did previously exist.

To some extent, then, 'Weberian' readings of counterinsurgency are accurate. They certainly mirror many of the actions and stated objectives of counterinsurgents, especially when they are talking among themselves, and can be found across each of the five cases examined in this book. Yet, elaborations of the Weberian ideal in counterinsurgency texts are primarily and partially descriptive. They are primarily descriptive because they do not provide analysis of the nature of counterinsurgency rule itself, but rather repeat the stated objectives of counterinsurgency states. Political realism is a famously practical philosophy, seeking to give historical and philosophical weight to the way elite state actors conceive of their actions, and to encourage them to conceive of their actions in political realist terms. This does not make political realism a reflection of political reality. Similarly, elaborations of the Weberian ideal are partially descriptive because political realism itself is a powerful and historically specific paradigm of social regulation, rather than an accurate description of political and military reality. Political realism is not grounded on some profound 'sociological' insight into the nature and character of politics and the state. It seeks to participate in the creation of a certain kind of state authority against (class or anti-colonial) insurgencies, and then describe this 'relation of men dominating men [sic]' as the natural outcome of the fundamental relation between politics and violence. In other words, as described further in Chapter 2, modern political realism was forged in reaction to revolutionary claims perceived to be emanating from the social realm, but it does not offer a convincing theory of the nature of counterinsurgency rule (see, for example, Luttwak, 2007).

The other leading – and much more popularly appealing – theory of counterinsurgency assumes the possibility of a far more benign and progressive form of war than followers of Weber, although these approaches are potentially compatible. *Realpolitik* is an unappealing vision in an age defined by notions of popular sovereignty in which states are supposed to act on grounds of *raison de la société* as much as *raison d'état* (Singer, 1986: 77). Moreover, even on its own terms, *realpolitik* needs to be supplemented by *sozialpolitik*. Hence, especially when addressing public audiences, describing populations targeted by armed social work or offering explanations for insurgency support, counterinsurgency texts are much more likely to emphasise themes drawn from the 'socialisation' of liberalism in late nineteenth-century France that is now usually associated with 'solidarism'.[24] Unlike Weber, who emphasised irreducible conflict, the founder of academic sociology, Émile Durkheim, argued that separate but functionally related and interdependent parts of 'society' were complementary and potentially harmonious; social structure was a moral order held together by *solidarité* and shared beliefs. This structural functionalism originates in broader and rather pervasive attempts through the nineteenth century to analogise biological and 'social systems'. All parts of society were imagined to be functionally interdependent just like the organs of a human body. Order and stability, not conflict, was the normal, healthy 'social' condition. But if that were true, what explained the violent and extreme disorder of the Third Republic, founded in 1870, and which Durkheim was politically committed to defend? Echoing Henry Sumner Maine's earlier social explanation for the Indian Mutiny, Durkheim claimed that it was the progressive transition from one type of society to another that created conflict, dissociation and *anomie*. Against the critics of state action and advocates of *laissez faire*, Durkheim and other solidarists argued that the collapse of capitalism into anarchy or communism would only be forestalled by state and non-state (family, church, community) interventions into the social *milieu* itself. Society, claimed Durkheim (1893/1984: 39), was a 'determinate system which has its own life'. 'Social facts' were real. The social contract was not a myth; it could be achieved through the proper application of bureaucratic techniques of risk assessment in cases of emergency, old age, unemployment and illness. If new moral and social norms and forms of solidarity could be created, then society's naturally healthy condition could be restored, a view attractive to many conservatives as well as liberals.[25] Rather than view 'social

[24] There is some overlap between solidarist accounts of counterinsurgency and those of humanitarian intervention associated with the English School of international studies (Wheeler, 2000) but these are not reducible to each other. The former has a much longer history and is more wide-ranging in its claims about the role of distinctly social norms in pacification war. IR solidarism is more narrowly focused on the sense in which state leaders and publics may feel ethical obligations beyond borders and act to prevent massacres during a military crisis through 'humanitarian intervention' (for criticism see Owens, 2004).

[25] 'Since a body of rules,' wrote Durkheim (1893/1984: 304), 'is the definite form taken over time by the relationships established spontaneously between the

problems' as an inevitable product of class exploitation or private contracts, they were contingencies of interdependence for which no one could be held responsible. Eventually, this powerful discourse of 'social solidarity' prevailed over – partially through combining – classical liberal, conservative and reform socialist answers to the Social Question; for many, it still underpins European welfare states and buttresses 'collective security' in international 'society' (Bourgeois, 1902; Stjernø, 2005).

Although the specific terminology is adjusted across the campaigns, reflecting different national, geopolitical and intellectual contexts, forms of Durkheimian structural functionalism and solidarism closely accompanied all the counterinsurgencies examined, from the most striking case of the official Committee to Enquire into the Sociological Causes and Remedies for Mau Mau to RAND Corporation social systems analysis of Vietnam, Afghanistan and Iraq. It is easy to see why such ideas have long appealed to military strategists seeking distinctly social (non-political) explanations of and remedies for violent revolt. Again, echoing Maine's (1886) patriarchal theory of 'traditional society', many explained support for insurgencies not in terms of the political attitudes and actions of those concerned but in seemingly 'deeper' terms; that is, of the 'passing of traditional society' and the failure of individuals, especially young men, to adjust to modern society; their violence, in that sense, was pathological (Pye, 1956; Lerner, 1958). These would become the social anthropological grounds for the co-optation of 'traditional leaders' to maintain despotic order in their miniature village or tribal 'societies'. Moreover, with its image of 'society as a whole', structural functionalism provided the grounds for a military strategy involving the *total* restructuring of local ways of life. For if society is 'organically interdependent', as Sitaraman has written, then counterinsurgents must grasp the 'mutuality between the parts: the individual elements cannot maintain themselves without each other ... it is full-spectrum, embracing ... military, political, economic, ideological, legal, and cultural' life (Sitaraman, 2012: 15; see also Davis, 2011b). Transformation in one segment of society requires

social functions ... a state of *anomie* is impossible wherever organs solidly linked to one another are in ... sufficient lengthy contact. Indeed, being adjacent to one another, they are easily alerted ... to the need for one another and consequently they experience a keen, continuous feeling of their mutual dependence.'

transformation of every other, legitimising the total, social revolutions pursued to the greatest extreme in Vietnam. Because these were liberal military campaigns, evidence of their more benign, solidarist character was also taken from the promise of electoral participation, the legitimation of social revolution through a highly managed form of democracy. The delivery of basic necessities to reduce the numbers of people dying *en masse* was also most often conceived in solidarist terms. Although 'counterinsurgencies are inherently degenerative' since 'brutality pays', viewed from a solidarist perspective, armed social work is potentially progressive and humanitarian (Merom, 2003: 47). The Weberian emphasis on the *selective* and *conditional* provision of basic necessities becomes the humanitarian delivery of relief that potentially 'wins over' the 'neutral majority' of the population (Kleinfeld, 2009; Sitaraman, 2012: 8).[26]

Military historians are well aware that the violent administration of populations in wars of pacification is not 'paradigm shattering', as suggested by many of its more recent and forgetful proponents (Sewall, 2007: xxxv; cf. Porch, 2013; Khalili, 2013). While there are obvious propaganda reasons for counterinsurgents to present their actions in such terms, to talk of 'progressive' counterinsurgency, of soldiers as social workers, is also more than mere talk. It is the paradigmatic form of this kind of war. In formalising and transforming assistance to some of the most needy, the rise and expansion of the new 'social sector' from the late nineteenth century dramatically increased the possibilities of seemingly humanitarian action. According to Barnett and Weiss (2011: 37), 'reform societies, social movements, and leaders ... spearheaded campaigns to humanize domestic society'. It is not a coincidence that the nineteenth century – the Age of the Social – has also been described as the moment of the 'humanitarian big bang' (Barnett, 2011: 49). However, recent efforts to locate the origins of humanitarian military intervention in the rise of intervention into the lives of exploited populations at 'home' misconstrue the causes, purposes and effects of the expansion of social regulation in nineteenth-century Europe (Bass, 2008; Mitcham and Muñoz, 2010). Similarly, armed social work is

[26] The crucial and often repeated claim is that 'in any situation', 'whatever the cause' there is a neutral majority that supports neither the insurgents nor counterinsurgents (see FM 3–24: 1–20, Fig. 1–2). The claim, first made by Galula (1963/2006: 70), is analysed in Chapter 7.

more than mere talk, but only if we adopt a different view of social work than liberal solidarists. There is indeed a correspondence in type and structure between armed social work during counterinsurgency and the distinctly social regulation and theory that emerged across European metropoles and empires during the nineteenth century. But solidarism is unable to properly theorise this homology. While solidarism itself was initially developed to counter insurgency by industrial workers, the explanatory power of Durkheimian writing on counterinsurgency is not confirmed because wars of pacification have been described as '*La guerre dans le milieu social*' (Nemo, 1956). Even leaving aside the well-known flaws of structural functionalism, solidarist theories of counterinsurgency obscure the way these wars are actually fought and how, if at all, victory is achieved. For example, in the large hagiographic literature on Britain's Malaya campaign, it is often taken for granted that the 'hearts and minds' policy defeated the insurgency (Nagl, 2002). In fact, Britain defeated anti-colonial insurgencies in Malaya and Kenya because its armed forces and local collaborators were able to isolate not very well-organised or supplied guerrillas through inflicting the greatest harm on the civilian populations. In their different ways, armed social work in Vietnam, Afghanistan and Iraq are also stories of collective punishment and rewards (O'Huiginn and Klevnas, 2005).

This highlights one of the paradoxes addressed in this book. It is the very nature of these interdisciplinary wars fought by soldiers, social anthropologists and social workers to directly target the life processes of populations. However, counterinsurgencies should not be defined in primarily social work terms, as usually understood, and not only because the funds allocated are only ever a tiny percentage of the costs of the overall campaign. To see the armed social work aspects of counterinsurgency as extensions of benign humanitarianism would be equivalent to theorising capitalism chiefly in terms of its accompanying social policies. Social security, the entire apparatus of the welfare state, as Piven and Cloward (1971: xiii, 3) argued, arose as a 'secondary and supportive institution' to capital accumulation, state and geopolitical order. Although its consequences are far-reaching, social policy has historically been 'ancillary to economic arrangements', best understood in relation to disciplinary and regulative functions in enforcing wage labour, gender and racial norms. Seen this way, we can indeed place the social regulation of different populations within a common historical and theoretical frame, but one very different than offered by liberal solidarism. Such a frame has already been suggested by some of those on the receiving end of social work. During the Vietnam War, Samuel F. Yette (1971) talked of President Johnson's 'Great Society Pacification Program' targeted at African-Americans. Charles Silberman (1964) spoke of 'welfare colonialism' in *The Crisis in Black and White*.[27] There is no such thing as unarmed social work; it always rests on the highly gendered fusion of penal and social policies, of the jailhouse and distinctly *social* housekeeping. We need a different way of conceiving the joint agency of the armed and social welfarist sectors of the state during counterinsurgency rule.

Within critical international theory, the dominant theoretical framework for understanding counterinsurgency is Michel Foucault's (1978, 2008) influential writing on biopolitics. From the eighteenth century, Foucault claimed, biological life itself became subject to government interventions and forms of scientific knowledge aimed at improving, but also normalising, human life. Novel forms of statistical and demographic studies justified and sustained government intervention into more and more spheres; it determined whether some groups needed more direct management than others, more targeted interventions in populations subdivided along national, class, gendered, sexualised and racialised lines. With 'the discovery of population', argued Foucault, power was exercised not only through the ability to destroy life, as in the sovereign model of power, but to foster it. Biopower regulated life through pastoral care, producing whole populations amenable to coordination and mobilisation in the face of new threats and vulnerabilities. While modern life was made healthier, more long-lasting, rational and productive, 'man-as-species' became an object of administrative control, intervention and normalisation. Crucially, for theories of sovereignty, the 'discovery of population' was not the product of sovereign power asserting the boundaries of the space that it would govern, enforcing its will through violence, as political realists would claim; it was a biopolitical technique of governing 'man insofar as man is a living being' (Foucault, 2003: 239–40). For Foucault (2007: 71), 'the variables on

[27] Critical legal scholars have suggested that there is a 'selfsame logic cutting across policy domains' that 'join penal sanction and welfare supervision into a single apparatus for the cultural capture and behavioural control of marginal populations' (Wacquant, 2009: xix).

which population depends are such that to a very considerable extent it escapes the sovereign's voluntarist and direct action'. In contrast to the solidarist stress on humanitarian intervention in 'society', Foucault and his followers point to the disciplining and coercive character of social welfare.[28] Biopolitics is an oxymoron, since for Foucaultians it is essentially de-politicising. Indeed, extending this point to law, Giorgio Agamben (1998, 2005) has argued that when states 'lawfully' suspend the law, when the exception to the normal functioning of the law becomes the rule, humans are reduced to 'bare life', subjects without meaningful speech and political freedom. Agamben uses the evocative term 'camp' to describe all spaces in which biological and political life cannot be distinguished and in which individuals can be subject to violence without legal consequence on territory outside the normal juridical order. In concrete and material 'zones of indistinction' (such as detention centres or refugee camps) humans are reduced to mere biological animals. Such states of emergency are not exceptional or marginal phenomenon, Agamben argues; they reveal the fundamental character of juridical and political order. The camp, he writes, 'is the biopolitical paradigm of the modern' (1998: 95).[29]

Counterinsurgents do not, of course, explicitly conceive their actions in biopolitical terms, although they repeatedly claim to have discovered the population as the 'human terrain', the centre of gravity, on which counterinsurgency is fought (FM 3–24; Gentile, 2009). Given the 'population-centric' language of the campaigns in Afghanistan and Iraq, it is no surprise to find a large literature on the biopolitics of counterinsurgency.[30] For Foucaultians, populations living under counterinsurgency rule could easily be seen as the ultimate biopolitical subjects, those who can be regulated and governed at the level of

[28] Chambon et al. (1999); Donzelot (1979); Hewitt (1983); Berend (2005).

[29] In more recent work, Agamben (2011) has sought to retrieve the concept of *oikonomia*, the 'government of men', in his theological genealogy of government. 'The concept of *oikonomia*,' he writes,'is the strategic operator that ... allows a temporary reconciliation of the [Holy Trinity] with the divine unity ... [As such, there is] a single activity of "economic" administration of divine life, which extends from the heavenly house to its earthly manifestation ... Christian theology is, from its beginning, economic-managerial, and not politico-statal' (2011: 66, 36–37).

[30] See, for example, Duffield (2007); Gregory (2008); Dillon and Reid (2009); Kienscherf (2011, 2012); B. Anderson (2011). For Foucaultian analyses of humanitarian intervention see Fassin and Pandolfi (2010) and Fassin (2011).

population in a military 'state of exception' outside the normal legal framework. This is why Britain's late-colonial campaigns in Malaya and Kenya were called 'emergencies'. Under dictate of military necessity, populations could seem to be reduced to 'bare life' inside various forms of camp-like spaces: detention centres, concentration camps, new villages and strategic hamlets, refugee camps, ethnic enclaves, family homes and the nation-state itself. In light of the Bush administration's scandalous claims to absolute discretionary powers in its 'War on Terror', including the unlawful detention and torture of prisoners, Agamben's writing on states of exception appealed to many critical theorists (Mirzoeff, 2009; Butler, 2004, 2009). When compared to political realism and solidarism, the biopolitical framework does, indeed, provide a more promising general framework because it addresses some of their flaws; biopolitics is not a paradigm of social regulation in the guise of an objective theory of politics or society; the approach is grounded in historical analysis, including the crucial period of the late eighteenth to nineteenth century; it explicitly addresses the extent to which the life processes of populations are targeted in counterinsurgency; and it emphasises, rather than obscures, the coercive character of armed social work. Although there are problems with this ugly oxymoron, much writing on biopolitics captures something important about counterinsurgency, namely its intervention into the biological life of populations.

However, the major problem with this approach to counterinsurgency is that an important part of Foucault's own, admittedly speculative, story about the discovery of population rests on a false premise. The 'discovery', he claimed, was only possible with the concomitant eradication of the family as the model of government. Since Plato, recall, most political thinkers had believed that the origins and model of all government was the household government of the family by the father: patriarchy. For Foucault, the appearance of populations with their own statistical regularities and cycles irreducible to those of the family made this older model redundant. 'The family will change from being a model to being an instrument,' he wrote, 'it will become a privileged instrument for the government of the population rather than a chimerical model for good government' (Foucault, 2007: 105). Creation of and intervention into small-scale family units would become a central feature of social policy, including during armed social work. Moreover, Enlightenment theorists of civil society would criticise mercantilist assumptions that the state could comprehend and control its subjects as the *paterfamiliās* governed his family. Recall Foucault's (2007: 71) claim that 'the variables on which population depends are such that to a very considerable extent it escapes the sovereign's voluntarist and direct action'. But Foucault is mistaken in his characterisation of the underlying historical and theoretical model that the discovery of population supposedly (but had not) eliminated. Not the family as such but the *household* was the origin and model of good government. Again, historically and conceptually, households and families are not the same. Households are the units of rule in which the life processes of members are reproduced, whether or not they are co-residents or kin. There is no historical or theoretical contradiction between the decline in the *familial* model of government, necessary to realise liberal theories of 'contract', and regulating populations through techniques of household rule. Moreover, household governance does not necessarily require 'the voluntarist and direct action' of a sovereign; it can be achieved through the anonymous machinery of bureaucracy. Contra Locke *and* Foucault, household rule was transformed rather than destroyed by the rise of commercial empires in the eighteenth century. Rather than unblocking the 'art of government' with the elimination of the family as the model, the historical rise of the social realm scaled-up and transformed the art and science of household governance. In more Foucauldian language, rationalities organised around a household logic continue to be inscribed within strategies of population governance.[31] By joining liberal thought in absorbing households into families, Foucault and his followers missed something fundamental: the modern social realm is not a negation of household rule; it is its modern capitalist form. This is despite the fact that Foucault was cognisant of the historicity of society, some of his own students and interlocutors wrote directly on this subject, and he never intended the terminology of biopolitics to become a general theory of 'society', as many of his followers in IR too readily assume.[32]

31 I am grateful for Lara Coleman for suggesting this formulation.

32 Baudrillard (1978/2007); Donzelot (1984, 1988); Smart (1990); Procacci (1995); Schinkel (2010); and Rojas (2005). The US *Counterinsurgency Field Manual* illustrates the new 'population-centric' strategy through a series of idealised anecdotes from past 'hearts and minds' campaigns; military doctrine and embedded journalists report on the great successes of the

Nonetheless, what happens when life processes are at the centre of politics and war? Are Giorgio Agamben's disquieting claims regarding 'bare life' and camps a better framing for the numerous 'spaces of confinement' (Khalili, 2013) in counterinsurgency? After all, one argument of this book is that counterinsurgents seek to reduce populations to purely social and non-political beings through their 'naked exposure to the exigencies of life' (Arendt, 1958: 254–255). Is counterinsurgency, then, not the perfect example of sovereign power producing and acting directly on 'bare life', 'a space in which power confronts nothing other than pure biological life without any mediation', Agamben's very definition of a 'camp' (Agamben 2000: 40)? The answer must be no. The relationship between sovereign power and 'life' is never completely 'unmediated', as suggested in Agamben's existentialist emphasis on 'life as such'. It is always forged through the historically specific relations of class, gender, racialised and inter-household hierarchies within which household rule occurs and through which it is transformed and resisted. In other words, it is always mediated by the *oikonomia* through which life processes are managed, and the specific configuration of contingent historical facts and events.[33] This also means that 'the domestic', as Laura Wexler (2000: 22) has put it, 'is a meaning that has to be produced; it is not simply found in nature but is selected from an array of available symbolic resources in accordance with historically specific needs'. Agamben's writing on the sovereign exception, under the influence of Carl Schmitt (1996, 2005), obscures the origin of sovereign models of power in household rule, the near absolute discretionary power of the despot. Agamben's unidirectional logic of sovereign power has been criticised for ignoring the historical origins of various forms of detention and concentration camps and the important distinctions between them (Owens, 2009).

population-centric strategy. Yet too much of the would-be critical literature also reproduces the notion of 'population-centric' war by primarily focusing on doctrine, instead of examining how the military campaigns have actually been fought. In other words, much of this literature accepts the counterinsurgency narrative regarding these campaigns, assuming that 'biopolitical' governance is also at work in counterinsurgency (Kienscherf, 2011).

33 Similarly, for Jef Huysmans (2008: 167), Agamben's writing on life 'as such' is a 'radical ontological erasure of the political conception of the societal'. Unfortunately, Huysmans' own notion of 'the societal', 'a realm of multi-faceted, historically structured political mediations and mobilizations' (2008: 166) is also ahistorical.

Similarly, the various spaces of confinement in liberal counterinsurgencies, the houses of corrections, collaborative tribal or village households, family homes, all the way up to the functioning nation-state are not 'camps' as Agamben understands this term. They are different forms of despotic household space.

Political realism, solidarism and biopolitics (when taken as a general theory of modern society) are inadequate to the task of properly historicising and theorising counterinsurgency. Liberal counterinsurgency is more specifically a form of *sozialpolitik*, a form of despotic and sociocratic household rule or *oikonomia*, than either *realpolitik* or biopolitics. For to claim that the late-colonial emergencies and counterinsurgencies examined were especially amenable to armed social work is only another way of saying that counterinsurgency itself is a form of household governance, seeking to create units of rule in which populations can be domesticated. It is a form of *oikonomia* by other means. There is an *oikosystem* to liberal counterinsurgency. Like all forms of household rule, counterinsurgency rule is despotic. However, the spatial organisation of this despotism may be indirect and decentralised (such as the use of local despots or client states), as well as direct and centralised (such as strengthening the patriarchal house or in establishing larger concentration and detention camps). Like most historical forms of household governance, counterinsurgency rule is based on violent compulsion. On grounds of military necessity, counterinsurgents seek the obedience of local populations through the issuing of commands that must be obeyed for pain of death, or the actual or threat of pain. Populations are forced to collaborate through the dictate of violent necessity, becoming objects of social administration rather than political agents or subjects. The effort to negate the political subjectivity of the governed is defining of household rule. This is because of the political potential of the governed and the consequences of their political agency for the would-be household masters. The issue is not simply a question of counterinsurgents portraying enemy and civilian populations as slavish/uncivilised, childlike, feminine and animalistic, those categories justifying subordination inside the ancient *oikos*. Pacification wars are wars of domestication in the sense that counterinsurgents seek to govern through strategies of household rule and is a form of war justified, in part, through domestic images and sentiments.

What is specifically 'social' about liberal counterinsurgency? This form of war clearly draws on traditions of both enlightened despotism and indirect imperial rule, which are not usually considered distinctively social. In fact, the former emerged in the eighteenth century alongside social philosophy and the Enlightenment conception of society; the latter is deeply rooted in new theories of traditional society that emerged from the middle of the nineteenth century (Scott, 1990). However, the distinctly social aspect of the counterinsurgency household is best understood as a form of sociocracy. French philosopher and founder of sociology, Auguste Comte coined *sociocratie* in 1851, from the Latin *socius*, companion, and *kratein*, from the Greek to govern. Sociocracy, for Comte, was a utopian end state only achieved once all forms of theocracy had been replaced and positivism had become the new religion. However, for the first President of the American Sociological Association, Lester Frank Ward, sociocracy was not a utopian end-goal, although he believed society had a telic purpose. By the end of the nineteenth century and at the height of the Progressive Era, he could claim that sociocracy was a really existing method of government by enlightened professionals in the name of the welfare of 'society as a whole'. Sociocracy, argued Ward, was the 'general social art, the scientific control of the social forces by the collective mind of society for its advantages, in strict homology with the practical arts of the industrial world'.[34] Neither a democrat nor a socialist, Ward described himself as a 'sociocrat', advocating for technocratic expert rule by 'sociological inventors working on the problems of social physics from the practical point of view' (1906: 339). Describing liberal counterinsurgency as sociocratic does not require the adoption of either Comte's or Ward's understanding of this term.[35] It is to retrieve a powerful but neglected name for the government form that accompanied the rise and transformation of the social realm. The rise of sociocratic household rule reflected a fundamental change in the structures of organising and managing life processes. New forms of

[34] Ward quoted in *The American Fabian* (1898: 11). For a rare discussion of Ward in the context of international relations, focusing on his beliefs on race and imperialism see Hobson (2012: 119–121). Comte's (1877: 375) teleology was directed towards 'the Sociocracy of the future' in which democracy and aristocracy performed a distinct historical purpose, preparing the ground for sociocracy.

[35] It should also be distinguished from the efforts of Dutch engineer Gerhard Endenburg (1981) to develop a practical and normative sociocratic approach to 'dynamic governance' in the workplace, including through cybernetic social systems theory.

rule and distinctions – between public and private and between economy, politics, the state and imperial/inter-state system – were particular to the modern social realm. In turn, the administrative techniques and ideological rationalisations of this mode of sociocratic governance would profoundly shape the nature and character of numerous counterinsurgencies.

Methodology and overview

The writing of this book was motivated by three problems with existing political and international thought: the ahistoricism of the recent 'social turn'; the neglect of the historical and theoretical significance of household governance and domesticity; and the related inadequacies of existing accounts of counterinsurgency. Corresponding to each of these problems, there are three main arguments relating to the historicity of the social; its ontology as a scaled-up and transfigured form of household governance; and the homology between distinctly sociocratic household rule and armed social work across five cases of counterinsurgency war. In making these historical, theoretical and empirical claims, the book draws on a range of sources, including existing historical and theoretical scholarship and a selection of primary sources related to the counterinsurgency campaigns. The historical literatures encompass writing on households; the breakdown of feudalism and the rise of commercial empires; international/imperial history; the history of social policy, the Social Question and social legislation; conceptual histories of social and society; and the history of political and international thought. It also offers close readings of distinctly social theories across a wide range of traditions and national contexts. Chapters 2, 3 and 4 draw together these literatures, offering historical and theoretical analysis of the rise and household ontology of the modern social realm and forms of thought in their international and imperial context.

Once we begin to pay attention to the history of household rule and notice its influence on the history of thought, it becomes difficult to underestimate the significance of household governance. However, the danger in seeking to forcefully establish the significance of household rule, including in liberal 'society', is that too much is swept into the concept of household. This is always a problem given the extent to which numerous phenomena and experiences can be understood through domestic metaphors and analogies, pointing to the all-pervasive character of household relations and related ideologies. 'The domestic realm', as Wexler (2000: 21) writes, 'can be figured as well by a battleship as by a nursery'. It is incredibly easy to re-describe all hierarchical relations as if they were households. Here the concept is limited to relations of governance based on the control of life processes, real bodies that need food, water and shelter. The fragility and vulnerability of these bodies in the face of life necessities makes household governance possible, it is how non-domesticated space is transformed into domesticated space. Put negatively, hierarchies not organised around the management of life processes are not fundamentally household hierarchies. For example, many workplace and educational hierarchies are not households in this sense. Yet they are always situated within a wider form of household rule, the organisation of life processes, which shapes the character of other hierarchical relations.

The particular way households are captured in the first part of the book – through an analysis of changes across ancient, feudal, early modern and modern households – reveals the household ontology of the modern social realm.[36] It is argued that the extent to which government is about managing the welfare of the governed (administering life processes) then the best way to generate knowledge of government, the best language for thinking through changing forms of government and the relations between them, is through the genealogy of households. We still require different names to capture historically specific, contingent and variable forms of household government. For example, 'kingdom', the king's domain (from the Latin *dominicus*), is the space over which the king governs. However, it is not possible to identify every variant of household rule, which would amount to naming every single unit of rule in history organised around managing life processes. Different scholarly literatures have adopted different terminology to describe the historically dominant forms of household, including

[36] The pragmatic decision to use such distinctions should not be confused with 'stadial thinking', the view central to the evolution of social science that assumes a natural evolution from one stage of 'society' to another (Meek, 1976). There are certainly pitfalls to distinguishing ancient, feudal, early modern and modern, including an inherent arbitrariness, the dangers of Eurocentrism and the fact of historical continuity. However, as used here for heuristic purposes, they can be defended as shorthand to identify specific periods and places with relatively identifiable ways of organising life processes and therefore the changing forms of household rule.

oikos, Roman households, feudal manors, villages, royal households, empire as 'political households', all forms of despotism, early modern *Polizeistaats*, mercantilism, *driot administrative*, cameralism and modern capitalist empires/states. For example, the Russian Imperial House, which ruled until 1917, conceived of itself as a monarchical family-state, pioneering enlightened/benevolent despotism over a largely feudal (non-social) sphere.

In lieu of identifying and naming the full diversity of household forms, this book distinguishes between them to the extent that they elucidate what is particular and distinctive about the modern social realm to illuminate, in turn, liberal counterinsurgency. This is not to assume that sociocratic governance extended out of Europe endogenously and automatically through an internal process of development (cf. Bhambra, 2007; Matin, 2012) or that there are no non-liberal forms of social governance. Just as all non-liberal social theories adopted some of the general features of liberalism, given its co-emergence with empires of global reach, there are no forms of social governance that were not shaped by the initial emergence of the social realm (Hoffmann, 2011), whether through inciting resistance or in adopting and transforming social forms of rule. Hence there is a necessary co-relation and interdependence between different household forms and distinctly social regulation. For example, nineteenth-century radicals in Bengal adjusted the terminology *samaj*, 'assembly' or 'gathering', to make sense of the bourgeois civil societies that were coming into being as a result of new methods of expropriating Indian labour. In addition, forms of patrimonial and decentralised household despotism were transformed and deployed during overseas counterinsurgencies prosecuted by liberal states.

Taking seriously the historical rise of social thought and its relationship to household governance raises serious questions about the current use of social concepts in contemporary social, political and international thought.[37] Social terminology is often used in a rather banal and casual way, while many scholars defend talk of 'social relations', 'social processes' and 'social norms' as shorthand for the simple

[37] This is not to endorse every criticism of sociology or to adopt a view that there are no structures, only associations between people and objects, as recently argued by Bruno Latour (2005). Manuel DeLanda (2006) also offers a critique of the notion of an existing 'society as a whole', but continues to adopt social terminology in his 'social ontology' (of assemblages against totalities).

fact of human interconnection and coexistence. For others, the social world is a reality that underlies and supports all other human institutions of culture and community, politics and law, gendering, racialisation, class and sexuality, which are then used to develop general theories of human history.[38] Yet, if these banal or descriptive notions of human interconnectedness were the only or even primary way in which social concepts had entered into scholarly discourse then the dominant theories would look very different. A great deal of the baggage of nineteenth-century classical social thought underpins the dominant political and international theories, going far beyond the notion of the secular relational constitution of the human world.

Hence this book avoids using the concepts of social and society in a casual manner as, for example, when scholars speak of Vietnamese society, the society of states or social relations. Although there can be no such thing as a pure language, every effort is made to use these terms and concepts analytically and historically, rather than casually and ahistorically. While desirable, it is probably not possible for scholars to abandon social language, given how deeply entrenched it has become. In any case, we do not need to excise the words 'social' and 'society' from language. The appropriateness of using social terminology depends on whether it is accompanied by an explicit understanding of the historicity of social concepts and the household ontology of the social realm. In other words, we need to distinguish between social theories of international politics (Wendt, 1999; Joseph, 2012) and a theory of the historical rise of the social. Here conceptual history takes on a greater importance. Language is considered as a repository, possessing an historical life that can be excavated to capture real phenomena and concrete experience. This is not an argument for the deconstruction of concepts and distinctions, an approach that rejects any stable meaning for language as an expression of

[38] For example, in their important work, Barkawi and Laffey (1999) write repeatedly of 'global social change', of 'social relations and practices' and 'social institutions and processes', of 'embeddedness in particular social contexts', of 'capitalist social relations'. 'Social relations' represent the relative thickness of world politics in contrast to the thinness of liberal peace theory, neorealism and positivism, the latter unable to account for the situated-ness of myriad elements of world politics in time and space (Barkawi, 2006). However, the 'social' here is always shorthand for something else. As discussed further in Chapter 6, the overlap between 'the social' and an image of depth and thickness is a regular theme in both the history of social thought and much writing on counterinsurgency.

something non-linguistic, something that cannot be reduced to pure language (Derrida, 1976). Instead, we can enquire into the original experience out of which certain concepts such as household and domesticity arise and are transformed and how such an understanding has become obscured through dominant traditions of social and political thought (Arendt, 1958).

The second part of this book examines in detail armed social work across five cases in three chapters. These are two British late-colonial emergencies in Malaya and Kenya; the United States counterinsurgency in Vietnam; and the US-led but multinational 'population-centric' campaigns in Afghanistan and Iraq. Although not serving as full case studies, there are lengthy discussions of important nineteenth-century precedents, linking the two parts of the book: the French tradition of colonial war and the US occupation of the Philippines from 1898. These cases and examples were selected because they have in common the phenomenon to be explained, the attempted creation and regulation of a functioning social realm as a strategy of overseas pacification by liberal capitalist empires/states.[39] However, they also illuminate how the forms and functions of social regulation vary across historical periods, ideological framings, locations and national/imperial contexts. The structure and dynamics of social regulation changes in relation to the level of organised resistance; the resources available to the counterinsurgency state; the perceived racial 'Otherness' of the target population and other racialised and gendered practices; and the degree of external support provided to insurgents. In other words, experiences of war itself forced counterinsurgents to reconsider and revise forms of household governance. Rather than simply assume that

[39] The analysis is restricted to overseas counterinsurgency administration undertaken by Britain, the United States and US-led coalition forces. Russia and China are not liberal states and accordingly have different ideological rationales for their wars of pacification. Moreover, they are seeking to *directly* rule Chechnya and Tibet and Xinjiang, as part of their sovereign territory. Nonetheless, despite their obvious differences, both the Soviet Union/Russia and China also inherited a particular modern conception of the social, including an idea of order, mastery and universal validity that could be carried forward by intervention and coercion. For discussion of China's distinctive approaches to counterinsurgency see Wayne (2012). The state of Israel is closer to a liberal democracy for its Jewish citizens. However, in the occupied territories and through the settlements, Israel is engaged in a form of settler colonialism that is distinct from overseas occupations pursued by the traditional imperial powers.

counterinsurgency wars directly impact existing institutions and populations, the cases show how the effects of war are mediated through social forms of household regulation and thought.

Given the need to ground the analysis of specific counterinsurgency campaigns in previously under-explored history and theory, the case studies are to a great extent one-sided, primarily focusing on the character of counterinsurgency. It would require another book to show how insurgents sought to govern populations through techniques of household rule. Similarly, there is only limited discussion of the role of different household formations in countering the counterinsurgents (see Gurman, 2013). This is not, by default, to assume there is no conflict or politics inside households or that household rule is always successful in domesticating struggle. Even in the classical *oikos*, patriarchs were resisted and defeated in various ways (Keuls, 1985). Resistance to household rule is readily apparent, otherwise what is being countered by counterinsurgency? For example, during the Mau Mau emergency, Kikuyu women turned to what black feminist theorists have called 'homeplace' as a site of resistance (hooks, 1990: 43); this is one of the reasons the British tried to destroy all the vestiges of Kikuyu home life. In other words, to emphasise the agency of counterinsurgents is not to reserve agency only to them or present this activity as self-generated and immanent within imperial thought and practice (Hobson, 2012). In the analysis of every case, there are examples of local agency and/or the co-constitution of social regulation and resistance, a specific case of the more general co-constitution of household despotism and struggle. Nonetheless, this book is concerned with establishing how households have been one of the most successful arenas for the *domestication* of conflict, for the attempted removal of resistance. It does not attend to conflict and political struggle inside various forms of household to the same degree.

Research for the case studies draws on existing historical scholarship, as well as original readings of a number of primary counterinsurgency texts: field manuals, memoirs, government reports, think tank publications and the large scholarly literature that both formally and tacitly adopts the government/counterinsurgency position. In both the counterinsurgency texts and the work of professional historians, it is not difficult to find material on armed social work. It is among the most publicised and controversial aspects of the campaigns. In addition, wider sociological accounts of 'native populations', their violence and remedies for it are examined as counterinsurgency texts. These include 1950s theories of psychopathology, ethno-psychiatry, and community development; 1960s theories of development psychology and modernisation; more recent 'cultural' explanations for why Muslims take up arms; biological metaphors explaining the health of 'Afghan society'; and the profound insights of social systems analysis, such as, 'over time, everything affects everything' (Davis, 2011a). To repeat, these texts are not examined because counterinsurgents themselves somehow sought to consciously apply social theories to practice (with the possible exception of modernisation theory in Vietnam, as already implied; its leading proponent became National Security Advisor to President Johnson).[40] Certainly counterinsurgents are highly selective in the social theories they adopt. However, critiquing the selective use and shallowness of specific counterinsurgency texts does not reckon with how and why social thought in general began as and continues to be such a powerful object of political and military strategy.

The homology between social theories and counterinsurgency derives from both the historical origins of social theories as well as the ontology of the social realm as a scaled-up and transformed household. Social theories first emerged in the context of efforts to counter forms of insurgency, that is popular uprisings by workers and natives against the disruptive effects of capitalism and imperialism. This made social theories incredibly useful in the context of armed social work, an intensive, military form of pacification/domestication. The late-colonial emergencies and counterinsurgencies examined are wars of domestication in the sense that military strategists sought to create units of rule over local populations as a means to the end of defeating insurgents. In every case, military exigencies related to population coercion were interpreted and justified in sociological terms, underpinning the total administration of the life processes of the local population. This is not a functionalist argument that particular social theories automatically emerged from the dictates of specific elites or in the more common sociological sense that assumes 'social systems' as

[40] Cf. the words of American conservative social reformer, Francis Greenwood Peabody (1909: 7): 'The theorist is like the commander who stands apart from the fighting, but directs the battle and foresees its end. The army accomplishes what the theorist has planned. Has not this detached view of things its place in the Social Question.'

a whole are stable and cohesive. Rather, the military campaigns were accompanied by social theories because military leaders themselves understood what they were doing in terms consonant with the basic premises of social thought and academics, intellectuals and 'experts' offered distinctly social explanations and remedies for insurgencies, borrowing from existing social theories and pioneering new forms of *oikonomikos*, the science of household rule.

Chapter 2 analyses the broader intellectual context for the earliest forms of distinctly social discourse, from early modern natural law to Enlightenment theories of bourgeois civil society through to the nineteenth-century rise of social theories and sociology proper. Such a conceptual history shows the problem of the ahistorical social in international thought and the extent to which the dominant international theories were forged during nineteenth-century debates about the Social Question. Chapter 3 analyses the historical and theoretical significance of forms of household rule, beginning with discussion of ancient and feudal households, their hierarchy and mobility, as well as the deep, continuing symbolic and ideological functions of domesticity. The discussion begins in a familiar place in the history of Eurocentric thought, the ancient Greeks and Romans. This is partly justified to the extent that the dominant language of household government in the capitalist West, and hence for the object of empirical study, originates in ancient household despotism. Several of the key terms now used to describe rulership and government originate here, further evidence that so-called 'political' domination in much Western thought is better understood as household rule. Yet, there is no singular history of origins 'in' Greece and Rome for the genealogy of households. The Orientalist, as well as gendered, character of Greek languages of *polis* and *oikos* is irreducible. Athenian 'politics' was defined in opposition not only to the *oikos*, but also to so-called 'Oriental despotism'. Moreover, this focus does not assume that all forms of domination and rulership originate in the *oikos*, as if they did not exist prior to the formation of the Greek city-states or in other contemporaneous locations. The chapter also analyses the material and intellectual context for the transformation of household rule that accompanied the rise of commercial empires and states from the eighteenth century; and ends with analysis of the dramatic, crisis-induced expansion of social regulation (national and imperial housekeeping) from the middle of the nineteenth century. Crucially, new concepts of society and the social were forged in an intellectual and political context dominated by expanding commercial empires and imperial rule.

Chapter 4 addresses the colonial limits of the new discourse of civil society and liberal improvement, leading to the adaptation of distinctly social forms of household rule and ideologies of domesticity for the ends of liberal empire. Through the work of Sir Henry Sumner Maine, we examine the invention of the notion of an original despotic and functionally interdependent 'traditional society' in India that came to underpin strategies of indirect rule and later became so important in wars of colonial pacification and counterinsurgency. To date, international theorists seeking connections between classical European imperialism and more recent military interventions turn to John Stuart Mill's defence of liberal despotism (Jahn, 2005; Duffield, 2007). Until 'barbarians' were 'capable of being improved by free and equal discussion...' Mill argued, 'there is nothing for them but implicit obedience to an Akbar or a Charlemagne' (1999: 14). However, the international historical sociological scholarship of Henry Maine is of greater significance for understanding the connections between European imperialism, social theory and the decentralised household despotism of counterinsurgency rule. Turning more explicitly to colonial military campaigns, the chapter ends with discussion of French colonial wars as shaped by *raison de la société* and notions of progressive housekeeping in the turn-of-the-century United States' occupation of the Philippines.

Chapter 5, incorporating the first full case study, examines two late-colonial emergencies in Malaya and Kenya. It was not economy in the use of force that defined Britain's strategy, if economy here means moderation. Rather, in drawing on and enhancing older forms of despotic and sociocratic household rule, *oikonomia* in the use of force defined Britain's 'successful' strategies of depopulation and concentration in Malaya and Kenya, and were accompanied by the latest structural functionalist social anthropology and postwar social welfare ideologies. Chapter 6 examines the multiple houses of counterinsurgency created by the United States in its pacification war in Vietnam, the most extreme and destructive military campaign examined in this book. The radical nature of the social engineering pursued during this war is not explained by the form of social systems analysis that dominated American social science in the postwar period, and was seen as providing the final answer to the Social Question. Strategy was driven by the perceived needs of military necessity. However, US conduct in Vietnam most frighteningly exposed what is latent in the West's social theories of choice to deal with the non-Western world. Chapter 7 turns to the most recent US-led 'population-centric' campaigns in Afghanistan and Iraq, examining social regulation in the age of neoliberalism at the levels of nation-building, tribal 'society' and the family home. It shows how military strategy was heavily reliant on the notion of a passive mass of people essentially neutral regarding the outcome of the military campaigns; a population swayed more by social necessity than political commitment. This fundamentally gendered construction underpinned the military strategy of population coercion, involving house searches, censuses and financial and military support for the sectarian and despotic militia that, at the time of writing, continue to kill thousands of civilians in Afghanistan and Iraq.

2 *The really real? A history of 'social' and 'society'*

For us, too, 'social' civil society is, as it were, the divinity on earth. Society is our God, the ontological frame of our human existence. The social (as anyone who presumes to question its priority is reminded) is our name for the 'really real'. It secures the existential grounds beneath our feet, presenting a bedrock of reality beneath the shifting sands of discourse.

Kenneth Michael Baker (1994: 96)

The idea of a social explanation for political and international affairs is now widely taken for granted. Political sociologists examine the sources of state power and social movements. International historical sociologists debate which social forces underpin and best explain changes in international order. Empirical studies of social norms and processes of socialisation fill the pages of major journals of politics and international studies. Philosophers of social science debate the relative weight of agency versus structure, individualism versus holism, and materialism versus idealism. There is widespread agreement that there is such a thing as the social in general, a universal, always present sphere of interaction on which every human institution is based (Wendt, 1999; Hobden and Hobson, 2002). Uncritical adoption of distinctly social language is indicated in the periodic discussions of whether international relations is an American social science (Hoffmann, 1977). Debate has entirely centred on the first and third words, the extent to which the field is dominated by American scholarship and foreign policy agendas and methodological debate over the meanings of science. To date, the principle and most powerful criticisms of social theory centre on the legacy of Eurocentric categories and, under the influence of liberal and Marxist thought, its relative neglect of war. In response, scholars have offered postcolonial and war-centred sociologies of international politics (Barkawi and Laffey, 1999; Barkawi, 2006; Bhambra, 2007).

But when and why did social explanations for political and international affairs first emerge? More than two decades after the so-called 'social turn' in international studies there has been virtually no discussion of the historical origins and conditions for the emergence of distinctly social concepts and theories. This is not only a problem of anachronism and Eurocentrism. The widespread and largely ahistorical adoption of social thought across social and political science has obscured the theoretical and historical significance of households and ideologies of domesticity. Each of the major traditions of political and international theory – political realism, liberalism, constructivism and the English School, Marxism and Foucaultian critical theory – have all largely accepted the basic liberal premise that large-scale forms of household rule were eliminated in modern capitalist states. In contrast, the next three chapters reconstruct and analyse the relatively recent rise of the social realm and accompanying social forms of thought. We find that household forms of rule were not thereby eliminated; they were transformed and continued to play a central role in state, imperial and international relations. However, to initially focus on terrain more familiar to international studies, this chapter largely brackets explicit analysis of households to first address the political and intellectual conditions for the rise of social thought.[1] The purpose is to historicise distinctly social theories and to highlight a number of its features – the many variations notwithstanding – that would anchor and be used to justify counterinsurgency war, as examined in the second half of this book. These include a search for deeper social causes for political action; a propensity towards grand teleological claims about the nature of historical development, almost always drawing analogies with biological sciences; and faith that the remedy for crises in capitalist and imperial order is the introduction of often violent and radical new forms of social intervention. The relation between social theories and counterinsurgency goes beyond analogy. There is a homology rooted in their common origin in the theory and practice of household governance, the historically variable units of rule in which the life processes of populations are managed and through which they are domesticated.

[1] This is not to suggest that IR scholars have failed to situate their theories and concepts within wider traditions of modern thought (see Walker, 1993; Bartelson, 1995; Alker, 1996). The point is that these analyses have not subjected 'social' and 'society' to proper scrutiny (but see Bartelson, 1996; Owens, 2012, 2013).

Historical attention to the specific idioms and underlying assumptions of distinctly social discourses tells us a great deal about the dominant schools of modern international thought. Consider political realism. Defined by its commitment to the autonomy and specificity of the state, it would seem at first glance that political realism has a relatively uncomplicated relationship to something called society. It is the domestic sphere internal to state territory enabling the state to pursue its superior interests in power and security (Weber, 1946; Morgenthau, 1948). The politically and militarily preeminent state is defined by its relative autonomy over something understood in social/ societal terms, whether domestic society or the organisation of the social relations of production, the major foci of liberal and Marxist schools (Waltz, 1979; Gilpin, 1981). In the end, *raison d'état*, not the fractious class interests of competing factions, directs state behaviour. In twentieth-century political science, states are defined as either strong or weak depending on their degree of autonomy over society (Migdal, 1988). Society is something the state governs, something over which it rules. However, what are the origins of this discourse of state autonomy from society? At issue is not the plausibility of the political realist claim regarding society, but the historical conditions for its emergence, a surprisingly late development. Thucydides, so-called founding father of realism (Freyberg-Inan, 2012), did not conceive Greek city-states acting autonomously from the interests and concerns of the members of the *polis*, or that the *polis* acted on or over citizens. Such a distinction would have been nonsensical. Even more surprisingly, it is anachronistic to trace this discourse to justifications for the actions of early modern absolutist states in either Machiavelli or Hobbes (Meinecke, 1957; Viroli, 1992). It was only with the rise of commercial empires in the eighteenth century – and accompanying notions of the independence of market forces from state direction – that the language of society with an autonomous non-political logic fully enters European discourse.

Thomas Hobbes did, indeed, target what he saw as the pernicious effects of the growth of clubs, religious sects and small societies in early modern England (Withington, 2010). But these societies were understood in purely associational terms; that is, in line with the Latin origins of the term 'society' in 'association' and 'fellowship'. The question of relative autonomy that defines political realism is not simply an issue of factions, or the dangers of civil war and disorder;

that is, the interest particular governments might have in maintaining their existence against potential internal and external usurpers. At issue for political realism is the threat to 'the political' – defined as the state – from the historical emergence of a seemingly separate and distinct social logic emanating from such a thing as society (Treitschke, 1916). This is a product of the late eighteenth century. The shift in discourse towards a new social philosophy reflected a major transformation in household governance. The rise and expansion of capitalist markets and commercial empires was accompanied by a new distinction between state-public administration and privatised economy. 'Politics' and something called '*œconomy*' were given new meanings and distinguished from each other in a novel and very particular way (Schabas, 2005: ch. 1). This created the conditions for a new intermediary discourse of civil society, a form of *raison de la société* that sought to distinguish itself from the state and excessive state regulation of its commercial affairs. Only in this context could nineteenth-century political realists reassert state autonomy from the newly emergent notion of society. The reassertion of *raison d'état* against *raison de la société* seemed especially important in the wake of increasingly violent resistance by industrial workers to the realities of an unrestrained market (Hintze, 1975; Steinmetz, 1993). More specifically, primarily German political realist arguments concerning the relative autonomy of the state emerge in reaction to the increasing hegemony of French and then Scottish Enlightenment discourses of *raison de la société* and challenges to these discourses from newly organised and increasingly radicalised workers. At issue for political realism in the tumultuous nineteenth century was the fate of the political in the revolutionary Age of the Social. But, of course, political realism is not the only theory with a social problem. Virtually the entire field of international theory is deeply, although largely unselfconsciously, constrained by its origins in the historical rise of the social and associated modes of thought.

The chapter is divided into four parts. Departing from the usual ordering of international theories, the first section establishes the historical novelty of the concept of the social in the history of thought, drawing attention to the specifically 'social' roots of liberalism and the liberal roots of distinctly social theory. Liberal thought is conceived as an evolving philosophy of and for commercial/capitalist society, which was powerfully shaped by – and also helped set the terms of – the rise of distinctly social forms of household governance. As discussed further in Chapter 3, what we now consider to be basic liberal premises were fundamental to the abstraction and scaling-up of household rule, providing the language to formulate new distinctions between bureaucratic-state 'government' and 'economy', public and private. We begin the discussion in this chapter with an analysis of the rise of sociability discourse in early modern theories of natural law. However, contra English School writing on the 'society of states', natural law theorists did not have a concept of society as the ontological basis of all forms of human organisation. This general meaning only arose in the eighteenth century with new Enlightenment theories of bourgeois civil society. The second part analyses the response of Marx and his followers to the violent crises of civil society provoked by the growing power of organised industrial workers. Marx adopted several aspects of nineteenth-century social theory, yielding to realism the meaning of politics (essentially control over violence), and resulting in the near unanimous adoption of social language in later critical theory. The third section returns to political realism. Frightened by the prospect of class revolution and sceptical of classical political economy, realists pointed to the fundamentally political character of social regulation, including the creation of governable national populations where they did not previously exist. For political realism, the state's regulation of society was necessary to preserve the distinctiveness and autonomy of 'the political' defined in a very particular and not very convincing way. The final section analyses the rise of a much stronger sense of society in the sociological functionalism and positivism associated with Émile Durkheim's influential theories of social solidarity forged in response to violent upheavals in the Third French Republic. The particular way Durkheim attempted to purge liberalism of ideology would be enormously significant for the way mainstream sociology would be imported into international studies, especially English School discourses of a society of states and social constructivism. The most significant origins of social constructivism are less a critique of rational choice theory than the nineteenth-century rise of socio-biological theories of norms. Durkheim's structural functionalism and solidarism would join political realism as the basis of the most influential social explanations of and remedies for counterinsurgencies.

The autonomous logic of *raison de la société*? Towards liberalism

Despite the effort to construct a coherent tradition of international thought, often harking back to ancient Greece (Gilpin, 1986), international theory is decidedly modern in its steadfast and ahistorical adoption of the language of society and the social. The ancients had no separate word for such phenomena. As already noted, Thucydides (431 BC/2000) may have been an historian of democracy and empire, but for him, like all ancient thinkers, the relevant distinction in human affairs was between *polis* and *oikos*, the political realm of free citizen action and the violence of the household. Even if we accept that the Western tradition of 'international' thought (to use another anachronism) began in 431 BC with *The History of the Peloponnesian War*, then there is a gap of at least 2,000 years between the start of international theory and the emergence of social theories of international relations.[2] But this would still be based on a generous interpretation of the extent to which the early modern tradition of natural law constitutes the beginnings of an entirely new kind of social theorising. To be sure, at the beginning of the seventeenth century, the meaning of sociability and then society shifts with the writing of Dutch jurist Hugo Grotius, but especially German jurist and philosopher, Samuel Pufendorf. Sociability, from the Latin friendliness, came to refer to a form of fellow-feeling uniting individuals within Europe's wider commercial empires. But when these scholars of jurisprudence wrote of the

[2] The origins of the term 'international' are in Jeremy Bentham's 1789 book, *An Introduction to the Principles of Morals and Legislation*. The use of the term 'international' to describe relations between sovereigns, Bentham claimed, was preferable to 'jurisprudence among nations' or the 'law of nations'. 'It is calculated to express, in a more significant way, the branch of law which goes commonly under the name of the *law of nations:* an appellation so uncharacteristic, that, were it not for the force of custom, it would seem rather to refer to internal jurisprudence' (Bentham, 1789/1823: 326, fn.1; see also Suganami, 1978). Stanley Hoffman's explanation for the relatively late arrival of a science of international relations compared to political and legal science is rooted in the rise of 'social government', although he does not explicitly put it in these terms. Political philosophy seemed to have a lot to say about 'the common good in the domestic order', and its apparent regularities could be more or less predicted. 'But international politics remained the sport of kings, or the preserve of cabinets, the last refuge of secrecy, the last domain of largely hereditary castes of diplomats' (Hoffmann, 1977: 42).

significance of human feelings of sociability they did not understand themselves to be offering a social theory as such. Still, into the eighteenth century the only way of conceiving humans in their totality in European thought was religious or legal-political.

As indicated, the origins of social and society terminology are Roman, meaning to be friendly or genial. It derives from the Latin *socius* meaning companion or friend and *socialis*, a partner or an ally, a loose federation for a specific purpose and later to particular fellowships and partnerships of various sorts. In Old English, *secg* similarly meant companion. Early modern England and France witnessed an upsurge in the use of 'society' to describe the rise of voluntary associations made possible by the breakdown of feudalism (Withington, 2010). But this is still largely an extension of its classical use. How and when did the notion of an autonomous social logic separate from sovereign political will or social explanations for human affairs first emerge? Hugo Grotius is significant because he represents the earliest attempt to derive a more general account of human association from the Latin *sociabilis*, companionship, and *socialis*, to live with others.

Citing the Stoic's use of 'sociableness', Grotius claimed that sociability was the 'fountain' of right (1625/1925: Prolegomena, paragraph 6). Humans are naturally desirous of society and friendship; they possess an *appetitus socialis*. There is 'an impelling desire for society, that is, for the social life – not of any and every sort, but peaceful, and organized according to the measure of his intelligence, with those who are of his own kind' (1625/1925: 11, paragraph 6). This inclination towards sociability was not merely due to the requirement to satisfy the needs of life, although humans possess the instinct for self-preservation. People seek the society of others even when there is no need. Sociability, Grotius claimed, is a general disposition of fellow-feeling. The prerequisites of sociability are revealed by natural law, which can be accessed through the use of reason. The enforcement of natural law extended to the prosecution of war, an activity that Grotius argued was analogous to the enforcement of law within states, and could thus also be governed by reason and law. On these grounds, the state possessed no powers that individuals or collections of individuals in nature did not also possess. It is no coincidence that such claims emerged during an upsurge of competition between European empires and corporations for global territory and trade. In arguing that there was no moral distinction between individuals in the state of nature and sovereign states, Grotius was famously defending the right of private Dutch chartered companies to make war like traditional sovereigns. The Dutch East Indies Company, he argued, possessed a corporate sovereignty, a war-making capacity and associated public international rights. Grotius' defence of these rights was part of a broader innovation in legal theory in light of the needs of the rising commercial empires and early modern republican thought.[3]

The first real attempt to theorise an autonomous social logic independent of state direction emerges with Pufendorf's (1682/1991) natural law theories of property and commercial sociability. In a similar context to Hobbes, the increasingly perceptible terminology of both society and company reflected the expansion of various forms of early modern corporatism, forming the model for Pufendorf's attempt to theorise an autonomous social logic. His first task was to formulate a principle of society prior to the founding of the state while retaining Hobbes's method of constructing the argument on a claim about the state of nature. Both Grotius and Hobbes moved directly from humanity's assumed natural condition to the state's founding. Pufendorf pointed to forms of order that pre-existed the state, specifically the institution of – and combination of several – households (Bates, 2011: 89). Thus, the state of nature was not a state of war, as Hobbes had claimed. There were two states of nature, not one. In the first, claimed Pufendorf, people lived alone. But in a second natural condition, small groups could be found living peacefully without a common government; that is, in households governed by a household head. In principle at least, violent conflict could be avoided even without the enforcement of state authority because humans became aware of the dangers of attacking others. In Pufendorf's words,

> Man ... cannot subsist ... unless he is *sociable*, that is to say, unless he wishes to live in a sound union with his fellows and act in such a way that he gives them no reason to think he will do harm but rather that he is engaged

[3] The constitutional order of the United Provinces (1581–1795), which later influenced the framers of the US Constitution, was an exemplary form of republican corporatism allowing the realm of inter-state law to be conceived as identical to intra-state law. Eric Wilson has argues that Grotius's claims in *De Indis* (1604–1605) need to be understood in the wider context of early Dutch republican theory and notions of 'Corporate Sovereignty' (Wilson, 2008: xii–xiii; see also Keene, 2002; Boucher, 2009; cf. Deudney, 2007).

in maintaining or advancing their interests ... It follows that everything that necessarily contributes to this *sociabilité* must be held to be prescribed by natural law.

(quoted in Gordon, 1994: 63)

Hobbes had argued that society was not possible without the prior creation of a set of institutions to limit the human capacity for violence. But if we are potentially more sociable than Hobbes assumed, then it was possible to collectively organise without the enforcement of the state. This move allowed Pufendorf to go beyond the more limited role for sociability found in Grotius; sociable interaction possessed its own logic of operation independent of both individuals and the state.

With the early modern tradition of natural law both religious and legal-political modes of representing human life were superseded by modes of thought derived from the language of commercial *société*. For new forms of association were being interpreted and reinterpreted to give intellectual shape and philosophical legitimacy to the rising commercial empires. John Locke would build on these claims to develop a new theory of property for the early capitalist age. The origin of property rights, he argued, was not the will of the sovereign, privileges the king could bestow or take away. They emerged within the society of the state of nature; that is, prior to the founding of civil government (Locke, 1689/1963). Still, for Locke, political society referred to state government. The adjective 'social' was not transformed into a noun until well into the eighteenth century (Heilbron, 1995: 88). Until then, the term would continue to mean companion or gathering and not a general field of human interaction on which everything else was based. Again, only in the eighteenth century did the concepts of society and social begin to acquire this more general meaning as the ontological basis of all human organisation; that is, with theories of bourgeois civil society. Religious and legal-political reasoning came under further assault. Politics was associated with absolutist state power or civic republican and ancient notions of citizenship unappealing to the newest proponents of *raison de la société*. The underlying basis of civilised order was no longer religion or even sovereign power. It was a social contract between rational, self-regulating individuals.

Early eighteenth-century French philosopher Montesquieu did not use the term 'social' to describe human relationships or institutions.

However, his distinction between the state's commanding use of force and what were imagined to be the more gentle mores of commercial *société* helped to found the notion of society as self-instituting. In *The Spirit of the Laws*, Montesquieu (1748/1989) drew a now well-known contrast between government forms. Yet he initiated an intellectual tradition in which the laws animating these regimes was an outcome of the underlying character of *société*. For Montesquieu, the distinctive quality of each nation was evident from the common psychological characteristics and practices from which corresponding systems of politics and law emerged. The most significant distinction between human institutions was not forms of government as such but the basic and largely natural attributes of their core – society – and these attributes could not be transformed simply through the power of human (sovereign) will. The notion that societal or social relations were the deeper, underlying basis of surface laws and institutions would become a staple of distinctly social thought and, as discussed later, was one of the reasons social theories would be so attractive to those countering popular insurgencies. In each of the cases examined, counterinsurgents attempted to transform precisely what Montesquieu argued could not be so transformed, the underlying core of a peoples' way of life: 'society'.

David Hume made a parallel claim; the form of society was more important than the form of government, or even the presence of government at all. 'Though government be an invention very advantageous, and even in some circumstances absolutely necessary to mankind,' he wrote, 'it is not necessary in all circumstances; nor is it impossible for men to preserve society for some time, without having recourse to such an invention' (Hume, 1738/2007: 240; Finlay, 2007). Again, commercial sociability contributed to Hume's revaluation of the traditional distinctions between government forms (democracy, republic, monarchy, aristocracy) that had defined the classical study of politics. The relevant division was less between republic and monarchy than between civilised and uncivilised regimes. The level of civilisation was judged by the degree of protection for private property and support for the arts and polite *sociétés* where the manners most suited to commerce were instilled. 'Private property,' in Hume's words, 'seems ... almost as secure in a civilized European monarchy, as in a republic ... Commerce ... is apt to decay in absolute monarchs, not because it is less *secure*, but because it is less *honourable*. A subordination of ranks is absolutely necessary to the support of monarchy' (1994: 55).[4] As Sheldon Wolin explains, Hume ranked the level of sociability in the *salons* and other polite *sociétés* as

> the highest form of human achievement and the vital condition for the development of morality and rationality. The interdependence of each on all, which was the marvellous secret of society, furnished the basis for the complex structure of cooperation and the division of labor which had enlarged man's productive power and extended his mastery over nature (Wolin, 1960: 369).

Note the shift in the meaning of society. Where Hobbes' society is still enwrapped in a critique of the discourse on friendship and association, and for Grotius and Pufendorf *sociabilité* is a powerful form of fellow-feeling, for Scottish and French Enlightenment thinkers, society is more than a genial relationship. It is the general, quasi-natural sphere in which civilised humans are found. *Civilised* society was not a contract binding the individual to the state. It emerged out of individual material interests and communal needs: trade and manufacture, the realm of private freedom and collective necessity, not free political agreement. The social relations between citizens and traders were evidence that order could be produced entirely by the will of individuals, not by the violence of an external Will. 'Commerce,' Montesquieu claimed, 'polishes and softens barbarian mores, as we can see every day' (1748/1989: 338, Bk 20, ch. 1). Trade itself was a form of sociable conversational exchange with equally civilising effects. Society's principle of organisation was found within itself, not in any higher order. For Adam Smith (1776/1793: 19–25), this underlying social order was potentially harmonious; society itself could be the model of order, a sphere of interdependence in which self-interested individuals could also appear benevolent.

This, of course, is bourgeois civil society: relations of market exchange between rational, legally equal, sovereign individuals. Contra Hobbes, the emerging economic and social system was not a function of the state. Market forces possessed a degree of independence; they were 'non-political' (meaning not the domain of government action).

[4] Having important consequences for the methods and rationale of social administration, Hume argued that 'monarchical government seems to have made the greatest advances towards perfection ... Property is there secure; industry encouraged; the arts flourish; and the prince lives secure there among his subjects, like a father among his children' (1994: 56).

Politics needed to conform to the natural conditions of society, not the other way around. 'The task of enlightened government', wrote Elias (2000: 39) of this view, 'is to steer this automatism so that society can flourish on a middle course between barbarism and decadence'.[5] Rather than the state acting as the external force reining in otherwise untrammelled passions, the purpose of the state was to steer and guide the natural instincts. As Holbach put it: 'The principle of politics, to be useful, should be based on nature, that is, they should conform to the essence and goal of *société*' (quoted in Gordon, 1994: 73). In civilised society, social reproduction was properly private, an arrangement between free individuals in self-regulating competition that was both anarchic and harmonious, the original 'anarchical society' (Bull, 1977).

Crucially, the rise and expansion of commercial sociability made possible new claims about and critiques of something called 'politics', most commonly taken as synonymous with state government. When representations of human life became secularised there was an obvious intellectual break with theology, but also with classical political thought. To be sure, much philosophical reflection continued to centre on the state and law; matters of 'political economy' were understood as part of the state's legislative function (Wood, 1994). Yet through the eighteenth century, social philosophy slowly usurped the place of political philosophy in analysing human collectives. Especially in the pioneering centres of Enlightenment thought, it was claimed that – prior to the formulation of any political philosophy – society needed to be understood and theorised as the fundamental grounds of human existence. 'Human conduct,' writes Heilbron (1995: 72),

> was no longer perceived in relation to obligations and duties, but in terms of motives and effects ... Compliance with religious and political obligations was not a precondition for political order. In defiance of church doctrines and the tradition of political theory (Machiavelli, Hobbes), a *société* had come into existence where people who solely followed their own interests and preferences nonetheless managed to live together in an orderly fashion.

Social philosophy was tasked with representing and monitoring the social world in its imagined entirety, incorporating the now mere

[5] For an excellent discussion of how 'liberal peace theory' ignores the extent to which eighteenth-century thinkers of commercial society feared that a peaceful commercial order was effeminising and a danger to martial virtues see Neocleous (2013).

subfields of politics and law. 'Social science,' as Mantena (2010: 70) has put it, 'began at precisely that moment when the traditional project of political philosophy was abandoned.' This is significant. Many subsequent thinkers, including many international theorists, have viewed the effort to think beyond state sovereignty, to provide social theory underpinnings to the state itself, as a virtue of social theory. In doing so, they have obscured the ideological origins of the new discourses of *société*, for power and hierarchy were still legitimated through 'societal' principles; and too readily accepted that political theory is adequately represented by Machiavelli and Hobbes (Bull, 1977).

There is now a growing body of literature on how liberal internationalism emerged out of the intellectual and historical context just sketched; on the connections between eighteenth-century discourses of sociability on the theory and practice of early Benthamite liberal imperialism; on theories of liberal democratic peace; and justifications of the global division of labour (Doyle, 1997; Boucher, 1998; Keene, 2005; Deudney, 2007; Jahn, 2013). However, at this stage we have only addressed *sociabilité* discourse up to the late eighteenth century, before the consequences of the industrial and democratic revolutions 'socialised' liberalism; that is, when notions of a self-regulating civil society were thrown into violent crisis in both the heart of the major European empires and colonies (Bellamy, 1992). The first social philosophers set out to examine the conditions under which autonomous individuals interacted as members of civil society. By the nineteenth century, the image of self-regulating individuals producing a coherent and knowable order gave way to images of society in need of organisation, of continual administration to ward off incoherence, uncertainty and disorder (Mazlish, 1989). When industrial workers began to conceive of themselves more consciously as objects of exploitation and part of a common class, new forms of social theory and practice emerged and older ones were revised. And when a series of mid-nineteenth century rebellions across the empires demonstrated the colonial limits of civil society, new theories of 'traditional society' and forms of imperial rule were forged. The transition from eighteenth-century social philosophy to the still influential social theories of the nineteenth century was a product of multiple and varied crises of order. The main competing social theories – social liberalism, Marxism, political realism and their many variants – all initially emerged as explanations of and remedies for the increasingly violent demands of labour and natives. We return to two different strands of nineteenth-century social liberalism momentarily, both of which exerted enormous influence on international and counterinsurgency thought. First, we address the embrace of the social by radicals who might otherwise have illuminated a truly revolutionary politics of the dispossessed.

Marxism and the Social Question

Into the nineteenth century, European governments continued to reorganise themselves into more exacting and rational vehicles of control, including by using professional soldiers whose ranks had swelled with the revolutionary wars and were used to suppress domestic dissent. In 1819, for example, Manchester workers protesting for political reform were met by a cavalry charge. Productivity and industry were increasing; Europe's bankers and merchants had become richer; the bourgeoisie gained greater influence, including over imperial policy; and the era of great famines and epidemics seemed to be ending. However, the masses of labourers were poorer and greater in size. Violent repression alone could not solve the problem of democratic politics and the necessity of better conditions of life. Prior to industrial capitalism, anxieties regarding 'the poor' centred on the threat posed by paupers and vagabonds, those who did not work, the destitute who needed to be supported by charity (Slack, 1988; Dean, 1991; Castel, 2003). This changed with the revolutionary wave of 1848 and more organised worker rebellions over pay and conditions and peasant revolts against excessive taxation. Insurrections occurred in almost every capital city of old Europe.[6] An alliance of monarchists, aristocracy, military and some peasants defeated the radical movement, although not without making further concessions to powerful commercial and property interests.[7] The threat to the hegemony of bourgeois civil society was not only the old feudal privileges and excessive government regulations. It was a threat to the order of civilised society by wage labourers themselves.

[6] The major exceptions are Britain, the Netherlands and Russia.

[7] These forms of internal and external violence seriously undermines the claim of Polanyi, Arendt and more recent sociologists of war that the nineteenth century was characterised by relative peace due to the absence of multilateral great power wars in Europe before 1914 (Joas and Knobl, 2013). As Halperin has shown, 'European states fought *in Europe* fourteen interstate wars and twelve wars against the populations of other states; outside Europe, they fought some fifty-eight wars' (2004: xvii, emphasis in original).

Prior to industrialisation, the existence of mass poverty did not call into question the prevailing organisation of governance. Wage labour and industrialisation produced a different order of worker precariousness. The significance of poverty and hunger had changed. Workers were now structurally integrated into the system of 'free' wage labour that was bought and sold as a function of market demand. Yet, the 'freer' the labour, the less it was secure; old forms of dependency were replaced with new ones. The intensity of fluctuations in the commercial markets left workers far more exposed. Employment was unstable, temporary and poorly paid. New forms of vulnerability were produced with wage labour, as well as novel dangers as labourers became organised. Industrial capitalism had created a very particular and violent breach between the organisation of production and the democratic ideals expounded during the Haitian, French and American Revolutions. It did not require any social theory for workers to observe and understand the clear gap between the founding ideals of the democratic revolutions of the late eighteenth century and the realities of industrial life. Similarly, no social explanation for the Indian Rebellion was needed to explain the collective decision of a group of Sepoys to 'mutiny' in May 1857 (Maine, 1878/1908, 1888). The founding of the first modern republics had put equality at the centre of the new political discourse. To make such ideas credible, the instabilities and gross inequalities of life under industrial imperial capitalism needed to be mitigated, or they would be overthrown.[8] How, if at all, could the chasm be bridged between the cohesion of civil society and capitalist development, between political legitimacy and accumulation? Was it possible to integrate the proletarian class into the new industrial order without overturning capitalism itself? What could account for the scale and ferocity of the rebellions across the British Empire at the end of the 1850s? What new forms of imperial rule would be required?

These are all variations of the Social Question that dominated nineteenth-century European thought: was it possible, and if so how, to meet the demands of newly organised workers and native peasants without simultaneously destroying capitalism and liberal empire? The question expressed the conflict between claims of legal and political equality

[8] This did not apply to the former slaves of St Domingue/Haiti (James, 1938/1963).

and the reality of poverty and un-freedom in the new industrial age. Since, as Judith Stone (1985: 1) writes, it was originally 'a polite euphemism for what to do about and for the working class', the spectre of Karl Marx would be ever-present in the posing of, and answers to, the Social Question (Moggach and Browne, 2000; but see Pilbeam, 2000; Arendt, 1963; Aisenberg, 1999). The response of European governments evolved over time, usually from initial forms of direct violence against unruly workers and socialist activists to more subtle forms of repression and the augmentation of state powers. Marx and his followers were important participants in the struggle over the meaning of the social and answers to the Social Question. For revolutionary socialists, 'social' instability was not a danger but an opportunity. As Engels (1872/1970: 49) put it, 'only by the solution of the social question, that is, by the abolition of the capitalist mode of production, is the solution of the housing question made possible'. However, rather than analyse the extent to which the organised labour movement was able to found a new organisation of labour and politics, here we are concerned with the degree to which Marxist thought, initially inspired by outrage at injustice, carried over into its theories a social discourse it might otherwise have abandoned rather than reformed.

Marx had most thoroughly exposed the degree to which the rise of *burgerliche Gesellschaft* had created new relationships of power and subordination, dependency and vulnerability. He mounted a powerful and unmatched critique of many bourgeois forms of thought and organisation in which, he wrote, 'the various forms of social connectedness confront the individual as a mere means toward his private purposes, as external necessity' (Marx, 1973: 83). Marx powerfully rejected classical liberalism's sharp distinction between state and civil society, arguing that state institutions could not be so abstracted (Jessop, 1990). The modern state was produced historically out of the evolving conflicts and alliances between 'social forces' and 'formations', a concept Marx had borrowed from the social evolutionists but adapted to refer primarily to classes, struggling for power and resources.[9] Marx also

[9] House (1925) suggests that the term 'social forces' originates in the work of English social Darwinist and coiner of the phrase 'survival of the fittest', Herbert Spencer (1820–1903). For an attempt to develop a Marxist account of 'social formation', a term Marx did not often use, see Hindess and Hirst (1977). In IR see Cox (1987); Halliday (1994); Harrod (1997). The term 'social formation' also migrated from Marxist to realist IR (Gilpin, 1981).

rejected the liberal abstraction of the autonomous individual. But in line with dialectical thought and his belief in the progressive tendencies of capitalism, the liberal abstraction was flipped on its head. 'Above all,' Marx wrote, 'we must avoid postulating "society" again as an abstraction *vis-à-vis* the individual. The individual *is the social being*. His manifestations of life ... *are* therefore an expression and confirmation of *social life*' (1975: 299, emphasis in original). In agreement with earlier social philosophers, Marx conceived of social life as an historical process, the product of the interactions of individuals who were 'socially' produced. Marx's materialist conception of society began with the simple premise that every achievement of human existence required the prior satisfaction of the needs of the life process. 'The first historical act,' Marx wrote with Engels, 'is thus the production of the means to satisfy these needs [food, water, shelter], the production of material life itself' (Marx and Engels, 1970: 48). Society was a set of material relations and social relations of production and, like other theorists of Enlightenment, Marx viewed these relations as the foundation, the underlying base from which systems of law and politics emerged.

In other words, while rejecting the bourgeois abstractions of the individual and society as ideological justifications for particular class interests, Marx nonetheless further pioneered social explanations of history and predictions for the future. Social interaction would become a general human condition discovered during the Enlightenment when the veils of religion and absolutist state power were lifted. On this view, the discovery and first analyses of social relations were made possible by *burgerliche Gesellschaft*. But they are not beholden to it. For Marx and his followers, it is possible, even necessary, to rescue social categories from the original project of justifying the expansion of commerce and the indignities of wage labour. Really existing social relations should become the legitimate object of scientific analysis and intervention in the tradition of classical social theory (Giddens, 1973). Indeed, precisely because of their origins in capitalism, the concepts of social and society are the best analytical categories for describing the multiple and complex systems formed through the course of human history, even in pre-capitalist times and places.[10] Such a defence of the social – primarily as an analytical category – is absolutely crucial to

[10] I am grateful to Justin Rosenberg for articulating this response.

certain strands of critical theory, especially those most influenced by Marx. For liberalism and political realism, a reformed bourgeois civil society is the reality to be defended; the historical conditions of its emergence are not an intellectual problem in the same way. In these traditions, social thought and government explain and justify capitalist nation-states and are worthy of defence either because these are good in themselves (liberalism) or because they are better than any revolutionary alternative (political realism). The charge of the ahistorical social is a bigger problem for critical international theory, especially in its Marxist vein.[11]

It is, indeed, possible to distinguish between the justificatory discourses of *burgerliche Gesellschaft* and the more general idea of a sphere of relations between humans that are self-instituted. Often when Marx talked of humans as social animals he used the term in the broadest possible sense, merging it with all forms of human interaction. 'By social,' wrote Marx and Engels, 'we understand the co-operation of several individuals, no matter under what conditions, in what manner and to what end' (1970: 50). This could be in accord with the earliest pre-capitalist meaning of *socius* as companion and partly resonates with the sociability discourse pioneered by early modern theorists of natural law. Yet Marx's embrace of the social was not only, or even primarily, as an analytical category to describe a general field of human interaction. It was central to his philosophical anthropology and philosophy of history, as distinct from the critique of capitalism and science of human relations. In other words, these two notions of the social – the historically specific *burgerliche Gesellschaft* and the 'discovery' of society – are joined by a third and, for Marx, more fundamental form. This is Marx's claim that humans are not social beings in the simple even banal sense that, like bees, we live with and interact

[11] As Adorno (2000: 34) put it, 'the concept of society … is indispensible, even though it should be seen not as a given but as a category defining relationships'. On Marxism in IR more generally see Rosenberg (1994); Teschke (2003); Anievas (2010); see also efforts by Rosenberg (2013), Matin (2013) and others to extend Leon Trotsky's theory of the Russian Revolution, uneven and combined development, to a theory of international politics for all world history, a 'universal law'. Still, in these accounts, 'politics' essentially means control over violence. This mode of sociological theorising has also been criticised for its 'articulation of a deductive-nomological covering law, leading toward acute conceptual and ontological anachronisms, premised on … radical de-historicisation' (Teschke, 2014: 1).

with others. The social was to be the source of human emancipation itself. Marx centred his philosophy of labour and the labouring process on a discourse of man as a social animal with the end goal of a 'socialised humanity'. Marx defined humans as social beings *as such*; that is, in the more fundamental and essentially biological sense of 'species beings', again in common with contemporaneous biological and evolutionary theories of historical development. Society is 'species-life itself' and humans are a 'species-being' (Marx, 1972: 41).[12] This is the more fundamental reason why Marx and his followers could not abandon the language of the social; only through its embrace – only through the right socialisation of the human world – could alienation be overcome.

In part, this argument about the fundamental nature of humans was made through misreading Aristotle's claim of what was distinctive about humans. In *Grundrisse*, Marx wrote, 'The human being is in the most literal sense a *zoon politikon* ... an animal which can individuate itself only in the midst of society' (1973: 84). Aristotle had no such concept. But this did not prevent Marx and many later sociologists from anachronistically rereading Aristotle as the first social theorist.[13] Such statements are only plausible if politics is taken to refer to any and every kind of human association, which was certainly not Aristotle's meaning. Specifically political interaction and the fact of human connectedness were not the same for Aristotle. When he defined humans as *zoon politikon*, Aristotle was suggesting that the distinctly human quality was the possibility of forming associations that were not primarily for the fulfilment of biological/material necessity, something we have in common with all living things, and which hitherto have only been fulfilled through violence and household domination (Arendt, 1958: 23–24). Humans may be a species being, like all living

[12] Darwin's *On the Origin of Species* was published the same year, 1859, as Marx's *Critique of Political Economy*. 'The individual *is* the *social being*,' wrote Marx. 'The manifestation of his life – even when it does not appear directly in the form of a communal manifestation, accomplished in association of other men – is, therefore, a manifestation and affirmation of *social life*. Individual and species-life are not different things, even though the mode of existence of individual life is necessarily either a more specific or a more general mode of species-life' (1992: 158, emphasis in original).

[13] Similarly, French sociologist Raymond Aron, echoing Marx, suggested that '"Social animal" is as good a definition of' Aristotle's notion of humans as '*zoon politicon* as "political animal"' (1968: 8).

creatures. The real question is under what conditions can humans also be *zoon politikon*. Put differently, can the needs of the life process be managed non-violently and democratically through new forms of political organisation? Of course, this was also Marx's question. Indeed, he looked to Aristotle for possible ways to politicise the household, to collapse the very distinction between household and politics.[14] What does it matter, then, that Marx and his followers based their understanding of 'man as a social being' on an anachronistic misreading of Aristotle? After all, not all ways of conceiving the social have the same political, economic and imperial implications.

In embracing man as a social being, Marx and his followers carried with them and then multiplied the historical and theoretical baggage of nineteenth-century social thought: appeals to developmental laws of historical change; faith in the progressive tendencies of capitalism; belief in underlying social forces; and confidence in technocratic and administrative solutions to political problems. 'Society' did indeed become 'the gigantic subject of the accumulation process' or in Marxist terminology, the '"collective subject" of the life process' (Arendt, 1958: 256, 116). But, as argued in the next chapter, this is a variation on, rather than a negation of, household rule. Marx was right to historicise *burgerliche Gesellschaft* and to search for a new way of conceiving of the secular relational constitution of the human world. However, he made a category error in adopting distinctly social theory for his critical science. We need not deny that every achievement of human community requires the prior satisfaction of life needs or that capitalism should be replaced by some other organisation of *oikonomia*. But these observations require no social theory. Both capitalist and socialist images of 'socialised mankind' are as historically conditioned as that of bourgeois civil society and its colonial equivalents. Moreover, the deeply burdened language of 'social' interconnection, if it is more than simply an obvious banality, is just one way of representing human interrelations. It emerged at a very specific time, for specific reasons and is based on numerous false premises about politics: that Hobbes and Machiavelli speak for the tradition of political thought;

[14] As Marx wrote, 'The veil is not removed from the countenance of the social life-process, i.e. the process of material production, until it becomes production by freely associated men, and stands under their conscious and planned control' (1976: 173).

the quintessential political form is the authoritarian state; and, most pernicious of all, politics is essentially violent. Social terminology is not the only available discourse through which humans can be understood as making and remaking their worlds. For society was not 'discovered' as the ontological grounds of human existence necessary for an authentic social theory. It was one of the most aggressive and contingent products of a particular and problematic period of history. The point is not to advocate for a wholesale rejection of Marx, far from it. But in reifying the social, his followers would join the liberal tradition in obscuring the household ontology of the modern social realm and, as a result, would be unable to properly theorise politics, abandoning this terrain to realism (Davenport, 2013).[15]

Realist reactions: from *realpolitik* to *sozialpolitik*

In the French *salons* of the eighteenth century, a *société* was imagined to have come into existence in which, to borrow recent and influential IR language, individual 'preferences were taken seriously' without erupting into anarchy and disorder (Moravcsik, 1997). The discourse of *sociabilité* emerged as the set of polite and moral rules governing civilised conversation; it was from this location that the earliest theories of society developed as more generalising accounts of humane conduct in the commercial empires, forming the basis of the first distinctly social arguments regarding the historical development of civilised nations. In a direct challenge to the traditions of thought inaugurated by Machiavelli and Hobbes, social philosophy shifted understandings of order away from religious authority and government enforcement to individual motives and seemingly deeper societal causes and effects. Especially in imperial England and France, the new scholarly fields of political economy and social philosophy supplanted the study of politics and governing regimes as contenders for the dominant intellectual and scholarly subjects. 'A sovereign,' claimed Holbach, 'is not master but the minister of *société*' (quoted in Gordon, 1994: 73 n. 109). And

[15] It is possible to read the beginnings of such a distinctive political concept in *Grundrisse* with its subtler account of the distinction between public and private than found in Marx's indictment of bourgeois government and related distinctions. There may also be some evidence of an understanding of the need for a political theory in his studies of classical Greece, close reading of Aristotle and limited praise for the *polis* (see Schwartz, 1979).

as Adam Smith claimed, 'in the great chess-board of human society, every single piece has a principle of motion of its own, altogether different from that which the legislature might choose to impress upon it' (1869: 207).[16] Montesquieu, Tocqueville, Comte and Burke had all seemingly shown that the authority of government was based on the underlying social and largely 'private' conventions without which civil society could not cohere. As we have seen, Marx largely agreed, although he rejected the particular way the early social philosophers distinguished between public and private and on the coherence and legitimacy of civil society.

Either way, with the rise of *raison de la société*, what would become of the state's ability to identify internal and external threats? In the wake of the revolutionary upheavals of 1848, Prince Metternich had despaired that 'the crisis "was no longer about politics" (*Politik*) but the social question' (in Rose, 1999: 117). It was as clear to political realists as it was to Marx that 'society' (*Gesellschaft*) was a bourgeois concept of the 'third estate'.[17] It was also clear that the threat to order emanating from organised workers could not be contained by the logics of classical political economy. As argued earlier, primarily German political realist arguments concerning the relative autonomy of the state emerged in reaction to the increasing hegemony of French and Scottish Enlightenment discourses of *raison de la société*. For many German nationalists, society's association with bourgeois men more

[16] Or in the words of Moravcsik (1997: 517): 'Socially differentiated individuals define their material and ideational interests independently of politics and then advance those interests through political exchange and collective action. Individuals and groups are assumed to act rationally in pursuit of material and ideal welfare.'

[17] 'The whole concept of society in the social and political sense', wrote Swiss jurist Johann Caspar Bluntschli (1808–1881) 'is not really a popular concept, but a *Third Estate concept*, although we have grown used to identifying the state itself with bourgeois society' (quoted in Gödde, 2000: 164, emphasis in original). Contrasting bourgeois society with the 'nation', Bluntschli (1921: 109) writes: 'The Nation (*Volk*) is a necessarily connected whole, while Society is a casual association of a number of individuals. The Nation is embodied in the state as an organism, with head and members; Society is an unorganized mass of individuals ... The Nation is endowed with the unity of will, and the power to make its will in the State. Society has no collective will, and no political power of its own. Society can neither legislate nor govern, nor administer justice. It only has a public opinion ... The Nation is a political idea: Society is only the shifting association of private persons within the domain of the State.'

concerned with private accumulation than affairs of state was a source of deep concern rather than celebration. Heinrich von Treitschke's neo-Hegelian explanation of geopolitics as a battle between national souls followed Bluntschli in criticising the notion of a science of society. He was acutely aware that the new science was a threat to the integrity of proper political science. In reaction to this attack on state autonomy, a strong defence of *Staatswissenschaft* was required. As Treitschke declared in his 1897–1898 lectures on politics,

> there is in fact no actual entity corresponding to the abstract conception of civil society ... Where do we find its concrete embodiment? Nowhere. Any one can see for himself that society, unlike the State, is intangible. We know the State is a unit, and not as a mythical personality. Society, however, has no single will, and we have no duties to fulfil towards it ... Society is composed of all manner of warring interests, which if left to themselves would soon lead to a *bellum omnium contra omnes*, for its natural tendency is towards conflict.
>
> (Treitschke, 1916: 45–46; see also Megay, 1958)

If useful at all, social policy had to be a strategy of class de-politicisation, as first Chancellor of the German Empire, Otto von Bismarck, had brilliantly shown. After all, one of the most heralded practitioners of *realpolitik* had founded Europe's earliest comprehensive *sozialstaat* for reasons of state order and geopolitics. Imperial Germany, not Britain or France, was the first to establish a comprehensive social security system with compulsory sickness, accident and old-age insurance passed in 1883, 1884 and 1889. Not only social liberalism and Marxism, but also modern political realism would be forged in response to the Social Question.

By the late 1870s, Chancellor von Bismarck had developed a form of social policy that has been aptly described as 'the domestic side of a foreign policy whose foreign policy dimension was economic and colonial expansion' (Wehler, 1985: 132). Conservatives and corporatists were more likely to call for repression as well as bargaining with the uneducated and property-less masses. Yet even those most sceptical of the new social policy understood that working-class rebellions could not be defeated by repression alone. The underlying premise of the *Verein für Sozialpolitik*, founded by Gustav Schmoller in 1872, was that radicalised German workers could be pacified through a mix of social security and patriotism in which their fate was explicitly linked to imperial success. For Schmoller and others, *kolonialpolitik* was a branch of *sozialpolitik*; mutual borrowings between 'internal' and 'external' German colonialism were extensive (Grimmer-Solem, 2003a, 2007; Zimmerman, 2013). In addition to repressive anti-socialist laws, the working poor were marked as direct targets of intervention. *Sozialpolitik* was a paternalistic humanitarianism. Basic needs had to be satisfied in order to pacify workers to ensure Germany did not fall behind the more advanced capitalist states (Shilliam, 2009). The Chancellor had decided to recognise the core (male) industrial proletariat but endeavoured to contain its power by assaulting its organisational and leadership base. In short, Bismarck provided a structure through which a dangerous population could be socially integrated; the German social realm was an entity to be monitored and regulated through social policy and studied by the newly created field of sociology. Bismarck's innovative use of national insurance attracted adherents from across Europe, many of whom travelled to Germany in the years before the First World War to learn of its application (Donzelot, 1988: 425).[18] Although there are distinct national traditions, sociology was not a straightforwardly European product; it was a transnational and colonial enterprise.[19]

Bismarck's domestic adaptation of *realpolitik*, the rise of *sozialpolitik*, was the context for Max Weber's influential political realist paradigm of social regulation – his demand for a strong autonomous state able to cultivate an internal populace willing to support the requirements of the struggle between nations and races. The provision of welfare remained the means to the end of state and geopolitical power. 'In the final analysis,' wrote Weber, 'in spite of all "social welfare policies", the whole course of the state's inner political functions, of justice and administration, is repeatedly and unavoidably regulated by the objective pragmatism of "reasons of state"' (1946: 334). Weber's answer to

[18] 'Relative to [US President] Wilson's ideals circa 1890,' notes Ido Oren (2003: 41), 'Imperial Germany appeared much more "normal", and more like the US, than it appears relative to present norms and in the democratic peace literature; that is, as in the "authoritarian" box'.

[19] For a survey of different national traditions of sociology by sociologists see Genov (1989) and Levine (1995: Part II). For a brilliant historical analysis of the reciprocal influences between German colonialism in Poland and Africa, American labour relations in the 'New South' and German and American sociology see Zimmerman (2010: ch. 5)

the Social Question was a product of his underlying political realist conception of politics as the struggle over control of violence; the state was an apparatus of coercion competing against other apparatuses of coercion. The social unification of the nation was required to counterbalance the fragmentation and antagonism caused by capitalism and a strong *sozialstaat* was necessary in the context of the power struggle within and between nations. Though an outspoken 'imperialist, a racist, and a Social Darwinistic nationalist' (Zimmerman, 2006: 53), Weber lacked Treitschke's hatred of England, his disdain for the proletariat and the emerging science of society. Critical of the paternalistic and egocentric elements of Bismarck's social policies, Weber advocated a more rational and progressive *sozialpolitik* in the overall national and colonial interest. Workers ought to be subjects and not merely objects of state policy. Here Weber emerges as a transitional figure for political realism, between the conservative reactionaries and what has recently been described as the 'progressives' of mid-twentieth-century realism (Scheuerman, 2011). With Weber, and his contemporary Émile Durkheim, social theory was fully incorporated into the European intellectual arena and his political realist version of politics as the struggle for control over the means of violence would dominate international and counterinsurgency thought.

Weber participated in founding a tradition of sociology that was compatible with many of the core tenets of political realism as well as comfortable with the transformation of bourgeois civil societies into social welfare states.[20] In Weber's words, a political association is capable of 'arrogating to itself all the possible values toward which associational conduct might be oriented' (1978: 902). In this regard, German jurist Carl Schmitt's polemical rejection of the social can be seen as anomalous for twentieth-century political realism. For Schmitt, like Weber and later Morgenthau, the limited redistribution of wealth demanded by welfare states was a fundamentally political act in disguise, a quintessentially liberal neutralisation and de-politicisation of the friend-enemy opposition of class antagonism. *Social* law, Schmitt argued, served to 'protect one and disarm the other' (1950/2006: 332 fn. 17). Although British governments had shown that imperialism was 'the solution to the social question' (Schmitt, 1950/2006: 330),

[20] In *Economy and Society*, Weber (1978) suggested replacing the term 'society' with 'communalisation' or 'association' (see Terrier, 2011: 111).

Schmitt sought to distance the very term social from the German language; it was a 'foreign word' better suited to French and English where at least the non-socialist connotations had been retained. Like Treitschke, Schmitt attacked the rise of the social for what he took to be its de-politicising effects, at the same time rejecting the bourgeois notion that society was a self-regulating domain with a plurality of values and norms. Society did not, in fact, possess its own automatic principles of self-regulation of which the political order was a mere articulation. For Schmitt, it was absurd to seek to domesticate the state to society through bogus social contract theories as if the state could be normatively restricted with reference to these idealisations of its founding. Society was – or should be – domesticated to the essentially authoritarian state. On this reading, Schmitt's 'decisionism' was a reassertion of the unity of the political against the fragmentation caused by the rise of society, the revolutionary consequences of capitalism, and the need to manage its exigencies. Schmitt's solution to the Social Question could be summarised thus: 'the political decree[s] its law to the economic and the social, reducing their division from outside and by force, subordinating the social to the economic in the name of the latter's subordination to the political' (Donzelot, 1988: 420). From Schmitt's perspective, the state *had* to be more than just the instrument of society if the concept of the political was to make sense. Yet, as argued later, Schmitt's effort to theorise politics as non-domestication is unconvincing; it assimilates politics to sovereign power, which is a variant of household despotism. Politics and domestication are, indeed, opposites. But not in the manner suggested by Schmitt. Unfortunately, after Schmitt, those wishing to think through the distinctiveness and autonomy of politics would risk being damned by association with the authoritarian polemicist (Owens, 2011; more generally see Odysseos and Petito, 2007 and Teschke, 2011).

Where Schmitt is 'an acquired taste', not so Hans J. Morgenthau, the political realist of choice for American social science (Rasch, 2005: 182). Yet Morgenthau shared with Treitschke, Weber and Schmitt a set of basic assumptions about the nature and character of the autonomous political, as distinct from the social, an autonomy that needed to be preserved against all that the Social Question seemed to represent. From what was the political autonomous? 'The autonomy of the political sphere,' Morgenthau wrote in 1952, 'is endangered not only by the misunderstanding of the nature and role of morality but also by the imperialism of other spheres of substantive action ... The economic attack upon the political sphere dominated the nineteenth and the first decades of the twentieth centuries. Marxism and liberalism are its outstanding manifestations' (1971: 20). The threat emanating from the social was as much of a problem as that posed by confusion over the place of morality in politics. As Morgenthau (1946/1974: 35) noted in *Scientific Man vs. Power Politics*, it was only in the nineteenth century – the Age of the Social – that the merging of ethics and politics was understood as a perfectly achievable goal. Echoing Schmitt's concern with liberalism's repudiation of politics, Morgenthau observed that the earliest social reformers of the nineteenth century assumed that social problems 'were of a nonpolitical, rather technical nature, analogous to those with which the physicist and the technician have to deal' (1946/1974: 27). Liberalism and Marxism shared essentially the same view that had dominated European politics in that century: 'liberal science ... meets socialism in its attempts at social reform. Marx simply transfers the liberal confidence in the rational powers of the individual to the class' (Morgenthau, 1946/1974: 33). The task of a more sober and historical realism was to advance social and political reform – even radical reform – but without naivety regarding the ability of science to temper the never-ending struggle for power. In this period, Morgenthau viewed the rise of social policy from the heights of realist high politics, as the statesman looked down on the 'social engineer' (1946/1974: 219). His reading of social policy was overly shaped by his attack on the general philosophy of science as applied to human affairs, downplaying the general and widespread crises of order – domestic, international, imperial; each threatening a class revolution and even global revolution – that made interventionist social policy necessary.[21]

[21] For Morgenthau, the application of scientific methods to social problems offered no definitive solutions; all answers to the Social Question could only be 'temporary and ever precarious'. Three conditions shaped the degree of order and the relative success of social regulation, according to Morgenthau (1946/1974: 217), 'social pressure which is able to contain the selfish tendencies of human nature within socially tolerable bounds; conditions of life creating a social equilibrium which tends to minimize the psychological causes of social conflict, such as insecurity, fear and aggressiveness; and, finally, a moral climate which allows man to expect at least an approximation of justice here and now and thus offers a substitute for strife as a means to achieve justice'.

After Bismarck's creation of the *Sozialstaat*, fierce ideological battles ensued over social regulation, defining competing social theories and much modern political (and international) thought. Different proponents of liberal, conservative, feminist and socialist ideology debated the meaning of the social, the best way to prevent its dissolution; the terms and rationale for social intervention; and the relative weight of violent repression, incarceration, moral reform, personal responsibility and outright revolution in response to open class antagonism. For modern political realists, who could adopt both liberal and conservative methods but were self-consciously anti-socialist, social policy performed a particular function in the context of state power, a power shaped by its foundational violence. It was the supreme task of the autonomous state to subordinate domestic social problems to the national requirements of geopolitics, colonialism and the realities of life under capitalism. This would form the rationale for so-called 'realist' foreign policies, including financial and military support for despotic, even genocidal, regimes in the name of counterinsurgency. For others unwilling to abandon *raison de la société*, the state was envisioned as the means through which society could be perfected, as long as the management techniques were right (Ward, 1903, 1906). Others were less idealistic but nonetheless took for granted that the job of an enlightened state was to engineer society according to the highest technical standards and out of 'humanitarian regard for the weakness of special classes of society' (Hobson, 1901: 197). In contrast to political realists, who at least were open about the inherently conflictual character of civil society and the depoliticising task of social policy, there is another strand of distinctly social theory that emerged in the middle of the nineteenth century with a major influence on twentieth-century international theory and counterinsurgency.

Society of states without a history of society

What is 'society'? German political realists avoided the pitfalls of defining – as distinct from partially and politically historicising the emergence of – *burgerliche Gesellschaft*. However, to place sociology on a secure institutional footing, as well as sidestep the need for explicit ideological politics, required a clearer scientific statement regarding the nature of society: a definition. 'Society,' argued Émile Durkheim, 'is a reality *sui generis*; it has its own peculiar characteristics, which are not found elsewhere ... The representations which express it have a wholly different contents from purely individual ones' (1912/1915: 16; see also Durkheim, 1982). The workings of society could not be explained through individual psychology. Norms, rules and institutions were all 'social facts' that required social, not individual, explanations; that is, something more than simply multiplying individual interests and motives. At the same time, the objective task was to explain rather than merely justify the existing political and economic order. Sociology could achieve such a non-ideological status if founded as an objective science. By grounding sociology in positivism, Durkheim attempted to rid liberalism of its most obvious ideological positions. Of course, Durkheim's political agenda was rather transparent. He wished to provide a more secure base for the crisis-ridden French republic, borrowing both socialist and conservative ideas. Faced with a crisis of political and economic order, Durkheim's central question, which defined all subsequent forms of social liberalism, was how to reconcile a maximum autonomy for the individual with the regulation of personal conduct necessary to maintain order in modern, differentiated society. The conception of the national society – on whose behalf the state was imagined to act – had to become much stronger. Analogies with the human body were irresistible.[22] While the language of pathology had long been associated with bodily disease, from the early nineteenth century the term was extended to the abnormal functioning of society. Social pathology required social intervention, the proper regulation of society's organs.

Against more radical and anarchist critics of society's inequalities, organicist sociology pointed to the functional and natural interdependence of society's unequal parts (Barberis, 2003). 'By the term society,' wrote the French aristocrat Arthur de Gobineau in his 1855 *Essay on*

[22] Unsurprisingly, given its rootedness in the household governance of life processes, social thought is pervaded by biological metaphors to determine healthy and unhealthy 'social development'. 'The social realm,' wrote Durkheim (1912/1915: 18), 'is a natural realm which differs from the others only by a greater complexity ... That is why ideas which have been elaborated on the model of social things can aid us in thinking of another department of nature.' Prominent evolutionary and development theories believed 'the very model of the new concept' of society was the 'biological process within ourselves' (Arendt, 1958: 116). In Polanyi's words, 'The biological nature of man appeared as the given foundation of a society that *was not of a political order*' (1957/2001: 115, emphasis added).

the Inequality of Human Races, 'I understand a union of men actuated by similar ideas, and possessed of the same general instincts. This association need by no means be perfect in a political sense, but must be complete from a social point of view' (in Terrier, 2011: 25). The social and natural worlds were continuous. Borrowing heavily from the new field of biology, Auguste Comte (1875) had already claimed that society was a totality comprised of interacting parts, providing what many saw as the basis for an authentic social science. Social structure would be the subject matter of this strand of sociology, specifically the workings and dynamics of social solidarity (Durkheim, 1982). Contracts were upheld, not primarily because they were in the rational interests of the separate contracting parties, but because of the existence of a pre-contractual solidarity, identification with a common goal (Durkheim, 1893/1984). For contracts to be possible, the fundamentally moral order of society had to already exist. For Weber, society was no such abstraction, but a complex network of stratified classes, groups and other organisations. But Durkheim claimed solidarity was a social fact; it was created through a sense of belonging, the existence of a 'collective conscience'.[23]

As indicated, Durkheim could not accept that class conflict, suicide and divorce were 'normal' phenomena in modern society because they were against his ideals and normative commitments. The sociological (and tautological) explanation for such phenomena thus went as follows. As each part of society becomes more differentiated under capitalism, the risks of *anomie* increased: 'if the division of labour does not produce solidarity it is because the relationships between the organs are not regulated; it is because they are in a state of *anomie*' (Durkheim, 1893/1984: 304). As modernisation theorists and many counterinsurgents would later repeat, social pathologies were most likely in the transition from one mode of society to another (Rostow,

[23] For Durkheim, morality itself was embedded in collective conscience or collective representations; these needed to be reconstituted as a solution to the problem of order. The 'general conclusion' of *The Elementary Forms of Religious Life* is that 'religion is something eminently social. Religious representations are collective representations which express collective realities' (1912/1915: 10). The essential traits given to God were all also the case for society, all-pervasiveness and all-powerfulness. And the functions were very similar; 'even with the most simple religions,' Durkheim wrote, 'their essential task is to maintain, in a positive manner, the normal course of life' (1912/1915: 29).

1960). For Durkheim, conservatives were partly right; the solution to the crisis of order was to increase moral cohesion. But it was no longer possible to rejuvenate the old cohesiveness of primitive, relatively small, undifferentiated (mechanical) societies. Pre-industrial modes of sociability were redundant with urbanisation, the declining authority of the established religions and customs, and industrial capitalism's far more complex (organic) division of labour. And yet, given the essential complementarity of its separate though functionally related parts, the capitalist division of labour could be the source of a new solidarity. Social cohesion was based on the degree of mutual dependence of the component parts of society. As discussed in more detail in Chapter 3, solidarists successfully argued that the solution to *anomie* was the creation of new rules and norms for resolving conflicts between capital and labour, above all intervention into those segments of society most at risk of dissociation, especially the working poor.

If society was a moral order founded on collective beliefs, then the solution to *anomie* was working on these beliefs, creating new norms and constituting objects of intervention. As Castel (2003: 270) has put it, 'there is a direct connection between the idea of society as a collection of interdependent parts and practical modes of intervention in that society'. New forms of solidarity could be found in society itself, through the creation of new social ties. Since social phenomena were not the product of sovereign will or the psychology of individuals, any transformation of society had to occur through working on social *norms*, the social environment itself. Taking inspiration from but also moving beyond Bismarck's social policies, and against classical political economists who favoured limitations on state intervention, solidarists turned to the discourse of popular sovereignty to legitimise state and non-state socialisation. The political legitimacy of the state rested on the will or consent of the national 'people', a collective able to constitute and work on itself. The state was the visible expression of the invisible bond uniting members of the same society (Donzelot, 1984). In contrast to political realism, the state and its representatives were not the agents of a deliberate transformation of the structure of society. Rather, the state provided the means to maximise the effective bonds of solidarity within the existing structure. In this distinctly sociological mode, grand appeals to the philosophy of history and the nature of political obligation gave way to more piecemeal and ameliorative social reform (Ward, 1906). This new form of political legitimacy and expression played an important role in fostering the view that society, conceived in this period as a 'national people', was a state responsibility, and is the foundation of later claims regarding international society's 'responsibility to protect' populations inside delinquent states.[24]

While European societies were in danger of disintegrating into open class warfare and their empires had embarked on their most ambitious and ferocious imperial conquests, there was a proliferation of claims regarding the greater humanisation of society: the nineteenth century as the age of the humanitarian 'big bang' (Barnett, 2011). As civilisation progressed with the division of labour, Durkheim argued, so did the willingness of humans to sympathise with suffering; the increasing expansion of the scope of these feelings was a marker of humanity's progress. Instead of the local customs and taboos of *Gemeinschaft*, of small and relatively stable pre-industrial villages, more general abstract principles and laws were imagined to bind society together (Tönnies, 1887/1955). The contents of 'collective conscience' became more principled, concerned with justice and fairness, hence more interventionary towards the needs of the poor.[25] Rather than view social problems as an inevitable product of economic exploitation, the discourse of solidarity rather vaguely represented the consequences of the division of labour as a product of the contingencies of interdependence between members of society, for which no one individual or particular economic model could be held to account. From this perspective, the central object of sociological study and intervention was the moral rules that governed a particular society, rather than

[24] Consider the leading role of international society theorists in discussions of military intervention in the society of states, now usually framed as 'the responsibility to protect' (Wheeler, 2000; Finnemore, 2003; Hurrell, 2007; Bellamy, 2014). There is a strong echo of these earlier formulations of solidarity – in which society became the common site and criteria for intervention – and more recent solidarist accounts of humanitarian intervention (cf. Owens, 2004, 2007b: ch. 7).

[25] Recent pre-histories, of 'humanitarian intervention' emphasise this nineteenth-century shift (Bass, 2008, Barnett, 2011). However, rather than a step towards the teleological completion of liberalism, the humanitarianism that emerged in this period is better understood as a response to a major crisis in the prevailing form of rule; that is, within a broader and more fundamental structural transformation of the social realm.

structural inequalities. Again, moral unity ensured social stability and continuity.

Only very late in his career, Terrier observes, did Durkheim 'envisage ... more than one level of society; that there could be ... a further social level with different functional attributions and a differently binding moral force ... national societies as embedded in international communities, larger than nations and of a different nature' (2011: 75). Yet, long before theories of modernisation and globalisation, Durkheim claimed that the expansion of the division of labour would contribute to internationalism, making possible a true society of states and even the formation of supranational communities (Lukes, 1972: 350). During the Great War, Durkheim attacked militaristic German nationalism exemplified in Treitschke's claim that the state was a primordial natural necessity, the highest political and military power with a specific dignity. Durkheim could not accept that the state acted over and above society, that its aims were pursued through violence and were ultimately beyond moral limit. Treitschke's position was a misguided 'pathological' form of distinctly German patriotism. Germany's defeat in total war was a prelude to a more enlightened national and eventually 'world patriotism' led by the civilised nations (Giddens, 1986: 22–23). Just as the individual could not exist outside of society, so national states are embedded in a society of states and must accept the constraints on behaviour that this entailed. Sovereignty was relative to the moral norms established in international society just as individual autonomy is relative to the moral norms of society. 'There is no state which is not incorporated into the broader *milieu* formed by the totality of other states, that is to say, which is not part of the great human community' (Durkheim in Giddens, 1986: 23; Durkheim, 1915). Much of the current international theory discussion about 'international society' is an updated version of Durkheim's critique of Treitschke.

Although scholars of international society consider themselves to be heirs to the grand tradition of modern natural law, especially Grotius, they are far more reliant on Durkheim's functionalist and ahistorical evocation of society.[26] Consider Hedley Bull's tautological

[26] Bull (1979); Bull et al. (1990); Wight (1991); Watson (1992); cf. Bartelson (1996). On Grotius's appropriation in IR see Keene (2006). Kenneth Waltz

definition of a society of states. Such a society exists, Bull wrote, 'when a group of states, conscious of certain common interests and common values, form a society in the sense that they conceive themselves to be bound by a common set of rules in their relations with one another, and share in the working of common institutions' (1977: 13). If international relations are 'social relations' then, as Edward Keene has written of Bull's view, 'order in world politics should therefore be conceived as a form of social order' (2002: ix). On this reading, theorists of *realpolitik* 'underestimate the importance and frequency of cooperation and regulated intercourse among states, based on the norms, rules and institutions of the modern "anarchical society"' (Keene, 2002: ix). Once again, a theory of society is formed through an explicit critique of political thought with Machiavelli and Hobbes taken as the exemplary political theorists.

In Bull's sociological functionalist account, society comes into being to meet the practical concerns of individuals or states. As Barry Buzan interprets, 'all human societies must be founded on understandings about security against violence, observance of agreements, and rules about property rights' (2004: 52). However, rather than address the origins and problems of sociological functionalism, discussed in Chapters 5 and 6, the 'functions' of society are simply asserted. Similarly, mirroring Durkheim's claim that the legitimacy of sociology depends on the existence of 'special facts', Martin Wight argued that 'international society is, *prima facie*, a political and social fact attested by the diplomatic system, diplomatic society, the acceptance of international law and writings of international lawyers, and also by a certain instinct of sociability' (1991: 30). Again, the meaning of society is demonstrated through tautology. For Wight, the human 'instinct of sociability' is the basis of a 'thick' characterisation of international society. Without such a natural inclination, society would be 'shadowy and insubstantial'. With this depth metaphor common to social

also made use of Durkheim's notion of 'mechanical solidarity' in his structural theory of international politics. As John Barkdull has put it, 'Durkheim's "social segments" become Waltz's sovereign states, or "like units", and the segmentation of anarchic international society becomes, likewise, an insurmountable barrier to international integration or interdependence and thus to global transformation' (Barkdull, 1995: 669; see also Waltz, 1979). On the wider structural functionalist influences on Waltz see Goddard and Nexon (2005). Indeed, structural functionalism is making a comeback in IR (Buzan and Albert, 2010; Albert et al., 2013).

theory, and drawing on the purposefully ahistorical natural law claims regarding sociability, Wight applies Bull's definition of a society of states across history. This is possible because the historicity of society is not subject to enquiry in any major English School text. Indeed, in some cases it is actively effaced.

Consider the appropriation of Ferdinand Tönnies' (1887/1955) distinction between 'community' and 'society' in Buzan's (2004) influential writing on international and world society. For Tönnies, German village household communities were defined by kinship obligations, communal ownership of property, shared beliefs and a sense of a common fate. Individual identity was rooted in and governed by relatively stable norms in a historically grounded order, *Gemeinschaft*. 'The village community,' Tönnies (1887/1955: 68) wrote, 'even where it encompasses also the feudal lord, is in its necessary relation to the land like one individual household. The common land was the object of household activity and care and is intended partly for the collective purposes of the unit itself, partly for the identical and related purposes of its members.' The rise of capitalist markets and bourgeois civil society initiated a revolution in collective subjectivity in the feudal households. Property and labour were privatised and made exchangeable with other commodities. The interactions of now 'free' and self-interested individuals constituted civil society for instrumental purpose; individuals were 'independent of one another and devoid of mutual familiar relationships' (Tönnies, 1887/1955: 87). In contrast to the historical customs and hierarchies of feudal villages, civil society – *Gesellschaft* – was regulated through abstract law and understood spatially. These were relationships of exchange, of means to ends, of specific voluntary and limited associations. Tönnies' writing on *Gemeinschaft* and *Gesellschaft* is mirrored in the near contemporaneous distinctions between theocracy/sociocracy, status/contract, mechanical/organic and *societas/civitas*, in the work of Comte (1875), Maine (1878/1908), Durkheim (1893/1984) and Gierke (1934).

What relevance, if any, might this late nineteenth-century literature – and its wider context – have for thinking through the emergence of something called 'society' and, in turn, for any notion of a society of states? While acknowledging longstanding debates about the meaning of society, Buzan suggests that Tönnies' distinction is 'freighted with German historical baggage not relevant to the IR debate about second order society', that is, between states (2004: 110). Instead of enquiring into the historical conditions for the emergence of a distinction between *Gemeinschaft* and *Gesellschaft* 'one can instead extract the essential distinction and use it to identify different types of social relations in any historical context'. This has the benefit, writes Buzan, of moving 'away from ... all of the political and intellectual battles associated with it' (2004: 111). If not history, politics or intellectual production, then what is essential in the distinction? In Buzan's words, 'society becomes essentially about agreed arrangements concerning expected behaviour (norms, rules, institutions), and community becomes essentially about shared identity (we-feeling)' (2004: 111). In other words, the concepts of and distinction between *Gemeinschaft* and *Gesellschaft* can be removed from their historical setting, cleansed of their specific meanings in this context, and applied to any and every form of human interaction where 'expected behaviour' or 'we-feeling' can be observed. The primary advantage of this sociological functionalism, according to Buzan (2004: 111), is that theorists of international society have no obligation to offer 'a particular interpretation of history'. Durkheim's effort to rid sociology of ideological politics and history is accomplished in sociological functionalist theories of international society. For the history obscured is not only 'German baggage', and the sociological concepts and distinctions of Tönnies, Comte, Maine, Durkheim and Gierke were not only a 'German debate', as if those were not significant enough. They only make sense as part of a wider and rather momentous series of struggles across Europe and the empires to come to terms with, and find remedies for, popular insurgencies and to constitute and to theorise the differences between Europe's commercial societies and the populations they were seeking to conquer and reform.[27] In other words, the very concepts of and distinction between *Gemeinschaft* and *Gesellschaft* were distinctively modern practices of *oikonomikos*, the science of household rule.

[27] These thinkers can also be placed in a distinctly nineteenth-century tradition of nostalgia 'for the archaic household, including at times the extended clan, the vertically integrated patronage group, and the (generally masculine) martial community; the lure of empire, with its coeval promises of profits, new beginnings, and exotic escape from the mundane constraints of civil society' (Pecora, 1997: 13). Pecora describes this nostalgia 'as a rather basic reaction to the economic rationalization of civil society and the feminization of the bourgeois domestic sphere' (1997: 13), and is discussed in more detail in the next chapter.

Conclusion

Most contemporary international theory is deeply, although largely unselfconsciously, constrained by its origins in the historical rise of the social and associated discourses of the relative autonomy of society or the adoption of other instrumentalist social modes of thought. There are several reasons. The seeming 'discovery' of society and social forms of thought is often presented as a methodological advance. If IR theorists know anything about Comte and Durkheim it is that they founded the *science* of society, bringing positivism from the natural sciences to the study of the human-made world, now conceived as the world of social construction. The 'holist' critique of individualism, for example, held that all institutions were social institutions and thus not the outcome of human will; that is, potentially perfectible, but the product of underlying social facts. The social is the really real. However, this reading of the rise of social theory and sociology from the perspective of the philosophy of social science – as primarily a methodological discovery – obscures what was fundamentally a very different kind of project. Social theories arose as part of a multilayered attack not only on political philosophy, but also older forms of civic republicanism and democratic citizenship lest they provide a model for radical political action in the *modern* world. It is not often noted that the sociological tradition's 'essential concepts and its perspectives place it much closer to … philosophical conservatism', than we might otherwise think (Nisbet, 1966: 17).[28] In the writings of Durkheim, and also Weber and Marx, central conservative moral categories of community, authority, alienation and status became basic sociological concepts and theories of integration and solidarity but in scientific garb (Nisbet, 1966: 13). In particular, mainstream sociology's 'holist' critique of individualism; claims about the functional character of institutions and the need for intermediate associations; and notions of 'collective conscience' all originate in the conservative critique of the 1789 Revolution in France.

Durkheim's major achievement was not his definition of society, but the assimilation of conservative responses to the violent upending of established class and other relations of authority into the basic categories of mainstream sociology. This was partly achieved through

[28] For a rare discussion of conservatism and IR see Welsh (2003).

a re-evaluation of the political heritage of ancient Greece. For many late eighteenth- and nineteenth-century radicals, including Marx, the model for democratic participation recalled the politics of ancient Athens. Central to the critique of this potentially radical view of political participation was a claim regarding the irreconcilable differences between ancient and modern '*societies*', a difference understood as far more profound and determinate than assumed by the radicals' hope for democracy and a revolution in ownership of property. For the conservatives, the achievements of European civilisation were fragile, the outcome of a long historical process. All would be lost in radical democratic experimentation. In an argument that would also be marshalled in the invention of 'traditional society' and in social explanations for colonial revolts, industrial society had wrenched individuals from older forms of group attachment; the task of distinctly social thought was to found a new form of solidarity to overcome modern forms of estrangement and alienation (Mantena, 2010). It was not enough, as political and moral theorists had argued, to declare moral and political truths or forms of existence. It was not enough to take the workers or the peasants in revolt at their own word. Deeper social explanations for politics were required. Not the nature of sovereignty or politics, but debate over the mechanisms of solidarity and intervention into society came to dominate, what Stefan Collini (1980: 214) has described as 'those intellectually megalomaniac nineteenth-century social theories which attempted to subsume politics within some larger scheme of social development'.

The conservative, de-politicising origins of social theories should not be surprising. Assertions of the hegemony of social modes of governance and thought were always accompanied by attacks on something understood as 'political'. This is true of every move in the rise of social thought already discussed, from celebrations of private *société* and bourgeois norms of commercial civil society; to the emergence of functionalist accounts of 'traditional' Indian society; to Marx's attempt to transcend the political sphere; to Bismarck's social policy; to Weber and Schmitt's political realism; to Durkheim's call for an interventionist state; and Bull's functionalist definition of a society of states. What politics meant in each context was obviously different, ranging from the democracy of ancient Athens; the government of absolutist states; government regulation of commerce; the politics of the dispossessed in both metropole and colony; and classical political philosophy. All distinctly social forms of governance and thought are united in their attack on real and fictitious images of something they call politics. Why did social thought make its forward march by attacking what was variously taken to be political? The answer is both historical and ontological. The rise of distinctly social thought must be understood in the historical context of the establishment of the social realm itself and crisis-driven transformations of this realm, leading to the rise of distinctly social forms of governance from the nineteenth century. However, to understand fully the nature and character of the social realm within which social thought emerged requires a claim about its ontology. It is no surprise that the material and intellectual rise of the social was accompanied by various attacks on politics because the social realm was the distinctly modern and capitalist form of household rule, the space in which populations are governed and domesticated, the space in which they are depoliticised. Distinctly social thought is the modern form of *oikonomikos*, the science of household management, the science of how to rule over – de-politicise – populations.

3 *Out of the confines of the household?*

By the public police and œconomy I mean the due regulation and domestic order of the kingdom: whereby the individuals of the state, like members of a well-governed family, are bound to conform their general behavior to the rules of propriety, good neighborhood, and good manners; and to be decent, industrious, and inoffensive in their respective stations.

William Blackstone (1765/1979)

It is difficult to underestimate the influence of household rule on political thought. Since Plato, numerous political philosophers have claimed that the model of good government was a well-run household. If there is one foundational source of the notion that politics is ruling over others, mastery and domination, it is found in household rule. In the Western tradition, only liberalism has explicitly sought to displace despotic power with its image of government as a freely chosen social contract. Yet, even the liberal tradition consciously turns to household rule over subjects not able to self-regulate, especially children and barbarians (Mill, 1999: 14). The art of household management is obviously at the root of modern economics and theories of political economy (Myrdal, 1953; Schabas, 2005). And yet historical and theoretical analysis of households is absent in international thought and even rather fragmentary in political theory. This is a glaring omission not only given the historical and theoretical significance of households, but the centrality of the 'domestic analogy' in the history of international thought and much contemporary international theory. We have already given a preliminary explanation for this oversight, the extent to which political and international theory has been constrained by its adoption of distinctly social modes of thought. We now examine in more detail how this was possible: social theories and social forms of rule are the modern capitalist forms of *oikonomikos*, the science of household rule. More specifically, rather than the antithesis of household government, nation-states are a distinctively modern and bureaucratic social form of household rule. To understand how this is so, and how liberalism and social theory have obscured this reality, we need an account of the historical ontology of households.

What kind of space is household space? How is non-domestic space transformed into domestic space? Even to begin to answer these questions we need to abandon the nineteenth-century European idea of households as primarily houses, homes or families. Those governed within households are not necessarily (or even usually) family or kin, although the way in which this form of rule has usually been understood is through familial relations and analogies. Households are constituted by the nature of relationships between people in a particular spatial arrangement. They are units of rule in which the life processes of members are reproduced and the collective unit itself – the household – is maintained. For Aristotle, the ancient *oikos* was established 'as a means of securing life itself' (1962: 28, Bk I, ch. 2). These means included tending to the young, sick and elderly; the cultivation of animals, plants and agriculture; all the labouring activities necessary to sustain the life of those residing in the household. However, households have taken many different forms and have many different functions, from production, distribution, reproduction and military defence.[1] Household rule is despotic (*despot*, again, master of the house); it is always hierarchical, shaped by gendered, generational, racialised and inter-household hierarchies. Through the art of household management (*oikonomikos*), the household head oversees the administration of the domesticated and this administration is usually justified in terms of the protection and welfare of the household as a whole. Those domesticated inside the household are expected to submit to the rule of the householder, whether the traditional *paterfamiliās* or the anonymous dictates of bureaucrats. Crucially, household space is not necessarily fixed space or strongly bounded. Forms of household rule are eminently portable, such as medieval noble households or indirect imperial rule, the conditional delegation of power to a local despot. At the broadest level, the construction of household space can be understood as a 'process of domestication, which entails conquering and taming the wild, the natural, and the alien' (Kaplan, 1998: 583). This

[1] Hunter (1984); Mundy (1995); Allison (1999); D'Altroy and Hastorf (2002); Barile and Brandon (2004); Netting et al. (1984); Trigg (2005); Nagle (2006); Faroqhi (2010).

is captured in one French meaning of *domestiquer*, the 'subjugation of a tribe to a colonizing power' (Bowlby, 1995: 75).

The term 'household', much like 'society' and 'social', possesses various meanings in different historical periods, geographical locations and scholarly traditions. Prior to the rise of liberal contract theories, most – if not all – units of rule were explicitly understood to be households or were analogised with familial forms of rule. Historical studies in comparative politics suggest that government-as-household was a near universal feature of human organisation before the rise of modern bureaucratic states, although this literature has often mistakenly assumed that modern state bureaucracy contributed to the destruction of large-scale households (Hunter, 1984; Faroqhi, 2010). Today, however, the fields of archaeology, architecture, literary and cultural studies, economics, political theory and international relations all use household and domestic terminology to mean quite different things (Herlihy, 1985; Cox, 1997; Netting et al., 1984; Elias and Gunawardana, 2013). This poses a methodological problem for a study that seeks to trace households as a historically variable form of rule, as foundational to the tradition of Western political thought, and the continuing relevance of household rule and the science of *oikonomikos*. This problem can be minimised through attentiveness to the historicity of thought regarding households, to language itself, and the historical transformations of some of the most influential forms of household rule. It is simply not possible to offer an exhaustive historical survey of every form of household government. Yet order and coherence is given to what could potentially be an extremely wide-ranging discussion by limiting the analysis to four very broad household forms in a particular part of the world – ancient, feudal, early modern and modern. The analysis of these household forms is also limited to analysis of the dominant meanings of 'public' and 'private'. This emphasis is not to make an argument about the value of any general or normative meaning of public and private and how they should be distinguished. In fact, as Michael McKeon (2005: xviii–xix) has pointed out, only under modern capitalism is there a 'division of public *from* private ... the separablility of what formerly had been most intelligible not "as such" but as parts of a greater whole'. Rather, attention to the associated transformations of public and private in the history of household rule is necessary to illustrate one of the fundamental claims of this chapter. With the modern rise of the social in the late eighteenth century, the management of life processes, household activities, acquired their own *public* domain; they became a collective concern bureaucratically and professionally administered by imperial states or their representatives in the name of 'society as a whole'.[2] This gave states an enormously powerful means for countering popular insurgencies.

The first section of this chapter analyses the ancient *oikos* and feudal households, noting their particular relations of hierarchy, mobility and the deep symbolic significance given to domesticity, a symbolism that continues to be enormously productive and revealing.[3] The second part examines the effects on household rule of the breakdown of feudalism and the rise of mercantilist commercial empires, which by the early eighteenth century ruled over 'society' like one household *œconomy* for the sake of state power. Building on John Locke's radical theories of labour, property and contract, Enlightenment theorists of civil society would criticise mercantilist assumptions that the state could comprehend and control society as the *paterfamiliās* governed his family, although analogies between household governance and 'economic' management would persist. Nonetheless, the rise of the new discourse of 'society', as either self-regulating or an object of government not reducible to familial models, would obscure the extent to which the modern social realm was a scaled-up and modified form of public household. The third section supports this claim through analysis of the new forms and ideological rationalisations of household governance that accompanied the rise of the modern social realm. Commercial 'society' reconstituted – rather than eliminated – household

[2] The claim develops an idea first noted by Gunnar Myrdal, then Hannah Arendt. Myrdal noted how, despite Locke's critique of patriarchal despotism, liberal 'economic' theory continued to draw analogies between capitalist economy and housekeeping. Its function was to give some coherence to the economic process and, more importantly, to the notion of a 'single subject with a consistent set of ends' (Myrdal, 1953: 145). However, Hannah Arendt went further, arguing that the modern social realm is the 'public organization of the life process'. In 'modern society', she wrote, 'we see the body of peoples and political communities in the image of a family whose everyday affairs have to be taken care of by a gigantic, nation-wide administration of housekeeping' (1958: 28, 46). Unfortunately, much of Arendt's writing on the social lacked conceptual and historical precision.

[3] As Pecora (1997: x–xi) has shown, the ancient *oikos* was the pre-eminent 'image of a precapitalist household … in the midst of modern political economy' and as a 'reaction against, the bourgeois household of modern Western capitalism'.

rule. The fourth section reconsiders the famous Social Question of the nineteenth century born of a major crisis of the social realm after the industrial and democratic revolutions, and the practical modes of intervention into 'society' that would be required to forestall anti-capitalist revolution in Europe and, as discussed in the next chapter, serious anti-colonial revolt. By the middle of the nineteenth century and across imperial Europe's ideological spectrum there was agreement that 'the social' realm now existed as an entity; debate centred on the justification, degree and technical method of intervention into it. As already noted, debates about how and whether to domesticate dangerous populations would inflect the major political ideologies of the nineteenth century. It was out of these ideologies that contemporary international theory emerged and through which colonial pacification and overseas counterinsurgency would be understood.

Classical *oikos*, feudal households

The ancient Greek household, the *oikos*, was an incredibly powerful institution, performing tasks far greater than any obvious modern equivalent. It was the fundamental building block of the entire systems of *poleis*, or city-states, not only in terms of reproducing the life of citizens but also in the moral formation of citizens able to participate in military and political affairs (Xenophon, 1923; Pomeroy, 1994: 46). The primary activity of the *oikos* was the satisfaction of the basic material needs, the life processes, of the household master. In other words, labouring activities were transferred to others for the benefit of the household head and were organised in accordance with the personal ranking of members – master, wife, child, servant, slave – each understood to have specific tasks and responsibilities. The gendered, parental and master–slave relations between household members was seen as natural and inevitable. To a large degree, this despotic household space was defined by stringent inequality, a realm of violence, necessity, hierarchy and privation.[4] This is the Greek origin of the modern term 'private': the privation,

[4] Again, to point to the fundamental inequalities structuring the organisation of the *oikos* and the *polis* is not to assume the impossibility of resistance in the *oikos*; that is, to adopt Arendt's (1958) polemical characterisation of *oikos* life as totally defined by despotism and necessity. Greek culture appeared obsessed by the possibility of female rebellion against the reining 'phallocracy' (Keuls, 1985). 'The motif of the rebellion of the Amazons was the most prominent

the deprivation, of a life lived entirely in and primarily for the *oikos*, the privation of being unable to escape the toil and material hardship of only labouring. 'In the public sphere of men,' writes Keuls (1985: 5), 'buildings were massive and surrounded by phallic pillars, whereas private dwellings, largely the domain of women, were boxlike, enclosed, and modest.' *Oikonomicus* was the practice of maximising the welfare of the household. To the extent that household rule was one-man rule, it was considered analogous to the rule of a military commander in wartime (Xenophon, 1923: 8, 23; Arendt, 1958: 221). The master of the house determined the best interests of the household and the *oikos* was organised to enable the household head to actively engage in the affairs of the *polis*, purposes that were not reducible to the ends of *oikonomia*.

The extent to which the *polis* was functionally dependent on the *oikos* is obvious. Household management was a form of expertise for the acquisition of life necessities. In *The Statesman*, however, Plato not only argued that the good management of both *polis* and *oikos* were inseparable; he made no distinction between the constitution of a large household and the *polis*. The best model for political rulership was the hierarchal household; the same body of knowledge covered both domains. This way of modelling the relationship between different forms of rule – conceiving the *polis* on the model of the *oikos* – would be incredibly significant in the history of Western thought.[5] In

expression of men's gynophobia, or fear of women. Many other myths – as well as drama, the law, and the practices of everyday life – document the same view of women, as caged tigers waiting for a chance to break out of their confinement and take revenge on the male world' (Keuls, 1985: 4). Also, in the words of Julia Kristeva(2001: 161), 'The busy household and the bodies of women and slaves it contains were not – and still are not – destined merely for an unhappy life of labor ("travail", from *tripalium*, "torture") … [T]he "economy" of the household [*oikia*] is not limited merely to ensuring survival, and to the simple world of the *animal laborans* and his painful and servile labors that metabolize nature in order to make the body last.'

[5] As Leshem (2013: 33–34) writes, 'the Stoics chose to follow Plato and Xenophon in rooting the *polis* in the *oikos* … Philo … writes that: … *œconomia* is a special instance of statecraft on a small scale, since statecraft and *œconomia* are related virtues which … are, as it were, interchangeable, both because statecraft is *œconomia* in the state, and because *oikonomia* is statecraft in the home'. The first Christians also used household terminology. Christian 'community is defined as "the house of God (*oikos theou*) – and that of *oikodomē*, and *oikodomeo*– terms that refer to the construction of a house – in the "edifying" sense of constructing a community'. For Paul the Apostle, 'the attainment of the promised redemption' is presented as an *oikonomia* – that is, the fulfilment of a task of domestic administration …

fact, as Arendt reported, 'all the Greek and Latin words which express some rulership over others, such as *rex*, *pater*, *anax*, *basileus*, refer originally to household relationships and were names the slave gave to the master' (1958: 32 fn. 22). Indeed, to the extent that politics is imagined in terms of relations between rulers and ruled, as in all sovereign models of politics we are still thinking in terms of household governance. Aristotle, of course, was the first to challenge Plato's claim that there was little if any difference between the nature of rule in the household and in the character of life in the *polis*. Although 'the state is made up of households', he wrote, the *polis* was not an expanded *oikos* (in Booth, 1993: 2). There was a direct *opposition* between the forms of human association taken to define each location. Where the *polis* required a multiplicity of equal actors and opinions to thrive, the household was founded on hierarchy where one opinion was enforced through violence and one interest (that of the household head) was meant to prevail. In Aristotle's words, the *oikos* was established 'as a means of securing life itself, [however, the *polis*] is now in a position to secure the good life' (Aristotle, 1962: 28, Bk I, ch. 2; Booth, 1981; Nagle, 2006; Patterson, 2001).

Our primary concern here is not whether Aristotle's distinction between *polis* and *oikos* reflected actual life in the ancient city-states, nor is it to downplay the forms of resistance to household despotism practised by women and slaves. Instead, note the degree to which assumptions about the character of life in the household *gave meaning* to the political and military activities of the *polis* whether or not the two domains were analogised or opposed.[6] We are interested in the

[and] the Gnostics [also presented] ... Jesus as "the man of the *oikonomia*"' (Agamben, 2011: 23, 25). Paul 'refers to himself and the members of the messianic community using exclusively terms that belong to the language of domestic administration: *doulos* ("slave"), *hypēretēs*, *diakonos* ("servant"), *oikonomos* ("administrator"). Christ himself ... is always defined with the term that designates the master of the *oikos* (that is, *kyrios*, or *dominus* in Latin) and never with terms that are more openly political, such as *annex* or *archōn* ... [T]he lexicon of the Pauline *ekklēsia* is "economic", not political, and Christians are, in this sense, the first fully "economic" men' (Agamben, 2011: 24).

[6] In one pseudo-Aristotelian book, *Oikonomikos*, 'Political *oikonomia* is distinguished from war based on the kind of enemy against whom the "strategems" are enacted: while in war the enemy is a foreign power, in the case of political oikonomia it is the citizens and subjects of the ruler' (Leshem, 2013: 35). And yet the term *oikonomia* also 'appears in strategic (military)

symbolism accompanying forms of household rule, how the different meanings of 'politics' that would become so influential in the Western tradition were drawn in contrast to or modelled on the household. For Aristotle, the basic processes related to maintaining life – the endlessness and repetitiveness of labouring – were not considered distinctively human, but limitations imposed by nature on all animal life, including human life. Women and slaves – as not fully capable of expressing their humanity by participating in the *polis* – were forced through violence to provide life-reproducing functions largely for the benefit of free (and thus considered fully human) male citizens (Anderson, 1974: 36–37). Only in the *polis* were men assumed to be among equals and therefore able to experience the freedom to engage in public affairs. The unfreedom of a life in the *oikos* stood in stark contrast to the unpredictability and extraordinariness of political action. Not only was the meaning of humanity and political freedom drawn from a contrast with the *oikos*; it also gave content to perceived hierarchies between civilisations. Greek writers explicitly compared the despotic 'barbarian empires of Asia' to the despotic 'organization of the household' (Arendt, 1958: 27).[7] Long after the ancient *oikos* and its *polis* disappeared, the class, gendered and Orientalist legacies of Greek thought and practice still structures much modern thought. Forms of household rule and associated domestic ideologies retain their deep symbolism and productive power and, as argued later, were of enormous influence in colonial and counterinsurgency military campaigns.

literature, to indicate "the proper arrangement and management of supply and military affairs ... for a general in charge of the army"' (Reumann quoted in Leshem, 2013: 37–38). Cf. 'The presentation of an indispensible correlation between the overt violence of the battlefield and the ostensibly non-conflictual embrace of the household is given paradigmatic form in Machiavelli's *The Art of War* ... and in *The Prince*' (Mitropoulos, 2012: 52).

7 The notion of 'Oriental despotism' originates in the fifth-century BC wars between the Persian and Greek empires. Aristotle later argued that despotism was the natural form of government for Asian barbarians and Aristotle's classification was utilised in the Spanish conquests of the New World in the fifteenth century. Early modern natural law thinkers – Grotius, Pufendorf, Hobbes and Locke – all adapted the notion of despotism to justify rule over newly conquered peoples. Eighteenth-century theorists of sociability, above all Montesquieu, negatively compared absolutist government in Europe with Eastern despotism. From their different perspectives, Hegel, Marx and John Stuart Mill all theorised Asia as essentially despotic, backward and unchanging unless forced by external pressure, whether capitalism or liberal government, to 'develop' (Grafton et al., 2010: 261–263).

Conflict and competition between Greek city-states contributed to the decline of the ancient *polis* and associated household forms. However, despotic rule over the household was given an enduring legal basis in classical Roman law with the concept of the *paterfamiliās*. The *patria potestas*, the power of the father, established the absolute authority of the head of the family over his family and its property. The *paterfamiliās*, who was always a Roman citizen, possessed absolute power over the persons and property in his estate, including the right to decide life, death and marriage.[8] But this disciplinary power was based on the obligation to tend to the welfare of the household. As discussed in Chapter 5's account of the colonial origins of 'traditional society', Sir Henry Sumner Maine, Legal Counsel in British India, would argue in the nineteenth century that the *patria potestas* was the primeval basis of all political authority in non-capitalist (non-'contract') societies. In Maine's words, 'many rules, of which nobody has hitherto discerned the historical beginnings, had really their sources in certain incidents of the Patria Potestas' (1876: 17–18). For large-scale landowners, nonetheless, the Roman state had become a far less reliable protector of its privileges and more expensive to support. More and more state resources were committed to defending against barbarian invasions. Landowners could increasingly avoid the taxes demanded by Rome's weak successor estates (Wickham, 1984: 16). With the collapse of the Roman Empire, the slave mode of production was replaced by feudalism; slaves became dependent tenants in 'a self-contained household economy' (Habermas, 1962/1991: 15; Tönnies, 1887/1955).[9] The basis of feudal authority in medieval Europe was not slavery and taxation, as in classical Greece and Rome, but the ability of lords to appropriate feudal rents from peasant tenants.

[8] Kate Cooper argues that by the 'end of antiquity … the older vision of Roman family life based on the legal powers of the *paterfamiliās* gave way to a new ideal, in which the *paterfamiliās* had essentially ceded to the Christian bishop his role of arbiter in matters of piety and justice … [However] the erosion of the powers of Roman heads of households … had more to do with tax-collecting than with religious ideas' (2007: ix).

[9] At this stage, the old 'society' [sic] of feudalism, according to Marx (1972: 42), 'had a *directly political* character; that is, the elements of civil life such as property, the family, and types of occupation had been raised, in the form of lordships, caste and guilds, to elements of political life. They determined, in this form, the relation of the individual to the *state as a whole;* that is, his *political* situation.'

The organisation of the feudal household was not simply the underlying foundation of the wider 'political' community as with the ancient *oikos*; 'private' and 'public' were fused into one. There was no clear distinction between *polis* and *oikos*. Indeed, to the extent that we can speak in terms of public and private here, these spheres were analogous rather than distinct and separated. Politics (meaning government) and household were versions of each other. Production, reproduction and government (as domination) combined through the institution of paternalistic lordship. The interests of the ruling householder and the household itself were imagined to be the same. The common land was organised as one household on which peasants laboured to ensure survival and reproduction. 'The village community,' to quote Ferdinand Tönnies' influential account once again,

> even where it encompasses also the feudal lord, is in its necessary relation to the land like one individual household. The common land was the object of household activity and care and is intended partly for the collective purposes of the unit itself, partly for the identical and related purposes of its members (1887/1955: 68).

Working on estates, peasants existed in a direct relationship of servitude. Production was organised around subsistence agriculture; peasant communities were self-sustaining. Labour was arranged around the extended family and associated relations of dependency. 'This is not simply any large household or one which produces on its own various products,' observed Max Weber,

> rather, it is the authoritarian household of a prince, manorial lord or patrician. Its dominant motive is not capitalistic acquisition but the lord's organized want satisfaction in kind. For this purpose, he may resort to any means, including large-scale trade. Decisive for him is the utilization of property (1978: 381; see also Riesebrodt, 1989).

Rent appropriation was based on the lord's superior organisation of administrative power and greater capacity for violence. However, although violent domination underpinned feudal authority, control over violence was diffuse. Monarchs were not in a position to directly govern within clearly defined territories and landed nobility were restricted in their ability to use force against competing lords. As a result, jurisdiction was dispersed among a number of overlapping actors in a system of shifting relations of hierarchy and subordination. There was no permanent and unitary executive; sovereignty was 'parcellized' (Anderson, 1974: 151, 153).[10] In Arendt's words,

> Within the feudal framework, families and households were mutually almost independent, so that the royal household, representing a given territorial region and ruling the feudal lords as *primus inter pares*, did not pretend, like an absolute ruler, to be the head of one family. The medieval 'nation' was a conglomeration of families [households]; its members did not think of themselves as members of one family [household] comprehending the whole nation.
>
> (Arendt, 1958: 29 fn. 14)

Note here that the royal or imperial household encompassed more than any biological family unit. Again, the term 'family' did not refer to blood relatives but to those who lived in the same household. Moreover, just as there was no separate 'state', 'economy', 'nation' or 'society' – abstractions specific to modern capitalist states – there was no clear differentiation between internal and external; the boundaries of households were fluid (Teschke, 2003: 62).[11] This is also evident from the mobility of households. Again, although households are always located in space, this space is not necessarily fixed. Medieval noble households in England, for example, were famously nomadic, fluid and adaptable; they 'acted as a combination of storm troop, bodyguard, moving van' (Mertes, 1988: 12). Elite households 'could move from place to place, residential manor to manor, and still remain a household' (McIntosh, 2009: 6). Recall that households are not defined primarily by their location but by the nature of the

[10] These are the feudal origins of the notion of territorial 'sovereignty'. In the words of Sir Henry Maine, 'during a large part of what we usually term modern history no such conception was entertained as that of "*territorial sovereignty*". Sovereignty was not associated with dominion over a portion or subdivision of the earth … Territorial sovereignty – the view which connects sovereignty with the possession of a limited portion of the earth's surface – was distinctly an offshoot, though a tardy one, of *feudalism*. This might have been expected *a priori*, for it was feudalism which for the first time linked personal duties, and by consequence personal rights, to the ownership of land' (1878/1908: ch. 4, emphasis in original).

[11] 'In these formations, there is no more "social", than there is an "economic" or "political" or "scientific"' (Castel, 2003: 10).

relationships between members: organised around the differential satisfaction of needs with activities arranged according to perceived biological and other status positions. This feature will become important in the analysis of forced relocation and concentration of populations in counterinsurgency.

Although there were no clear-cut distinctions between public and private in feudal and medieval households, ancient notions of good household management as *benevolent* despotism thrived. This paternalist relation between governor and governed clearly persisted in medieval and feudal households; hierarchical relations were founded on personal, patrimonial rule by feudal princes (Dorwart, 1971: 11). All residents of the king's domain were members of the household and, while all were not equal to each other, all were equally subject to the king's authority and protection. 'The king, as the householder', writes Dubber, 'had his own *mund*', that which he protects or guards, and 'as any householder, the king had the power to protect his *mund*, and everyone and everything within it, against external attacks ... The expansion of royal power ... is simply the expansion of the royal household and its *mund*, the royal peace' (2005: 15).[12] The king was to act on behalf of the protection and welfare of the household as a whole. By the sixteenth century, royal power in England was understood to emanate from the king's household and cover the entire realm of the kingdom.[13] Departments of government were divisions of the royal household, including the exchequer, the courts and the army. And as monarchists would argue, royal power was derived from

[12] Foucault cites sixteenth-century French writer, Guillaume La Perrière who argued 'a good ruler must have patience, wisdom and diligence', with diligence being 'the principle that a governor should only govern in such a way that he thinks that he acts as though he were in the service of those who are governed. And here, once again, La Perrière cites the example of a head of a family who rises first in the morning and goes to bed last, who concerns himself with everything in the household because he considers himself to be in its service' (Foucault, 1991: 96).

[13] 'Henry VII,' writes Wood (1994: 11), 'personally directed affairs of state through the royal household, as medieval monarchs had done since time immemorial. By dexterous management of a variety of dispersed feudal bodies ... he was able to tighten his grip on state business and win the cooperation of the great magnates of the realm. By Elizabeth's reign, however, the royal household was no longer the hub of governmental power. The queen set the broad lines of policy but left the day-to-day implementation to her privy council.'

nature and God, just as the father's rule over his household was a reflection of God's will.

The 'good government' of the royal *mund* was facilitated by the monasteries, which became the main administrators of charity. The first state-run apparatus of poor relief in early modern England and then across Western Europe were established after the dissolution of the monasteries and alongside more general 'security' anxieties regarding threats from vagabonds (Slack, 1988).[14] Financed by taxes and, in the case of England, supervised by government and administered by local authorities, the poor laws of 1601 included assistance with food, outdoor relief, orphanages and compulsory apprenticeship of poor children and the founding of almshouses and hospitals through private charity. In the context of large demographic growth and accompanying sense that 'the poor' were a threat to the general order, new forms of poor relief were aimed at keeping them in check. Chinese and Islamic regimes also recognised obligations to subject populations, such as relief-giving, well-digging and the management of food and water supplies especially in periods of famine and drought. Confucian paternalism in late imperial China (1368–1911) meant that the Chinese poor were just as well (or badly) supported by state elites as they were in Europe.[15] Early modern forms of government assistance draw attention, again, to the persistent expectation that the householder is tasked with managing the welfare of household subjects.

The classic early modern statement of the specifically patriarchal origins of royal despotism is Sir Robert Filmer's *Patriarcha*, in which '*the natural and private dominion of Adam* [is] the fountain of all government and propriety' (Filmer, 1680/1984: 71). It was absurd to think of the king as somehow answerable to law when the law was the word of the king. 'The Father of a family governs by no other law than by his own will,' said Filmer, 'not by the laws or wills of his sons or servants

[14] The greater institutionalisation of assistance at the beginning of the sixteenth-century was 'occasioned by … crises of subsistence, increased food prices, unemployment linked to a strong demographic surge, … agrarian reforms … Poverty became the object of widespread public debate fuelled by the controversies of the Renaissance and the Reformation' (Castel, 2003: 27; see also Dean, 1991).

[15] Although there was a deep decline in the ability of state authorities to offer welfare in the post-imperial period, during the major armed conflicts that defined Chinese history in the early twentieth century the communist regime provided extensive welfare (Wong, 1997; Bayly, 2004: 82).

... And yet for all this every Father is bound by the law of nature to do his best for the preservation of his family' (1680/1984: 95). The legitimacy of the patriarchal family and absolute monarchical power was underpinned by appeals to the naturalness of both. Again, patriarchal power is accompanied by the duty to maintain the welfare of those residing in the household. Disciplinary authority, like that of a father over his family, was imparted for the benefit of the household as a whole; that is, as a corporate entity rather than for the personal benefit of all household members. Hence, his actions were not subject to limitation. The ends of preserving and protecting the household justified the means, grounding royal prerogative and eventually absolutist state power as a form of enlightened despotism, of household mastery. All subsequent contract theory would be united in attacking classical patriarchy as the basis of civil government. Most famously, Locke (1689/1963) distinguished between paternal and political power. The natural right of the father was not political but familial.[16] Legitimate political power was based on consent, a form of contract and convention that was prior to political rule. Locke developed early modern natural law claims regarding the existence of autonomous societal relations independent of state power to offer a new theory of property for the age of commerce. His enormously influential attack on unchecked despotic and personalist power did much to obscure the extent to which modern 'contract society' was a form of – rather than a negation of – household governance. It is not that all patriarchy disappeared in the modern age, but as a model of government it could not have the same power, especially in liberal societies defined precisely in opposition to it.

From household status to contract society?

In the classical patriarchal household, all those receiving protection from the household head and labouring in and for the household are subjected to the tutelage of the *paterfamiliās*. If this arrangement was sanctioned by God, if the earth was divided between patriarchs and kings, then property rights were fundamentally political, subjected to

[16] However, as feminists argued, 'a specifically modern form of patriarchy is established' through the means of contract, a sexual contract, in which women are 'the subject of the contract' (Pateman, 1998: 6, 1).

and conditional on the will of the absolute monarch. In his *Second Treatise*, John Locke developed an entirely new account of the relationship between labour, commerce and government, a new theory of property to counter Filmer and naturalise wage labour. The origin of private property, Locke claimed, was not the political discretion of kings. Property rights emerged within the 'society' of the state of nature; that is, prior to the founding of any civil government. As evidence, Locke cited what he took to be the untamed and natural life of Native Americans who made use of the earth and in doing so turned the products of their labour into personal property. 'The Fruit, or Venison, which nourishes the wild *Indian*, who knows no Inclosure, and is still a Tenant in common, must be his, and so his, *i.e.* a part of him, that another can no longer have any right to it, before it can do him any good for the support of his Life' (1689/1963: 328, Bk. II, ch. 5 sec. 26, emphasis in original).[17] Through the '*Labour* of his Body, and the *Work* of his Hands', man makes something out of nature 'and thereby makes it his *Property*' (1689/1963: 329, Bk. II, ch. 5, sec. 28, emphasis in original; see also Irvine, 2009). The effect of this argument on the form and theory of household governance was revolutionary. In the words of Richard Schlatter, 'before 1690 no one understood that a man had a natural right to property created by his labour; after 1690 the idea came to be an axiom' (1951: 156; Arendt, 1958: 110).

If the origins of private property preceded the formation of civil government, then government had no right to make a claim on private property without the consent of the rightful property owners, and this was true of both fixed land and of the mobile profits from commerce. Man, wrote Locke, is 'Master of himself, and *Proprietor of his own person*, and the actions or *Labour* of it' (1689/1963: 341, Bk. II, ch. 5, sec. 44, emphasis in original). However, labouring was not conceived in Aristotelian terms as the necessities of life and the life process, 'but rather', as Castel writes, '*of the necessity of the liberty to labor* ... and the concomitant establishment of a free market for labor' (2003: 155, 153, emphasis in original).[18] The liberty to exchange

[17] For a discussion of the significance of such claims about 'wild Indians' for the history of international thought see Jahn (2000, 2013).

[18] Castel writes, 'until modern times, labor is coterminous with the fact of finding one's self *outside* the order of wealth ... It is only with liberalism that the representation of labor will become "free", and the imperative of the liberty to work will be imposed' (2003: 152, 149, emphasis in original).

labour for a wage became a fundamental freedom. If individuals were owners, proprietors of themselves, then unchecked despotic and personalist power over equal (or potentially equal) others was unjustified since it infringed on a fundamental liberty. Against the absolute power of the despotic household head, Locke theorised the limited power of the state and limitations on the power of the householder over his sons and eventually even his slaves and wife. The governorship of the parent over the child is reasonable because it is temporary; it is limited given the potential ability of the child to self-govern. But, for Locke, paternal power was not the model of legitimate government as such. Liberal political theories would henceforth begin not with the patriarchal household as the basis of government but with the individual consenting with others to be governed in exchange for the protection of private property and 'security' of the wider dominion. With Locke's contract theory, human subjects were individualised, theoretically freed from the bonds of feudalism and conceived as rational and formally equal. Liberal subjects self-regulate. More specifically, they can be trusted to participate in their own self-government without threatening the lives and property of other self-regulating persons. Far from being the lot of slaves and other subordinated groups, the status of labour and labouring activities were elevated, subject to contract rather than tutelage.

Before describing the effects of this new 'liberty' on the structure of feudal households, briefly consider how Locke's 'societal' theory of property transformed the classical purpose of *oikonomia*. For Locke, it was the moral duty of landowners to utilise land in such a way that maximises the common wealth. But this is not the same as arguing that landowners – like the ancient head of the household – had a duty to pursue common political purposes, as Aristotle had argued. The despotism of the household and *oikonomikos* were not ends in themselves; they were means to the higher ethical and political ends determined by the free citizenry. The satisfaction of basic material needs, all *oikonomia* in the household, was subordinated to the political community.[19] For Aristotle, recall, a particular conception of political freedom

[19] Rather than the basis of the accumulation of ever-greater wealth, property was understood as a private enclosure from which men were able to enter into the public world. This vision of a largely use-value, needs-oriented economy was attractive to Karl Marx, who commented favourably on the democratic possibilities of the Greek model. Marx expanded on Aristotle's distinction

and community life was the end purpose of *oikos* activity; *oikonomia* was distinct from but embedded in wider community needs. In the first instance, household activities were subordinated to the needs of the patriarch, but ultimately they were arranged around the political and military requirements of the *polis*. Locke explicitly rejected this ancient notion of the embedded status of commerce and the priority of the public, political realm, as well as more contemporary republican renditions of the priority of civic virtue, a legacy of Rome. Justifying an attack on the despotism of ancient slavery and the servitude of peasant life, capitalism *appeared* not to require 'economic' activity to be embedded in the same way, into a think set of moral and political values to which *oikonomia* was subordinated. The stated liberal concern, recall, was to preserve the autonomy of self-governing subjects and to theorise relations between them. 'Interests to be pursued,' Booth (1992: 251) notes, 'replace the good life as the binding cement of the new economy.'[20] Rather than indicating deprivation, privacy became the site of negative freedom from illegitimate interference. Political action was not conceived as an end in itself; government was established as the means to the end of protecting liberty. Rather than achieving one's full humanity through active participation in the political sphere, by the nineteenth century the private person in the bourgeois home would become the definition of the human with moral rights.

Through the eighteenth century, European governments were taking on 'political œconomy' tasks such as regulating public investments and seeking to sway 'private' commercial ventures to maximise revenue and increase the military power of the state (Smith, 1776/1793). The growth of chartered companies, as arms of mercantilist state power, allowed imperial states to mobilise and exploit 'private' resources for trade far beyond those immediately available to the exchequer.

between the simple exchange of commodities in a needs-based economy and one directed towards the accumulation of surplus. Marx's ideal of an economy embedded in and determined by the needs of genuinely free subjects had no role for the patriarchal despot of the classical *oikos* or slavery (McCarthy, 1992; Booth, 1994).

20 The rising bourgeoisie 'only had interests and no glory to pursue, and everybody *knew* this pursuit was bound to be *doux* in comparison to the passionate pastimes and savage exploits of the aristocracy' (Hirschman, 1977: 63).

Mercantilism reigned as a product of royal absolutism and mercantilist empires competed with each other to harness the resources of the core territory over which they governed, as well as oversee commercial relations in pursuit of a positive balance of trade and the further acquisition of territories. These empires developed far-reaching strategies to increase their capacity to tax, put down peasant revolts, modernise armies, encourage industry and increase surveillance (Dandeker, 1990; Tilly, 1992; Downing, 1992). With the support of increasingly sophisticated state bureaucracies able to raise capital and provide military protection, national territorial 'economies' began to form, as did clearer distinctions between legal jurisdictions. The reproduction of life, as it were, was no longer a matter primarily left to the feudal household or medieval manor. It required state regulation and protection in the interests of what could now be conceived as the national 'society as a whole'. These empires were *Polizeistaats*; œconomic activities referred to the general administration of the community as a whole on the model of a well-ordered household. 'The science of policing,' wrote Johann von Justi in 1768, 'consists, therefore, in regulating everything that relates to the present condition of society, in strengthening it and improving it, in seeing that all things contribute to the welfare of the members that compose it' (in Hoffmann, 2011: 17)

Like the head of the ancient and feudal household, monarchs determined the general welfare under the *ancien régime*. The common thread linking all previous forms of *oikonomikos* to English mercantilism, French *droit administrative* and German cameralism and *Polizeiwissenschaft* was the competitive struggle to improve the productive capacities of the domesticated subjects of power. Eighteenth-century *Polizeiwissenschaft*, an adaptation of the earlier German notion of *Polizei*, legislative regulation, was comprehensive, incorporating moral behaviour, public works, city sanitation, medicine, public health and laws for the marketplace.[21] As William Blackstone wrote in the passage cited earlier, 'public police and œconomy' referred to the 'due regulation and domestic order of the kingdom: whereby the individuals of the state, like members of a well-governed family, are bound to conform their general behavior to the rules of propriety' (1765/1979; for the

[21] As early as the fifteenth century, for example, the House of Hohenzollern, pursued legislative regulation of poverty, vagabondage and lawlessness in the interests of protecting trade and order (Dorwart, 1971: 14).

US context see Novak, 1996). In other words, as a theory of government, police science was in line with the earlier approaches to household rule. Commerce was understood as simply a part of statecraft, a more general governmental concern, with no independent logic of its own (Small, 1909; Raeff, 1983). The kingdom remained a large household constituted by smaller households that were vehicles of royal power, and sources of revenue. The heads of lesser households were given aid and protection to maintain their household and thus wider public order. To be sure, late eighteenth-century 'enlightened absolutist' reformers were influenced by new ideas of science, reason and administration. But this despotism only improved the lives of subjects to make them more useful to the household (increasingly conceived as 'society') as a whole (Scott, 1990). Colonies too were in the king's dominions. 'The model of household governance ... applied with particular force to the colonies,' notes Dubber (2005: 29), 'even though the enormous distances often interfered with the king-householder's exercise of his patriarchal power.'

The concerted effort to expand royal sovereignty through the cultivation of 'society' unleashed forces that would eventually undermine absolutism itself. Under *Polizeiwissenschaft*, society had no independent logic. Police regulation was for the sake of *raison d'état*, not *raison de la société*. By the end of the eighteenth century, the discourse and practice of 'public police and œconomy' would come under assault from liberal proponents of something called 'political economy'. To be sure, Locke had already argued that society was a domain of order and stability unto itself that could establish legitimate government through consent.[22] Early modern England and France witnessed an upsurge in the use of 'society' to describe the rise of voluntary associations with the breakdown of feudal arrangements. Recall Withington's observation that, '"household" and "family" figured much less frequently in the printed horizons of readers ... This contrasts with the increasing visibility in print of "society" and "company" and the concept of deliberate and purposeful association they

[22] Locke moved 'straight from "conjugal society" and the "society betwixt Parents and Children" to "*Political Society*", which he defines as "those who are united in one Body, and have a common established Law and Judicature to appeal to, with Authority to decide Controversies between them, and punish Offenders, *are in Civil Society*"' (Locke quoted in Withington, 2010: 130, emphasis in original).

invoked' (2010: 112). Nonetheless, for Locke, 'political society' was still coterminous with the state. With Montesquieu, Smith and Hume, in contrast, civilised society emerged out of individual material interests and trade, the realm of private 'freedom'. As already discussed, the underlying form of 'society' was viewed as more important than the type of governing regime. Turning the relation between state and society on its head, Scottish Enlightenment theorists claimed that society instituted itself and abided by laws not amenable to police science. Absolute monarchs were in no position to observe, let alone control, the operations of this self-regulating domain. The French Revolutionaries too had shown that 'society' was imminent to itself, its own creation. It could represent itself to itself without reference to anything exterior, either God or the state. From Locke's attack on the familial analogy to the new liberal economists pushing back against market regulation, including by dismantling the old system of poor laws, the notion of the monarch as despotic head of one large family managing its *oikonomia* appeared to be in terminal decline.

Proponents of the new liberal political economy called for the removal of protectionist legislation, reductions in poor relief, the closure of the guilds and the repressive workhouses, and the end of all forms of forced labour, including slavery. The old system of poor laws was an anathema to adherents of liberal political economy. In addition to systematically abusing inmates, the workhouses were an inefficient means for utilising the 'labour power' of the masses. A more rational and productive organisation of labour had emerged with the rise of civil society. In addition to protection from external threat, the role of the state was to contain and eventually eliminate all feudal institutions that hindered the market, including the market for labour. The attack on the traditional poor laws and guilds were central to the freedom to labour, but more importantly of freeing access to labour. From the early seventeenth century, poor relief was provided in the context of fears about the disordering effects of population growth and pauperism due to the commercialisation of agriculture. The form of regulative state that emerged to promote the 'general welfare' of the population through police ordinances was in line with *Polizeistaat* and paternalist ideas that the welfare of the people was the personal responsibility of monarchs overseeing the royal household as a whole. However, from the beginning of the eighteenth century, historians have observed a transformation in the posture of elites: 'the poor came to be seen as a threat to be controlled, or as opportunity for social and economic engineering, rather than as an object of charity' (Slack, 1988: 205).[23] Poor relief, it was increasingly claimed, increased indigence.[24] If left to their own devices, the virtuous poor thrived through their own industrious activity. The autocratic state, fully aware of the need for a productive workforce, instituted a series of mechanisms to compel the able-bodied to work, including vicious attacks on the moral character of vagabonds. The removal of older mercantilist regulations did not mean the end of discipline. In common with feudal and paternal practices of *Polizeistaat*, the basic life and moral needs of the poor were to be more actively managed.

In England, the Poor Law Amendment Act of 1834 replaced the Poor Law legislation of 1601, creating a centralised system of administration of paupers, including the establishment of workhouses that consolidated distinctions between deserving and undeserving poor, usually based on the perceived ability to work. The collection of poor relief and the administration of poor houses were now to be overseen at the national level. The system was based on the principles that aid should in no way undermine the incentive to work and the

[23] Based on a survey of the available literature, Castel (2003: 142) argues that in the period prior to the Industrial Revolution, 'in the average year between 5 and 10 percent ... were dependent for their survival on various forms of relief, whether as the ward of a hospital or "charity", or as the recipient of partial relief in the form of ... distribution of food or of occasional subsidies. In the country, there were no such specialized institutions ... This was maintained at what appears to be a more or less constant level for several centuries, affecting the whole group of countries then composing "wealthy" or "developed" Europe.'

[24] Although written a few decades later in reaction to the eventual updating of the older poor laws, Joseph Townsend's infamous attack on the new 'social' legislation captures the sentiments of the new political economy. He wrote (1786/1971: 19–20), 'There never was greater distress among the poor: there was never more money collected for their relief. But what is most perplexing is that poverty and wretchedness have increased in exact proportion to the efforts which have been made for the comfortable subsistence of the poor; and wherever most is expended for their support, their objects of distress are most abundant; whilst in those counties or provincial districts where the least provision has been made for their supply, we hear the fewest groans. Among the former we see drunkenness and idleness clothed in rags; among the latter we hear the cheerful songs of industry and virtue.'

Malthusian belief that poor relief should not contribute to unsustainable population increases. The wealth of nations now depended on the rational organisation of the market for labour based on the principles of the liberty to labour (for the labourer) and free access to labour (for employers) (Smith, 1776/1793). Yet attacks on existing provisions occurred in a context of a dramatically increasing vulnerability in the mass of the population with a decline in agricultural employment and inflation caused by the Napoleonic Wars (1803–1815). After these empire-wide campaigns, dynastic police states and imperial regimes were re-imposed across Europe with the help of experts in administration and representatives of the bourgeoisie. By the 1830s, it was clear that a fundamental disjuncture had emerged between the political rights of citizens proclaimed during the democratic revolutions and the industrial system that spread a new kind of structural poverty. As Halperin (2004: 70) reminds us, from the end of the revolutionary wars in 1815 through to 1850, 'approximately one third of the population of Europe lived below the level of subsistence and "at the brink of starvation"; another one-third lived at subsistence level but with no reserves for periods of unemployment or high food prices'. It would take a crisis in charitable and paternalistic forms of poor relief in the face of revolutionary insurrection for distinctly 'social' welfare and 'social insurance' to emerge as major stabilising institutions for the modern capitalist and competitive empires.

Polizeiwissenschaft was measured by and continuous with the government of the extended family (non-synonymous with kin). Liberalism defined itself against such a model, primarily focusing on the wrongs and inefficiencies of patriarchal rule. But it is not only liberalism that obscures the continuing relevance of household forms of rule. For Michel Foucault, it was not primarily the free workings of the market that was threatened by police science. Rather, in the eighteenth century, he argued, a new form of 'biopower' joined older forms of sovereign and disciplinary power, and its 'discovery' was dependent on the eradication of 'the family' as the model of government. For Foucault (1991: 92), the issue for *Polizeiwissenschaft* was 'how to introduce this meticulous attention of the father towards his family into the management of the state ... To govern a state will therefore mean ... to set up an economy at the level of the entire state, ... a form of surveillance and control as attentive as that of the head of a family over his household and his goods.' However, according to

Foucault, the eighteenth-century emergence of 'populations' with their own statistical regularities and cycles irreducible to those of the family made the familial model of government redundant. It was, he wrote, simply 'too thin, too weak and too insubstantial' to grasp the complex mechanisms necessary for working on and through the biological life of 'populations' (1991: 98).[25] Foucault goes on,

> prior to the emergence of population, it was impossible to conceive of the art of government except ... in terms of economy conceived as the management of a family; from the moment when, on the contrary, population appears absolutely irreducible to the family, the latter becomes of secondary importance compared to population, as an element internal to population: no longer, that is to say, a model, but a segment (1991: 99).[26]

Only when the immobilising model of the family was abandoned could a new art of government emerge – the governance of humans as population (Foucault, 2003, 2007).[27]

To be sure, the life process of populations became subject to a variety of normalising and controlling interventions. Moreover, the 'family' would, indeed, become a segment of the 'population' and an instrument of government. However, in these passages just cited, Foucault fundamentally misconstrued what the underlying historical and theoretical model of *Polizeiwissenshaft* actually was. It was not the patriarchal family as such but the patriarchal *household*. As Wood (1994: 106) writes,

[25] 'Statistical investigations, which were initially concerned with estimating and comparing the wealth of nations and examining the relation of national wealth to population size ... gradually revealed the population as a domain with its own specificity and irreducibility. Investigations ... inscribed the nation in terms of a set of aggregated statistics with their regular fluctuations, and as knowable processes with their laws and cycles' (Rose, 1999: 113).

[26] In important respects, Foucault's writing on 'governmentality' is a corollary of biopolitics. He defined governmentality as the 'ensemble formed by the institutions, procedures ... calculations and tactics that allow the exercise of this very specific albeit complex form of power, which has as its target population ... resulting ... in [the] formation of a whole series of specific governmental apparatuses' (1991: 101–103).

[27] Foucault (2003: 223) was right to note that with the rise of 'society', 'The essential function and the historical role of the nation is not defined by its ability to exercise a relationship of domination over other nations. It is something else: its ability to administer itself, to manage, govern, and guarantee the constitution and workings of the figure of the State and of State power. Not domination, but State control.' 'It is the power to "make" live and "let" die' (Foucault, 2003: 241). But this is the purpose of household governance.

'the Latin *familia* is properly translated "household" instead of "family", the latter unlike the former customarily denoting blood relationship'. From Nicholas Delamare's *Traité de la Police* (1722) to Adam Smith's *Lectures on Justice, Police, Revenue and Arms* (1762–1763) and William Blackstone's *Commentaries on the Laws of England* (1765), the 'science of policing' was not modelled on the biological family as such. The science of public police and œconomy concerned the regulation of the household order of the state. Everything Foucault cites as the focus of biopolitical government – 'the welfare of the population, the improvement of its condition, the increase of its wealth, longevity, health' (1991: 99) – was and would continue to be integral to household governance. The point is not to suggest that there was nothing new with the rise of the modern social realm, which did indeed involve extensive intervention into and management of the life processes of populations. Feudal households did indeed slowly disappear in parts of Europe. However, several of the activities, mentalities and oppressions associated with ancient, feudal and early modern households did not dissolve; they were transformed. 'Liberal thought,' Foucault (1997: 74–75) rightly noted, 'starts not from the existence of the state ... but rather from society, which is in a complex relation of exteriority and inferiority with respect to the state.' But what is 'society'? The rupture in the mode of production introduced by industrial capitalism transformed the character of household governance. It did not destroy it. This suggests that Foucault's notion of 'biopolitics' is less the essence of contemporary relations of power, as many of his followers suggest, than one element of something more fundamental: the modern rise of the social realm as the major new arena for the management of collective needs including, especially from the nineteenth century, the life processes of increasingly radicalised populations.[28]

The household ontology of the modern social realm

The bloody religious wars in seventeenth-century Europe demanded great commercial and financial innovation from state rulers, consolidating the power of administrative and military bureaucracies. Significant elements of private exchange became the concern of bureaucratic state apparatuses. Labour, land and exchanges of goods were increasingly

[28] On the difference between biopolitics and Arendt's analysis of the rise of the social see Owens (2012).

absorbed into the market, exchangeable for other commodities and subordinated to the pursuit of surplus. The primary unit of production was no longer the feudal household but the commercial, soon to be industrial, national and imperial marketplace. With the forcible expropriation of land in much of northeast Europe, small peasant property ownership and serfdom were destroyed (Brenner, 1985). From the middle of the eighteenth century, common agrarian land in England was appropriated for private use through a series of parliamentary and local government acts, creating a landless class of cheap labourers for emerging industry. Abandoning the feudal household, primarily male workers would now exchange their labour for a wage. With peasant labourers separated from the land, the accompanying mode of production, relations of authority and connections to territoriality, kinship and co-residency were also destroyed. Wage labour, understood in terms of private contractual market exchange, was distinguished from the labouring activities undertaken in the newly conceived 'private' intimate family 'home'. Large numbers of peasant women were deprived of customary agricultural labour and would instead labour inside houses increasingly reconfigured into units of consumption and reproduction. No longer subordinated in the household of the feudal lord, the new proletarian class would struggle instead with the 'economic' precariousness of wage labour and the 'political' laws of the administrative state. These terms – 'economic' and 'political' – would be given new meanings and distinguished from each other in a new way.

The despotic but embedded household of the feudal manor was slowly and haltingly destroyed in much of the core of the powerful commercial empires of northwest Europe, although not in the overseas empire itself. The global expansion of commerce produced a new set of distinctions between state-administrative (public) power and (privatised) economy. These, in turn, were the ideological and material conditions for the rise of a separate social realm, the hybrid space between capitalist economy and state-political institutions. The administrative structures associated with the state became the new narrow conception of 'politics'. Influential early formulations of the role of government in commercial society centred on national defence and the protection of private property. Government should protect the rights and freedoms of those who own property against the claims of those who relied merely on their labour. As Adam Smith

(1896) put it, the purpose of government was justice, peace, revenue and arms.[29] There was not yet a central place for state-led 'social policy' in either Enlightenment theories of civil society or state practice, although government could play a role in cultivating individual freedoms in a self-regulating civil society. State-public authority was distinguished from and imagined to act above 'civil society', the new location of private commercial exchange (Kaviraj and Khilnani, 2001). Civil society, distinguished from the state, would be comprised of two different forms of privacy: capitalist exchange and the intimate 'domestic' sphere of the family, the 'household' now divested of an explicit economic function aside from reproduction and consumption. Although public administration was not directly concerned with the productive economy, the new private sphere of economic reproduction was of enormous 'public' (state) relevance. 'Public power', recall Habermas's claim, increasingly 'concentrated in national and territorial states, rose above a privatized society … The "social" could be constituted as its own sphere to the degree that on the one hand the reproduction of life took on private forms, while on the other hand the private realm as a whole assumed public relevance' (1962/1991: 127). The social realm was the intermediary between these newly constituted, newly separated, spheres of public and private.

Labour, recall, had been redefined as the source of wealth; it needed to be properly and rationally organised for the benefit of a new unified object, not the feudal household, but the national or imperial 'society as a whole', the new modern unit of rule (Polanyi, 1957/2001). The exchange of labour for a wage would now occur in a newly conceived private realm. Yet the circumstances of capitalist exchange – the working of the market and the conditions of labour – were necessarily a matter of imperial state concern. 'The economic activity that had become private,' notes Habermas, 'had to become oriented toward

29 Smith's lectures were delivered in 1763. Interestingly, Wood (1994: 216) argues that 'Smith used the household analogy to exemplify some basic economic concepts. Although he never explicitly maintained that the state was like a household, sometimes only comparing the proper action of the state to that of a prudent farmer, his parallels between state and household are nonetheless too noticeable to be discounted. Following Aristotle, Smith in *Republica* saw the origins of the first state in the patriarchal household, and in general he viewed the rule of the family as similar to the government of existing polities: the aristocratic regime of the parents and the democracy among their children. But in the *Discourse* he implied that the state was the household in macrocosm by his comparisons of the economic life of each.'

a commodity market that had expanded under public direction and supervision; the economic conditions under which this activity now took place lay outside the confines of the single household; for the first time they were of general interest' (1962/1991: 19). Civil society was capitalist economy distinguished from state politics defined as government. It was grounded on the security of property and the capitalist requirement that labour-power be 'free' and separated from the means of production.[30] However, labour and the market still needed to be administered. Political economy emerged as the new scholarly and practical field examining the scientific laws regulating economy in the interests of 'society' (Schabas, 2005: 102–124; Maifreda, 2012). No longer restricted to the activities of the *oikodespote*, the workings and the analysis of economy were abstracted to designate a new sphere of reality and intervention. This abstraction made plausible the notion of invisible laws of supply and demand, a market able to self-regulate unlike all previous systems of exchange. Always an object of statecraft, capitalist economy was supported not by the will of an *oikodespote* but by bureaucratic action. Nonetheless, classical political economists would argue that society was a structure of interaction distinct from the state and, given the seeming homology between the abstractions of economy and society, the whole of society could eventually be remade in the image of the market. The economy, as a self-regulating domain, was theoretically unhindered by and distinct from the other abstractions of the soon to be called 'social system' (Comte, 1875). However, as Gunnar Myrdal pointed out, since political economy purported to be in the interests of 'society as a whole' it necessarily assumed a willing and unified subject that could scientifically coordinate economic activities on behalf of the general welfare (1953: 145; Arendt, 1958: 47–48 fn.). The model of this 'single subject with a consistent set of ends' relied on the analogy between the running of a household and 'social housekeeping' as a form of 'collective "economizing"' (Myrdal, 1953: 145). 'Society' itself was conceived as one entity with a unity of

[30] 'It was only very gradually,' writes Bourdieu (2005: 6), 'that the sphere of commodity exchange separated itself out from the other fields of existence and its specific *nomos* asserted itself…; that economic transactions ceased to be conceived on the model of domestic exchanges, and hence as governed by social or family obligations…; and that the calculation of individual gain, and hence economic interest, won out as the dominant, if not indeed exclusive, principle of business against the collectively imposed and controlled repression of calculating inclinations associated with the domestic economy.'

interests, the national household 'as a whole'.[31] This fiction of a unity of interests facilitated the management of populations stratified along class, gendered, sexuality, nationality and racialised lines.

Under these ideological and material circumstances, the meaning of the term 'household' narrowed dramatically, but its symbolism and the reach of household activities did not. Liberal capitalism defined itself by its abandonment of household rule. And yet only with the rise of industrial capitalism does the notion of a distinct 'domestic domain' as synonymous with the idea of a biological family enter political thought and, rather ironically for many feminists, alongside liberal ideas about autonomy and consent as a critique of patriarchal despotism (Nicholson, 1986).[32] There is an irony since, in Pateman's words, 'civil society, including the capitalist economy, has a patriarchal structure' (1998: 38). In this system, the intimate household would emerge as the most fundamental element of civilised society, a sphere of privacy and 'personal' freedom, of security and comfort, with enormous ideological power.[33] And yet for many women and domestic servants, this household-as-bourgeois-home would remain a place of patriarchal and racialised subordination, suffocation and immobility (Friedan, 1963; Elshtain, 1982). In other words, we are speaking of two new and very closely related conceptions of the private realm in civil society, the capitalist market and the intimate sphere of the bourgeois family home. Their co-emergence was not a coincidence. As

[31] For Arendt (1958: 29), 'the collective of families economically organized into the facsimile of one superhuman family is what we call "society", and its political form of organization is called "nation"'.

[32] As Corrigan and Sayer (1985: 135) have pointed out, 'although ... one might be able "in theory" to imagine a non-patriarchal capitalism – patriarchy cannot be inferred from the concept of capital, and attempts to do so are invariably reductionist – ... all real capitalisms have in practice been constructed through patriarchal forms of social relationship, which have history independent of that of capitalism'.

[33] Yet alongside the fetishisation of a new form of bourgeois home in the nineteenth century there is the rise of nostalgia for earlier noble households as reaction against what was seen as 'the increasingly feminized and market-oriented bourgeois European households' (Pecora, 1997: xi; see Comte, 1875; Maine, 1878/1908; Tönnies, 1887/1955; Durkheim, 1893/1984). Yet, as Pecora also maintains, while in 'Victorian culture ... the growth of a distinctly domestic sphere ... functioning as the necessary complement (or even impetus) to masculine conquest and progress ... is not particularly salient in the classical literature. It exists, for example, neither in Homer's account of the warrior nor in Aristotle's account of the household in the *Politics* nor in Xenophon's treaties on agriculture, *Oeconomicus*' (1997: 4).

historians have noted, the 'private' family home was conceived as the foundation of Western civilisation at the same time that expropriated peasants had to abandon older household networks of interdependence, communal life and extended families.[34] Just as 'more and more people' were forcibly losing a 'commitment (physical, legal, and emotional) to a particular small unit of land', including in the colonies, there was an idealisation of the new small-scale household of the bourgeois family (Wallerstein, 1991a: 19; Habermas, 1962/1991: 28). With the displacement of the classical and feudal *oikos*, the household in this narrower sense lost its direct 'economic' function aside from reproduction and consumption.

Relations of material dependency in the new household of the intimate family were limited to the reproduction of individuals. This reproductive labour was represented as pre-contractual and pre-capitalist, neither properly 'political' nor 'economic'. Identities continued to be regulated along a hierarchical gender binary, which was useful for valorising certain forms of labour and devaluing others (Hartsock, 1983; Pateman, 1998). To the new 'political economists', households were the small organising units of consumption dependent upon the larger 'market economy' (Lord, 2002; cf. Folbre, 1986). In turn, the interpretation given to the market economy was shaped by gendered and sentimental notions of privacy and home in the bourgeois family, naturalising the relationship between the intimate sphere and the 'private' realm of the marketplace. The new 'domestic' realm was presented as a safe place, free from the interference of power. The self-image of the bourgeois family man in his castle tallied with the image of the individual private property owner participating in the unregulated ('free') capitalist market. The ideal individual was the property-owning man and 'head of house', an image taken to define the civilised human being as such. In fact, the family household became the primary location of discipline and encouragement, of cultivation of new 'social' norms. Indeed, despotic household governance and cults of domesticity would be central to running not only the Greek but also modern empire, spreading bourgeois family ideology to the working classes and subjects of empire (McClintock,

[34] In the words of E.P. Thompson, '1760 and 1820 are the years of wholesale enclosure in which, in village after village, common rights are lost' (1963: 217, 237; on the political theory of enclosure see Brown, 2010).

1995). The forcible reorganisation of domestic space and ideologies of domesticity were central to how colonisers and colonised transformed each other. As discussed later, new ideologies of domesticity would play an important role in giving meaning to imperialism and counterinsurgency.

The well-ordered family household remained the model for the well-ordered and self-regulating society, a society composed of the relations between household heads and protected by the state. However, the rise of society nonetheless coincided with the erosion of traditional sources of charismatic and religious authority. The monarch, religious leaders and the *paterfamiliās* all experienced a decline in authority in favour of the impersonal rule of 'society'. Increasingly anonymous administration substituted for the dictates of the *paterfamiliās*; 'society', Arendt observed, 'becomes the substitute for', rather than represents the elimination of 'the [extended feudal] family' (1958: 256). 'An individual no longer gets protection from the household and kinship groups,' noted Weber (1978: 375) 'but rather from political authority, which exercises compulsory jurisdiction.' This ruler-ship was not founded on the power of an individual patriarch, although systems of patriarchy and despotism remained fundamental to modern society (Coward, 1983). Relations of power and violence did not evaporate, but were often mediated by contracts and administrators rather than directly enforced through physical force. These contracts and bureaucratic decisions would be recognised under the law and backed by public and organised (police and military) violence. This was ruler-ship through permanent bureaucracy, of Weber's 'specialists without spirit' (1958: 182). Not one-man rule as in the ancient *oikos*, but as Arendt said, 'a kind of no-man rule' defined the national and imperial household (1958: 40). For note that while the Lockean contract tradition was completely opposed to individual submission to personal authority, it appeared far less concerned about submission to the impersonal power of markets and bureaucratic decree. For example, as Sheldon Wolin has noted, many liberals did, in fact, seem willing to surrender to power as long as this 'power was impersonal and was directed at all the members indifferently ... The entity which satisfied these longings was society ... Society was no single individual: it was none of us, yet it was all of us' (Wolin, 1960: 348; see also Booth, 1993: 145). Yet Edmund Burke saw conservative advantage in the continuation of a 'personalist analogy'. Imagining society as a person made it easier for people to identify with it, encouraging fidelity to something higher increased 'social' cohesion.[35]

The individual despotism of the household head was retained in sovereign executive power and, as discussed in the next chapter, was useful as a form of decentralised despotism in the colonies. To be sure, the new term 'society' was pitted against the undiluted power of the royal prerogative; against the divine right of kings; against an understanding of sovereignty as the unitary will of the king. However, even with Locke, the familial mode of despotic governance was not entirely replaced, as long as it was presented as the 'exception'. Where legislative power, the making of law, was only legitimate when derived from the consent of the governed, Locke claimed there was an important distinction between the making and the executing of law. For the sake of protecting society from internal and external threats, the executive had *prerogative* power to act for the general good, even if it involved a breach of the law. 'These two powers…' Dubber (2005: 46) notes, 'were analogous to the internal and external aspects of the householder authority to maximise the welfare of his family.' As long as the sovereign acted on behalf of the welfare of society as a whole, it (just not 'he') may claim the same rights as the absolutist state. As Wolin has put it, since executive authority extends to both 'internal' and 'external' affairs, 'the distinction serves to create a domestic domain for *Staatsräson* while lodging it in the same constitutional hands as power over foreign affairs' (1987: 485).[36] *Salus populi suprema lex esto* was the epigraph of Locke's *Two Treaties of Government*: the welfare of the people shall be the supreme law. This is the basic structure of the modern capitalist and imperial nation-state form of household rule.

Onto the Social Question

To think historically about the modern rise of the social realm is to think through the consequences for household governance of the transformation of ancient and feudal *oikonomia* to a complex capitalist and nation-state system. If households are units of rule in which

[35] For a discussion see Terrier (2011: 181–182). On the argument that states are persons see Wendt (2004).

[36] This suggests that Schmitt (2004a) was wrong to argue that liberalism has no theory of sovereign decision and the exception. For an assessment of the recent turn to Schmitt in IR see Owens (2011).

populations are domesticated, then it is no surprise to find distinctly *social* policies primarily targeted at populations most threatening to the internal cohesion of national and imperial households and emerging at the intersection of capitalist economy and the newly empowered masses after the democratic revolutions. Thus far we have established the household ontology of the modern social realm. This section returns to the Social Question, drawing attention to the much more concerted intervention into 'society' and the forms of sociocratic household government this intervention produced.

To be sure, states always had a regulatory and population management role; this function was not entirely new with the rise and expansion of distinctly social welfare through the nineteenth century. Nonetheless, the classical bourgeois public sphere of civil society was subsumed into an expanded and deepened social realm in a context of class conflict and imperial crises. As noted in the previous chapter, working classes had become more organised and radical, resulting in numerous strikes and threats of insurrection, culminating in the revolutionary wave of 1848. This was the context of the Social Question, an expression of the conflict between claims of legal and political equality and the reality of mass poverty and precariousness in the 'age of capital' (Hobsbawm, 1975; Jacoby, 1870). The leading empires were forced to respond to the demands of labour at the industrial heartland, including by partially admitting labouring classes into the official political (government) scene. If order and existing property relations were to be maintained, then more concerted and organised forms of state-led 'socialisation' would be required. In lieu of revolution, organised labour could claim 'social rights'. How to manage the new social sector of state action became the primary content of ideological debate between moralistic conservatives, supporters of *laissez faire*, and revolutionary or reformist socialists.

In its earliest incarnation, recall, social philosophy was characterised by an absence of doubt concerning the possibility of knowing the social world. Clearly, ideas about the initial shape and form of the social realm were strongly influenced by liberal political economy and the vision of bourgeois civil society as a self-regulating domain. This notion gave way to one of society needing greater order, something to be more actively controlled and regulated.[37] Basic liberal doctrines

[37] While political economy strived for the authority of 'hard' natural sciences, when confronted with the Social Question, the discipline was forced to meet its

such as the separation of (private) capitalist economy from (public) state-politics were not wholly undermined, but eighteenth-century distinctions between state and society and public and private began to wither away. As long as exchange relations occurred between 'private' individuals, state and civil society could be imagined as separate. However, it became increasingly difficult to represent civil society as a private sphere when 'the powers of "society" themselves assumed functions of public authority', such as the administration of social insurance and social policy (Habermas, 1962/1991: 142). The arrival of organised labour also disrupted classical liberal notions of the power of reason and rational debate among civilised persons. Where rational public reason had reined in bourgeois civil society, liberals such as John Stuart Mill (1861/2010) and Alexis de Tocqueville (2003) now feared that the rule of the majority would be dangerously coercive; free and equal discussion was problematic for those not prepared for self-government: women, the labouring classes and natives.[38] Any political participation by *les peuples* had to be mediated through representation, with loyalist political parties competing over how best to administer the welfare of the population over whom they wished to govern. 'Political' debate would centre on the how best to regulate industry and labour, and appropriate arrangements for taxation and spending on social services. Social policy, Castel has written, would answer the problem of 'a representative regime which protects itself from the power of numbers' (2003: 212).

By the end of the nineteenth century, all the major European powers had introduced protectionist and labour legislation. As Karl Polanyi put it:

> Victorian England and the Prussia of Bismarck were poles apart, and both were very much unlike France of the Third Republic or the Empire of the Hapsburgs. Yet each of them passed through a period of free trade and laissez-faire, followed by a period of anti-liberal legislation in regard to

limitations while also seeking to protect itself as a discipline. Classical political economy was joined by 'social economy'. On the transition from the confident 'political economy' before 1840 to the more defensive 'social economy' in the French context see Sage (2009).

38 In his *Memoir on Pauperism* (1835), Tocqueville worried that a 'permanent, regular, administrative system' of poor relief would 'in time reduce the rich to no more than farmers of the poor, dry up the sources of savings, stop the accumulation of capital' (quoted in Wacquant, 2009: 39).

public health, factory conditions, municipal trading, social insurance, shipping subsidies, public utilities, trade associations and so on.

(Polanyi, 1957/2001: 153)[39]

For Polanyi, this convergence in social regulation was explained by the general needs of 'society as a whole' being favoured over those of the self-regulating market of orthodox liberal political economy. In any case, there was no such thing, he famously claimed, as a self-regulating market. This last point is certainly true. However, Polanyi's evocation of the interests of 'society as a whole' obscures the extent to which the Social Question was not about human suffering *per se*. The problem was not primarily with the existence of mass poverty itself, but with its consequences on 'social' cohesion and political order (cf. Jones, 2004). The essential challenge for Victoria's England, Bismarck's Prussia, the Third French Republic and the House of Hapsburg was how to contain the threat of insurrection while strengthening the state and bourgeois freedoms. More extensive forms of social housekeeping would be required. As a result, the first populations constituted as objects of social intervention would not be the poorest as such, but those most threatening to the security and stability of the prevailing order: the industrial proletariat and the objects of colonial rule. The function of social policy was restoration, to reinstate or create binding ties between members of the new industrial 'society'. Then as now, the place of different groups within the 'social division of labour' would

[39] For an excellent discussion and critique of Polanyi see Halperin (2004). On the German and French cases see Beck (1995); Stone (1985). Although state institutions did not reach into the entirety of the countries, by the mid- to late nineteenth century, China and Japan had already developed systems of taxation and control of labour movement to help forestall internal revolt, and partly in response to European expansion. Many responded to 'the pressure put on them by the East India Company's own hybrid polity, which taxed and counted like a western European state, but allowed many social functions to be monopolized by groups of indigenous administration and landlords' (Bayly, 2004: 259). Imperial China's welfare system is analogous to the poor law relief system that developed from the 1600s in Europe, both of which were aimed at the poor. Social welfare was not targeted at the poor as such, rather for wage earners who may be in or out of work (Hu, 2012; Tang, 1998; Hu and Manning, 2010). The expansion of healthcare systems in imperial Japan, China, and the Ottoman Empire can be seen, in part, as reactions to the establishment of these systems by their European rivals, and in some cases as a result of petitioning by the commercial classes in those states.

be fundamental to the extent to which they could access (or be subjected to) social protections.

The proliferation of regulations dealing with wage labour conditions and worker protection, factory regulation and industrial tribunals helped to bring an end to workers' *direct* subjection to their employers. Social insurance made public something that had previously been absorbed as a 'private' risk. Rather than view workplace accidents, loss of employment or sickness as purely a matter of individual responsibility, insurance transformed these into a collective concern; life risks became 'socialised' and were relieved by financial compensation (Donzelot, 1984: 131; Ewald, 1991).[40] As Castel has explained, membership in an order of social insurance 'is of a qualitatively different kind than that afforded by the proximate protections of kinship and the tutelage of strategies of patronage', the dominant forms of household rule prior to the rise of capitalist states (2003: 288). Insurance also served an important ideological function, billed as an expression of the bonds of 'solidarity' between individuals and classes, making concrete everyone's functional interdependence. As a result, conflict over the nature of the system itself was mitigated by technical solutions to social problems (Beck, 1992, 1999). In powerful solidarist and social democratic discourses, individuals and groups were eligible for compensation not because their labour was exploited by capital, but due to their position in the 'social' division of labour and membership in national society. 'Membership in a social class', Arendt noted, 'replaced the protection previously offered by membership in a family, and social solidarity became a very efficient substitute for the earlier, natural solidarity ruling the family unit' (1958: 256; Hobsbawm, 1990). Familial language did not completely disappear. If populations were like members of one family, then the state could appear as a neutral arbiter between kinsmen, a benign body that could administer the rule of law on behalf of the entire family. The notion of the nation-state as a family was more than a metaphor; the government was both disciplining and, increasingly into the nineteenth century, nurturing of many of its citizen-children. Although elements of industrial paternalism would linger, such personalist relations were increasingly outmoded in the context of ever-greater rationalisation of the

[40] For an analysis of this development in relation to 'accidental' civilian death in military intervention see Owens (2003).

labour market. As Corrigan and Sayer pointed out, state inspectors 'acted to establish and standardize a range of civic institutions which could concretely symbolize the extension of "Society"...beyond the efforts [of] ... paternalistic capitalists' (1985: 126; see also Scott, 1998). In short, the rise of social insurance was tacit acknowledgement that fundamental inequality would be a permanent situation in capitalist society, that an ever-growing disparity of wealth was integral to the system, but that something needed to be done to manage its effects (Castel, 2003: 284; Donzelot, 1984: 128).

These new social rights and solidarities involved a redefinition of the role of the state in fostering 'social' bonds. The new social sector became the common site and criteria for state and non-state interventions, creating a set of powerful new instruments and institutions to be used by the state. Although the state would increasingly take over and transform a number of services formerly provided by churches and philanthropists, marking a qualitative shift from traditional forms of poor relief, social regulation can exist and come into effect with or without 'sovereign' intervention. In other words, not all answers to the Social Question are statist. Numerous non-governmental actors played a role in social intervention, including religious and women's groups, unions, civil servants, city-planners and, most recently, international organisations, NGOS and private contractors.[41] Rather than state leaders proclaiming moral or political maxims that individual subjects were supposed to consciously follow, social policies provided a means through which individual behaviour was altered through intervention in the wider social 'milieu', a term adopted from biology (Rabinow, 1989: 31). Individuals were social beings, they were rather malleable if their social conditions were transformed and, of course, some populations were assumed to be more malleable than others.

As governments and social philosophers were speaking of 'society as whole' they also distinguished between separate parts of that society, especially the poor as a special segment. The distinction allowed theorists and reformers to treat one segment of 'society' as posing a particular social problem while signalling the mutual interests uniting all parts of the 'social whole'. In other words, there is a close and

[41] On the explosion of 'social intervention' through post-World War II foreign aid and development programmes see Ferguson (1994); Escobar (1995); Li (2007); Owens (2012).

necessary relationship between the rise of the social sector (as distinct from state politics and capitalist economy) and 'the aggregation of distinct populations' with a specific set of problems that need to be cured (Poovey, 1995: 4; Horn, 1994). Put differently, social *intervention* was central to the emergence of 'society' as an object of more concerted government action through the nineteenth century. As such, it is no surprise that the language used to conceive of social intervention was deeply shaped by the biological metaphors that have always accompanied distinctly social thought, indicating the vital functional interrelatedness and mutual interests between different parts of the body. One of England's earliest sanitary reformers, physician Thomas Southwood Smith, viewed 'individual human bodies as composed of constituent "particles"; the social body in turn was made up of the entirety of the particles entering and leaving all living creatures' (Joyce, 2002: 106). The use of biological metaphors to conceive of the social whole was not an accident of timing ('biology' was also invented in the nineteenth century). As the scaled-up modern public household, the social realm was the space in which the life processes of its members were reproduced and ordered, and was again justified as activity taken in the interests of the household (now 'society') as a whole.

In addition to managing labour, the Social Question eventually fanned out to various other heterogeneous 'social problems', related to family, health, education, housing, crime, immigration and so on. Each became subject to distinctly social discourses, knowledge and intervention with the goal of instilling better, more productive behaviour in specific populations. The scope of intervention into society appeared to be endless. Consider the huge proliferation of activities to which the prefix 'social' would be appended. 'Socialise' – to make social – appeared in 1828 and 'socialisation', the process of making something or someone 'social', in 1840. 'Social' and 'socio' became increasingly common in compounds from the 1880s. 'Socio-economic' appeared in 1883, as did 'asocial'. The notion of 'social work' took on its modern meaning in 1890, 'social worker' from 1904 and 'social security' from 1908.[42] By the end of the nineteenth century,

[42] 'British liberal reformers gathered in 1856 to form the British Social Science Association' and in '1856 the American Association for the Promotion of Social Science was founded, with guiding advice from John Stuart Mill' (Collins and Makowsky, 1972: 84). Mill described the term 'sociology' as a '"convenient barbarism" of the Social Science' (Mill, 1843/1988: 83).

social relations had become the subject of active state management across the industrialised West. Social policy and social work was professionalised, with organisations housing specialists and experts with power to distribute conditional aid and assistance. The functions of the state were separated into discrete departments underpinned by a new professional and scientific culture of expertise. The institutional growth and acceleration of social interventions was partly driven by logic crucial to the social realm as a scaled-up public household, its 'irresistible tendency to grow' (Arendt, 1958: 87). It is a cliché that bureaucracy, 'the most social form of government', expands to meet the needs of an expanding bureaucracy. This bureaucracy, Arendt suggested, is constantly produced and reproduced because 'the life process itself ... has been channelled into the public realm' (1958: 45, 40). The multiple and complex 'social problems' that arise from the system of wage labour and empires – unequal access to health services, food and water, basic housing – demand urgent action into the most basic conditions of human life. These conditions are 'born of a great urgency', Arendt continued, 'and motivated by a more powerful drive than anything else, because life itself depends on it' (1958: 87). This is another way of saying the social sector is the location of modern household rule, the unit of rule in which life processes of populations are managed as a form of domestication.

It is no surprise that the intensification in social housekeeping led to innovations in the art and science of household management, and that could take many different forms. Catherine Beecher's *A Treatise on Domestic Economy*, published in 1841, has been described as 'a prime document of the cult of domesticity because it combined citations from the work of Tocqueville with explicit instructions on laundry' (Matthews, 1987: 7, 110).[43] Through the production of endless statistics, censuses and surveys, the 'social system' became a discrete and abstract object of scientific knowledge, allowing social scientists and social housekeepers (state managers)

[43] 'Indeed, by 1850 the home had become the mainstay of the national culture ... [taking] the home beyond the boundaries of the "women's sphere" and into the national arena ... [H]ome provided a touchstone of the values for reforming the entire society ... In fact, when the cult of domesticity reached its height, middle-class women began to organize for exerting influence on the world as never before and in such a way that public and private values were genuinely intermingled rather than dichotomized' (Matthews, 1987: 35).

to distinguish which populations most urgently required intervention. Such an abstract conceptualisation of the social enabled social engineers and sociocrats to imagine of ways in which the bonds between people, the environment in which they interacted, could be massaged and shaped to modify the behaviour of particular 'social' types. If social laws could be uncovered then they could also be manipulated for social and humanitarian ends. There was a proliferation of rules governing who was eligible for assistance based on assumptions about the impact of incentives on mass behaviour, particularly populations defined in terms of biological and other attributes related to 'what' they are (what gender, age, nationality, illness, race or combination of these). There was, of course, a pull from below to the extent that various groups and movements sought social reformist intervention on their behalf and, in doing so, often fully embraced their 'socially' determined identities. While some social policies acted on what were conceived as pre-existing problems such as 'women's issues', others defined new social groups like 'youth' and 'homosexuals'. As Procacci has put it, state-led social interventions functioned through 'a redistribution of social identity, much more than a redistribution of economic wealth. At its center, there was the constant production of the "social tie" – that is, surfaces of interaction which delineated a network of social inscriptions for the individual' (1995: 142; Donzelot, 1988). A whole series of new social identities were established alongside the new agencies and forms of expertise to manage social problems, including those of 'international society'. Colonial populations and eventually new postcolonial nations would become objects of social scientific expertise and engineering.

Middle-class social workers, many of them women, had replaced the traditional *paterfamiliās*. Social workers were the bureaucratic rather than personal trustees of problem populations, empowered to decide their best interests within the existing structure of power. Through 'the "benevolent empire" of female charitable activity', middle-class women were among the earliest advocates for social reform given the perceived affinities between 'women's work' and social engineering, and between 'women's work' and empire (Matthews, 1987: 134). For if good government was a form of good housekeeping then there was even more reason to extend the suffrage to women and fully incorporate them into national housekeeping and the domestication of the empire.[44] Bourgeois ideologies of domesticity would play an important role in the moral panics about crime, sex, gambling, sedition and radicalism that often sparked an intensification of social regulation; that is, when advocates of the cult of domesticity, 'male and female, began to carry domestic values outside the home' (Matthews, 1987: 36). Moral panics would be expressed through the new language of social deviance and anti-social behaviour. Vast numbers of desperately poor urban workers living in 'domestic squalor' disturbed political and bourgeois elites. 'Scenes of distant battles with savagery...' observe Comaroff and Comaroff (1992: 267), 'became the cautionary currency of an urgent moral offensive in the urban "jungles" of Victorian Britain ... where the poor were seen to be as uncivilised as the most beastly blacks in the bush.'[45] In addition to increases in the prison population, social interventions into the lives and habits of the labouring poor were necessary steps in the longer-term process of 'socialisation'. The 'natural' family played a central role in underpinning the physical and moral health of the state and empire.

Alongside the rise of social insurance, which was primarily aimed at labouring men, intervention to improve 'families' was primarily

44 In an article for *Ladies Home Journal* in 1910, the enormously influential public intellectual Jane Addams 'contended that the American city was in a bad way precisely because it lacked "domesticity". The humblest farm dwelling is more presentable than an urban landscape because a woman is directly involved in its maintenance, she argued. In order to redeem the city, even the most traditional women must begin to understand their social responsibilities in the areas of hygiene, education, child-labor legislation ... Thus, domestic feminism was a vital part of the American political landscape for decades' (Matthews, 1987: 89; see also Rynbrandt, 1999; Addams, 1905; Gottlieb, 2001).

45 According to Anne McClintock (1995: 17), 'the mass marketing of empire as a global system was intimately wedded to the Western reinvention of domesticity, so that imperialism cannot be understood without a theory of domestic space and its relation to the market'. 'The cult of domesticity,' Wexler (2000: 22) also writes, 'was a crucial framework for American imperialism in the late nineteenth century. In the United States, apologists for colonialism used conceptions of domestic progress as both a descriptive and a heuristic tool. Customary ways of life need protection and advancement at home; they also, apparently, needed conquest and continuing domination of foreign lands. At home, American domesticity was a potent concatenation of ideas of scientific racism, social Darwinism, and economic pragmatism that could be used to orchestrate consent for expansionist policies. In the colonies, and in the institutions and social agencies that dealt with subjugated peoples ... such ideals of domestic life were also disciplinary structures of the state.'

targeted at working-class and poor women. For the French engineer and social reformer Émile Cheysson (who coined 'social engineer'), working-class families were laboratories for observing broader social dynamics; and they should be objects of reform, since it was in the home that class antagonism was disseminated and self-regulating subjects could be produced. Social policies related to child labour, housing and education were to support the 'normal' functioning of stable working-class homes. As Donzelot has suggested, this social legislation related to the family and children produced 'a gradual transfer of sovereignty from the "morally deficient" [poor] family to the body of philanthropic notables, magistrates, and children's doctors' (1979: 83). The family did, indeed, shift from being a model to an object of government, but with a paradoxical result. With the rise of children's rights and restrictions on some forms of patriarchal domination 'the more the strangle hold of a tutelary authority tightens around the poor family. In this system, family patriarchalism is destroyed [sic] only at the cost of a patriarchy of the state' (Donzelot, 1979: 103).[46] Similarly, the rationalisation of labour relations, and the professionalisation of social work, did not signal the end of (now even more enlightened) tutelage (Castel, 2003: 232). The recipients of social welfare would be heavily supervised; the ever-present aim was to alter their asocial behaviour. 'The relationship of assistance,' Castel writes, 'may be likened to a flow of humanity that runs between two persons ... The benefactor serves as a model of socialization ... The benefactor and his beneficiary form a society, whose moral bond is also a social bond' (2003: 219). The benign despotism of the social worker was humanitarian, targeted at the basic life processes of human beings as such for the sake of the welfare of society, the national and imperial household as a whole.

Conclusion

Scholars in the discipline of international relations, like other social scientists, have not been very good at thinking historically and conceptually about households, suggesting again their deep dependence

[46] To clarify, Donzelot here is incorrect to imply that 'family patriarchalism' is completely destroyed with the rise of child protection interventions by the state.

on distinctly modern and liberal categories of thought (Walker, 1993). Before the rise of modern contract society, the homology between forms of household governance was obvious and was the grounding for almost all so-called political thought, so-called because it was too often based on *oikonomia*. After liberalism's attack on the familial mode of government, and the conflation of household and family, it became almost impossible to think of modern capitalist states as a form of household itself. Even those writers who suspected as much never fully developed the idea and were roundly criticised for the very suggestion (Myrdal, 1953: 145; Arendt, 1958: 47–48fn.).[47] The explanation for this oversight in political and international theory is the hegemony of social forms of thought, including among critical theorists; 'society' replaced the household as the object of serious scholarly enquiry and theorists have struggled to develop an adequate theory of politics as a result. Politics is reduced to government administration and/or is placed on a continuum with violence. This is household rule, not politics if the latter is to have a meaning of its own. By the middle of the nineteenth century, debate about the nature and character of modern politics, economy and international and imperial affairs was conducted almost entirely in the lexicon of sociology. As a fragment of the major social theories of the nineteenth century – liberalism, Marxism and political realism – international theory could not help but reproduce its terms and mode of thought. This is despite the intellectual possibilities not very well hidden in the 'main stock and trade' of the field, the *domestic* analogy. Even feminists, the most attentive to the significance of patriarchy and domesticity, and Foucaultian critical theorists seemingly attentive to the historicity of modern categories, have failed to notice the household ontology of the modern social realm.

Households are the units of rule in which the life processes of members are reproduced and the collective unit itself is maintained. With the rise of commercial empires, the organisation and management of life processes underwent a major transformation: they were emancipated from their containment within feudal households. This chapter has argued that techniques and organisational

[47] Arendt, in particular, was accused of crimes against socialism and feminism for suggesting that the modern social realm was, problematically, a scaled-up form of household rule (Pitkin, 1998; Benhabib, 1996).

devices of household governance in modern society are homologous with older forms of paternalistic and despotic forms of household rule. So what, then, is distinctive about the modern social realm? If the forms of governance examined here are variations on household rule, then what is particular to social regulation, to sociocratic household rule? The rise of the social realm was a product of a fundamental change in the structures of organising and managing life processes; it represented a transformation or shift in the basic structure of human life when, for the first time, life processes acquired their own public domain. As such, the new capitalist 'society' inaugurated forms of rule peculiar to itself: altered distinctions between public authority and private spheres; the emergence of civil society; the relative de-politicisation of 'economy' and 'property'; a new distinction between economy, politics, the state and imperial/inter-state system; new scholarly fields of 'political economy' and social theory. Commodity exchange 'burst out of the confines of the [feudal] household' (Habermas, 1962/1991: 28). But the organisational and administrative techniques of this mode of governance would take on new forms and ideological rationalisations: the welfare of 'society as a whole' was purportedly maximised by political economy; a new cult of domesticity would form the marker of civilisation; personalist authority was replaced by bureaucratic administration, yet despotic government was retained in executive/prerogative power; and the science of society would replace classical political theory.

These are the forms of rule and distinctions that were particular to the modern social realm and, as shown in the analysis of counterinsurgency, wars of pacification would be deeply shaped by *raison de la société*. Contra near unanimous claims of its demise, the household was scaled-up and transformed in the late eighteenth century. The social realm was a newly configured household that stretched from the core territory of the English and French imperial states to their empires overseas. Crucially, the rise of the social was not purely a feature of European development transferred to other societies through empire. Rather than a timeless and wholly 'European' entity, something that developed through internal reference to a particular national 'society', the social realm was an imperial entity, as were new discourses of 'traditional society'. Distinctly social forms of household governance were imperial and highly portable.

4 *The colonial limits of society*

[T]he concept of Society represents ... a claim advanced and enacted in order to construct a state of affairs that previously was not. The name is not the thing; and that thing had first to be built up in space and time. It is as much an invention as the intersecting guilds, cult fealties and royal domains of precolonization East Africa.

Eric R. Wolf (1988: 757)

The 'improvement of the world' through the spread of commerce and good government would become a major ideological and practical component of overseas imperial rule just as governments were increasingly developing more elaborate methods to 'improve' the lives of some of Europe's working poor. The mercantilist policies of the eighteenth century seemed anachronistic to the rising class of free-marketeers, who by the 1830s and 1840s were successfully agitating for the repeal of the Corn Laws. Achieved in 1856, the repeal reduced the price of grain for British and Irish workers, but factory wages also decreased. These workers were now to be fed with foodstuffs imported from the rapidly expanding empire. In an alliance between organised capital and the new interventionist state, the major European empires expanded their possessions through the nineteenth century partly to ward off the consequences of internal class conflict, partly in competition with each other. The term 'social imperialism' would refer to attempts to maintain domestic peace in an age of more open class antagonism, where further imperial expansion seemed to promise not only new revenues and markets but also a way to undermine organised labour, an alternative to more radical transformations (Semmel, 1960; Wehler, 1972).[1] In his famous Crystal Palace speech of

[1] John Stuart Mill also viewed settler colonialism as a potential solution to the Social Question, as well as of general benefit to humanity as a whole (Bell, 2010).

1872, Benjamin Disraeli set out a vision of progressive conservatism in which social reform and imperialism were conjoined to reduce class tensions; 'the idea of the *mission civilisatrice*', writes Richard Drayton, 'embraced both the working classes and the Irish at home, and the Jamaicans and Egyptians abroad' (2000: 225).

The terms of trade between Europe and the empire rapidly deteriorated, as did the general balance of power between world regions. Imperial domination and the increasing extraction of resources from Asia and Africa exposed most of the world's population to economic crises emanating from the 'core', while the global wealth differential exploded. Capitalist markets were dependent on overseas labour and markets; that is, expansion in the colonies as much as, if not more than, the expansion of markets in Europe itself. This meant that 'rural, pre-industrial, feudal, and autocratic structures of power and authority' remained in place in most of Europe throughout the century (Halperin, 2004: 14). Newly uprooted members of colonial territories had little access to the ameliorative 'social policies' that were slowly being established by central authorities in European states. To be sure, small public health schemes and philanthropic paternalism often accompanied colonial expansion, especially after 1870. But these were primarily for the benefit of European colonists and soldiers. Nonetheless, new nineteenth-century social discourses were applied to an array of 'social' problems in the colonies, also providing a vehicle for proto-nationalist leaders to advance their aims (Ray, 1984). New indigenous middle classes constituted embryonic bourgeois 'civil societies' in cities such as Calcutta, Bombay and Penang. Political radicals in Bengal, for example, selectively appropriated the abstract terminology of 'society' and used it to subvert some aspects of British rule, if not commercial practices. 'When radicals in Bengal adopted the notion of "society", a dispassionate community of interacting interests,' Bayly notes, 'they also adopted the same linguistic and conceptual shift that their European exemplars had pioneered ... The word *samaj*, which meant "assembly" or "gathering", took on this striking new sense' (Bayly, 2004: 292; Kaviraj and Khilnani, 2001). This new class formed clubs, societies and missions, integrating themselves into central positions and developing distinctive modes of sociability and claims to land and markets and advocated for 'social' reform through municipal projects related to housing, hygiene, education and the regulation of vagabonds. Despite the imperial rhetoric of 'improvement', alongside the expansion of roads, markets and irrigation, colonial offices were less interested in providing for the welfare of indigenous populations. Only the exigencies of managing increasingly restless and politicised populations gave impetus, for example, to the belated establishment of Indian famine codes.

By the 1885 Berlin Conference, chaired by Bismarck, some discussion of the humanitarian treatment of 'native tribes' was included in the General Act. The Conference extended the Concert of Europe system to Africa by establishing a common set of rules for the 'great game', especially in relation to trade, navigation and annexation of territory. Article VI declared: 'Powers exercising sovereign rights or influence in the aforesaid territories bind themselves to watch over the preservation of the native tribes, and to care for the improvement of the conditions of their well-being.'[2] The idea that the preservation and welfare of tribes should be incorporated into the calculations of imperial rule had been established at least three decades earlier, a construct of mid-nineteenth-century social thought. The immediate political origins of the discourse are the increasingly violent rebellions across Britain's colonial holdings, in Ireland and Jamaica, but above all the Indian Mutiny of 1857, which led to the end of East India Company rule and major revisions in British attitudes regarding how its subject peoples ought to be ruled (Chakravarty, 2005; Metcalf, 1964). Exemplified by James Mill's *History of British India*, the dominant pre-Mutiny ideas of imperial rule were underpinned by the rational and universalist assumptions of Bentham's utilitarianism with 'sophisters, economists and calculators' directly overseeing the wholesale imposition of new forms of rule. 'The sword was to be exchanged for the pen, and the soldier-diplomat to give way before the administrator and judge' (Stokes, 1959: 13). As evidenced by the number of violent rebellions, however, utilitarian models of social contract, discourses of improvement and attempts at legal and economic reform had catastrophically failed. The persistence of native revolt and then imperial retribution with slaughter and floggings suggested that European 'civil society' could not be as easily universalised as the Benthamites had assumed.

[2] Article VI goes on: 'They shall, without distinction of creed or nation, protect and favour all religious, scientific or charitable institutions and undertakings created and organized for the above ends, or which aim at instructing the natives and bringing home to them the blessings of civilization.'

In an admission of the colonial limits of 'civil society', a different 'social' form and mode of imperial governance was invented, 'traditional society' and indirect rule. What could explain violent rebellions against such relatively benevolent empire? Of particular political and intellectual significance in this context is the work of comparative jurist, historian, and colonial administrator Sir Henry Sumner Maine (1822–1888). Legal Member of the Governor-General's Council in India between 1862 and 1869, Maine's writings provided the social theory framework to account for native resistance and formed the basis of a new form of imperial governance, a form of decentralised household despotism. With Maine's work, colonial administrators could leave aside the awkward and unpleasant political answer that many of those living under colonial rule had decided to actively and violently resist their own exploitation. An explanation was found in the very nature of pre-modern 'societies' themselves. The arrival of modernity in the form of the British Empire had thrown caste-based and tradition-bound societies into crisis. Maine's elaborate history and theory of comparative 'social' development challenged utilitarian philosophy and reform as applied to both native populations *and* to understand the achievements of bourgeois civil society at home. The advances of modern individualist society remained fragile. In the Age of the Social, conservatives and utilitarians were united by belief in the underlying importance of 'society' as determining the character of all other human institutions. But conservative historicism pitted itself against utilitarianism's *a priori* approach to politics and law. The traditional Indian village could not suddenly be replaced by a system of contractually based rights and duties between individuals (Maine, 1878/1908: 165–166). They were structured functional wholes based on longstanding customs and the authority of the patriarch. Utilitarian reformers had misunderstood the definite function and purpose of 'traditional society'. Maine raised powerful questions regarding whether natives were ready for rapid liberal reform and, more practically, whether earlier ways of conceiving and implementing reform were even necessary to the maintenance of empire.

Sir Henry Sumner Maine's conception of native society as a self-sufficient household would provide the theoretical foundation and normative justification for the notion that imperial rule was for the sake of *protecting* the native population. Crucially, this population was not to be viewed as a collection of individuals but as groups governed, depending on the location, under village patriarchs or tribal elders. In other words, the intellectual and practical solution for imperial rule was to rehabilitate and revise a form of despotic household rule, decentralised household despotism. The first social contract theories of civilised society, recall, were explicitly constructed in opposition to patriarchal theories of government in which political rule was modelled on the government of the family by the father. It should come as no surprise then to find the first theories of pre-modern 'traditional society' centre on the enduring household despotism as explanations of – and cure for – native revolt. Protect and preserve the native tribes, let village elders run their day-to-day affairs. The unbridled liberal reformist agenda gave way to a more conservative, even romantic, emphasis on culture and history as limitations on the wholesale reform of colonial subjects. This was domestic containment in the language of protection. Transferred from British India to Africa and Asia, social theories of 'traditional society' would long influence the relationship between 'local knowledge' and imperialism, including imperial war and counterinsurgency.

It is possible to make many criticisms of Sir Henry Maine's work.[3] However, as Edward Shils has claimed, 'no one writer has entered so penetratingly and so pervasively, into the fundamental outlook of sociologists of the twentieth century' (1991: 144). His central dichotomy between 'status' and 'contract' would have an immense influence on the future course of sociological thought, as evidenced by its centrality to Tönnies, Weber and Durkheim (Shils, 1991: 162).[4] In 'status

3 As Kate Millett has written, citing the work of Victorian ethnologist and Maine critic, John Ferguson McLennan, 'Roman *patria potestes* was an extreme form of patriarchy and by no means, as Maine had imagined, universal. Evidence of matrilineal societies (preliterate societies in Africa and elsewhere) refute Maine's assumption of the universality of agnation. Certainly Maine's central argument, as to the primeval or state of nature character of patriarchy is but a rather naif rationalization of an institution Maine tended to exalt. The assumption of patriarchy's primeval character is contradicted by much evidence which points to the conclusion that full patriarchal authority, particularly that of the *patria potestes* is a late development and the total erosion of female status was likely to be gradual as has been its recovery' (Millett, 1969/1977: 34; see also McLennan, 1885). Maine's reading of the *patria potestas* in Roman law has also been accused of lacking ground in empirical evidence, of being more 'polemical ... than scholarly' (Kuper, 1991: 103).

4 As noted in Chapter 2, this also suggests that there is more at stake for international studies in the 'German historical baggage' underlying the

societies', Maine argued, individuals exist only as members of a collective performing certain roles of the collective. In 'contract societies', individuals are freed from collective constraints and act only in their own interests. Surprisingly, Maine's work has largely been overlooked by international theory. This is surprising given his influence on the sociological tradition, including in later Cold War theories of modernisation; but also his writings on the primitive bases of international law; and his place as one of the earliest 'historical sociologists' (Maine, 1888).[5] Building on and extending the recent revival of his significance in political theory, this chapter offers the first sustained treatment of his work in the context of international relations (Mantena, 2010; Mamdani, 2012). International political theorists have paid far more attention to John Stuart Mill's defence of liberal despotism, but Maine's distinctly social explanations and remedies for native revolt are of equal – if not greater – significance for the actual conduct of imperialism, the canon of social theory and later counterinsurgency rule.[6]

This chapter is divided into four parts. The first section analyses the influence of eighteenth-century discourses of sociability on the new genre of global and comparative history that accompanied the rise of the commercial empires, its influence on utilitarian liberal reformers in India, and conservative criticisms in the wake of the Sepoy Rebellion. The second section sets out Sir Henry Sumner Maine's patriarchal theory of 'traditional society' in which custom, tradition and caste would be understood as the underlying 'social' bases and fundamental units of India's social structure. The third part of the chapter shows how in reviving and revising older theories of despotic household governance, Maine laid the groundwork for the theory and practice of late

distinction between *Gemeinschaft* and *Gesellschaft*, than claimed by an influential theorist of 'international society' (Buzan, 2004: 111).

[5] However, there is some discussion in Koskenniemi (2002). While rejecting the view that international law was not possible without a global sovereign, Maine did not believe international law (rules of conduct between states) would follow the same path as the transition from status to contract. These 'rules of conduct, which, whatever be their origin, are to a very great extent', Maine argued 'enforced by the disapprobation which attends their neglect' (Landauer, 2002: 247). There is also reference to Henry Maine's *Village Communities in the East and West* in Lester Frank Ward's theory of sociocracy (1903: 226–227).

[6] This is not to deny the independent effect of imperialism on classical sociology, for example on Marx's theories about the Asiatic mode of production and despotic village communities.

nineteenth-century indirect rule that, in turn, would be important for understanding counterinsurgency. His claim that the patriarchal household was the origin of all political association is deeply revealing of the ever-present need of liberal 'contract societies' to revert to forms of household rule when non-compliant subjects require domestication. The fourth section shifts focus from British theories of 'traditional society' to radical French and American experiments in social paternalism during wars of colonial pacification in which rule through local despots would form a central plank of military strategy. The interdependencies between these colonial experiments and contemporaneous social reforms in the homeland are well-documented. Here we specifically address the intersection between the nascent ideology of counterinsurgency and the distinctively *social* regulation that it was increasingly understood to demand; that is, the 'equivalences between nation-building and household management' (Wesling, 2011: 122; Guha, 1988). Colonial occupation was both practised and understood as a form of good housekeeping, as a domestication of imperialism.[7]

Civil society meets mutiny

Early social philosophy was closely associated with what were taken to be the civilising aspects of sociable, polite, and benevolent conversation between equals in *salon société.* The etiquette and norms that developed in eighteenth-century *société* were the quintessence of civilised conduct and could be enlarged to humanity as a whole (Hume, 1738/2007; Montesquieu, 1748/1989). The basis of universal morality, new forms of sociability underpinned civilised 'social' order in general. According to Norbert Elias, the earliest use of the term 'civilisation' was as a tool of a new middle-class French intelligentsia in its struggles against the old court 'high society'. But with the coming to national political power of the bourgeoisie, the term also came to 'epitomise the nation, to express the national self-image' (Elias, 2000: 43). What the bourgeoisie considered barbaric – such as restrictions on trade – was also first and foremost deemed to be against the nature of 'society' itself. Not forms of government or

[7] 'To "domesticate" is to bring the foreign or primitive or alien into line with the "domestic" civilization and power, just as a "domesticated" animal is one that has been tamed into home life' (Bowlby, 1995: 74).

individual actions, but the coherence and stability of underlying 'social relations' determined the qualities and health of a nation. By the latter half of the eighteenth century, the distinction between so-called civilised and 'polished nations' and those that were 'rude and barbarous' was common in both Britain and France (Ferguson, 1767/1995). The terminology of 'polished nations' almost certainly derives from its likeness to the language of *adouci*, sweetened/softened, and the more widespread language of the *douceur*, of pleasantness, commerce and other forms of polite social intercourse. New eighteenth-century forms of comparative and global history, most influentially the four stages theory, ranked populations in terms of race, culture and degree of civilisation, largely on the degree to which they had developed into polished and polite commercial societies with a state apparatus able to undermine feudalism, regulate labour and protect private property.[8]

The intellectual task of the new social philosophy was to describe the conditions for social harmony in an emerging capitalist system and colonial order. Enlightenment ideas about the structure and development of European societies were conceived in direct contrast to what was assumed to be the case among 'savages', or what Adam Ferguson (1767/1995) called 'rude nations'. In other words, notions about a self-regulating civil society possess an important colonial genealogy. The social contract between citizen and state, the idea of sovereign individuals creating a bourgeois civil society, was obviously absent in colonial contexts. 'Founded in force', writes Gyan Prakash of a dominant imperial view,

> the colonial state was a Hobbesian colossus that acted upon and constituted a society deemed unable to self-constitute and self-regulate. Because the indigenous society did not resemble the European bourgeois civil society, [many] colonizers concluded that society *qua* society was absent ... What was acknowledged to exist prior to the colonial state [administered by Europeans] was not society, but something else – races, tribes, castes and

[8] As Adam Smith put it: 'A nation that founds a colony in an unoccupied territory, or in a territory occupied only by savages, makes it subservient to the benevolent purposes for which it was destined by Providence, and extends the empire of civilization to it' (in Bhambra, 2007: 133). The irony of the language of the *douceur* was not lost on Marx 'who, in accounting for the primitive accumulation of capital, recounts some of the more violent episodes in the history of European commercial capitalism and then exclaims sarcastically: "Das ist der *doux commerce!*"' (Hirschman, 1977: 62).

> clans. Not surprisingly, the colonies became the location for the development of the discipline of anthropology, not sociology, ... the classic discipline of European modernity.
>
> (Prakash, 2002: 82)

The dominant theory of 'socio-economic' development in the eighteenth century held that there was a natural historical progression through the stages of development in different modes of subsistence: hunting, pasturage, agriculture and commerce (Ferguson, 1767/1995; Meek, 1976). In savage society, there is no ownership of property; in barbarian society there is limited individual and some communal ownership. Only in civilised society is 'social' reproduction properly private, an arrangement between free individuals in self-regulating competition that was both anarchic and harmonious, the 'anarchical society' again.

The early modern theorists of natural law, Hobbes, Grotius and Pufendorf, had all theorised human nature in universalistic terms. However, divergences between nations in the levels of sociability allowed for deviation and the preservation of hierarchy while still speaking of universality. This was and continues to be one of the main functions of the language of sociability and its descendants. 'In its meaning as politeness,' Gordon (1994: 75) writes, 'sociability referred to the disposition and manners of humans who understood that their interests were entwined with others ... With religion and other myths obstructing the growth of sociability, the degree of sociability varied from people to people and required time to achieve perfection.' In the less elegant language of contemporary international theory, some regime types are more 'sociable' than others. These arguments developed in an international and imperial context that assumed that not all nations were equally sociable, but that they all *potentially* were; the role of government in relation to its 'society' depended on the level of sociability displayed by its subjects. By the 1830s, leading liberal thinkers in both Britain and France had turned to empire, and claimed that imperial order was best secured by creating native elites in the image of their more civilised tutors, a form of direct rule through assimilation (Mehta, 1999; Schultz and Varouxakis, 2005). Different, less civilised modes of sociability could be overcome through legal and economic reform. It was taken for granted that indigenous legal and political traditions were a hindrance to overall liberal improvement. However, once stripped of pre-modern identities, once the all-important distinction was made between existing (arbitrary) laws and the rational laws that could govern all humankind, individuals would respond in similar, rational ways given similar structures of incentives, or so utilitarian philosophers believed. Direct rule through a civilised native elite and major legal reforms would, in turn, transplant the universal values of civil society to the colonies. In this guise, wrote Eric R. Wolf, 'the concept of Society was aggressive ... in claiming universality, applicable at all times and everywhere, as part of universal Enlightenment' (1988: 759).

Then as now, Europeans understood themselves to be agents of progress, delivering good government because they understood the underlying laws of society. It was but a short step from eighteenth-century discourses of sociability to the early nineteenth-century justifications and methods of imperial domination through native assimilation and liberal reform. Certainly, as Jennifer Pitts has noted, Jeremy Bentham's 'belief that colonial rulers and administrators could never be trusted to rule well, and his suspicion of aspirations to civilize non-Europeans, stand in sharp contrast to the technocratic and cultural confidence of Bentham's successors' (2005: 104).[9] The most articulate exponent of a technically and culturally confident liberal despotism in the colonies (in addition to children and the working classes) was John Stuart Mill, of course. A significant figure in the transition from classical to social liberalism, Mill wrote of the need for colonial administration of barbarians while the English working classes were also conceived as objects of social administration (see also Kurer, 1991). Colonial subjugation and representative (as opposed to direct) democracy were justified because they gradually improved the conditions of the barbarous or dangerous without undermining the basic structures of either imperial or capitalist rule. At issue in the colonies was how to be a good despot. Like his contemporary Henry Maine, Mill rejected the idea that humans were all essentially the same and could be governed through similar arrangements. But unlike Maine, Mill was in thrall to

[9] Majeed (1990: 209) argues that the 'radical rhetoric of Utilitarianism expressed by Jeremy Bentham, and especially James Mill ... was an attack on the revitalized conservatism of the early nineteenth century, which had emerged in response to the threat of the French revolution; but the idea of the struggle between this conservatism and Utilitarianism increasingly became defined in relation to a set of conflicting attitudes towards British involvement in India'.

the 'spirit of improvement' as the justification for despotic rule. As he wrote in *On Liberty*:

> a ruler full of the spirit of improvement is warranted in the use of any expedients that will attain an end perhaps otherwise unattainable. Despotism is a legitimate mode of government in dealing with barbarians, provided the end be their improvement, and the means justified by actually effecting that end, and if less violent forms of transformation toward *liberal social progress*, such as persuasion, will not suffice.
>
> (Mill, 1999: 13–14, emphasis added)[10]

With schemes of liberal social progress, good despots should encourage the capacity for self-government among natives by encouraging forms of peasant proprietorship. In addition to instilling good habits, such as self-control, liberal improvement encouraged the more efficient use of land.

Thomas Macaulay, member of the Supreme Council of India in the 1830s, had called for the creation of 'a class of persons Indian in colour and blood, but English in tastes, in opinions, in morals and in intellect' (in Sinha, 1995: 4). But what if liberal improvement did not work, or not work quickly enough? Schemes of improvement had evidently not succeeded given the scale and ferocity of native resistance, especially the disastrous Mutiny that scandalised British civilised society. With their 'chilly dogmatics', utilitarians were accused of failing to understand how backward peoples really lived. Pre-modern societies were inextricably tied to their traditional customs and this could not be calculated away (Stokes, 1959: 14). More than simply a crisis in imperial administration and law, the rebellions across the British Empire at the end of the 1850s were read as failures of knowledge.[11] On this view, colonial administrators had paid insufficient respect to distinctive local cultures, native beliefs and forms of rule, and they paid the price. In the case of the Sepoy Revolt, how could Muslim and Hindu soldiers have been asked to use rifles greased with the fat of beef and pork?

[10] For a sympathetic discussion of Mill's theory of 'enlightened despotism' in the colonies see Chiu and Taylor (2011). For more critical readings see O'Malley (1996); Valverde (1996); Helliwell and Hindess, (2002); Jahn (2005).

[11] The emphasis of this chapter is not intended to downplay the military response, including the revival of notions of 'martial races' after the Mutiny, a response that was highly gendered (Streets, 2010).

Utilitarianism stood accused of failing to understand properly what it means to talk of the essentially *social* basis of political and legal institutions, in both modern and pre-modern culture. As a result, all subsequent colonial practice and ideology would hail the importance of understanding the deep-seated 'social' base of all indigenous community. For emphasising these social and cultural factors was preferable to any alterative – more political – account of rebellion.[12] After all, if the explanation for native revolt was social-cultural, then its remedy was social-cultural too. The figure most closely associated with both the new theories of 'traditional society' and the practical implementation of its consequences, was Sir Henry Sumner Maine, leading administrator in British India and one of founders of social anthropology.

In a claim that would be repeated in mid-twentieth-century modernisation theories of anti-colonial and postcolonial resistance in Kenya, Malaya and Vietnam, Henry Maine's explanation for the fact and ferocity of revolt centred on what would later be called a 'crisis of transition'. Absorption into the British Empire and associated liberal reforms accelerated India's evolution to modernity, destroying its customary property and village governance norms, and hence its internal cohesiveness. 'For the separate, unchangeable, and irremovable family lot in the cultivated area, if it be a step forwards in the history of property,' wrote Maine, 'is also the point at which the Indian village-community is breaking to pieces' (1876: 112). Traditional communal and status-bound village relations were shattering in the face of new norms of absolute private property and contractual labour relations. This was Maine's distinctly 'social' explanation for native violence, a theory of violence based on a structural-functionalist account of Indian village society (that is, before 'structural-functionalism' explicitly emerged as a dominant approach in twentieth-century sociology and much counter-insurgency thought). Like the organs of a human body, he claimed, all 'societies' were functionally interdependent and hierarchically ordered. Maine's conception of the 'holistic' Indian village in crisis would be the colonial forerunner of Émile Durkheim's writing on *anomie*, in which

[12] Cf. Guha's (1988: 47) study of peasant rebellions in India in which 'an explanation will be sought in an enumeration of causes – of say, factors of economic and political deprivation which do not relate at all to the peasant's consciousness or do so negatively – triggering off rebellion as a sort of reflex action; that is, as an instinctive and almost mindless response to physical suffering of one kind or another (e.g. hunger, torture, forced labour etc.)'.

the breakdown of regulative 'social norms' disrupted conventional modes of socialisation resulting in deviant behaviour (Pope, 1975). Maine argued that disturbance of the core elements of Indian village life had led to dissolution of the coherence of the social system (or household) as a whole. Since all the parts of the system were understood as functionally interrelated, fundamental changes in the use of land and form of law caused the otherwise inexplicable violence against British interests. Given the vulnerability of traditional society after the arrival of modern contract norms, imperial administrators needed to find new grounds for reconciling themselves to the customary institutions and structures of authority in the villages. Unless colonial administrators somehow revised the nature of colonial rule, violent reaction was inevitable (for an excellent account see Mantena, 2010).

Before analysing in more detail Maine's account of the precise nature of traditional village society and his proposed remedy for anti-British violence, it is important to appreciate the significance of its underlying basis in the conservative critique of utilitarianism, for it would have a lasting impact on the entire course of modern sociology and distinctly social thought. The greatest crime of utilitarianism, conservatives argued, had been 'to eradicate in the name of utility all the historical associations connected with the rise of British power; and in the cause of efficiency, simplicity and economy, sought to reduce the historical modes of government to one centralized, uniform practice' (Stokes, 1959: 14). Drawing on now well-developed 'social philosophy', French conservatives such as Louis de Bonald similarly maintained the priority of the social and historical order over the individual and its imaginary contracts (Klinck, 1996). After all, it had been the universalising and individualistic maxims of the French Revolutionaries that led to the disastrous upending of all authority, a Reign of Terror and war. Order could only be maintained on the basis of semi-natural 'social relations' that provided stability and legitimacy to counter the disordering effects of industrial society, as witnessed again by the 1848 revolutions. Conservatives maintained that the progressive, historical achievements of all commercial societies were deeply precarious. For Maine, the triumph of British civilisation was not the discovery of some universally perfect form of rule. It was a product of historical progress and convention (Burke, 1790/1993). They could not be transplanted at will without endangering the very foundations of liberty. Similarly, conservative insistence on the radical contrast between 'traditional' (including ancient Greek) and modern 'society' inaugurated a major 'historical' and 'comparative' methodological innovation, the basis of 'a new science' (Maine, 1876: 225).[13] Collective ideas (later 'holism') would counter individualism; ordered structures were produced from the interactions of separate parts that required theorising in their own, structural terms.[14] Not the cold claims of utilitarian philosophy, only an historical, conservative and romantic sensibility could understand the fragility of Europe's civilised conventions. Such conservative reactions to the revolutions furnished the assumption, accepted by much of the sociology tradition, that authority and power were natural in human relations. These were attractive propositions to those searching for the basis of solidarity in crisis-ridden industrial society. No one played a greater role in the reciprocal transfer of 'social' knowledge and imperial rule than Sir Henry Sumner Maine, developing a new theory of the historical modes of government for imperial purpose.

Sir Henry Sumner Maine and the patriarchal theory of traditional society

Following the basic socio-biological thought of his day, Henry Maine held that the structure and function of social systems developed in self-organising and self-sustaining entities through processes

[13] As discussed in Chapter 2, the nineteenth-century revaluation of the political heritage of ancient Greece, a form of democratic political action that could lead to the violence of the French Revolution, was a central part of the devaluation of political action in favour of 'social norms'. Representative government, not direct participatory democracy, was more suitable in commercial societies. However, the ancients could nonetheless be a source for the earliest anthropological studies of 'kinship', on which the content of Maine's theory of 'traditional society' was based. For a good discussion see Mantena (2012). At the same time, however, Pecora has pointed to an 'underlying relation between [aspects of] the [British] imperial project and the redemptive resonance of the classical *oikos* in modernity ... The image of the colonial plantation, whether as fictional reality or fantasy ... [recalled] on the one hand patriarchal transcendence of the petty bargains and contracts regulating civil society and on the other lordly abundance and leisure' (Pecora, 1997: 18).

[14] The term 'holism' was first deployed for social theory in the 1920s by Jan Christian Smuts (1926, 1994), the South African statesman, military commander in the Boer War, segregationist, social philosopher and writer of the preamble of the UN Charter. In Churchill's war cabinet during World War II, he has a statue in Parliament Square, Westminster.

of evolutionary adaptation.[15] Stable societies cohere around a set of interdependent social, economic, political and legal institutions that find their more or less equivalent counterparts in all locations, allowing the comparative analysis of universal institutions in radically different epochs and places.[16] One of the first concepts to receive such an elevated comparative status was kinship, providing the grounds for Maine's historical and comparative account of the evolution from ancient village communities to modern contractual society. Such analysis, Maine argued, revealed that the beginning of 'political society' was not in some fictitious social contract but the historically conditioned Roman family structured on the power of a father, *patria potestas*. Subjection to the power of the patriarch was the primordial condition of human 'society'. In Maine's words again, 'many rules, of which nobody has hitherto discerned the historical beginnings, had really their sources in certain incidents of the Patria Potestas' (1876: 17–18). The original state of nature was not Hobbes' anarchy composed of individuals but more or less ordered relations within and between family households, each unit with its own controlling patriarch.[17] 'The points which lie on the surface of the history are these ... The eldest male parent – the eldest ascendant – is absolutely supreme in his household' (Maine, 1878/1908): 109). The 'primeval condition of the human race' was the subjection of all members of the household to the patriarch (Maine, 1878/1908: 122; 1886; Starr, 1985).

This patriarchal theory of the origins of society inverted John Locke's theory of the original state of nature, in which individuals choose to form a government through a social contract. In Maine's words, 'society in primitive times was not what it is assumed to be at present, a collection of *individuals*. In fact, and in the view of the men who composed it, it was an *aggregation of families*. The contrast may

[15] 'When he wants to emphasize the fact of continuity ... Maine speaks in an evolutionary, "gradualist" manner. But almost equally often he speaks in terms of a straight dichotomy–status and contract, progressive and non-progressive, barbarous and civilized' (Burrow, 1966: 159).

[16] This claim also underlies the comparative analysis of forms of 'international society' (Watson, 1992; Buzan and Little, 2000; Buzan, 2004).

[17] 'Ancient society, in a fundamental sense,' writes Mantena of this view, 'was *imperium in imperio*, a society of commonwealths, an aggregation of families. The closest modern analogy to archaic public law therefore was international law, where a minimal set of rights and duties extended only to the head of the family, who was sovereign in his own domestic domain' (2010: 77; see also Kuper, 2005: 11).

be most forcibly expressed by saying that the *unit* of an ancient society was the Family, of a modern society the individual' (1878/1908: 111, emphasis in original). Moreover, the state of nature was not one of freedom but *despotism*, the original unit being the patriarchal family, 'a group of men and women, children and slaves, of animate and inanimate property, all connected together by common subjection to the Paternal Power of the chief of the household' (Maine, 1876: 15). For Maine, there was no other conceivable basis for political association than the primordial collective of the patriarchal household. 'All the forms of Status taken notice of in the Law of Persons,' Maine wrote, 'were derived from, and to some extent are still coloured by, the powers and privileges anciently residing in the Family' (1878/1908: 170). However, Maine did not dispense with the idea of contract. Rather its location shifted from the origins of civil society to its end. Societies formed through contract were the highest *historical* achievement of bourgeois civilisation. Maine not only inverted Locke. He reversed Robert Filmer's *Patriarcha*, in which the first kings were the fathers of families. For Maine, it was the first fathers who were kings.[18] The basic and essential 'sociological' unit was the patriarchal family and all other 'political' institutions (except those found in liberal contract societies) were extensions of the family. All social formations in 'Indo-European' civilisation, the Hindu Joint Family, the East European House-Community and medieval Germanic, Teutonic township and Indian village-communities, evolved from this base. 'What was obviously true of the Family was believed to be true first of the House, next of the Tribe, lastly of the State' (Maine, 1878/1908: 114).

Maine created a legal basis for despotic kinship relations, in which the father has unfettered control over the people and things within the property of the household. However, once again the patriarch was understood, Maine wrote,

> [to] lay under an equal amplitude of obligations ... He had no privilege or position distinct from that conferred on him by his relation to the petty commonwealth which he governed. The Family, in fact, was a Corporation; and he was its representative or, we might almost say, its Public officer.
> (Maine, 1878/1908: 163)

[18] Comte (1875: 305) also argued that the Roman 'idea of Fatherland ... [is] the necessary forerunner and the permanent support of the idea of Humanity'.

The criterion for membership of the household was territorial locality and kinship with 'status' determined by biological attributes. The fate of individuals was bound by their position – their *status* – in the hierarchical, patriarchal order of affiliations between people based on kinship, cultural and religious ties. These were small in scale, largely agricultural and economically self-sufficient households in thrall to irrational and religious forms of thought. These primordial, primitive communities were nonetheless conceived by Maine as functional wholes in which 'Authority, Custom, or Chance are ... the great sources of law' (1876: 110–111). Maine believed he had uncovered the evolutionary trends leading societies in the direction from status to contract, from patriarchy to liberty. As he wrote in *Ancient Law*, there was a slow, historical transition from 'the Family expanding into the Agnatic group of kinsmen, then the Agnatic group dissolving into separate households; lastly, the household supplanted the individual; and ... each step in the change corresponds to an analogous alteration in the nature of Ownership' (in Mantena, 2010: 80; Maine, 1878/1908: 261). Over time, Maine argued, it was possible to trace the evolution of primordial patriarchy into more complex systems, the *Gens*, an aggregation of families, to the Tribe and the Commonwealth. But again these are extensions of the original patriarchal form of rule and modelled on the image of a family.[19] For Maine, only with the rise of liberal contract society through the progressive transition from ancient to modern does patriarchy lose its absolute authority.

Patriarchal relations of dependency and control, Maine argued, were increasingly undermined by the slow progression of public law and the privatisation of property in land. The territorialisation of authority and the privatisation of land drove the shift from tribal status to individual contract. Maine's entire theory of progress and comparative, historical method depended on this distinction between status and contract with their underlying 'sociological' base. In fact, mirroring the better-known dichotomous accounts of Tönnies, Gierke,

[19] As McClintock (1995: 357–358) has put it: 'The family trope ... offers a "natural" figure for sanctioning national *hierarchy* within a putative organic *unity* of interests ... The metaphoric depiction of social hierarchy as natural and familial – the "national family", the global "family of nations", the colony as a "family of black children ruled over by a white father" – depended ... on the prior naturalizing of the social [sic] subordination of women and children within the domestic sphere.'

Comte and Durkheim, there are really only two kinds of societies in Maine's scheme, those based on status founded on collectivity, kinship and locale and those based on contract in which forms of affiliation are based on legal contracts between sovereign individuals, territorial proximity and individual ownership of property. The customary laws of primordial societies were defined in terms of their concreteness and particularity. Modern law, in contrast, would claim universality (Shils, 1991: 164–165). In status societies, heads of households were sovereign in their own domain and related to other household heads as sovereigns. The modern territorial state was now sovereign over its land, and only then over those who resided within it. The rights and duties that had formerly been given to heads of household were eventually transferred to individuals defined by their ability to exercise self-regulation and self-discipline, the definition of the sovereign individual. 'The individual is steadily substituted for the Family, as the unit of which civil laws take account' (Maine, 1878/1908): 149).[20]

In Maine's anthropology, the traditional patriarchal family and the agricultural village community were the universal institutions out of which modern civilisation was built, but had left behind. The Indian village community represented a halfway position between societies of hierarchy and those defined by territorial sovereignty, between status and contract. These villages were the cornerstone of the history of civilisation, revealing at once the Indian present and the European past, 'united by the assumption of common kin-ship, and of a company of persons exercising joint ownership over land' (Maine, 1876: 12).[21] As Maine put it, 'the Indian and the ancient European systems ... in village-communities are in all essential particulars identical' (1876: 103). As such, they served as a crucial marker of the progressive development of individual legal rights, contracts and property relations, a base of comparison between past and future. In Burrow's words, there was an unrecognised '"Aryan" past, including both India and Europe. It permitted [Maine] to make, within its limits, the dashing

[20] As Shils (1991: 154) put it, for Maine, 'when society extended beyond the limits of the family and lineage and when spheres of activity emerged which could not be covered by the traditional norms and legal fictions of the primordial society, a qualitatively different kind of regulation was needed'.

[21] 'It ceased to be simply the Indian village community; it became the early European village community *extant*' (Dewey, 1972: 307; see also Dumont, 1966).

comparisons, the equation of the past institutions of one society with the present ones of another' (1966: 161). Modern legal order was fundamentally alien to the patriarchal villages of India. Nonetheless, these villages needed to be respected; their unity and independence should be protected and preserved under colonial rule. The crisis of imperial legitimacy provoked by the Sepoy Revolt was eventually resolved with the invention of 'traditional society', theorising about its nature and character, and making these theories part of the underlying rationale for a revised form of imperial governance: decentralised household despotism.

Decentralised household despotism: on indirect rule

Mid-nineteenth-century conservatives used the Mutiny to attack liberal utilitarian assumptions about how modern legal and political institutions had evolved and could be transplanted overseas. To be sure, John Stuart Mill had argued that until 'barbarians' were 'capable of being improved by free and equal discussion ... there is nothing for them but implicit obedience to an Akbar or a Charlemagne' (1999: 14). However, rather than being destroyed or used as a laboratory for utilitarianism's legal experiments, native 'social' structures and patriarchal-household authority would now be mobilised in the delivery of imperial rule. For utilitarians, the traditional village had been an obstruction to economic progress; it needed to be radically reformed. Maine turned this image on its head. The notion of 'traditional society' and related arguments about its coherence and stability provided what would now be referred to as the 'international historical-sociological' basis for a major revaluation of British imperial strategy. There were important elements of village life to be preserved, especially those offering a seeming solution to the problem of colonial order. The very nature of traditional society itself, its simultaneous vulnerability and longevity, became the justification for imperial presence in the face of the sweeping and all-powerful processes of modernity associated with the rise and expansion of contract societies. The natives were so bound up with their customs and traditions that their acquiescence to imperial rule relied on Britain adopting a protective role. As Evelyn Baring, Earl of Cromer, put it, 'the real Indian question was not whether the English were justified in staying in the country, but whether they could find any moral justification for withdrawing from it' (quoted in Mantena, 2010: 148).[22]

The liberal-utilitarian agenda of improvement was joined and partly forced to give way to an imperial discourse of working with already existing 'customs'. In Stokes' words,

> To take the peasant in all his simplicity to secure him in the possession of his land, to rule him with a paternal and simple government, and so to avoid all the artificialities of a sophisticated European form of rule – these political aims surely spring directly from … the Romantic movement.
>
> (Stokes, 1959: 13)

Thus emerged a new form of rule that incorporated 'native traditions' into the quest for imperial order and stability. Conservatives and colonial administrators, interprets Dewey, 'were attracted by the village community's apparent ability to preserve, amidst the disintegration of larger forms of political and social organization, ordered societies in miniature' (1972: 295). In practical terms, this meant the partial shift of land policy away from commoditisation towards more 'traditional' and communal land uses and the consolidation of patriarchal village life through conceding power back to what were presented as natural and traditional native rulers. The 'women question' – previously a topic of great debate among both English and Bengal reformers – was also given over to 'tradition', to be located in a newly conceived sphere of 'domestic' intimacy.

Within colonial discourse, India was presented 'as an assemblage of timeless traditions and communities' (Prakash, 2002: 85). Hindus were subordinated to religious edicts; Brahmanical religious texts were responsible for the insufferable conditions of women. Social reformers argued that indigenous peoples needed to be educated not only in the ways of commerce and good government but also in how to treat 'their' women (Metcalf, 1994). In this context, Indian nationalists

[22] Franz Fanon (1967: 88) later referred to this logic frequently used by liberal-left proponents of imperialism as 'technocratic paternalism'. 'After breaking all links with France, it is argued, what will you do? You need technicians, currency, machines … The colonists tell the French people in their propaganda: France cannot live without Algeria. The French anti-colonists say to the Algerians: Algeria cannot live without France … What is involved here is a kind of terrorism of necessity on the basis of which it is decided that nothing valid can be conceived or achieved in Algeria independently of France.'

developed a new sense of the importance of the 'private' domain in Indian culture, a notion given even greater weight in the absence of political autonomy under the Raj. The question of the status of women could thus be constituted as one of authentic tradition that was properly located in an inner, domestic realm where colonial power must not be allowed to enter. Privatised domestic space came to define important elements of proto-nationalist Indian culture, a space of resistance to colonial discipline, in distinction to the political sphere of external subordination. Building on the gendered distinctions between public and private spheres, Indian nationalists cast women and the 'domestic' home as the carriers of tradition, a sacred and hence superior realm to the worldly and material sphere of colonial state sovereignty. The 'women question' was taken off the agenda of elite debate, writes Chatterjee, due to 'nationalism's success in situating [it] in an inner domain of sovereignty, rather removed from the arena of political contest with the colonial state' (1993: 117). The gendered separation of spheres not only impacted on India's 'women question', but also the attempt of British women seeking to make 'home in the empire' and configure imperial power as a kind of household (George, 1993/1994).

Historians have written extensively on how a particular spatial division between public and private 'became concrete during the rapid industrial urbanisation of Victorian England when a domestic ideology dominated the lives of, in the main, middle-class women, secluded in their suburban homes while their husbands ventured into the bustle of "the outer world" to make a living' (McDowell, 2002: 818). And yet few activities disrupted the boundary between domestic and foreign than overseas imperial rule, the foreign policy of domestication that created new forms of public domesticity. Consider the middle-class women setting up a domestic home in the colonies, whose special expertise in social housekeeping was deemed particularly useful in managing an empire of unruly, childlike subjects. The empire itself was an enlarged domestic space and the well-run domestic home, in which any visible signs of conflict and dissent were erased, was a model for a well-run empire. In this context, 'colonialism was not a one-sided affair' as Comaroff and Comaroff write. 'For in seeking to cultivate the "savage" … British imperialists were actively engaged in transforming their own society as well, most explicitly in domesticating that part of the metropole that had previously eluded bourgeois control', through social work in urban slums (1992: 292). Then as now, masculinised forms of imperial violence were accompanied by feminised homemaking, legitimising the former through the 'sublimation of the entire background of colonial warfare into the furniture of domesticity' (Wexler, 2000: 47). In the process, some women were offered a chance to be included in the 'public, political' realm. In the context of racial and civilisational hierarchy, many British women claimed to have experienced for the first time the sense of 'authoritative self', of being a 'full individual', supposedly defining of the liberal subject in the contract societies theorised by Maine (George, 1993/1994: 97)

Henry Maine's work, so well received by imperial administrators, was instrumental in founding a new methodological approach, a historical, 'sociological' and comparative jurisprudence, to properly capture the primordial human condition and subsequent stages of progress. Colonial anthropology and ethnography were marshalled to provide cultural knowledge of local kinship relations, customs, marriage and funeral rituals, all theorised in social and structural-functionalist terms. For anthropologists themselves, being asked to discover the key to local law and order for colonial administrators was a dramatic advance over earlier practices of merely describing local habits, food and diseases (Dirks, 2001: 46; Feuchtwang, 1973).[23] Anthropologists were still to observe the day-to-day life of the natives, but its underlying logic was governed by deep-seated customs and traditions, the more profound and underlying 'social relations' of which daily life and activity was a mere expression. They were called on to identify how native systems of stability and internal cohesion worked. Like the sociology out of which it emerged, 'social anthropology' was functionalist, pointing to small-scale tribal divisions as the most stable form of 'traditional' order. After all, the imperial 'respect' and 'protection' afforded to traditional society was based on the assumption that traditional villages constituted *societies*. These were not 'civil societies' to be sure, but rationally and functionally ordered, internally structured, corporate wholes, like the human body that was its model.[24] These

[23] The Royal Anthropological Institute was founded in 1838 with an evangelical purpose of civilising the colonies. Founded in 1842, the Ethnological Society of London was more liberal than the Anthropological Society of London, founded in 1863, which was more supportive of notions of natural aristocracy.

[24] This was also true of castes in India and tribes in Africa. As Dirks (2001: 50) writes, 'in cultural as well as biological terms castes in India were like individuals in the West'; natives should be governed as communities,

small-scale group formations were understood as complete social systems that could be theorised in terms of their role in maintaining order.

Indirect rule would offer a degree of local autonomy, but ultimately involved even greater extensions of colonial power: define and rule. For, of course, the notion of protecting and preserving native customs was fantastical, based on the 'illusion', as Prakash writes, 'that all the [imperial] government did was to secure the conditions for the autonomous functioning of customary communities, when, in fact, it was deeply immersed in shaping their existence and functioning' (2002: 86–87). Indirect rule worked precisely through identifying the aspects of native 'custom' most useful for colonial purposes. It required the identification of 'the authoritarian strand so as to sculpt it and build on it, sanctioning the product officially as customary law' (Mamdani, 1999: 865). The particularities of native life were less important than the 'social fact' that everything specific was a mere expression of what was 'customary', taken as radically distinct from universal civil law. Above all, this worked to solidify seemingly natural caste and tribal differences through classification and censuses, the forging of an ethnographic state (Dirks, 2001: ch. 3). Of course, these privileged customs and rulers were invented by empire as much as they were ever 'discovered' by anthropologists. In other words, 'the colonial notion of the precolonial was really a faithful mirror reflection of the decentralised despotism created under colonial rule' (Mamdani, 1996: 39). More specifically, the delegation of power to village elders led to a form of mediated (indirect) rule that was a form of decentralised *household* despotism.

The narrative of a deep-seated cultural resistance to modern norms, like so many social explanations for native revolt, was a veiled assault on a properly political account of violence. Maine's theory of traditional society could not be anything but apolitical given the emphasis on its functionally coherent corporate wholeness that internally reproduced itself through customary norms and kinship. More generally, as we have argued, social theory in both metropole and colony was

rather than individuals. And as Mamdani puts it, in Africa, '*tribes* were governed under separate laws, called "customary" laws, which were in turn administered by ethnically defined native authorities … With *tribes* … cultural difference was reinforced, exaggerated, and built up into different legal systems, each enforced by a separate administrative and political authority' (2012: 48, emphasis in original).

motivated by a concern to demote politics and political philosophy in favour of an account of the seemingly 'deeper' sociological determination of political action. The culturalist and sociological theory of the Indian village community shifted analysis away from political contestation both within the reified village and, of course, between the village and the empire. This image of the village community would later reappear in counterinsurgency wars, in which the inhabitants of entire 'traditional' villages would be forcibly moved into 'New Villages', transplanted and reconstituted, but ideally able to self-regulate after sufficient developmental assistance and liberal 'social' progress.

French connection: colonial pacification as *raison de la société*

The immediate military response to the Sepoy Revolt was brutal and indiscriminate. More generally, rebellions provoked policies of wholesale exemplary attacks on civilians; define, divide and rule; and, of course, 'liberal improvement' (Gwynn, 1934; Loyn, 2008). The British fought numerous imperial 'butcher and bolt' wars through the nineteenth and twentieth centuries. Without denying the variety of tactics deployed during colonial pacification wars – ranging from negotiations with the leaders of favoured tribes to the extermination of entire communities – by the end of the nineteenth century, Britain and France pursued more or less successful pacification strategies that sought to combine the decentralised household despotism of co-opting native leaders, direct repression of the civilian population and 'liberal improvement' to assist in the extraction of raw materials and the opening up of territory to trade (Kiernan, 1998; Vandervort, 1998; Grob-Fitzgibbon, 2011).[25] During the 1860s and 1870s, for example,

[25] The greatest impetus towards sociocratic governance came with the rise of the 'New Imperialism' towards the end of the nineteenth century, in which increased military capabilities, geopolitical pressures and liberal ideology all made territorial control and then the 'improvement' of native populations more likely (although not inevitable, uniform or complete). White settlers in North America and Australia were less concerned in governing native populations as such than with forcing them onto smaller and smaller tracts of infertile land. Hence there is an important distinction between often exterminationist colonial wars fought by white settlers and overseas imperial wars where 'liberal improvement' was intended to transform the local 'social milieu'.

British Colonel Sir Robert Sandeman, who had aided in the suppression of the Sepoy Revolt, ruled the province of Baluchistan through the duel strategies of governance through tribes and liberal improvement. This 'was not military conquest' writes one admirer. 'His leading motive, so strong that it was almost a passion, was love for his fellow-creatures' (Tucker, 1979: 5; Bruce 1932).[26] When necessary, the 'peaceful conqueror' oversaw brutal suppression of uprisings and applied heavy financial penalties on tribal leaders who failed to put down revolts. Peaceful conquest also involved the expansion of trade through the construction of railways, roads, telegraphs, hospital buildings, irrigation and forest preservation, post offices, savings banks, courthouses and jails (Thornton, 1977: 187–188, 213).

After his role as leading administrator during the Second Boer War (1899–1901), Alfred (Viscount) Milner (1908) came to advocate a policy of 'progressive social reform' as central to 'constructive imperialism'. Crops and livestock were destroyed; civilian homes burned; and mainly women and children were transported to racially segregated concentration camps.[27] Crucially, this newer, more intensive concern with the population in the midst of fighting was accompanied by military discourses of civilian 'protection'. This oft-repeated language originates in the late nineteenth-century gendered and racialised discourses in direct response to the most controversial aspect of depopulation and concentration in the Boer War, as it related to white Boer women and children. Almost 30,000 Boer women and children died in the camps as a result of disease and starvation. At least, 20,000 black Africans died in their separate camps. While the treatment of black Africans did not require justification beyond military exigency, in response to widespread criticism of the handling of white people, Britain's Secretary of War St John Brodrick argued that Boer women had been 'deserted' by their men; it was Britain's duty to protect them in the camps (Krebs, 1992, 1999: 44–79). Also in line with

[26] Sandeman's 'instincts were always those of a soldier, rather than a civilian; his methods were of the "rough and ready" order, and, as such, commended themselves to the people, who were not yet prepared for a full draught of civilization, but they were inspired by thoughts that looked forward to the great results, that are in a far way of being achieved' (Thornton, 1977: 300; cf. Dutta, 2002).

[27] Social reformist campaigns for 'national efficiency' grew in strength after the Boer War and complaints about the fitness of British troops (Searle, 1971).

nineteenth-century ideas related to the humanitarian treatment of the most vulnerable, it was argued that the camps were needed to protect white women otherwise exposed to rapacious African men. Despite the many enquires and calls for improvements in camp conditions, Field Marshall Lord Kitchener consistently emphasised the military reasons for confining and punishing the population that had or could provide material and moral support to enemy fighters (Concentration Camp Commission, 1902)

This chapter began by noting some of the connections between social reform and regulation and classical British imperialism. Later we examine two British cases of late-colonial wars conceived through the prism of 'traditional society' and in which concentration camps were justified for the sake of civilian protection. However, in the classical imperial period, the most articulate claims regarding pacification war through distinctly social regulation is found in the French colonial school associated with Thomas-Robert Bugeaud (1784–1849), Joseph Galliéni (1849–1916) and Hubert Lyautey (1854–1934) (Porch, 1986; Singer and Langdon, 2004; Finch, 2013). As exemplified in French military and political conduct in Algeria, Tonkin and Morocco, the notion of a French tradition of colonial warfare became influential in the United States during its crisis in Vietnam and was resurrected most recently during the threat of imminent military defeat in Iraq (Galula, 1963/2006, 1964; Kuehl, 2009). Through the writings of French officer David Galula (1919–1967) and their absorption into the most recent US *Counterinsurgency Field Manual*, Galliéni and Lyautey's claims regarding the 'primacy of politics', the need for 'social' and economic development, and close civil and military coordination would become clichés of the counterinsurgency genre. Like British 'protection' of white Boer women and children, these now staples of counterinsurgency 'best practice' were originally developed in response to a national political crisis in France caused by Bugeaud's open defence of indiscriminate terror tactics against civilian populations in Algeria, the *razzia*. Indeed, since France was the location of some of the most sophisticated and developed discourses of *société* during the nineteenth century, it is no surprise to find that the most articulate renderings of colonial pacification are French.

Joseph Galliéni pioneered the theory of pacification war during the early 1890s in what has been described as the 'neo-Lamarckian pacification of Tonkin' (Rabinow, 1989: 145). Heavily influenced by the biosocial evolutionism of Herbert Spencer and the naturalism of Jean-Baptiste Lamarck, the presumed significance of the 'social environment' on military strategy gained a sophisticated exponent (Galliéni, 1941). By the end of the nineteenth century, European social theorists claimed that the most successful means of modifying or civilising humans was by first modifying their 'social' environment. The actions of the state in France, or the colonial army in Tonkin, could transform the social milieu through progressive occupation, the stages of which have become well-known and much emulated as *la guerre dans le milieu social* (Nemo, 1956). The French army used conventional military tactics against Chinese and Vietnamese forces to take control of points of strategic significance. Rather than fan out as widely and quickly as possible, units were instructed to spread out slowly from these pacified centres across territory, as oil spreads on paper. Military columns would then be replaced by civil administrators in a kind of 'creeping' or 'progressive' occupation of new territories. The acquiescence of the civilian population was essential to protect the supply lines of French forces and their local allies tasked with suppressing rebellion. These strategic sites would become the location of markets to attract local traders. Schools and other amenities were established to draw in populations. Realising their own interest in the French military presence, it was claimed that locals would more actively resist Chinese brigandage and eventually local militia could be armed. 'Piracy,' said Galliéni, 'is not a necessary historical fact. It is the result of an economic condition. It can be fought by prosperity' (in Maurois, 1931/1932: 69). In line with new social administrative practices in France, economic and civil affairs were elevated, although military officers initially took direct responsibility for matters such as the local budget, public works and construction projects, legal reforms and agricultural and economic policy. Thus, in Tonkin emerged a theory of pacification that would be ventriloquised for more than a century: the correct combination of force and politics can socialise, pacify and domesticate a population into regulating itself.

Exemplified by Galliéni's later role from 1896 as both Commander-in-Chief and Governor-General of Madagascar, French commanders oversaw colonial administration. However, in North Africa, Galliéni theorised the strategy of *politique de races*, the incorporation of forms of decentralised despotism in which tribal differences were used to full advantage, after which 'liberal improvement' could take place. As Galliéni put it: 'An officer who has successfully drawn an exact ethnographic map of the territory he commands is close to achieving complete pacification, soon to be followed by the form of organization he judges most appropriate' (in Thomas, 2008: 57; Galliéni, 1900). In exchange for intelligence and cooperation, leaders of favoured tribes were recognised with a level of autonomy to govern 'their' population. Once the population, divided into tribes, had been conquered, the purpose of the reorganisation of civil and economic affairs was to impose forced or wage labour and associated social forms of governance; that is, the creation of new 'norms' through land expropriation and population resettlements, often fronted by local enforcers. As French sociologists increasingly claimed, military and political conflict could be replaced by administration because individuals and communities were able to adapt to their local environment through what sociologists now call 'norm diffusion'. In 1840, Bugeaud had justified the indiscriminate slaughter of the *razzias* on the grounds that 'war cannot be waged in the spirit of philanthropy' (in Khalili, 2013: 14). Bugeaud had died in 1849 before the old moralistic and personalist ideologies of philanthropy had given way to a rising cast of sociocratic technicians empowered by the French state. Although *razzia* tactics would continue, by the time Lyautey was pacifying North Africa not the spirit of philanthropy but the science of social regulation – and *razzias* – had come to prevail.

The 'French school' of colonial war has been so prominent in counterinsurgency writing because there is no late nineteenth-century British equivalent of the charismatic and erudite Hubert Marshal Lyautey, who appeared on the cover of *Time* in 1931, and whose sociocratic vision of how colonial cities ought to be constructed and governed is unmatched in terms of articulacy and ambition.[28] Assigned to Indochina, then Madagascar and Morocco, where he was Governor-General from 1912 to 1925, Lyautey believed he had found among Arab populations the raw material on which a new, distinctly modern and yet conservative society could be built through socialist means. The aristocratic Lyautey explicitly theorised the 'social role' of the colonial soldier, writing of the imperial army as 'organization on

[28] Apparently, Lyautey was a 'man with a brain so extensive that the top of his head is somewhat flat', *Time*, 11 May 1931.

the march' (Lyautey, 1891; Ramsay, 2000). The challenge was to establish French authority over native populations, 'protecting' and 'preserving' what was most valuable in pre-existing forms of order, while also imparting the technical, scientific achievements of modernity. Rather than native assimilation and direct rule, the task of the *bureaux arabes*, for example, was to identify and work with the hierarchies imagined to already exist and use them to indirectly administer the population. 'Good policy,' as Bugeaud had already argued, 'demands that for secondary jobs, we should have Arabs administering Arabs' (in Rid, 2009: 626).[29] At the same time, it served the French purpose to have local leaders 'respect those that they administer' (in Rid, 2009: 626).[30] The building of schools, hospitals and new roads would 'inculcate new needs and wants' (Conklin, 1997: 18; see also Berenson, 2011: ch. 7; Scham, 1970; Gillet, 2010). Lyautey certainly believed that war could be waged in the spirit of the new *société*, even if it was only haltingly and imperfectly being created in democratic France. 'Islam, he thought, sustained an aristocracy that France had unwisely cast aside. Only by taming and working with the Moroccan elite could France maintain its control over the colony' (Nightingale, 2012: 215; Lyautey, 1920). All societies contained natural aristocracies, Lyautey believed. Working with Morocco's was the key to a well-order colonial household. 'The French of 1900 … had no desire to be commanded … In a wild and happy country he was a man of providence' (Maurois, 1931/1932: 158).

Lyautey's numerous dicta on the military and political art of governing colonies would later be ventriloquised by eager counterinsurgents seeking charismatic and intellectual legitimacy for their thoughts and deeds. Above all, it would be said, social administration was as important as military conquest. In other words, empire involves domestic work. David Galula, recall, did most to propagate this view. 'The soldier must … become a propagandist, a social worker, a civil engineer, a schoolteacher, a nurse, a boy scout. But only for as long as he cannot be replaced, for it is better to entrust civilian tasks to civilians' (Galula, 1964: 62). Yet, as Lyautey had put it, in such circumstances administrative control is 'neither military nor civilian any more, but simply

29 Cf. 'Arabs rule … they do not administer' (McCallister, 2007: 15).

30 'Madani el Glaoui virtually ran Marrakech like a Mafia chief, down to the control of the city's 34,000 prostitutes. "You cannot run a colony with virgins", was all that Lyautey could say in his defense' (Porch, 1986: 395).

colonial' (in Rid, 2010: 754). In a lecture at the US Naval War College in 1964, Bernard Fall would similarly claim that 'the insurgency problem [in Vietnam] is military only in a secondary sense, and political, ideological, and administrative in a primary sense' (Fall, 1965). And in the most recent, post-Petraeus, discourse:

> Progressive counterinsurgency embraces the idea that war-fighting is state-building and that the only way to achieve a sustainable order in a territory is to gain the trust, obligation, and support of the population ... While progressive counterinsurgency does recognize the need for force, its central thrust consists of operations designed to win over the population.
>
> (Sitaraman, 2012: 8)

This entire discourse was made possible by the rise of social regulation and thought in the nineteenth century; here we are concerned with its colonial forms. Yet is Galula's story of soldiers as social workers an accurate reflection of how French colonial campaigns were actually fought? This question matters since later appropriations of the French experience often assumed that the discourse of soldiers as 'social workers' was a reflection of the reality of these wars, or if not, then it would be left to the United States to practice what the French had only preached (Sewall, 2007).

Certainly Bugeaud, who had led the conquest of Algeria and become Governor-General in 1840, supported colonial settlements in the hope of eventually establishing the 'good society' he wished to see in France; 'civilian and military colonies ought to be patterned on Utopian socialist lines' (Sullivan, 1983: 142; d'Ideville, 1884). Both Galliéni and Lyautey, the most articulate French practitioner-theorists of colonial pacification, were influenced by heated debates over the Social Question that dominated the French political scene through the wave of colonial expansion at the end of the nineteenth and early twentieth century. Asia, North Africa and France were all laboratories of the new social government and, as several scholars have noted, there was a reciprocal exchange of forms of repression between colony and metropole. But social experimentation was no substitute for war itself. It is well-known that in Algeria, indiscriminate slaughter through raids known as *razzias* were intended to produce terror among the population, as well as access to food and other supplies for ill-equipped French troops. In the words of one French officer:

> We have found a more efficient way than burning crops: waging an incessant war which impacts the population through individuals and in all their interests. The flights, the continuous alarms, the enormous losses inflicted by the razzias and even by mere relocations, the women and children we captured; the old, the women, the children and the herds who perished from fatigue and hunger; the necessity to live the entire winter in the harshest mountains, on summits covered with snow – that is what for better or worse pushed the Arabs into submission.
>
> (quoted in Rid, 2009: 624)

Razzia tactics by French flying columns in North Africa, including incinerating entire communities taking refuge in caves, became notorious in France and Europe during the 1840s. But they were not only associated with Bugeaud's conquests in Algeria. In Morocco, the French army still lacked the mobility and intelligence to defeat local armed resistance. As Porch has written, the 'Lyautey method boiled down in practice to a series of reprisal raids for damage inflicted. The dreadful *razzia* was institutionalized and perpetuated' (1986: 393).[31] Intelligence gathered through the *bureaux arabes* supplied the French army with targets for collective punishment. In this context, waging war in the spirit of the new *société* 'increasingly sounded like so many hollow clichés', Porch (1986: 394–395) continues; '"hearts and minds" was more a public-relations exercise with the French people than a workable military formula in Morocco'.

However, there is more to armed social work than mere public relations, although public relations were and continue to be a central aspect of it. Lyautey's emphasis on military-led social development was conceived, in part, to distance French actions in Morocco from those associated with Bugeaud's total and indiscriminate slaughter. But if armed social work is not the gentler, kinder form of war it purports to be, then it is also more than window-dressing. The question is not whether French or British armies 'advanced at the points of their bayonets' or 'with smiles and trade treaties' (Porch, 1986: 395). This question answers itself and there is nothing in the argument of this book that seeks to dissemble the reality of war as the reciprocal organised destruction of things and the killing and tormenting of people.

[31] As Rid notes (2009: 620), 'the booty [was] significant: goods, grain, produce, livestock, horses, and prisoners, often women and children as the men were more difficult to come by'.

Europe's imperial wars, much like more recent counterinsurgencies, proved amenable to claims regarding armed social work because they involved policies that directly targeted the life processes of populations through various techniques of household governance, whether in the form of liberal improvement or the collaboration of native tribal patriarchs. These were accompaniments of, rather than substitutes for, war. However, they were necessary accompaniments to the extent that these campaigns were prosecuted by liberal empires, seeking the 'improvement of the world', which requires the expansion of markets and the forced compliance and then 'socialisation' of local populations. For further illustration we now turn to the United States, which by the end of the nineteenth century had joined Britain and France as a leading global power with its own distinctive national-imperial household, forms of domestic ideology and military 'policies of attraction'.

Progressive housekeeping in the American Philippines

By the end of the nineteenth century, the United States Army and Marine Corps had occupied several islands across the Caribbean and Western Pacific, including Cuba, Puerto Rico, Hawaii and the Philippines (Musicant, 1990). In almost every case, the forcible removal and concentration of populations was accompanied with programmes of labour, education, health and sanitation reform, and the creation of police constabularies and census bureaus. The most extensive occupation was in the Philippines, which was incorporated as an insular territory of the United States in 1898 after victory in the Spanish-American War. A war of independence between US forces and Filipino republicans continued until 1913, but most of the territory was under US control by 1902, by which time 200,000 Filipinos had died and 4,200 of 70,000 US soldiers were killed (McCoy, 2009b: 5; Evans, 2008). The passing of the Philippine Organic Act in 1902 signalled the defeat of the Philippine Republic; the US occupation and administration of the islands lasted until 1942. A great deal has been written on America's largest turn-of-the-century experiment in overseas colonial rule, not least the so-called 'policies of attraction' aimed at civilians. The schools programme, in particular, was especially significant, symbolically representing the transition from military 'policies of chastisement' to civilian government, from direct American tutelage to 'the self-governing Filipino' (American League of Philadelphia, 1900).

Here we are especially interested in the extent to which these policies of attraction were homologous with the social reforms that defined US history in the Progressive Era (Rodgers, 1998; McGeer, 2003). Given that civilising missions involve the domestication of dominated others, how did these Progressive Era policies represent a distinctly social forms of modern domesticity? The American empire, like the nation and bourgeois home, was to be an efficiently and well-run household.

Contemporaneous with the British and Spanish use of concentration camps in South Africa and Cuba, the United States Army established a system of camps in the Philippines as a means of population control and to deny food and intelligence to revolutionaries (Brody, 2010). Once the majority of the population were so quartered, US soldiers laid waste to all outside, burning villages and killing 'everything over ten years old' to create among the people a 'burning desire for the war to cease' (Elliott, 1916: 30). Terror operations, including the torture of the 'water cure' (later water-boarding), were intended to make life so intolerable that Filipinos would renounce revolutionary 'bandits' in return for a reduction in the level of violence (Rejali, 2007: 280). The 'simple soldier philosophy' was this: 'there were to be no neutrals. Everybody was to be made to "want peace and want it badly". Those who were friends must come out in the open' (Elliott, 1916: 27). Then as now, professional counterinsurgents described the process of 'reconcentration' and 'protection zones' as 'humane to the point of military weakness' (in Gates, 2002: 5) since – if the population complied – the discomfort of the camps and exemplary massacres was surely less cruel than outright slaughter of everyone (Elliott, 1916: 27). Guerrilla leaders that renounced the cause were granted positions in the civil administration and rewarded with confiscated land. Moreover, with greater forward planning than its Spanish predecessors, the United States pursued a much more ambitious scheme of 'social improvement', establishing new schools, healthcare and drug laws, and a new system of policing, roads and environmental supervision (McCoy, 2009a: 16).[32] In the context of a severe labour shortage, a partial system of wage-labour was established, reforming the Spanish organisation of compulsory labour (Bankoff, 2005). The 'Army's expertise in

[32] By 1902, 'education, health, and justice ... consumed nearly half the 1912 colonial budget of 17.4 million pesos, with education first ... followed closely by the constabulary ... and public health' (McCoy, 2009b: 54; see also Amoroso, 2003).

human leadership and management', claims one historian, 'made it an ideal instrument for social engineering' (Birtle, 1998/2009: 92). Under these seemingly ideal conditions, 'armed Progressives' – a coalition of military, colonial administrators, and business-leaders – pursued the 'benevolent assimilation' proclaimed by President McKinley (Birtle, 1998/2009: 92). The United States, he declared, had come to 'protect the natives in their homes', 'supporting the temperate administration of affairs for the greatest good of the governed' (McKinley, 1898). Partially echoing the language of the 1885 Berlin Conference, McKinley's Proclamation of Benevolent Assimilation declared that the United States had arrived 'not as invaders or conquerors, but as friends, *to protect* the natives in their homes, in their employments, and in their personal and religious rights'. However unlike French and British indirect rule, the philosophy behind 'the notion of ruling through a despotic Asian potentate was distasteful to Americans ... [P]rogress ... could only be achieved by replacing tribalism with individualism – a goal that appeared incompatible with the perpetuation of despotic *datos*' (Birtle, 1998/2009: 160).

As discussed in Chapter 3, the notion that government has an obligation to decide on and rule for the greatest good of the governed can be traced back to medieval paternalism and police power. To what extent, then, was colonial policy and ideology in the Philippines shaped by the Progressive Era's distinctly social reforms? The answer relies on a reading not only of the military occupation, but also the nature and character of the 'progressive' solution to the Social Question in the United States (Jordan, 1899; Peabody, 1909). Much like their social-liberal counterparts in Europe, American progressives sought to reform the worst excesses of industrial capitalism as an alternative to the more radical solutions many workers were beginning to demand (Brands, 1995; Brown, 1990; Tone, 1997). With great zeal, a coalition of social reformers successfully legislated to reduce the power of business monopolies and robber barons, machine politics and government corruption, and ameliorate working and living conditions in urban slums. A distinctly American vision of a 'well-regulated society', reform extended to municipal, education and health, public safety and morals, with many ideas borrowed from contemporary Germany (Novak, 1996). Prominent journalist Albert Shaw toured European cities to observe advances in municipal housekeeping in sewage, gas-works, water, street-cleaning, housing, disease and poor-relief. 'There are, in the conception of a German city government, no limits whatever to the municipal functions. It is the business of the municipality to promote in every feasible way its own welfare and the welfare of its citizens' (Shaw, 1894: 380).[33] Progressive reform in the United States was explicitly conceived in terms of social housekeeping, of creating an efficiently managed household (Addams, 1905; Rynbrandt, 1999; Gottlieb, 2001). The art and science of 'municipal housekeeping' was guided by faith in the rational solutions to social illness determined by professional 'sociocrats' and 'human engineers' (Ward, 1893). As 'the science of welfare' (Ward, 1906), the first university Department of Sociology was founded in Chicago in 1892 (Collins and Makowsky, 1972: 84).[34] Lester Frank Ward, the future first President of the American Sociological Association and exponent of 'sociocracy', would claim that the purpose of the state was 'securing the welfare of society' and 'its mode of operation is that of preventing the antisocial actions of individuals' (Ward, 1903: 555). The regulation of virtually every aspect of American life would be justified in terms of the people's welfare.

Many wished to see such sentiments, including the prevention of antisocial actions, extended to state-building projects overseas. Surely, then, the apparent 'urge to engage in progressive reform…[in the Philippines] was something that the officers had brought with them from home' (Gates, 2002: 6). Indeed, the movement of 'progressive' ideas and institutions did not travel in only one direction. The occupation contributed to greater and lasting activism by the US federal government and influenced reform of the military itself; there was a progressive movement within the army seeking to apply more rational principles to the organisation and projection of American armed force (McCoy and Scarano, 2009; Go and Foster, 2003; Linn, 1989, 2009). It has therefore been easy for many to claim that 'progressivism's philosophy of government by enlightened experts dovetailed quite nicely with the Army's own brand of firm, yet benevolent, paternalism' (Birtle,

[33] Distinctive about the American tradition of *salus populi*, however, was the stronger emphasis on local governance, even after the expansion of federal programmes much later under the New Deal, and the heavy reliance on local government and private profit-making businesses to deliver even federally funded social policy programmes (Skocpol, 1992).

[34] The American Association for the Promotion of Social Science had already been founded in 1856.

1998/2009: 92). But what is the nature of this agreeable union, this apparent dovetailing between complementary and mutually dependent modalities? How were progressive ideals of uplift so adaptable and thus so portable to the empire? Proponents of pacification campaigns certainly have a strong incentive to present these most brutal of wars in benevolent terms. If military and political leaders can persuade public opinion that social improvements are made amidst violence – that the violence is part of the process of social uplift – then they are less likely to face accusations of war crimes or successful agitation for withdrawal. Moreover, to imagine oneself as part of a civilising mission is an understandable way for ordinary soldiers to rationalise their own brutality as a regrettable means to a well-justified end (Adas, 2006: ch. 3). However, at this level, the connection between progressivism and pacification remains largely propaganda and, of course, too readily assumes the benevolent character of social regulation in both the United States and the empire. Numerous critics have drawn attention to the fundamentally coercive character of the Philippines occupation – and not only the massacres, torture and camps, but also the compulsions attendant the 'good works of an enlightened colonial government' (Gates, 2002: 3–4; 1972). As Captain Albert Todd, director of the Department of Public Instruction openly put it, 'the primary goal of the army's teaching program was not to educate Filipinos but rather to pacify them ... The army's schools were, in effect, a mere adjunct of its military activities' (in May, 1980: 79; Go, 2003). School building and curricula were 'targeted' at its recipients; they were objects of the military offensive. In the distinctly social language of the period, sending in the 'army of instruction' in which children would learn to speak English and other forms of civilised conduct was 'both a means of political education and a mechanism of social control' (McCoy, 2009a: 23).[35]

It has therefore been relatively easy for progressive critics of the Philippines occupation to disassociate this war and its 'policies of attraction' from the more 'genuinely' progressive reforms in the United States. For Glenn Anthony May, Progressive Era legislation was motivated by 'majoritarian and humanitarian' concern for the most downtrodden of America's citizens. 'The chief U.S. policy-makers in the Philippines definitely were not men of that

[35] Use of the term 'social control' would eventually decline.

type' (May, 1980: xviii). Suffrage was restricted, not expanded in the colony. Rather than seek to regulate the power of big business, conservatives created an attractive environment for corporate investment and the exploitation of native labour. While progressives in the United States 'showed concern for the urban poor', the Filipino poor were largely neglected (May, 1980: xix). While these statements are surely correct, the attempt to save good social engineering at 'home' from bad social engineering abroad is problematic, idealising social policy in the United States (Piven and Cloward, 1971). The violent socialisation of the Filipino population was not so alien to the social regulation enacted under the progressive banner in the United States. Just as the 'policies of attraction' aimed to forestall an independent Philippine republic, the concessions towards a more managed democracy in the United States forestalled the realisation of the more radical claims of organised labour and direct forms of democratic rule. The wave of social regulation in the Progressive Era may seem attractive in an age of neoliberalism, but it was a defensive rearrangement of American society, creating new elites and distinctly social forms of control. Social work in both the Philippines and the United States were presented as benevolent gifts towards eugenic and social inferiors. They were attempts to contain different forms of violence and politics. In place of strategies of annihilation in the colonies and open class war at home, natives and workers were to be domesticated through social-civilisation work. In both crises of class and colonial assimilation, distinctly social and gendered forms of domesticity were deployed to contain resistance, to counter insurgency. To grasp the heart of the dovetailing of benevolent military paternalism with enlightened expertise requires moving past both colonial propaganda and the idealism of 'social' progressives.

The specific manner in which (benevolent) 'social control' was enacted – and through which the contradiction between violent coercion and 'socialisation' was managed in the Philippines – relied on colonial and gendered forms of housekeeping and domesticity. Teachers engaged in the practical work of civilian uplift, signalling the benevolence of American colonial rule to both Filipinos and American publics back home. Then as now, the turn to 'policies of attraction' was presented as a feminisation of the war effort 'whereby the healing sympathies of the feminine home are to spread their influence outwards, taking over the uncontrolled masculine spaces of strife'

(Bowlby, 1995: 84).[36] Although male soldiers built and taught in the first new schools and the majority of the civilian teachers were male, white bourgeois women were the most visible embodiments of the transition from violent occupation to more peaceful forms of tutelage, from the masculine world of war to the more feminine but nonetheless publicly useful forms of housekeeping. This 'manifest domesticity', Kaplan writes, served as 'an anchor, a feminine counterforce to the male activity of territorial conquest' (1998: 583). In place of the violent antagonism of military occupation, the 'paradigm of imperial domesticity', Meg Wesling has suggested, was more 'a family drama of errant children and benevolent mothers' (2011: 111).[37] Much like their counterparts in British India and Australia, bourgeois American women were viewed as singularly capable not only of counterbalancing military with civilian rule, but of creating and then upholding norms of respectability among half-civilised natives (George, 1993/1994; Myers, 2009; Fee, 1910/1988). Similarly, through their special role in domesticating the empire, these women would acquire a level of freedom and independence still denied to them in the United States, becoming 'a class of "civilization workers"' spreading social progress (Wesling, 2011: 111).[38] 'The world', as Patricia Hill (1984) has put it, was 'their household'. Needless to say, these new freedoms were acquired at the expense of the Philippines political independence and of the domestic labour of Filipino servants and maids.

'Imperialism as a form of good housekeeping,' writes Rafael, 'was meant to forge a sentimental affiliation or "special relation" between colonizer and colonized more like the bond between parent and child

[36] This extended to media presentations of the war effort, including photography. Middle-class women photographers were viewed as especially useful because they 'could be trusted literally to see, and therefore to show, a domestic scene where someone else might see a man of war' (Wexler, 2000: 47). The erasure of violent struggle, argues Wexler, made photography 'useful for the purposes of imperial consolidation'. In the Philippines, photographers were given access to 'American military might on its off time, that is, in domestic time'. This 'domestic photography hoped to make the visible disappear. By definition, the imperial house of horrors was outside the frame' (2000: 35, 32).

[37] The metaphor of the family, writes McClintock, 'offered an indispensible figure for sanctioning social hierarchy within a putative organic unity of interests ... Imperial intervention could thus be figured as a linear, nonrevolutionary progression that combined hierarchy with unity: paternal fathers ruling benignly over immature children' (1995: 45).

[38] The term 'civilisation workers' is from Newman (1999).

than that between master and slave' (1995: 642, 640). Indeed, the entire Filipino population was viewed as infantile. According to an American legal official in the colony, these people should be forced 'as children are forced ... to meet the requirements of the next stage of their growth' (Elliott, 1916: 254, 261). Within this discourse, the paternalist authority of male teachers would shape this malleable population into subjects fit for self-rule. In a process familiar from contemporary anxieties about the effects of armed social work on military masculinity and effectiveness, male teachers enacted forms of domestic-imperial masculinity that was 'civilized but not feminized' (Wesling, 2011: 130, 137). Paternalist rule would seek to instil male norms of individual and eventually national autonomy. In other words, practices of American empire were inseparable from masculine as well as feminine domestic subjectivities, specifically fatherly oversight of progress towards self-government. Teaching Filipino subjects how to behave, constituting them as putatively independent 'dependents' able to self-rule, claimed Governor-General William Taft, would lead to the end of 'the open presence of the US military' (in May, 1980: 15). At some future date, properly socialised Filipinos could be in control of their own homeland. The principle mechanism of 'socialisation' was not found in the schools, of course, essential though they were. Above all, it was the creation of new labour norms that would instil the ideals of individual autonomy and self-regulation; natives should be taught 'how to work' (Taft in Elliott, 1916: 253; see also Kramer, 2006: 366–404). The establishment of a free market for labour and a landowning class would transform unproductive peasants into productive workers and eventually self-regulating citizens in their own independent sovereign national household.[39] For, as Elliott put it, 'when the Filipino working man has acquired a knowledge of and a desire for the things that make life worth while to an American or European, he will perform the labor necessary to enable him to obtain them' (1916: 254, 261). And once these Filipino men had been taught how to work, 'American imperialists would teach them to exercise paternalist authority as heads of households' (Hoganson, 1998: 135). Instilling bourgeois and patriarchal forms of colonial domesticity permitted some Filipino men to claim a form of masculine power lost through the re-imposition of colonial rule.

[39] As such, some limitations were placed on the size of public lands that could be sold to private corporations.

Conclusion

Sir Henry Sumner Maine's turn to the despotic patriarchal household illuminates the extent to which violent reactions to liberal empire are countered both practically and intellectually through distinctly 'social' means. The failure to transplant bourgeois civil society, as evidenced by the persistence and violence of native resistance, did not become part of a political argument for the retreat of empire. Rather theories of a crisis of transition from tradition to modern, and claims about the nature of 'traditional society', became the basis of a social and anthropological argument for empire's continued existence. The colonial limits of 'society' led to the invention of 'traditional society' as a space of despotic household government that could be co-opted and mobilised for the end of imperial rule. As part of a critique of unsuccessful utilitarian efforts to radically transform native society, British imperial administrators adopted a policy of working with native collaborators. Functionalist theories of traditional village society became both an explanation and remedy for native violence. In practice this involved a decentralisation of despotic power and authority in apparent deference to local customs. The related turn to anthropological knowledge reified native 'society' as the source of order, and therefore a necessary part of imperial governance. Political conflict and change were downplayed in favour of an image of static, essentially rigid, tradition-bound societies governed by fundamentally irrational but nonetheless powerful belief systems. Rather than simply work with what anthropologists discovered in the villages, imperial administrators themselves helped to craft and elevate forms of despotic governance.

The liberal empires vacillated between reforming subjects that were understood as essentially malleable and, when met with violent resistance, turned to social anthropological discourses of native customs and tradition as an alternative pacification strategy. The homology between forms of distinctly social regulation goes beyond questions of the transference of practices or justificatory and high-minded talk of civilisation and liberal improvement. British and French colonial wars and the stories told about them are important not only given their oft-noted influence on contemporary theories of counterinsurgency. In particular, the singular French influence on *société* discourse and experimentation had a profound impact on the way subsequent counterinsurgency campaigns would be fought and conceived. The point is not to make some crude historical leap *from* social regulation and theory in Europe *to* colonial pacification or from colonial pacification to twentieth- and twenty-first-century counterinsurgency. Pacification developed as a distinctive form of colonial war due to the exigencies of overseas empire-building. The relation is ontological. When imperial administrators or colonial warriors needed to pacify the violent resistance of native populations they turned to the organisational devices of household governance, and they understood and justified what they were doing in terms of distinctly modern *oikonomikos*.

Liberal despotism is not the only form of household governance. Of interest is the way governments purportedly founded on contract socially administer non-liberal subjects, and why distinctly social theories are so useful in this task. Part of the answer is found in the conservatism of much distinctly social thought. The tension between the 'modern' values and realities and the need for something 'traditional' to provide order and stability structures an enormous amount of social theory, past and present. Consider again the deep nostalgia for past systems of medieval household order found in early sociological thought: Comte's utopian future 'sociocracy', Tönnies' *Gemeinschaft* and Durkheim's occupational guilds. Lyautey, of course, was able to build his *villes nouvelles* in Morocco. This is the *romanticism* of much sociology, where modern society is understood in relation to a lost community ideal, one that – perhaps ironically – colonial subjects and the imaginary state of nature came to appear as flawed but nonetheless authentic 'others'. The lost ideal of the archaic or traditional household was a place from where lessons may be drawn and, if necessary, through which the subjects of empire could be governed (Pecora, 1997). For many, including both nineteenth-century conservatives and radicals, the village household represented an authentic way of life, an alternative to modern industrial society that could represent either the progress or degeneration of the present. The symbolism of the traditional village is central to both the rise of modern social theory and is intimately related to the 'social revolutions' that would accompany mid-twentieth-century liberal counterinsurgency rule. In the context of late-colonial emergencies and the US war in Vietnam, the traditional village household was no longer a source of stability and order, as Maine had argued. By the end of World War II, imperial states were finding it much harder to pacify the traditional village. Anti-colonial, nationalist and communist insurgencies were mobilising peasants to their cause. Now constituted as a military and political threat, traditional village society would have to be totally destroyed and socially reconstituted.

5 *'More than concentration camps': the battle for hearths in two late-colonial emergencies*

> Maladjusted individuals whether they become so through economic, social or ideological causes are very susceptible to such disruptive movements as Mau Mau. It is therefore in my view most important that a plan for Social Welfare should be evolved. Social work in civilized countries became the safeguard of society. Without it hardship would, as it has in the past, lead to brigandage and even revolution.
>
> Tom Askwith, Commissioner of Community Development, Kenya, 1953[1]

At first glance, counterinsurgency and classical social theory seem to possess very little in common. Destroying an insurgency and thinking through the deeper social basis of human behaviour and identity appear to be fundamentally different endeavours. Yet, examining the historical rise of social thought suggests several homologies between counterinsurgency and classical social theory. First and foremost is the anti-insurgency origin of distinctly social thought. The search for sociological causes of – and remedies for – political conflict became a staple of national and imperial government since the nineteenth century. The first self-consciously sociological theorising was written to diagnose and cure increasingly violent class revolt in industrial cities and native revolt in the colonies. The Social Question was precisely the problem of how to manage and administer insurgent workers. Moreover, the first social theories of 'traditional' or 'native society' were developed in the effort to forestall violent uprisings across the British Empire. Also, consider the grounds on which social theories asserted their priority and autonomy from classical political and legal thought. Political action, laws and institutions were demoted to the realm of appearance, of mere superstructure, the exterior manifestation of something more profound. The pathologies afflicting society

[1] In Elkins (2005a: 108).

could be diagnosed and cured only with knowledge of the deeper causal logics and developmental tendencies of social organisation. Denying the autonomy of political ideas and activity, social forces were of greater ontological significance than the outward appearances of government and law, significant though they were for maintaining order. If reality itself is hierarchically arranged, then social theories claim to be a uniquely deep mode of knowing the human world. Depth metaphors are pervasive in social theory. Now consider the parallel grounds on which counterinsurgents claim to be fighting a unique and uniquely subterranean form of 'sociological warfare' (Galula in Mathias, 2011: 37).[2]

If, as T.E. Lawrence maintained, insurgency 'is more intellectual than a bayonet charge', then counterinsurgents too have long claimed to be pursuing 'graduate level' war (Ricks, 2009). As Sir Henry Gurney, British High Commissioner in colonial Malaya, claimed in 1950, 'The enemy in Malaya is Communism, with all its implications, and is not merely some 3,000 bandits' (in Grob-Fitzgibbon, 2011: 125). Like social theorists excavating the deeper underlying causes of political facts and events, good counterinsurgents go beyond mere surface symptoms and appearances, such as the views of 3,000 bandits and their supporters, to attack the inner core of insurgent violence, forms of life in which communism is rife. If insurgency is not primarily a military act, then – short of totally annihilating all insurgents and their supporters – there can be no such thing as a purely military response to even semi-popular armed uprisings. As one United States Army Lieutenant Colonel more recently put it, 'The deeper that personnel ... dig into local society, the better their ability to assess which groups threaten ... and which should be left alone' (Renzi, 2006: 21).[3] Good counterinsurgents burrow into society to affect a cure for its social ills, attacking the underlying 'root' causes of insurgency violence. French General

[2] In the post-World War II period, so-called sociological warfare was also the site for the generation of new forms of sociological theory, including critical social theory. In the French context see Bourdieu (1958, 1979, 2012, 2013; see also Goodman and Silverstein, 2009).

[3] In his analysis of the 'surface and subsurface elements of an insurgency', David Kilcullen (2010: 8) also talks of a 'mass base' that is 'largely undetectable to counterinsurgents, since it lies below the surface and engages in no armed activity'.

Hubert Lyautey also compared pacification war to the ploughshare. In his words,

> Supposing that a piece of land overran by rank weeds has to be brought under tillage, it is not enough to extirpate these weeds; that will only mean starting again next day; but it is essential that, where the ground has been ploughed up, the conquered soil should be isolated, fenced, and then sowed with the good grain which alone will make it impervious to the tares. Similarly with regard to territory given over to brigandage: armed occupation, with or without fighting, is as the ploughshare.
>
> (in Maurois, 1931/1932: 74)

Less eloquently, but no less forcefully, Sir Harold Briggs, Britain's Director of Operations in Malaya, declared that destroying communism 'was similar to that of eradicating malaria from a country. Flit guns and mosquito nets, in the form of military and police ... effected no permanent cure. Such a permanent cure entails the closing of all breeding areas. In this case the breeding areas of the Communists were the isolated squatter areas' (in Nagl, 2002: 74).[4] These are distinctly sociological claims about the underlying causes of anti-colonial violence and they provide the rationale for a distinctly sociological cure. In Malaya, sociological warfare involved the forcible removal of hundreds of thousands of people, 10 per cent of the population, into concentration camps to be 'socially' reformed.

The alliance between counterinsurgency and distinctly social thought and practice is more than analogical. There is a homology between social theory and counterinsurgency. To homologise, recall, is to claim a correspondence in type and structure between seemingly different things. Both counterinsurgency and distinctly social thought and practice seek to repudiate politics through administering and regulating the life processes of populations for military and *oikonomia* ends. They are forms of *social* regulation and government, the distinctly modern and capitalist form of household rule. This claim is substantiated in this chapter through a close reading of two military campaigns, the late-colonial 'emergencies' in British Malaya (1948–1960) and Kenya (1952–1960). Taking control of the life processes of populations in these colonies, and administering them through despotic household

[4] 'Squatters' were workers living on state or private-owned land.

rule, gave the late-colonial British state a new and powerful means of collective punishment and reward. In both campaigns, the domestic living arrangements of dispersed peasants were viewed as incubating resistance, making them more difficult to pacify. As Sir Harold Briggs claimed in regard to Malaya, if the British were engaged in a 'competition in government', then victory was to be achieved through the brutal elimination of subversives, de-population of their base of support, and then social administration (in Markel, 2006: 38). Hence, colonial authorities proceeded to destroy and reconstruct small-scale homes as a strategy of domestication. From 1950, 600,000 peasant families were forcibly removed from their farms into more than 400 houses of correction: interrogation, detention and concentration camps, new functional and self-contained 'social units'. In colonial Kenya, and borrowing directly from Malaya and other precedents, the British army forcibly resettled more than one million Kikuyu people into more than 800 punitive camps.[5] Under the legal cover of 'emergency', civilian populations were subjected to a highly racialised and sexualised system of household despotism of colonial officers, loyalist 'Home Guard' proxies, and social workers in an effort to shore up the crumbling household of the late-colonial state.

Core elements of Britain's population strategies in Malaya and Kenya – mass incarceration, civilising ideology, concern with exit strategy – were not new to this period or these cases. Social 'improvement' of the population and competent administration were central to the legitimacy of imperial government of any 'liberal' sort. However, by the middle of the twentieth century, Britain was forced into a more intensive focus on the local population as an object of strategy, leading to experiments in massive forced displacement, villagisation and the military administration of the basic needs of hundreds of thousands of people. Hence, British conduct in these campaigns marks a transition from the 'high' imperialism of the late nineteenth century. In this earlier period, revolts were violently repressed without much concern for the underlying political conditions they expressed, although roads

[5] In addition to Malaya, other detention camp precedents included those used for Ethniki Organosis Kyprion Agoniston (EOKA), or the National Organization of Cypriot Fighters, an anti-colonial paramilitary group that sought to end British rule on the island and to unify with Greece. The campaign against British occupation lasted from 1955 to 1959, during which time British forces detained and tortured EOKA fighters (Holland, 1998; Elkins, 2000: 38)

were built and markets opened for imperial commerce. Given the massive discrepancy in technology, organisation and discipline between imperial and local armed forces, uprisings were relatively easy to quell (Vandervort, 1998). With the exception of the Boer concentration camps, in which large numbers of women and children were detained, Europeans gave little thought to administering populations in the midst of fighting. However, with the imperial upheavals of two world wars, the military and political organisation of anti-colonial resistance vastly improved, providing insurgents with a popular base of support (Wolf, 1969). 'For those within colonial societies willing to follow Britain's timetable toward sovereignty and to do so within the confines of the Commonwealth,' Grob-Fitzgibbon writes, 'the government promised education, social welfare, training in the arts of administration and security' (2011: 4). For those unwilling to accept these terms, or where they were not offered, the colonial state responded with brutal and indiscriminate force (French, 2011). The most serious crises after 1945 were in Palestine, Malaya, Kenya, Cyprus, Aden, Oman and Dhofar. Malaya and Kenya were the most violent and intense. The combination of liberation ideology and guerrilla tactics forced the late-colonial state into a more urgent concern with the population, leading to innovations in despotic and sociocratic household rule.

Britain's conduct in Malaya spawned a particularly large 'lessons learned' literature because a communist insurgency was eventually defeated after 12 years and because similar de-population and concentration strategies were pursued during the US war on Vietnam. As one admiring British journalist would put it, the British attempted to 'implement at speed the largest social revolution ever known in Asia ... a brilliant, unorthodox tactic ... which military leaders would study in every future Asian war' (Barber, 1971: 100). The transfer of lessons from Malaya to Vietnam was aided by British military advisor and first 'counterinsurgency expert' Sir Robert Thompson (1966) and his classic text *Defeating Communist Insurgency* (see also Beckett, 1997; Paget, 1967).[6] Subsequent generations of counterinsurgents would celebrate Britain's apparent ingenuity in coordinating civil-military affairs in the camps; the way colonial authorities seemed to undercut communism's appeal by providing social services and setting a date

[6] There are several lengthy quotations from this book in FM 3–24, the updated US *Counterinsurgency Field Manual* (see also Kitson 1971; Mumford 2010).

for formal independence (Thompson, 1966; Nagl, 2002). In these counterinsurgency texts, the peasant population is imagined to have submitted to the political and economic regime of Britain's choosing in exchange for a faster end to extreme violence and a minimal level of 'social improvement'. In fact, Britain discovered no successful formula for winning 'hearts and minds'. Its population strategies did not translate into a coherent, well-planned and well-funded effort to persuade people to reject insurgent ideology. Neither 'hearts and minds' policies in Malaya nor 'rehabilitation' policies in Kenya – at least as they are commonly understood – had an independent impact on the outcome (as distinct from the violent effects) of the military campaigns. In both cases, colonial state terror and the forced resettlement of hundreds of thousands of actual and potential guerrilla supporters – not any health, education and social services – defeated armed resistance to the colonial state.

This is one of the paradoxes of this book. While it seeks to highlight the significance of the historical rise of distinctly social forms of government for liberal counterinsurgency rule, it does not accept that armed social work – as commonly conceived – is *defining* of this form of war. 'Hearts and minds' in Malaya originally referred to propaganda and psychological wars both in relation to the population in the midst of fighting and the public back home (Carruthers, 1995; Ramakrishna, 2002). Given the success of *this* propaganda campaign, 'hearts and minds' has become shorthand for 'winning over' the local population through social programmes. This is a misrepresentation of both the original meaning of 'hearts and minds' and also the way social programmes worked in late-colonial emergencies. In both campaigns, detention without trial, summary executions, massacres, torture and other forms of punitive and extreme cruelty defined these wars (Hale, 2013; Porch, 2013: 246–267). Especially in Kenya, the campaign was closer to annihilation than rehabilitation. Senior British officials sanctioned torture, including rape, castration and burning people alive. Evidence of high-level authorisation was concealed in a secret archive, only recently exposed through legal action.[7] Even Kenya's attorney

[7] 'Any ministry or department that dealt with the unsavoury side of detention was pretty well emptied of its files, whereas those that ostensibly addressed detainee reform, or Britain's civilizing mission, were left fairly intact' (Elkins, 2005a: xiii; see also D. Anderson, 2011; Elkins, 2011; Bennett, 2012).

general at the time, Eric Griffiths-Jones, suggested that British practice was 'distressingly reminiscent of conditions in Nazi Germany or Communist Russia' (Cobain and Hatcher, 2013). The regimes of compulsions in Kenya applied not only to forced labour and torture, but also the 'socialisation' in the clubs and societies in which women and men were expected to learn the behaviours of their more civilised white superiors, as well as changes to land tenure, the transformation of peasants into proletarian workers, and the arming and empowerment of loyalist enforcers. Rather than winning over the population, collaboration was violently extracted because British armed forces and their local collaborators were able to inflict the greatest harm, the epitome of despotic household rule. Crucially, military exigencies related to population coercion were interpreted and justified in sociological terms. Proponents of the latest theories of primitive societies and social welfare accompanied and sought to justify these military policies at every turn. Social anthropology and ethnopsychiatry were especially useful in reducing political and violent resistance in Kenya to psychopathology. Of course, the alliance between late-colonial war and distinctly social thought and practice did not arise because social concepts were somehow superior in explaining insurgencies than some alternative account. Rather social theory's focus on the deeper, underlying causes of violence was homologous with the colonial military's desire to affect a 'permanent cure' and to deny the political basis of native resistance.

'Good government in all its aspects': emergency in Malaya

Japanese forces easily defeated Royal Navy and land forces in and around Malaya soon after the start of the Pacific War in late 1941, temporarily bringing an end to Britain's colonial control of the Peninsula. The most active military and political resistance to Japanese occupation came from Chinese living in Malaya, whom the British had originally imported as unskilled and obedient labour. The Chinese-dominated Malayan Communist Party (MCP) decamped to the jungles to fight a guerrilla war against the Japanese, receiving weapons from the British. After the Japanese surrender in 1945, the interim British Military Administration established the conditions for the founding of the Federation of Malaya in 1948. Despite the wartime alliance, the citizen rights of non-Malays – above all, the Chinese, around 10 per cent of the population – were especially limited. Drawing on the Indian residential system of indirect rule, the late-colonial government sought the allegiance of the Malay majority and the collaboration of Malay sultans. Britain's abandonment of its wartime allies increased communal tensions, but consolidated its power over the essentially racial-colonial state.

Approximately 8,000 anti-colonial and communist guerrillas, many former resistance fighters from the Japanese occupation, founded the Malayan National Liberation Army (MNLA) and duly prepared for another armed struggle by retrieving their weapons from hidden arms dumps in the jungles. Unsurprisingly, many people of Chinese descent turned to the MCP with its compelling explanation for their continued exploitation. The MNLA also found support among the large numbers of landless workers in the British-owned rubber plantations and tin mines. Significantly for the colonial military campaign, these 'squatters' 'lived largely unadministered along the jungle fringe', which facilitated MCP mobilisation of civilian helpers, the *Min Yuen* (Komer, 1972: 54). A series of labour conflicts and attacks on British settlers and plantations sparked white settler revolt and colonial repression. Under the legal cover of emergency legislation enacted in June 1948, initial colonial policies included the mass detention without trial of 30,000 people, deportations of more than 12,000, and the destruction of property owned by presumed communist sympathisers. In the words of Sir Henry Gurney, British High Commissioner and former Chief Secretary in Palestine, Chinese people were 'notoriously inclined to lean towards whichever side frightens them more' (in Stubbs, 1989: 76). As such, Chinese were subject to travel control, curfews and identity card checks. Rather than simply recognising 'ethnic' distinctions, the British strategy was to reify and harden national and racial cleavages (Hack, 1995, 1999). In this case, the purpose of targeting the Chinese population was to marginalise support for communist anti-colonialism by constituting it as a foreign Chinese import, to create support for colonial policy among favoured (more compliant) groups. Targeting the population seen as most likely to support the guerrillas allowed the government to crush an already narrowed base of support.

Drawing on earlier imperial policing traditions in which uprisings were 'nipped in the bud', Britain's military response was fast and devastating. British army units were brought in from Palestine, Rhodesia,

Nyasaland, Fiji, Australia and New Zealand. MNLA military cells were weakened through Special Branch infiltration and terror operations were mounted to intimidate *Min Yuen*. In a now notorious incident on 12 December 1948, members of the 2nd Scots Guard executed 24 unarmed detainees, workers from the rubber plantation near Batang Kali (Mumford, 2011; Bennett, 2009). After any serious MNLA attack on government positions, all civilians in the area were collectively punished. Hooded native informants pointed to 'collaborators' in identification parades. Crops were destroyed through chemical defoliation. Food, especially rice, was rationed and enforced with house-to-house searches by mobile 'food-check' teams. These food denial operations were intended to force hungry guerrillas out of their bases, making them easier targets for government assault. With more and more squatters forcibly moved from real or potential guerrilla strongholds, armed forces could assume that anyone remaining in a so-called 'black area' was a guerrilla and could therefore be attacked. From the perspective of the colonial state, there was a need to separate insurgents from their main source of supplies and intelligence; control the space in which the population and the guerrillas could interact; isolate the scattered anti-colonial forces; and intimidate the population into providing intelligence.

By 1950, state and police terror tactics were complemented by more organised population control and intimidation strategies. Appointed as Director of Operations in April 1950, Sir Harold Briggs had called for a more 'permanent cure' for guerrilla activity: 'the closing of all breeding areas ... the isolated squatter areas' (in Nagl, 2002: 74). Briggs' systematic resettlement plan involved the forcible removal and relocation of 600,000 people into more than 400 detention camps. Dispersed and scattered peasants were difficult to coerce. Thus, 10 per cent of Malaya's population were forcibly removed and resettled into camps later named 'New Villages'.[8] By 1952, a number of privately owned mines and plantations also 'regrouped' their workers; that is, moved them from their homes into the mine or plantation property. By 1947, the export of rubber from Malaya was Britain's largest income from the empire and was being used, in part, to fund the expansion of social welfare in postwar Britain. Hence to protect

[8] The creation of compounds, camps and resettlement villages is part of a long line of coercive British colonial practices (Home, 2013: 192–217).

the revenues contributing to 'social peace' in the metropole, colonial rubber facilities, including factories, offices and shops, were surrounded by barbed wire. Resettlement locations reflected commercial as well as military logistics: easy surveillance, control of the roads, rail systems and supplies, but also a concern to transport labourers in and out of their places of work. Chain-link fences and barbed wire surrounded compounds; entry and exit was through military checkpoints. Guards in towers watched over inhabitants with floodlights. Surrounding vegetation was destroyed to reduce cover for guerrilla fighters. The Emergency Food Denial Organization strictly accounted for all food and continually searched houses for surplus rice holdings (Leng, 1998). In some areas, rice was circulated and consumed in community kitchens to allow greater surveillance; centrally cooked rice was distributed by local troops. According to a contemporary report, the depopulation strategy 'practically eliminated the dispersed Chinese peasant farmer by withdrawing him from his little wooden hut set in a few acres of farmland, into a town or village sited within a mile or so of his original clearing' (Dobby, 1952/1953: 167–168). In other words, people were transferred from communist 'breeding grounds' into more controllable 'social units'. While Briggs compared operations against bandits to eradicating malaria, real doctors were 'concerned about the increased incidence of malaria, enteric fever, and dysentery' (Stubbs, 1989: 105).

After Sir Henry Gurney's assassination in a roadside ambush in October 1951, General Gerald Templer became High Commissioner. Templer, the 'Tiger of Malaya', was granted exceptionally comprehensive powers to manage the village-level campaign (Cloake, 1985). At the core of the new population control strategy were limited and selectively distributed 'social' provisions and extensive psychological operations. These powers and activities have been described as 'Templer's New Broom' (Stubbs, 1989: 143–151). This metaphor unwittingly captures something of how the 'hearts and minds' strategy was imagined; that is, as an exercise in good housekeeping. Not simply emergency treatment for communist disease, the new villages were to be reimagined as offering the comprehensive modernisation of homes and communities at every level. As discussed in the previous chapter, there is a long tradition of envisaging the management of homes, villages and the empire itself as part of the same project. At the village level, forced removal and resettlement for military expediency was justified as a means to a 'social' revolution of a more liberal and benign sort. For the first time in Malaya's history, labour would be rationally organised. Modern land tenure rights for farmers, albeit to smaller often less fertile plots, replaced the fragmented or open villages in which squatting and communism were rife. Programmes designed to 'improve the lot' of the peasants were imagined as compensation for the 'adverse net effect' of displacement. 'In this way,' wrote one observer, 'the new towns and villages have made major strides to enlightenment of a kind unknown to the villagers' (Dobby, 1952/1953: 176). However, where farmers had once been able to make a modest living on their land, many were now forced to become wage labourers on British-owned mines and plantations, or for the colonial state. No longer isolated on their detached farms, peasants were becoming 'suburbanized, living in areas that were provided with basic social and health services' (Hamzah, 1962: 43). Social engineers, then and now, marvelled at the new standards being set for building construction, hygiene, food, water and electricity (mostly used for surveillance floodlights). As Dobby put it, 'at official cost ... farmsteaders ... were now for the first time brought into touch with these public utilities and public services. Thus it was hoped to offset the admitted nuisance and hardships of resettlement' (1952/1953: 169; see also Dobby, 1953; Hamzah, 1961). Basic medical supplies, community halls, makeshift schools and the occasional children's party were all promised. In his glowing evaluation for the US Department of Defense, Robert Komer wrote that 'every effort would be made to see that the communities did not degenerate into mere detention camps' (1972: 55). More recently, the co-author of the current United States counterinsurgency field manual, John A. Nagl, insisted that the displaced were being housed in '*More than concentration camps*', for they included 'schools, medical aid stations, community centers, village cooperatives, and even Boy Scout troops' (2002: 75, emphasis added).

Since Britain's hearts and minds campaign in Malaya had been highly publicised globally, welfare officers duly arrived from Australia and New Zealand keen to offset the hardships faced by peasants and to help the population progress 'from their scattered farms to a defended area or village located, designed, and organized by the state' (Dobby, 1952/1953: 167; Taylor, 2007). Again, then as now, many were attracted by the chance to be involved in the social work of integrating the non-integrated into society. Templer had conceded that out of military necessity too many resettlements had been 'hurried'. The rush had not allowed for the 'careful sociological and economic surveys and planning which would normally precede so abrupt a disturbance of a long established pattern of rural life' (quoted in Stubbs, 1989: 105).[9] Nonetheless, the detained population's most intimate relations of dependency had become a matter of colonial-social regulation. Hence, the provision of basic services required new levels of coordination and expertise. A panoply of actors were involved in the identification, provision and implementation of the social dimensions of the military campaign. The leading architect of the Strategic Hamlet programmes in Vietnam later praised Britain's 'unusual, unified civil-military command structure ... the wide range of civil and military programs tied together by unified management' (Komer, 1972: v, vi). As already noted, colonialism relies on and subverts conventional distinctions between civilian and military as well as domestic and foreign. Recall French General Hubert Lyautey's identification of such administration. It was 'neither military nor civilian any more, but simply colonial' (in Rid, 2010: 754). Extending Lyautey's point to the late-colonial state in Malaya, we might describe the 'abundant public aid and private assistance in the form of both money and personal services' as neither public nor private, but simply social (Hamzah, 1962: 43). Put differently, Britain's colonial-social administration of the hundreds of thousands of people it had displaced and concentrated was so amenable to the propagandistic version of 'hearts and minds' because it was an exemplary instance of despotic household governance.[10]

In each of the counterinsurgency cases examined in this book, household despotism evolved from direct and centralised control of the population to the indirect and decentralised rule of local proxies, the financing and arming of local despots to govern 'their' populations. In Malaya, the 'Malayan Chinese Association [MCA], the British Red

[9] As Franz Fanon (1965: 64) observed in 1957: 'Colonialist intellectuals consistently use the "sociological case study" approach to the colonial system. Such and such a country, they will say, called for, was crying for conquest. Thus, to take a famous example, the Madagascan was described as having a dependency complex.'

[10] This is not to assume British success at pacifying resistance. 'Resettlement,' writes Karl Hack, 'did not instantly domesticate villagers ... Min Yuen ... told shopkeepers not to enter all stock into their books, passed food over the wire, hid food under fertilizer, or bribed police to look the other way' (2013: 45).

Cross Society, the St. John Ambulance Brigade, the Women's Voluntary Services, the Boy Scouts' Association, church and missionary councils' all delivered social welfare for the colonial state (Hamzah, 1962: 43). Civil improvement teams provided limited but much commented on healthcare, education and demonstrations in childcare, cooking and sewing. Chinese affairs officers 'patiently ... extolled the virtues of their New Village – water, electricity, medical facilities, education for children who did not even know what a school looked like' (Barber, 1971: 103). Native loyalists served as adjuncts to the state in other ways. Established as a political party by Chinese businessmen in 1949, the MCA later became a useful vehicle for incorporating 'the Chinese community' into the Malayan national household. Deals were done; in exchange for its social work in the villages, the MCA – previously a 'group of leaders in search of followers' – would become part of the ruling coalition (Stubbs, 1989: 208). The Malayan Trades Union Congress, created in 1950, served a similar purpose. Formed with the advice of British trade unions, the goal was to channel workers' grievances through loyalist organisations.

Large-scale military operations did not cease with the heightened focus on population control. For example, the Royal Australian Air Force conducted Operation Termite in the summer of 1954 with aerial spraying of herbicide to eradicate food crops (Tyner, 2009: 85). However, the turn to managing populations in the camps provided a discourse in which the application of repressive colonial power seemed to be replaced by more productive and distinctly social forms of regulation. This was evident not only in the emphasis on social welfare, but also the highly managed experiments in 'democratic' participation. Sociological warriors had long claimed that with the correct combination of civic administration and economic activity new and healthy social groupings would emerge. But people needed to be given greater responsibility for their own governance; it was important to be seen to be accommodating the population's minimal political demands, not just their basic 'social' needs. In other words, greater emphasis on 'self-help' and self-government might encourage villagers to be better liberal citizens. Well-worn social work language was used to describe the governance agenda of 'establishing political consciousness at the "grass roots"' (Coates, 1992: 120). The creation of elected Local Councils and other civic action programmes would 'awake civic consciousness and responsibility' (King,

1954: 36).[11] Through participation in Home Guard units, peasants could be invested with new forms of self-understanding, community cooperation and ethics of self-reliance. However, since villagers were demonstrably reluctant to join in and stand for elections, British military officer Robert Thompson was asked to apply 'administrative dynamite where it was most needed' (Coates, 1992: 120). Clearly, this governance strategy should be seen in the context of the ideologies that accompanied Britain's disengagement from formal empire, the desire to manage a transition to the right kind of independence. British talk of self-government and its setting a date for formal independence was later viewed as ingenious, undermining communist arguments for socialist versions of national liberation. In fact, Britain's disengagement policy was primarily aimed at ensuring postcolonial states possessed police and military capacities able to maintain internal order, including British settler property rights (Louis and Robinson, 1994). The repressive laws and forms of colonial household despotism during emergency rule contributed directly to political and violent repression after independence in which 'states of emergency' became a normal feature of post-independence government in Malaysia (Hale, 2013).

In an argument constantly repeated by later counterinsurgents, it is claimed that British strategy in Malaya was successful because it delivered basic social needs to newly housed populations, thus making state authorities seem responsive to the aspirations of local people, and further rob the insurgency of its supportive base. Most influentially, Robert Thompson (1966: 113) claimed that social programmes in the villages gave Malaya's 'people a stake in stability and hope for the future, which in turn encourages them to take the necessary positive action to prevent insurgent reinfiltration and to provide the intelligence necessary to eradicate any insurgent cells'. Well-administered social programmes convey to the population the permanent nature of government. '"Winning" the population can tritely be summed up,' Thompson said, 'as good government in all its aspects' (1966: 112). If certain legitimate (social) grievances are met, then illegitimate (political

[11] Cf. 'Most counterinsurgents do not think of themselves as participating in the process of constitutional design, but counterinsurgency can actually be a form of constitutional design' (Sitaraman, 2012: 224; for a related discussion of Malaya see Harper, 1999).

and military) agendas are dropped. Such notions underpinned the many subsequent celebrations of British military ingenuity in Malaya, in which it is often suggested that village peasants 'came to prefer the villages' to being starved and/or killed (Komer, 1972: 56). However, rather than 'winning' over uprooted people, British forces violently extracted collaboration because they were able to inflict the greatest harm on the civilian population. This is not only in terms of physical coercion used to force people to leave their homes. Collaboration was obtained because the British military and its proxies were in a position to deprive people of basic life necessities through physical coercion. Unless civilians cooperated by providing intelligence, they faced food rations, extended curfews, torture and even death. Communal fines were imposed on villages near the location of guerrilla attacks and suspect populations were subjected to greater administrative control. Of course, many people 'cooperated' as a matter of survival. Instead of transferring meaningful 'support' to the armed forces, the population was forced to acquiesce to the despotic household rule of the army with territorial control. So-called 'hearts and minds' policies provided new means of collective punishment and reward, not the means of winning over 'hearts'.

By 1957, insurgent numbers had been reduced to less than 2,000 from its 1952 peak of 8,000 with only around 10 per cent of these active fighters (Markel, 2006: 40). The guerrillas were finally defeated after 12 years due to failed tactics; lack of widespread support among the wider population and outside powers; their isolation from civilian support through depopulation and concentration; and unexpected revenue for the colonial government, which financed resettlements and increased employment and wages, hurting MNLA recruitment.[12] 'Rather than having discovered the formula for effective counter-insurgency,' noted one observer, 'it now seemed as if the British could

[12] Failed tactics included the weakening of civilian support due to 'overemphasis on violence and sabotage, such as derailing trains and slashing rubber trees' (Hack, 2013: 23). The British also benefited from revenue from the tin and rubber export boom after the outbreak of the Korean War. Authors provide different figures for the costs of the Malayan Emergency. French (2011: 179) gives the figure of £84 million as the amount paid by British taxpayers. Mumford (2011: 159) puts the total cost at '£70 million, from the outbreak in June 1948 to Malayan Independence in August 1957. The British shouldered £52million of this cost, with the rest being provided by the Malayan authorities.'

not have lost' (Mockaitis, 1990: 10). Nonetheless, the discourse of winning hearts and minds first made its way out of Malaya and into the armoury of almost all subsequent counterinsurgency campaigns through the near-simultaneous discourse of rehabilitating the Kikuyu population during Britain's late-colonial war in Kenya. The mythology surrounding benevolent British conduct in Malaya has in no small measure been reproduced in light of colonial state terror during the war against Kenya's Land and Freedom Army, or Mau Mau. Much of the *Handbook on Anti-Mau Mau Operations* was borrowed directly from the conduct of operations in Malaya (Federation of Kenya, 1954). Somehow British conduct in Asia is redeemed because brutality did not reach the depths it did in Africa, where Britain is said to have 'imported the Malayan model wholesale ... without the sensitivity and restraint that had characterised Britain's conduct of the Malayan Emergency' (Markel, 2006: 41). Similarly, looking for precedents in her introduction to the updated United States *Counterinsurgency Field Manual*, Sarah Sewall disavowed elements of British practice, namely starvation, 'ethnic cleansing' and torture. However, 'British actions in Malaya *and Kenya*', she writes 'may look relatively civilized compared to the excesses of the Ottoman or Roman Empires' (Sewall, 2007: xxxiv, emphasis added). While such statements acknowledge the brutality of the war in Kenya, the comparison also serves to redeem British conduct in Malaya and reproduce longstanding claims that Europe's imperial despotism was more civilised than that of their Roman ancestors or Ottoman or Oriental contemporaries. In the words of James Mill, 'Even the utmost abuse of European power is better, we are persuaded, than the most temperate exercise of Oriental despotism' (in Pitts, 2005: 125). At least European imperialism was *liberal* imperialism defined not by theft of land, massacres and the concentration camps but the civilising mission that accompanied these acts. It did not seem this way for those living under colonial emergency in Malaya, of course. 'The Japanese,' many recalled, 'had never burnt whole villages, arrested women and children, and destroyed their livelihood' (Stubbs, 1989: 76). Yet despite the brutality by the 'red-haired devils' (Luo Lan in Khoo, 2004: 123) – not to mention the rather unimpressive nature of Britain's victory – the Malaya campaign spawned a vast 'lessons learned' literature and formed the basis of one of the most influential texts of 1950s American social science, Lucian Pye's (1956) *Guerrilla Communism in Malaya*. Still, although it is

Malaya – and not Kenya – that is held up as the model for emulation, might the war on Kikuyu civilians show the real face of late-colonial British armed social work?

Sociological causes and remedies: rehabilitating Mau Mau in Kenya

Numbering around 29,000 by the early 1950s, the notoriously white supremacist British settler population dominated the economy and politics of the Colony and Protectorate of Kenya. Settlers seized the most fertile land, compelling displaced Africans to provide cheap farm labour and domestic service. Africans could not own land designated for whites and were forced to carry 'ethnic' identity cards when leaving the reservations or the farms where they lived as 'squatters' (Elkins, 2005b). Standard British practices of white supremacy and class exploitation provoked the armed resistance to the colonial government, including attacks on white settlers. The uprising for land and freedom primarily from the most exploited 1.5 million Kikuyu (but also Meru and Embu) was then brutally put down by colonial authorities and their loyalist supporters (Alam, 2007: ch. 2). While capturing something of the context, the sequencing just presented obscures the pre-emptive character of colonial state repression. Rather than merely reacting to violent resistance, the declaration of the emergency on 20 October 1952 was an anticipatory strike against the increasing popularity and effectiveness of Kikuyu labour and political activism, often led by the new generation of ex-soldiers who had fought during World War II. The coercive Emergency powers were used to pre-empt this political action, including through night raids, mass arrests, detention without trial, torture, curfews, control over media, banning of publications and the confiscation of property (Elkins, 2003: 194).[13] In other words, the emergency 'was not', as Berman writes, 'a sudden and discontinuous outbreak of violence, but rather a logical, if major, escalation of the established organisational processes for dealing with African politics' (1976: 171).[14] Once

[13] Of these imprisoned leaders, the best known was Jomo Kenyatta who had founded the Pan-African Federation with Kwame Nkrumah in 1946 and became the first Prime Minister and President of independent Kenya in 1963 (Kenyatta, 1938/1953; Castro and Ettenger, 1994).

[14] Colonial state repression provoked armed resistance, writes Berman, 'particularly the repatriations and chaotic repression which encouraged

the war against Kenya's Land and Freedom Army had begun, Britain's primary mission in the colony was to reassert government control over the colonial household, including through the implementation of major structural reforms involving further theft of land.

With the support of Prime Minister Winston Churchill, General Sir George Erksine oversaw Britain's most savage anti-insurgency and police state-terror campaign of the late-colonial period. Mau Mau forest fighters were not especially adept at surviving away from the urban centres and villages, although they avoided direct military confrontation with the better-equipped and organised colonial forces. Through a slow war of attrition involving the cutting of food, medical supplies and intelligence, Erksine's military campaign against the disorganised and poorly armed guerrillas was effectively won by late 1954.[15] Kikuyu loyalist militia were mobilised to do much of the fighting and dying, undertaking the most brutal acts so British armed forces did not always have to. Loyal Kikuyu provided intelligence, leadership and control of their population, and were the mechanism through which targeted 'social' incentives and sanctions would be delivered. As if aware that the real and potential support for armed resistance was much stronger in Kenya than Malaya, the 'second prong' of the war against Kikuyu civilians would continue for another six years (Elkins, 2005a: 54; Branch, 2009). Governor of the colony, Sir Evelyn Baring, had oversight of policy towards civilians, although the military exerted considerable influence over policy, especially targeting those evicted from land and large numbers of urban poor in Nairobi who were most

thousands of young men … to move into the forests to escape the depredations of the security forces and continue the struggle' (Berman, 1990: 349). At the same time, Mau Mau also represented 'a defensive struggle to stem the tide of land losses and proletarianization and force open greater access to the sphere of commodity production blocked by state "developmental" policies, as well as by the position of settler estates and wealthy African farmers' (Berman, 1990: 363).

[15] The government claimed that, of the roughly 20,000 active resistance fighters, it killed 11,500 in combat and executed 1,090 by hanging. Anderson suggests that even 20,000 active fighters killed is a conservative estimate and compares this with the 32 European civilians killed by rebels, as well as a few dozen European soldiers; roughly 1,800 loyalist fighters and 2,800 mostly Kikuyu loyalist civilians dead (Anderson, 2005: 160). For Elkins (2005a: xvi), the total Kikuyu toll is almost certainly much higher given the number of people unaccounted for after the war; well over 130,000 of the Kikuyu population could be assumed killed in the longer campaign.

supportive of resistance (Bennett, 2012). In April 1954, Nairobi was purged of all Kikuyu in Operation Anvil, at the time the largest urban cordon-and-search operation ever carried out by British armed forces (Mumford, 2011: 57; Bennett, 2007). The capital was surrounded by 2,500 troops and 600 police, who forcibly detained and interrogated *all* Africans, around 30,000 people. 'Screening' teams comprised of British officers and Kikuyu loyalists, many of them hooded informers, carried out interrogations. Again, the centrepiece of population control was the forced resettlement, initially into concentration camps and then into emergency villages in the Kikuyu reserves. Eventually, more than one million Kikuyu were forcibly resettled into 854 punitive encampments, called 'protected villages', surrounded by trenches and barbed wire.

While Baring viewed Mau Mau and its supporters as irredeemable savages, some other justification was required for detaining this many people without trial. Sociological talk of 'rehabilitation' answered questions about the rationale for such sweeping and aggressive incarceration while also underpinning one of the most notorious ideological constructs of British military and political history, that of Mau Mau disease. The 'disease theory' of Mau Mau resistance resolved a classic dilemma of late-colonial legitimacy (Anderson, 2005: 281; Lonsdale, 1990). For the British government, it was imperative to deny the authenticity and politics of Kikuyu resistance. At the same time, widespread support for rebellion had to be explained and addressed *within* the framework of colonial power. The reconciliation of these two positions was the central task of the official government Committee to Enquire into the Sociological Causes and Remedies for Mau Mau (Report to the Secretary of State for the Colonies, 1954). Governor Baring appointed to the Committee a diverse group of 'experts': Tom Askwith, former municipal native affairs officer and commissioner of Kenya's Community Development Department and co-founder of the racially integrated United Kenya Club; Dr J.C. Carothers, an 'ethnopsychiatrist', whose professional training was a six-month course in psychiatry in London; Louis Leakey, 'paleontologist, self-professed "white African", and Special Branch officer' (Anderson, 2005: 283; Clough, 1998: 35); social anthropologist, H.E. Lambert (1956), author of *Kikuyu Social and Political Institutions*; Sidney Fazan, defender of government land policy; David Waruhiu, a loyalist Kikuyu and member of the movement for Moral Rearmament; and Harry Thuku, loyalist

Kikuyu, 'moderate' African nationalist and critic of Mau Mau for perverting Kikuyu customs. Carothers, Leakey and Askwith were the most influential members of the sociological committee, with Askwith the perfect alibi for Britain's war on Kikuyu civilians. Given the homology between social theory and counterinsurgency, it was no surprise to find military strategy turning to sociological means and ends to justify the destruction and reconstitution of Kikuyu households. Sociological causes, if properly diagnosed, could lead to a sociological cure.

In a Freudian update of Sir Henry Sumner Maine's theory of traditional society and Durkheim's writing on normal and pathological behaviour, J.C. Carothers applied to Kikuyu peoples the latest ideas regarding the psychological trauma and violent disorders of the 'African in transition'.[16] Although its core assumptions were found in the earliest forms of colonial anthropology, structural-functional social anthropology was especially important in the post-World War II period when the cooperation of local populations in their own government became even more urgent (Stocking, 1995). Throughout the 1950s, social scientists were drawing connections between the functioning of individual egos, wider 'societal' conditions and political radicalism, now increasingly perceived as a form of psychic deviance. Lucian Pye's (1956) *Guerrilla Communism in Malaya*, for example, would draw on developmental psychology to suggest that these adolescent societies were struggling to come to terms with their colonial and postcolonial fathers.[17] The turn to political radicalism was presented as a form of juvenile acting out, an identity crisis common in the adolescent stage of the life cycle. Echoing Harold Lasswell's (1930) primer *Psychopathology and Politics*, Carothers similarly argued that Mau Mau violence was psychopathological. Comparing the mental characteristics of 'untouched rural Africans' with 'African psychology in transition', Carothers claimed that the arrival of European civilisation had caused great psychological disturbance. Formerly functional

[16] The phrase is also repeated in Colony and Protectorate of Kenya, *The Origins and Growth of Mau Mau: An Historical Survey* (1959/1960: 9). F.D. Corfield wrote the report, but its claims about Kikuyu people rely heavily on Leakey's work.

[17] Pye adapted these notions from the work of psychosocial development theorist Erik Erikson (see Stevens, 2008) and can also be seen in the context of conservative claims regarding 'the exhaustion of political ideas in the fifties' (Bell, 1960).

and coherent traditional 'social systems' had been destroyed; the essential elements of African psychology were being transformed. With older integrating social systems stripped away, individuals were more prone to crises of mental health, especially those transitioning from rural to urban environments. For Carothers, mental illness and dislocation were not fundamental to civilised society as such, but a problem of the shock of transition from one system to another. Abnormal behaviour, such as anti-British violence, was almost unavoidable. The Kikuyu were unable to cope with the transition; to shield themselves from change they had turned inward to older forms of magical thinking. Not authentic native fighters, Mau Mau exhibited a forest psychology. Mau Mau leaders were presented as 'sophisticated egoists' and forest savages, exploiting the mental dissonance of ordinary people (Carothers, 1954: 15; Vaughan, 1991; Cooper, 2004). As Carothers explained, 'Mau Mau arose from the development of an anxious conflictual situation in people who, from contact with alien culture, had lost the supportive and constraining influences of their own culture, yet had not lost their "magic" modes of thinking' (1954: 15; 1970: 76).[18] The problem was especially acute with Kikuyu youth. Young people were less constrained by 'indigenous behavior patterns' compared to their elders, especially women, who are more conservative and fearful of change. Corroborated with fantastical stories of rampant oath-taking and bizarre sexual rituals, evidence of Mau Mau's anti-white and anti-Christian beliefs also included the witchcraft and magic used to indoctrinate ordinary Kikuyu. The *Manchester Guardian* duly reported that Mau Mau 'is essentially reactionary. Such an attitude, known to psychologists as "regressive", is not infrequent in primitive societies confronted with an advanced society' (in Kennedy, 1992: 253).[19] The very Durkheimian conclusion of the psychosocial

[18] The World Health Organization (WHO) originally published the *The African Mind in Health and Disease: A Study in Enthopsychiatry* in 1953. For analysis see McCulloch (1995: ch. 5).

[19] These were not just esoteric British views. A 1956 US State Department memo, 'Africa: A Special Assessment', stated, 'Western-introduced innovations have set off a chain reaction ... which is resulting in prodigious social dislocation. The validity and importance of traditional ... institutions and values have been directly challenged by ... Western institutions and ideas which seem both more powerful and more promising ... For the individual ... caught between the emotional pull of old cultural patterns and the enticing rewards of modernization there is no easy answer. And even when he seems to have

experts was that cultural confusion and maladjustment was the proper framework for understanding Mau Mau fighters and their most ardent followers.

Emphasising psychological disorders meant that the British could acknowledge 'social' and economic resentment and backwardness among Kikuyu without suggesting that these were the 'root cause' of resistance. 'On the question of "grievances"...' Carothers (1954: 12) claimed,

> by virtue of the type of mental structure that develops in Africans, misfortunes are seldom seen as one's own fault. They are seen as the work of evil "wills" and, since the power of these wills is now largely replaced by the power of the European, the latter is apt to be regarded nowadays as the sole author of all evil.

Only through applying a speedy cure to the entire population could new and healthy social norms be created. As a Parliamentary Delegation to Kenya suggested, 'Constructive measures are needed' (Report to the Secretary of State, 1954: 6). These 'deep' psychosociological explanations for anti-colonial violence were naturally accompanied by proposals for its cure: detention, cleansing and rehabilitation. Tom Askwith, in charge of rehabilitation, did not believe Mau Mau was a product of mass psychosis.[20] Several Kikuyu grievances were legitimate and could be remedied. In a first step, higher wages and land reform could address real problems of poverty and overcrowding. Askwith's broader approach to rehabilitation was articulated through a liberal welfare discourse that was distinct from, but not incompatible with, the emphasis on social-psychological factors. While accepting certain Kikuyu grievances, Askwith could still speak in Durkheimian terms of 'maladjusted individuals' in need of integration. Askwith's *The Story of Kenya's Progress* was the liberal counterpart to Carothers' *Psychology of Mau Mau* and Leakey's *Defeating Mau Mau*, and is replete with household analogies.[21]

found the answer in modernism, the old ties continue to disturb him' (quoted in Shafer, 1988: 80–81).

20 Like Askwith, many in the British army 'knew that the "disease" theories of the psycho docs were bunk' (Anderson, 2005: 286).

21 In a section on 'The Foundations of Government', Askwith writes, 'Let us again compare this matter to a house ... When the house has been built, the owner goes in and then walks round to find out where all the rooms are. He does not straightaway tell his wife to light a fire in the middle of the living

Askwith's very British discourse of community development and self-help represents a distinctive phase of late-colonial government. Administratively, it was the responsibility of the colonial governor to oversee a transition to modern civilisation. A certain level of social and economic 'improvement' substituted for political self-determination, especially since natives were not able to exercise the necessary self-restraint required for democratic self-government. However, even before World War II, indirect rule had started to give way to a model of 'partnership' and a new spirit of welfare imperialism to improve the lives of the natives. Welfarism had long been part of the Victorian ideology of liberal empire.[22] But the Exchequer was always reluctant to allot significant resources, preferring to rely on 'traditional African solidarity' and Christian missionaries. Social policy was limited to basic health services for colonial administrators, labour legislation and penal policy. However, in response to late 1930s labour riots in the West Indies, the Colonial Office began rethinking social policy, reflected in the 1935 Government of India Act and the 1940 Colonial Development and Welfare Act. The latter included £5 million per year for economic and social improvements, including psychiatric hospitals and schemes for rural development. The Social Welfare Advisory Committee was created in 1942 as part of postwar colonial planning. After 1945, the existence of large numbers of demobilised African soldiers gave even greater impetus to plans for a new form of trusteeship.[23] Many social workers with experience of administering Britain's poor joined the colonial service, transferring ideas about the functions of social policy from 'home' (Lewis, 2000a, 2000b; Payne, 2005: ch. 10; Midgley, 1981; Eckert, 2004). With the social work mantra of helping people to 'help themselves', these social workers

room without finding out if there is a kitchen ... So too with government; one would not expect that a simple council of elders would be the best government for a country with a railway system, roads and factories' (1954: 34; 1961; 1995).

[22] However, in Britain, *comprehensive* social provision came later than in Germany with the growth in power of the Labour Party from its founding in 1900 and the reforms pursued by Lloyd George. 'In fact, in the British Empire, it was in the colonies of European settlement that the idea of "cradle to grave" state provision was first introduced' in New Zealand and Australia (Bayly, 2004: 273).

[23] In Uganda, there were plans to turn 200 demobilised soldiers into rural social workers (Lewis, 2001: 10).

received modest funding for schemes such as welfare centres, women's groups and vocational training. In addition to, but certainly lagging behind, new thinking in the metropole, liberal attitudes towards race were gaining support even among Kenya's notoriously racist white settlers (Frost, 1978: 60; Throup, 1987). Carothers' emphasis on psychological deficiencies was obviously de-politicising but, to some extent, acknowledged the increasingly unacceptable and counterproductive *open* racism towards Africans. Racism became sociological rather than purely biological, a kind of 'neo-racism' (Balibar, 1991). While new liberal discourses were seen as a threat to those who preferred to freely express their racial superiority, the discourse of 'community development' offered a different method of racially constituting governable African subjects.

Askwith was evidently predisposed to view the potentials of rehabilitation strategy as a benign civilising mission, even perhaps leading to African self-government. Among his first tasks was to spend the summer of 1953 in Malaya. Reporting back to Governor Baring on his tour, Askwith delivered the first of a long sequence of commentaries filled with what have now become clichés about Templer's hearts and minds strategy. Rather than the means of collective punishment, starvation and control, Malaya's New Villages were sites of liberal social reform. While the situations were very different – the authorities in Malaya could deport Chinese and had revenues from the rubber boom – Templer seemed to offer Askwith a model of how to persuade Kikuyu to renounce Mau Mau violence and potentially trust the colonial government. In exchange for confessing oaths, repudiating Mau Mau and providing intelligence to colonial authorities, a radically reformed idea of community development might rehabilitate the entire Kikuyu society. Even some white settlers such as Michael Blundell, Minister Without Portfolio to the Emergency War Council, and one of the two 'last British liberals in Africa', extolled the reforms the new villages might bring (Blundell, 1994; Mungazi, 1999). Askwith's own perspective was directly influenced by the new generation of professional social workers and the latest social scientific expertise. Kikuyu needed to be constituted as subjects able to help themselves through participating in empowering projects in community centres. The late-colonial state could facilitate Kikuyu self-help if it established schools and medical services, basic civics lessons, economic development aid, welfare programmes and boy scouts, women's groups and training. With an earnest pro-African and sympathetic character like Askwith in charge, things seemed to be in place for a progressive course of social rehabilitation both inside and outside the concentration camps: a liberal paternalist overseeing social improvement; the application of the latest social work theory in Kenya's Community Development Department; a number of trained social workers sent from Britain; gender-specific interventions targeted at women; anthropological and WHO-acknowledged expertise of what is now called the 'human terrain'; the presence of large numbers of indigenous Kikuyu in the security forces; and no shortage of captive Kikuyu.

'The gulag never looked so good'[24]

The detention and rehabilitation process in colonial Kenya amounted to pure unadulterated violence, unmodified by even face-saving liberal inducements. From the declaration of emergency, arbitrary detention of Kikuyu civilians was pervasive. All Kikuyu suspected of Mau Mau disease were detained and 'screened' (Leakey, 1953, 1954; Berman and Lonsdale, 1991). The magnitude of raids, interrogation, detention and forced removals – the Pipeline – dwarfed even that of Malaya. More than 70,000 civilians were detained for interrogation and large numbers were tortured; more than 150,000 Kikuyu were held in prison camps; and more than one million were forcibly resettled (Anderson, 2005: 5; Branch, 2005). The colonial goal of the Pipeline was to pacify Kikuyu, but with far less financial support and much greater emphasis on racial vengeance than even practised in Malaya. The official purpose of the 'dilution technique' of physical and psychological torture was to cleanse detainees of their oaths. The actual 'socio-military' strategy was to destroy anti-colonial Kikuyu unity and rid ordinary people of their politics. Having confessed their political illness and performed the appropriate cleansing rituals, detainees progressed through various houses of correction. The truly despotic character of this process was cloaked behind the revitalised discourse of social improvement and community development. If released from interrogation, detainees were sent to transit and labour camps and/or a new village, overseen by loyalist Home Guard.[25] In

[24] Elkins (2000: 39).

[25] 'The frequency of brutality was particularly high in settler units of the KPR [Kenya Police Reserve], especially those composed of the Nairobi petty

violation of the 1930 International Labour Organization Convention on forced or compulsory labour, inmates built trenches, placed barbed wire around 'villages' and constructed watchtowers for their own surveillance (Elkins, 2005a: 129–130). The inmates of these domesticated spaces were subjected to despotic social administration by a motley crew of loyalists, prison and rehabilitation officers (Anderson, 2006). Administered in the name of their 'welfare' and 'protection', Kikuyu were offered 'more opportunities for social living' (Carothers, 1954: 22). In other words, they were subjected to despotic household government in detention centres, New Villages and ultimately in a reconstituted national household, a sovereign Commonwealth state.

As in Malaya, where scattered homes were viewed as incubators of communist violence, colonial officials in Kenya were concerned that the domestic arrangement of Kikuyu populations made them more prone to rebellion and more difficult to pacify. In contrast to bourgeois ideals of domesticity, with clear boundaries between family homes and a distinct 'domestic' domain synonymous with the biological family, rural Africans lived in dense kinship groups, homesteads rather than villages. Functionalist anthropologists were duly asked to study and describe the household 'social structure' of Kikuyu territorial organisation, especially 'the joint [land] rights of an extended family' over 'scattered' homesteads (Lambert, 1956: 2). More than just an offence to liberal understandings of property rights, the dispersed and isolated character of Kikuyu households played into insurgent military strengths. As the Parliamentary Delegation noted, 'the Mau Mau, by using the traditional African channels of spreading rumours, in other words "the bush telegraph", holds the initiative in this field' (Report to the Secretary of State, 1954: 12). The forcible removal of populations from their homesteads, the tearing down and burning of homes and the concentration of the displaced into forced labour camps were thus a means to a primarily military end. 'Villagisation' deprived insurgents of food, recruits, intelligence and moral support. In the familiar euphemisms of the Parliamentary Delegation, 'The Emergency has shown how difficult it is to provide these scattered families with adequate

bourgeoisie ... Drawn from the collaborating elite of chiefs and headmen and the class of wealthy farmers and traders, as well as from a fanatically anti-Mau Mau Christian fundamentalist revival movement ... the Home Guard acted without fear of reprisal' (Berman, 1990: 357; also see Doty, 1996: 99–124).

protection, so that they are not easy prey for the determined terrorist' (Report to the Secretary of State, 1954: 9).

Social anthropological accounts of Kikuyu domestic arrangements offered a sociological gloss to military strategy. Recall how the late nineteenth-century notion of society as a systemic whole borrowed heavily from current theories of evolution. In order to establish the reality of something called 'society', Auguste Comte and Herbert Spencer drew analogies between biological organisms and society, whose institutions similarly evolved out of simpler forms. Spencer was one of the first to seek a general theory of social evolution analogous to how evolution worked in the natural world. Societies, like organisms, were functionally integrated wholes. In *Principles of Sociology*, Spencer (1877) claimed that the overarching dynamic of society was integrative and this dynamic was the basis for comparing the evolutionary development of different types of society around the world. 'Society' grows ever stronger, he argued, when the web of relationships between its parts grows increasingly dense.[26] These differing levels of integration could account for many of the differences between the historical stages of society: gatherer, traditional village and modern. Building on these earliest structural functionalist theories of society, the psychosocial rationale for villagisation in Kenya was that scattered populations were not as *socialised* and *integrated* as those grouped into compact villages; 'it is very difficult for him to cleanse his soul of any filth that has adhered to it' (Carothers, 1954: 19). As Carothers pointed out, Mau Mau 'forest psychology' was born of isolation from wider social norms, 'the voice of the group is less insistent ... Such people learn to live in their own company and must tend to rumination on more personal lines, to secretiveness, to suspicions and to scheming ... Social conformity was not, here, so dominant a note' (1954: 5). All classical social theories agreed that modernity was defined by an integration deficit; the competing traditions simply disagreed regarding the causes and remedies.

The influence of Spencer and Durkheim on the tradition of colonial anthropology is clear, as is the role of colonial anthropology in

[26] Darwin was an important influence on Spencer's eugenicist ideas. Interestingly, 'Darwin's logic rested not on genetics, unknown as the time, but rather on how breeders of domestic animals can breed for desirable characteristics with a measure of success' (Matthews, 1987: 118).

justifying late-colonial military strategy.[27] As Spencer had argued, societies 'progressed' to the point that a coherent structural order existed that was increasingly observable and specific, 'from indeterminate arrangement to determinate arrangement' (1867: 372). 'Physics,' Spencer (1867: 19) wrote, 'regulates more completely our [modern, industrial] social life than does his acquaintance with the properties of the surrounding bodies regulate the life of the savage.' He goes on,

> A wandering tribe of savages, being fixed neither in its locality nor in its internal distribution, is far less definite in the relative positions of its parts than a nation. In such a tribe, the social relations are similarly confused and unsettled ... Any one of those primitive societies that evolves, however, becomes step by step more specific.
>
> (Spencer, 1867: 372)

Hence, the perfect antidote to their 'rather isolated ways of living' (Carothers, 1954: 23) was to regroup Kikuyu into new villages, little functional societies in miniature. Following Durkheim, overcoming *anomie* required the creation of new social norms, through intervention into the parts of the social whole at risk of dissociation; that is, to transition Kikuyu from its sick and violent phase to a functionalist and normalising (sociological) one. 'African children,' Carothers duly claimed, 'need to be taught to see themselves as part of a vast human organization with tentacles that stretch a long way off in four dimensions ... [T]he essential thing about all folk to-day is that they are only local examples of a highly homogenous humanity' (1954: 25).

If, as Governor Baring and the psychosocial experts agreed, this was a war against Mau Mau savages, then rehabilitation was part of

[27] Durkheim's influence was transferred most directly through his nephew, the French anthropologist, Marcel Mauss (1922/1990), and later forms of structural anthropology. As Pecora (1997: 175–176) notes, 'a certain strand of romantic anthropology in the nineteenth and twentieth centuries would also look to savage or primitive societies in an attempt to recover the virtues of noble mastery no longer supportable at home ... [It] rediscovered Aristotle's mastery and noble *oikos* ... as an element of "primitive", "archaic", or "traditional" society itself. Aristotle's proud magnanimous man ... his position in a network of noble, rather than necessary, exchanges – is rediscovered by a variety of anthropological and sociological discourses as the basis of primitive or archaic modes of exchange. In Mauss's synthesis of this tradition of thought ... it is precisely primitive (noble) exchange that establishes the basis for economic exchange in general.'

the war in defence of civilisation and its standards. For much colonial sociology, the strength and permanence of European civilisation was underpinned by the stability of European family life, understood in terms of patriarchal domesticity. In fact, as already noted, this bourgeois notion of the family home as the basis of civilisation also emerged alongside the forcible removal of peasants from their more communal households and extended families. Subsequent social scientists had seemingly shown that social dysfunction increased when family ties were weak, for it is in the family where 'general principles of social conduct' are instilled (Carothers, 1954: 26). Hence, intervention into the 'family' – government through family – had been central to social regulation since its inception, including in the colonies (Donzelot, 1979).[28] For example, during the high-colonial period, writes Zimmerman (2010: 18):

> German colonial attacks on African economic autonomy concentrated on the independence of women's households in polygamous marriages and on women's physical, sexual, and economic mobility. Colonial authorities sought to replace the individual autonomy of the Togolese extended household with the personal and sexual constraint of a patriarchal family farm.[29]

Late-colonial British military strategy similarly extended the scope of gendered and sexualised social regulation into the most intimate forms of Kikuyu life. The pacification and rehabilitation of Kikuyu civilians was inseparable from the remaking of domestic space and subjects into something presented as 'natural and universal in the first place' (McClintock, 1995: 35). For example, the absence of a 'secure'

[28] For example, in British South Africa, writes McClintock, 'Missionaries and colonists voiced their repugnance for polygamy in moral tones ... Yet colonial documents readily reveal that the assault on polygamy was an assault on African habits of labor that withheld from the resentful [white settler] farmers the work of black men and women. The excess labor that a black man controlled through his wives was seen as a direct and deadly threat to the profits of the settlers ... But the family would be gradually modified by diverting the profits of female labor out of the homestead into the colonial treasury in the form of hut and marriage taxes' (1995: 254–255). In other words, 'colonization inflects itself as a *domestication* of the colony, a reordering of the labor and sexual economy of the people, so as to divert female power into colonial hands and disrupt the patriarchal power of colonized men' (McClintock, 1995: 364).

[29] See also Wildenthal (1996: 371–395; 2001).

two-parent home was used to explain asocial Kikuyu behaviour and why young men were so attracted to Mau Mau. 'If ever Africans are to develop ... they must be given opportunity to live as families in stable homes. This above all' (Carothers, 1954: 23–24). Kikuyu women had a special role in producing healthy and responsible social subjects and were most in need of practical lessons in 'housecraft, cleanliness (of persons, of homes, of food), general health and diet, infant welfare, and so on' (Carothers, 1954: 25). Kikuyu women had participated in every aspect of the military and political resistance, including organising weapons, food and medical supplies and intelligence to the fighters, administering oaths and leading opposition in the villages (Presley, 1992: 130).[30] During the initial period of state terror, large numbers of women were accordingly detained, interrogated, tortured and raped. When broken by extreme physical and mental assault, women were expected to confess their oaths. 'It will be necessary to cleanse the women in the same way as the men before they are permitted to rejoin them', Askwith had stated,

> as there is evidence that wives have in many cases persuaded their husbands to take the oath and are often very militant. They are also said to be bringing up their children to follow the Mau Mau creed. It is therefore more important to rehabilitate the women than the men if the next generation is to be saved.
>
> (in Elkins, 2005a: 109–110)

In the prison camps for women, self-help groups such as 'Progress among Women Club' were vehicles of 'socialisation', as well as intelligence-gathering. They were used to disseminate acceptable 'norms', enacting ideologies long part of colonial welfarism and to serve as a diversion from political activity.

The level of women's involvement in the movement violated British conventions about appropriate feminine conduct. Anti-colonial political and military activism among women was not only a threat to

[30] In the words of Louis Leakey (1954: 145): 'Those who have close knowledge of Mau Mau, know only too well how many teenage girls in the towns have dropped into membership of the movement and have even become very active members of murder gangs – often out of sheer boredom at having nothing to do all day ... I can see no reason why, for some of them, the answer should not be domestic service.'

Kenya's colonial hierarchies, but also to bourgeois notions of masculinity and femininity (McClintock, 1995; see also Stoler, 2010). They were viewed as a threat to the small-scale family patriarchies central to the stabilisation of the concentric circle of household formations defining of the modern social realm. It should come as no surprise, then, that Kikuyu women's domestic 'homeplace' was subjected to invasions and reconstitution in the psychological war against Mau Mau. Colonial occupation is a form of expropriation, 'the deprivation for certain groups of their place in the world and their naked exposure to the exigencies of life' (Arendt, 1958: 254–255).[31] Postcolonial and critical race scholars have written of 'the importance of homeplace in the midst of oppression and domination, of homeplace as a site of resistance and liberation struggle' (hooks, 1990: 43). While there is no domestic realm that is not also a place of power, occupied peoples, especially women, have created and tended to domestic spaces potentially outside the reach of the most obvious forms of colonial control (Alcobia-Murphy, 2006). They have drawn on the resources of homeplace to actively fight and hold onto a place in the world, including through organising and fighting against colonial occupation.[32] It is this possibility of a site of resistance that made Kikuyu homeplace a military target, something to be actively destroyed and reconstituted. In Elkins' words:

> Only when there was a total obliteration of the Kikuyu domestic landscape in the villages did women begin to confess their oaths and leave Mau Mau. Their home front was the battlefield, and it was also their last line of defence ... It therefore took the annihilation of everything of domestic importance – the atomization of families, the death of children, the violation of Kikuyu social beliefs, the violation of their bodies, the destruction of homesteads and the loss of land and livestock – to force the women to submit.
>
> (Elkins, 2003: 217–218)

31 'For the security of the boundaries of the place one called home must have dissolved long ago' (Massy, 1992: 10).

32 Cf. 'The Algerian woman's ardent love of the home is not a limitation imposed by the universe ... It is not a flight from the world ... The Algerian woman, in imposing such a restriction on herself, in choosing a form of existence limited in scope, was deepening her consciousness of struggle and preparing for combat ... This withdrawal ... constituted for a long time the fundamental strength of the occupied' (Fanon, 1965: 66).

There were ample military reasons for burning down scattered homes and concentrating on the civilian population. These homeplaces were absorbed into the war and physically destroyed. But there were psychological as well as physical reasons to break peoples connection with homeplace: the real battle for hearths and minds.

Embodying portable domesticity, and thus seeming to mitigate some of the effects of colonial violence, middle-class British social workers helped oversee camps and train Kikuyu women to save their men and children from Mau Mau. Through such reformist schemes, European women had long participated in imperial projects, imparting healthy modes of family life and potentially greater loyalty to the colonial state. In seeking to improve the order, cleanliness and stability of Kikuyu homes, these social workers were often unwittingly participating in the destruction of homeplace as a refuge and form of anti-colonial defence. However, social workers were also among the first to expose the Pipeline, its white supremacy, torture, starvation, rape and castrations, and children dying of malnutrition and typhus. In her 1956 essay *Truth about Kenya: An Eye Witness Account*, Eileen Fletcher, an experienced social worker posted to rehabilitate women and girls in Kamiti, described prisoner of war camp-like conditions. For the colonial state was unwilling to provide more than minimal funding for food and basic services necessary for detainee survival, let alone ambitious schemes for social improvement. At the height of the emergency, there were approximately 250 rehabilitation workers, overseeing almost 1.5 million Kikuyu. By 1955, there were only six community development officers for women in the whole of Central Province, the main theatre of war. In the same year, the already paltry funding for rehabilitation was halved (Elkins, 2005a: 231, 149, 236).[33] The Korean War rubber boom subsidised Templer's plans in Malaya but since Mau Mau fighters did not identify as communists there were no geopolitical justifications for extra resources. With lack of funds, inadequate water and sanitation, thousands of civilians were subjected to starvation and disease. In the midst of a widespread famine in the villages, the colonial government refused to increase funds for the relief of hunger. Instead, the Red Cross and Christian missionaries provided limited food and medicine; a small number of social work volunteers

[33] 'In Kenya's Development Plan for 1954–57, Ernest Vasey allocated the Community Development and Rehabilitation Department £103,000, or .5% of the colony's total budget' (Elkins, 2005a: 148).

in Malaya travelled to Kenya; and Askwith transferred the already limited support for rehabilitation to famine relief. The colonial government denied reports of famine and emphasised the positive effects of the social revolution in the villages (Kennedy, 1992: 253). When his complaints about the accompanying abuses became too loud, Tom Askwith was forced out of his post.

Askwith is a tragic figure. In his acceptance of the liberal creed of social welfare and community development, he was a man of – rather than ahead of – his time (Askwith, 1995).[34] The worst aspects of colonial coercion were supposed to be ameliorated by delivering on the real promise of liberal empire: the 'imperial politics of inclusion', multiracial cooperation and African self-help in the community centre (Midgley and Piachaud, 2011; Hodge, 1973). The extreme violence of the Pipeline undermined all talk of rehabilitation. The brutality was not simply a question of 'Liberal [rehabilitation] remedies ... administered by conservative hands, since there were far more of these', as though liberal remedies for anti-colonial resistance were laudable (Lewis, 2001: 55). And yet for a short period, rehabilitation served as cover for gulag conditions, as well as for more structural transformations of the colonial household through which Kikuyu were to be bound to land, families and their 'ethnic' and 'racial' groups. The government and land reforms in Kenya that accompanied the emergency had profound and deliberate long-term effects. Limited land concessions were not extended to Mau Mau supporters, as they had been to some Chinese in Malaya. Land consolidation and the intensification of capitalist economy made the racially organised class exploitation even more punitive, providing further opportunity to punish rebellious Kikuyu and reward the most compliant. As advocated in the Swynnerton Report of 1954, African agricultural production was intensified; more territories were opened up for cultivation; and there was land reform to expand the size of the landed and landless classes. In the words of the Report,

> In the past, Government policy has been to maintain the tribal system of land tenure so that all the people have had bits of land ... In future ... Government policy will be reversed and able, energetic or rich Africans will

[34] 'Freedom is a great privilege. It cannot be given but can only be earned. It is only safe in the hands of those who know how to use it' (Askwith, 1954: 115).

be able to acquire more land and bad or poor farmers less, creating a landed and a landless class. This is a normal step in the evolution of a country.

(Swynnerton, 1954: 10)

Only loyalist Kikuyu benefited from these spoils of war, including entitlements to land confiscated from open supporters of Mau Mau. Many returning detainees and village inmates went back to largely feudal labour and squatting on white settler farms, the 'normal' relation in Kenya's stage of social evolution. Although there would be elections to the civil service, no real attempt was made to co-opt Kikuyu into the political and economic system. As with Malaya, the ground was being prepared for eventual independence with a household structure of Britain's liking.

Conclusion

In the rush of counterinsurgency texts that materialised with the United States occupation of Iraq, late-colonial British history was often presented as a model for emulation (Sewall, 2007: xxiv; cf. Branch, 2010; Strachan, 2007). In this writing, the Malaya emergency plays a singularly important role as a successful hearts and minds campaign. To defeat its enemies in Afghanistan and Iraq, the United States could apparently do worse than update this older and even potentially noble British tradition. Here the origin of British success is generally assumed to be twofold: a focus on winning hearts and minds and appreciation for an 'economy of force' (Sepp, 2005; Nagl, 2002; Betz and Cormack, 2009).[35] To 'win over' the population, the British army had learned how to fight with careful discrimination and socially administer the basic needs of the population. Needless to say, the notion that Britain's Malaya campaign represents a hearts and minds success or an example of its army's philosophy of 'minimum force' is a fabrication (Bennett, 2012). However, the language used to disseminate this version of British colonial history is close to accurate in one very important respect. Not economy in the sense of moderation, but *oikonomia* in the use of force was central to Britain's late-colonial military campaigns. Political and military strategists in

[35] For other criticisms of this narrative see French (2011, 2012); Porch (2011); Ledwidge (2011); Dixon (2012).

Kenya and Malaya explicitly drew on the art of household management to pacify and domesticate insurgent populations. In its competition in government with anti-colonial forces – insurgents and populations – British forces deployed techniques of *oikonomikos*. That is, they borrowed from and innovated despotic household rule to address what were presented as the deeper social causes of and remedies for resistance. Populations were forced to live under the tutelage of household heads of prisons, detention camps and New Villages. They were subject to administration: pacification and domestication. In Kenya, it really was as if the British believed that they were domesticating wild animals. While in the *Handbook on Anti-Mau Mau Operations* there are several passages discussing wild elephants and buffalo, and how to care for horses and mules, there is no discussion of the civilian population at all.[36]

Referring to Britain's policy of 'rehabilitating' Kikuyu, one Defence Ministry official stated, 'the whole thing is window dressing anyway' (in Elkins, 2005a: 296). Armed social work can easily appear like a mere façade since its function, in part, is to disguise one activity (population coercion and control) as something more pleasing (social improvement and development). If armed social work adorns the windows of the household of late-colonial emergencies, then perhaps it also offers a view *into* the nature of this form of household rule. In the art of window-dressing there are certain principles of display; 'the window may be styled an index to the house; if carefully kept, it should be as reliable to refer to as the index of a book' (*Warehouse and Drapers' Trade Journal*, 1883: 9). The proper dressing of windows is necessary not only for the sake of appearances; that is, to attract positive attention and divert the eye from the less than pleasant. It is necessary for one's own sense of decorum. The conduct of the war in Kenya would seem to be such a stain on Britain's reputation not because the fading empire violently and despotically resisted a legitimate liberation struggle, including through torture and starvation. This happened in Malaya. The embarrassment among counterinsurgents is Britain's failure to adorn the campaign against the Kikuyu population with better-funded schemes of rehabilitation. Although it seemed, for a

[36] The *Handbook* does, however, contain some tips on how to interact with local African trackers. 'Although their physical needs are a great deal less than ours, do not disregard the Africans comfort' (Federation of Kenya, 1954: 16).

while, to have everything necessary on show, the British colonial state violated its own lessons in pacification respectability. Rehabilitation in Kenya was a charade, but what if the programme of liberal reform had properly performed, if the window-dressing was less shabbily handled? Britain was 'successful' in defeating Mau Mau. Hence, if more funds had been available for rehabilitation, and the conditions in the camps had been a little better, perhaps even the Kenya campaign would have received a similar hagiography as that in Malaya. It is the Kenya campaign – not Malaya – that provided the real lesson for future counterinsurgents: resources are almost everything. The Malaya campaign suggests that relatively high spending on hearts and minds can be made alongside extreme repression and population coercion. But this does not make the campaign laudable; such a combination was a defining feature of Stalin's Soviet Union. As David L. Hoffmann (2011: 1) notes, 'as the number of incarcerations and executions grew exponentially, Communist Party leaders enacted sweeping social welfare and public health measures. Extensive state surveillance of the population went hand in hand with literacy campaigns, [and] political education.' It would take the United States war in Vietnam, when vast resources were spent on the 'Other War', the war for the social reconstruction of millions of Vietnamese peasants, that the worst excesses of the homology between counterinsurgency and non-Marxist social theory would be revealed. When combined with unprecedented technological and financial capabilities in the postwar period, the destruction unleashed was out of all proportion. Millions were killed by both the United States and the Soviet Union, pursing their own modern paradigms of social regulation, mostly in the Global South and in the same theatres as the old colonial empires.

6 *Society itself is at war: new model pacification in Vietnam*

Social patterns and institutions in most under-developed nations are extremely malleable.

United States Overseas Internal Defense Policy (1962)

American popular culture in the 1950s is known for its well-defined gender roles and stereotypes of the good suburban housewife. In this postwar version of the cult of domesticity, the ideal woman accepted her place in and tended to the household; she performed her duty on the American home front after men had completed theirs in World War II. Women were expected to support home life, but also embrace consumer culture, automobiles, televisions and the promise of Tupperware (Vincent, 2003). Supported by the Servicemen's Readjustment Act of 1944 (the 'GI Bill'), hundreds of thousands of veterans took advantage of low-cost mortgages to move their families out of the cities and into mass-produced houses in the newly developed suburbs. In popular culture and advertising, these homes were places of containment and order, despite – or perhaps because of – deep anxieties about nuclear annihilation and communism.[1] Rejecting these postwar ideals of American domesticity, feminists were more vocal in describing suburban homes as places of suffocation and confinement. By the early 1960s, Betty Friedan's *The Feminine Mystique* described the tangible experiences of many middle-class women. The ideal domestic life was actually a prison, or worse. Life for many in the suburban home was 'progressive dehumanization', like living in 'a comfortable concentration camp' (Friedan, 1963: 307; see also Heller, 1995). As Friedan was writing one of the most important American books of the postwar period, the soon to be defunct *Times of Vietnam* announced that 1962

[1] According to Elaine Tyler May, 'cold war ideology and the domestic revival were two sides of the same coin' (1988: 10); on the 'militarization of the house' in postwar America see also Colomina (2007) and Castillo (2005).

was 'Year of the Strategic Hamlet', America's counterinsurgency version of the comfortable concentration camp.

Nineteen sixty-three was a bad year for good housekeeping. In November, the *Times of Vietnam* was shut down following the violent collapse of the House of Ngo, the despotic but non-communist national household of President Ngo Dinh Diem (Ahern, 2000; Karnow, 1963; Hatcher, 1990: ch. 5). Created under American tutelage, Diem's household was too unruly; excessive repression and internal division provoked further violent resistance. With CIA ascent, Diem and his brother were arrested and assassinated in a military coup to create more effective local leadership in the war against the communist north.[2] The United States sought to domesticate not only local populations and their traditional leaders, but also an entirely new nation-state. In an activity that many imagined to be an exercise in good housekeeping, millions of peasants were removed at 'forced-draft' into New Villages and Strategic Hamlets. Each of these households – the idealised version of the suburban home, the real Strategic Hamlets and national household of South Vietnam – were partially or even totally destroyed by 1968. More or less consciously, all three were created as units of rule in which populations – women, children, peasants, Vietnamese; sometimes all four – were to be governed through the more or less openly despotic rule of a household head, if necessary through physical force, in the name of the welfare of the household as a whole. This war contributed to a radical (although not revolutionary) transformation of gender and race relations in the United States, making suburban domestic bliss more difficult, although not impossible, to sustain. By 1970, the year four unarmed Kent State student demonstrators were fatally shot by National Guard troops, family horror films in which monsters came from within the American family itself joined westerns and Disney animations as forms of mass entertainment (Williams, 1996: ch. 6).[3]

[2] Diem's brother was in charge of paramilitaries and South Vietnam's secret police.

[3] Also during the 1970s, American feminists mobilised against the decision by the US Bureau of the Census to lead with the question of who was 'head of household', and successfully had the question and concept of 'head of household' removed. The Bureau defended the use of the concept as a convenient 'basis for structuring relationships within the household, and it has provided a consistent set of data over a long time' (quoted in Presser, 1998: 148).

The war in Vietnam is one of the most written about episodes in history; and there are numerous critiques of the United States military campaign (Herring, 1979; Aronson, 1983; Kolko, 1985). This chapter sheds new light on a central aspect of the war, the convergence between the despotic and sociocratic techniques of household governance and counterinsurgency rule. Under the expert guidance of the leading social scientists, the households of counterinsurgency built by the United States radicalised practices that had been central to imperial British and French pacification campaigns. The United States was much more ambitious than its European predecessors, seeking to constitute and protect not traditional village 'society' but an entire nation-state. These policies are not fully understood outside a framework of social-colonial thought and the rise of the social realm itself as the arena for administering populations, as the distinctly modern and sociocratic form of household rule.

Sir Henry Sumner Maine, recall, had theorised 'traditional society' as a structured whole based on longstanding customs and the authority of the patriarch, an essentially natural system defined by kinship. As self-sufficient household economies, traditional villages were the more or less benign symbol of a functionally integrated society following its age-old customary norms, one that could be co-opted into Britain's system of imperial rule. Before the social science theory of 'modernisation', that dominated the postwar American academy, Maine had established the basic contours of the first distinctly social explanation for native revolt in the crisis of transition to modernity (Maine, 1876; Shils, 1991). As the United States Official Overseas Internal Defense Policy would put it almost a century later, 'the revolution of modernization can disturb, uproot, and daze a traditional society' (United States, 1962: 3, II B-4). By the middle of the twentieth century, British late-colonial wars had already upended Maine's observations regarding the stabilising norms of 'tradition'; that is, of despotic/patriarchal household rule. The postwar heirs to Sir Henry continued to conceive traditional societies as functional wholes. However, these once coherent 'social systems' had been totally destroyed by the world wars, with profound psychopathological consequences that could not be remedied by traditional means. Such was the sociological rationale for Britain's late-colonial military strategies of depopulation and concentration in Kenya and Malaya. Such policies helped to end the formal empire at least partially on Britain's terms, including the protection of British-owned businesses and white settler property.

By 1960, the 'village' – to many American eyes – reflected something even more apocalyptic. For US political and military strategists there was much more at risk than *realpolitik* and particular race and class interests in how the 'crisis of transition' was managed. Modern civilisation itself appeared to be at stake. As Eugene Staley, the Stanford economist and advisor to Diem put it: 'Either the benefits of modern civilisation in the form of better living conditions and greater human dignity will also become widely available to the non-Western world ... or these benefits will be lost even to us in the West' (in Latham, 2000: 172; Staley, 1961). The American way of life at home was in danger. Thus, where Maine had argued that the traditional village should be protected and preserved, US military and political strategists transformed the imperial construct of the 'traditional village' into a far more frightening menace (Cullather, 2006). For the Americans in Vietnam, the problem was not that isolated villages were disintegrating in the face of modernity. Rather, a perversion of modernity – communism – was making the village more politically and militarily coherent. 'The village' came to embody resistance to more than just the power and reach of the House of Ngo, but that of the United States itself. In the past, claimed MIT political scientist Ithiel de Sola Pool, external despots had left internal village matters to elders, to the local *paterfamiliās*. When peasants pay the requisite taxes, '"the Emperor's writ stops at the village gate"' (Pool, 1968: 7). However, the United States was no ordinary empire; its domesticating mission was much more ambitious. 'Vietnam,' Pool claimed, 'is the greatest social-science laboratory we have ever had' (in Mazower, 2008). Entire villages would be wiped out and millions of peasants would be swept up, killed or socially re-engineered in the literally toxic hurricane of American land and air power.[4] Put differently, the US war in Vietnam was the most extreme attempt at *oikonomikos* in the history of overseas empire.

[4] 'Between 1967 and July 1972 the US Army in Vietnam [unsuccessfully] attempted to modify Vietnam's weather through rainmaking [and] attempts to intensify the normal monsoon rainfall over the Ho Chi Minh Trail; clouds were seeded with silver and lead iodide from aircraft' (Tyner, 2009: 93; see also Cable, 1986).

This chapter is divided into three parts. The first section situates the motivating ideology most closely associated with the United States war in Vietnam, modernisation theory, in the socio-biological thought of nineteenth-century imperial Europe and the early self-conscious attempts to develop a seemingly non-ideological social science for the American scene. In fact, deeply rooted in the ideological battles of the nineteenth century, modernisation theorists were no less zealous or revolutionary than those who first quarrelled about the meaning of and solutions to the Social Question. The second part examines the United States attempt to create the state of South Vietnam as the House of Ngo, explicitly conceived in such household terms in the official (now declassified) CIA history of its involvement in Vietnam (Ahern, 2000). The gigantic building that was to house this nation was to be comprised of a strong client government, police and armed forces, and capitalist economy. The effort to 'socially construct' a South Vietnamese state was the United States' most ambitious and costly attempt to 'create at forced-draft the bone structure of a modern nation' (Rostow quoted in Gilman, 2003: 155). The third part examines the forcible depopulation and concentration of millions of Vietnamese peasants into camps, most famously referred to as Strategic Hamlets. As with earlier military experiments with population enclosure, depopulation and concentration drew on social work mantras of self-help and development, allowing crimes against humanity to be described, in the words of a State Department document, *Quiet Warriors: Supporting Social Revolution in Viet-Nam*, as an 'enormous venture in human rehabilitation' (United States, 1966: 39). Using the latest techniques of 'rational engineering control', American social science would play its most advanced and controversial role in justifying this pacification strategy and scientifically measuring its effects. Modernisation theory was not directly responsible for military strategy. However, the level of resources the United States was able to expend on the destruction of Vietnam, and the way in which this destruction was ideologically conceived, took to an extreme something inherent to distinctly social thought. Several commentators have pointed to the role of social *scientists* in conceiving of and justifying this level of destruction. To date, however, we are without an account of what it is about distinctly *social* science, rather than science *per se*, that makes it so amenable to counterinsurgency.

The end of the Social Question?

By the middle of the twentieth century, the Social Question – always also an Imperial Question – was reoriented to reflect the United States' global designs. Was it possible, and if so how, to oversee an orderly transition from a world order of European empires to a US-centred *global*, not merely hemispheric, hegemony? What forms of social regulation could address the rising demands of colonial and postcolonial peoples, while forestalling a fundamental shift in the hierarchy of relations between Global North and South? How could the 'new nations' be persuaded to base their revolution on Locke rather than Marx?[5] While this Eurocentric choice was first posed in nineteenth-century Europe, there can be little doubt that the dominant answer to these questions, indeed their very framing, appeared in the lexicon of American-style social science. Older European philosophies of history and ideological struggles would be subsumed into seemingly more professional, rational forms of knowledge. Leaders of the new political and social sciences in the United States implored intellectuals to substitute ideology for ostensibly value-free sociology and adopt a methods-driven commitment to empirical data and 'value-neutral' observation (Buxton, 1985: 167–181; Gilman, 2003). Postwar American social science was dominated by a broad elite-led consensus that embraced the promise of the modern social welfare state. Stripped of class conflict and inequality, imperial wars and civilising missions – stripped of history – postwar discussions of the Social Question were increasingly reformulated through the language of behavioural, value-free social science. In the process, nineteenth-century social systems analysis received a makeover and 'modernisation theory' became the twentieth century's foremost conceptual and rhetorical framework

[5] As Arthur Schlesinger Jr. famously put it, the 'Charles River approach' to foreign aid represented 'a *very American effort* to persuade the developing countries to base their revolutions on *Locke* rather than Marx' (quoted in Packenham, 1973: 63, emphasis in original). Charles River connects the Cambridge campuses of MIT and Harvard where American-style social systems analysis and modernisation theory were pioneered. The emphasis in the discussion here is on the social science theory of modernisation in the context of counterinsurgency. Again, this is not to suggest that 'modernising missions' were only limited to the counterinsurgents. Numerous indigenous movements throughout the decolonising world engaged in modern practices of 'social engineering'.

to formulate United States policy towards the decolonising world, the distinctly American answer to the postwar *global* Social Question.

The analysis of 'society' as a corporate 'social system', recall, emerged in the middle of the nineteenth century. French philosopher Auguste Comte had argued that society was a totality comprised of interacting and functionally interrelated parts, just like the human body. The context of Comte's theory was the seeming passage from one 'social system' to another; that is, from feudal households to capitalist states. Eventually, he argued, industrial society would be surpassed and the inevitable end state of 'sociocracy' would emerge, when the science of positivism became the new religion of humanity: 'sociolatry' (Comte, 1875: 306).[6] Even more forcefully than Comte, English biologist Herbert Spencer (1877) argued that the evolutionary processes of societal development were analogous to how evolution worked in the natural world, especially in relation to organism growth. Stable societies, like healthy organisms, cohered around a set of interdependent institutions with more or less equivalent counterparts in all societies. The dominant tendency of society was towards integration; individuals and groups were drawn into dense networks of interdependence through 'socialisation', a term increasingly used from the middle of the nineteenth century to refer to the internalisation of 'norms', another term (like 'organisation') adapted from nineteenth-century biology. Those outside the core of industrial society – the proletariat, peasant societies – were being incorporated into bourgeois society, taking their functional place in its interdependent whole. Émile Durkheim and Henry Sumner Maine departed from Comte's organicist sociology, arguing that not all social formations followed the same developmental path. Nonetheless, in their different contexts, both Durkheim and Maine claimed that evidence of societal dysfunction – working-class unrest or continued native violence – indicated maladjustment in the transition from one stage of society to another. As discussed, the enduring tasks of social science would be to offer 'social' explanations and practical solutions to societal dysfunctions, almost always through

[6] 'To give an ideal embodiment of Sociology and still more of Sociocracy, such is the aim of our system of Sociolatry', wrote Comte (1875: 116). The transition from theocracy to sociocracy could be hastened by the advent of positivism (Comte, 1875: 209). The goal was to gain 'a clear idea of the necessary extension of Western Positivism to the Theocracies of the East' (Comte, 1875: 207).

intervention into problem populations – individuals, classes and eventually entire 'societies as a whole' – to integrate them into national or international society, the new modern system of household rule.

'The American Spencerians' that dominated the formative, 'progressive' years of American sociology believed in the possibility of social harmony if unfettered capitalism was regulated, while also precluding more radical solutions to the Social Question (Breslau, 2007). Lester Frank Ward, first President of the American Sociological Association, viewed sociologists as physicians, analysing the causes of and providing remedies for the pathologies that accompanied the modern 'social' condition. Ideally, society was moving in the direction of 'sociocracy', a term Ward adopted from Comte. A form of government and 'an art which corresponds to the science of sociology', sociocracy involved the 'fearless application of those principles ... in the interest of the whole social organism' (Ward in Chugerman, 1939: 327). The purpose of sociocratic government was to oversee 'a series of exhaustive experiments on the part of true scientific sociologists and sociological inventors working on the problems of social physics from the practical point of view' (Ward, 1906: 339).[7] Ward may have been called 'the American Aristotle', but his highly idiosyncratic worldview based on philosophical premises of his own making did not form the basis of a social science 'paradigm', hence his marginal role on the canon of sociology largely created for an American audience by the most influential sociologist of postwar America, Talcott Parsons (1937). Despite Ward's attempt to conceive an alternative to 'the negativism of the dominant *laissez faire* school' *and* the excesses of socialism, the term 'sociocracy' also never caught on, perhaps sounding too socialist. The more professional Parsons undertook fewer branding errors or lapses into eccentricity. He founded the Harvard Department of Social Relations in 1946 to provide a secure, well-resourced and highly prestigious institutional base for his equally ambitious goal of synthesising all forms of knowledge of the human world into one totalising theory.

[7] 'It is the special characteristic of the form of government that I have called sociocracy, resting as it does, directly upon the science of sociology,' wrote Ward (1893/1906: 330), 'to investigate the facts bearing on every subject, not for the purpose of depriving any class of citizens of the opportunity to benefit themselves, but purely and solely for the purpose of ascertaining what is for the best interests of society at large.'

Of all scholarly enterprises, *social system* theorists could plausibly claim to be paramount, offering the basis of a new intellectual hegemony. Social system analysis alone was able to conceive of the world as one interconnected whole. Political, economic, military and legal systems were all special cases of the more general social system, a biological metaphor Parsons (1951) adopted from Pareto (Gerhardt, 2002; López, 2003: 90–114). Knowledge of this total 'system' allowed social theorists to adjudicate between the more parochial but nonetheless functionally vital social sectors (such as economy, government and law) and to formulate domestic and foreign policy interventions. Like Durkheim and Ward, Parson's social systems analysis continued social theory's longstanding critique of neoclassical economics. The 'economy', Parsons claimed, was a special case of a more general theory of the social system (Parsons and Smelser, 1956). Moreover, the classical economists were wrong to put such weight on utility maximisation. Economic rationality could not comprehend societies outside the industrial West since their populations were deeply connected to consistent patterns of local cultures and institutions. On the other hand, Marx and his followers were also wrong. According to Parsons, Marxists failed to account properly for long-term social stability in democratic nations such as the United States. After all, Max Weber (1958) had shown that essentially cultural rather than economic forces determined the nature and character of capitalist societies, especially the level of class conflict and social stability. In part because of Parsons' reading of Weber, including his translation of *The Protestant Ethic*, much postwar American sociology eschewed lengthy discussions of irreducible political conflict and the bureaucratic 'iron-cage', as emphasised by Weber's more critical readers (Adorno and Horkheimer, 1944/1979). Moreover, Weber's concept of modernity was no longer historically situated in Europe nor associated with a very particular form of Western rationalism (Habermas, 1985/1987: 2). Instead, Weber was read almost entirely as a critic of Marx. Parsons' project for a non-ideological American social science relied heavily on this revaluation of Weber's legacy. Moreover, as Howard Brick has written, Parsons' social theory also hinged on an explicitly '*noneconomic* concept of society defined as the sphere of family, other primary groups, and community organisation; of norms governing a range of civil institutions from school to church; and of relations and interactions that shape personality' (Brick, 2000: 492, emphasis added). Civil society was no longer *burgerliche Gesellschaft*, rooted in relations of capitalist exchange. It was reconceived as an aggregate of non-governmental organisations, a place of integration, solidarity and community. The social system, of which civil society was a part, was a corporate body whose harmonious existence was the end goal of progressive 'social reform': a sociocratic vision in all but name.

Mid-century sociology in the United States was virtually identical with structural functionalism, a neo-evolutionary theory of social development that can be traced to Comte, Spencer, Durkheim and Maine. As already noted, societies were conceived as integrated social systems and elements within any social structure were differentiated by their functions. The social system comprised separate but interrelated spheres – political, economic, legal and cultural – and change in the system as a whole was produced by interactions between these domains. Stable societies, Parsons argued, possessed a common set of values against which individuals oriented their social behaviour; hence behaviour was fairly predictable and observable through scientific study (Parsons and Shils, 1951). One of Parsons' major innovations was his emphasis on the consistency of patterns of behaviour based on individuals conforming to their social roles. Individuals conformed when roles became institutionalised and moral and other sanctions were applied to non-conforming behaviours.[8] As structural functionalists had long argued, social dysfunction arose when institutions and value systems were not powerful enough to integrate individuals or groups, which corresponded to unpredictable behaviours that, in turn, were less amenable to social scientific analysis. Structural functionalism assumed the natural tendency was for social systems to be in equilibrium, for stable societies to exist like a healthy body. Moreover, if stable societies cohered around a set of interdependent social, economic and political institutions, then one of the most important tasks of social science was to describe how the point of social equilibrium transformed over time.

[8] 'Very quickly,' writes Isaac (2012: 173), 'human scientists convinced themselves that the men and women they studied were plastic creatures, whose beliefs and patterns of behavior were programmed by the culture in which they had been framed, but which, in conditions of social dislocation produced by mass mobilization and total war, could be decoded and manipulated by those with training in the psychology and sociology of "human relations".'

Despite enormous variation across human ways of life, structural functionalists suggested it was possible to compare the fundamental institutions of human societies across time and place given the functional character of the components of any social system; they fulfilled a basic set of human needs. Parsons' other major innovation was his method for measuring 'social change'. He created a developmental index of five so-called 'pattern variables' along which all societies could be placed and seen to progress. Personalities, cultures and entire societies could be categorised according to whether behaviour was underpinned more by self or collectivity; universalism or particularism; achievement or diffuseness; affectivity-neutral or affectivity; and achievement or ascription. These 'pattern variables' purported to be more scientifically rigorous than the older imperial distinction between primitive and modern, affording the possibility of objectively locating every society along the progressive spectrum from tradition to modern. Claims regarding the degree to which societies had so progressed, Parsons wrote were based on 'criteria congruent with that used in biological theory, calling more "advanced" the systems that display greater generalised adaptive capacity' (1966: 110). Following Spencer and Weber, there was a tendency for social systems to move in the direction of rationalisation, or 'structural differentiation'. Each form of social organisation was to be superseded by a progressively higher one, forming the basis of a neo-evolutionary and teleological theory of 'social' development. Structural functionalism was appealing to many because it was all-encompassing, providing the grounds for identifying a distinct social domain and an historical understanding of its forms, which were assumed to be converging over time towards one specific type.

The abstract character of structural functionalism provided the basis for universal, trans-historical, comparative studies of 'societies', concurrent with its origins in colonial anthropology (Stocking, 1984). 'Modernisation' became the more concrete social evolutionary theory of comparative political and economic 'development' for the US-led postwar, postcolonial order. Structural functionalism had always assumed historical convergence. However, economic historian Walt Rostow (1960), later advisor to President Kennedy and National Security Advisor to Johnson, gave content to the specific 'stages of economic growth'. All societies, claimed Rostow, developed along an evolutionary path through objective and observable stages. These stages progressed from traditional society to one in which the 'preconditions' of modernity take root, to 'take-off', then 'maturity', all culminating in the pinnacle of growth and development: the stage of 'high mass-consumption'. On this view, modern society had a single origin in the commercial societies of seventeenth-century northwest Europe. All societies were a variation of one of the five stages; all were moving towards capitalist markets and representative democracy. By this logic, the new 'developing' and postcolonial nations after 1945 should naturally evolve along the same path towards greater autonomy and self-reliance, building infrastructure and becoming more efficient. The movement or 'development' of societies along this path was conceived as a perfectly natural process, the 'normal' path to growth, albeit something that might happen at different speeds. Moreover, since all social orders were interdependent functional wholes, changes in one variable, or social sector, led to changes in every other. Hence it was an article of faith in modernisation theory that the healthy transition from peasant to industrial society would involve not only the 'economy' of these 'new nations', but a wholesale cultural and social revolution in their entire ways of life, including kinship structure and family (Levy, 1949/1968). Social theories of the 'stages of growth' were not 'merely descriptive', Rostow claimed. 'They have an inner logic and continuity. They have an analytic bone-structure, rooted in a dynamic theory of production' (1960: 12–13). To emphasise these points, Rostow evoked what he called the 'essentially biological field of economic growth'. In an argument no less '*oikonomia* determinist' than the most vulgar readings of Marx, societies were natural, organic wholes, 'interacting organisms' driven forward by changes in the modes of production (Rostow, 1960: 2, 3).

Unlike the socio-biologist Herbert Spencer, Parsons and Rostow did not believe that the healthy functioning of self-equilibrating societies was necessarily automatic. Nations at a particularly vulnerable stage in their development were susceptible to a dreadful developmental disease, the perversion of modernity that was communism.[9] When society's natural tendencies towards equilibrium were at fault – or an

[9] In fact, as many have noted, 'Rostow's "stages of growth" were little more than Marx's dynamic of historical materialism with a happier, capitalist ending' (Milne, 2007: 170; Engerman et al., 2003). Indeed, Rostow's claims are the mid-twentieth-century rendition of the stadial thinking that accompanied European theories of history since the 'discoveries' (Meek, 1976; Jahn, 2000).

alien force such as communism was attacking from outside – there was a need for stabilising interventions to act as a remedy. Limited bursts of progressive activity could also come from outside 'society' to counterbalance and even eradicate the threat from deviant, abnormal modernisation. In accordance with the first theories of social policy in industrial society, modernisation theorists argued that it was perfectly possible to normalise the movement from traditional to modern society through targeted, expert- and US-led intervention in the 'developing' world. As American 'progressive history' itself had apparently shown, the state was the most efficient and effective bureaucratic instrument for intervening into problem aspects of society. Rather than socialist revolution, modernisation could be achieved through planned capitalism and foreign aid in the postcolonial world; that is, through infusing the 'spirit of capitalism' into traditional societies. Modernisation theorists, many of whom like Rostow, Lucian Pye and Ithiel de Sola Pool would become government advisors, proscribed a number of remedies for development dysfunctions for hundreds of post-independence countries, ranging from economic assistance to the establishment of military dictatorship to full-scale military assault (Kolko, 1988; Simpson, 2008; Karabell, 1999).

Modernisation theorists shared an essentially sociocratic liberal vision. The purpose of the state – which was analytically distinct from society – was to transform society in the desired progressive direction, one that promoted welfare, efficiency and social order. In line with many of the proponents of Progressive Era reform in the United States, modernisation theorists believed that political agendas could be transformed into technical projects. All political and economic problems were amenable to technical and social solutions.[10] Seen this way, the ideals of modernisation theory were those of American liberalism in the immediate postwar period. As Nils Gilman summarises, these were 'state-guided industrialism; an exaltation of rationalism, science, and expertise as the guide for democratic institutions; and convergence on

[10] Here modernisation theory also drew lessons from the organisational theories of the nineteenth century. Among the earliest of such theorists was Saint-Simon who built on a distinction between the 'social' and the 'political' to separate (social) 'administration' from (political) 'government', a contrast that was central to Engels and Lenin. Politics could be taken out of administration, to 'replace', in Engels later formulation, 'the government of persons with the administration of things' (Wolin, 1960: 376–379).

a consensual model of social organization based on progressive taxation and state provision of social benefit' (2003: 2–3; Hartz, 1955).[11] In its most idealistic form, modernisation theory claimed to be underpinned by a similar sense of social solidarity between the 'developed' and 'developing' world that, since Durkheim, has been said to define liberal society from the nineteenth century and many claim is the origin of all essentially 'humanitarian intervention', domestic and overseas (Bass, 2008; Barnett, 2011; Barnett and Weiss, 2011). For modernisation theorists, the United States was on its own path towards a benevolent welfare state; abundance was making class conflict irrelevant; managed democracy, guided by technocratic elites, mitigated disorder. In the new nations, similarly meliorist and technocratic governments would slowly integrate the world's poor into the capitalist system, undermining the evident and widespread appeals of communism.

Needless-to-say, modernisation theory was based on a revisionist account of the rise of industrial capitalism in Europe, downplaying, even erasing empire, class exploitation, political conflict and constant war (Halperin, 2004; Gendzier, 1985). Moreover, despite its affiliation with social liberalism, modernisation theory contributed to a conservative agenda in the United States. To be in a position to tell the rest of the world the right way to be modern required the US to have achieved modernity. If already modern, then US society and economy did not require extensive reform, let alone anything more radical or revolutionary. Furthermore, Talcott Parsons had claimed that the trajectory of all social systems was towards social conformity. The accompanying theory of government became known as 'elite democracy'; the so-called 'political system' created order and stability around a broad ideological

[11] This vision of broad consensus did not correspond to how the United States actually was, rather what many social liberals wanted it to be. The summers of 1965–1968, for example, 'saw more than three hundred episodes of civil disorder, resulting in two hundred deaths and the destruction of several thousand businesses ... In several cases, quelling urban riots became a domestic job for military troops' (Light, 2003: 4). According to Samuel Yette (1971: 15), the United States was 'in the midst of two wars: (1) a war of "attrition" (genocide) against the colonized colored people of Indochina, and (2) an expeditionary "law and order" campaign (repression – selective genocide) against the colonized colored people of the United States. Although nonaligned, both colonized groups ... [were] victims of the *same* war, though in different theatres ... The colonized blacks inside the United States were the subject of numerous and extensive studies, special programs, White House conferences, and plain gawking curiosity.' Yette was fired from *Newsweek* for expressing these views.

consensus that was legitimated through the periodic electoral competition between officials who shared in this ideological consensus.[12] Although not explicitly articulated in these terms, the notion of consensus implied nothing less than the final answer to the Social Question. In Parsons' distinctive formulation, 'Do we have or can we develop a knowledge of human social relations that can serve as the basis of rational "engineering" control? ... The evidence is unequivocally affirmative ... It is here, and that fact ends the argument' (in Latham, 2000: 49). The Social Question that had dominated Europe since the nineteenth century had finally been answered in twentieth-century America and was articulated through the social theory of modernisation. Its equally revisionist theory of world history became the most influential starting point for analysing all social systems, from the United States itself to the 'new nations' and the emerging worldwide international system (Parsons, 1961; 1967). It was surely difficult to doubt the power and reality of an independent, self-regulating 'American society'. It was a short leap from structural functionalist claims about the reality of this entity to a corresponding vision of the wider 'developing' world organised into bounded national societies with discrete, functionally interrelated social systems. Under American hegemony, the new postcolonial order would be steered in the direction of a system of self-regulating nation-states, functioning national households, interacting in the largest social system of them all, international 'society'.[13] If, in certain circumstances, a self-regulating nation-state did not exist, then a functioning national household might have to be created.

The passing of traditional society: building the House of Ngo

Both France and the United States expected Viet Minh guerrillas, led by Ho Chi Minh, to be easily defeated with the resumption of French colonial rule in Vietnam after the withdrawal of Japanese forces at the

[12] Daniel Bell (1960) argued that the major ideological struggles that defined nineteenth-century Europe were at an end in 1950s America.

[13] '"Society",' as Giddens put it, 'has a useful double meaning ... signifying a bounded system, and social association in general. An emphasis upon regionalization helps to remind us that the degree of "systemness" in social systems is very variable and that "societies" rarely have easily specifiable boundaries – until, at least, we enter the modern world of nation-states' (1984: xxvi; see also Albert and Buzan, 2013).

end of World War II. Despite Mao Zedong's success in China, guerrilla tactics were never a truly formidable obstacle to the global ambitions of imperial states. Throughout the nineteenth century and into the twentieth, Europe's empires had proven highly adept at repressing local rebellions. In the immediate postwar period, French forces were confident in their ability to pacify Indochina relatively quickly through a massive show of force. Instead, as Singer and Langdon (2004: 253) put it, they wound up fighting 'a nineteenth-century colonial war in Indochina through to 1954'. In addition to the use of conventional forces, drawn from both metropolitan France and its colonies, General Pierre Boyer de la Tour also attempted the *tauche d'huile* ('oil spot') method in Cochin-China, which was first conceived by Galliéni and Lyautey in their late nineteenth-century forays into Vietnam. Civil and military authorities coerced local populations into abandoning national or socialist aspirations. After French forces had 'secured' a village, Mobile Administrative Groups for Operations attempted to purge Viet Minh political leaders, assign new more 'traditional' ones, and reopen markets (Andradé, 1990: 21). While such techniques may have garnered some French gains in the high imperial period, the global upheavals following World War II had generated the historical and ideological conditions to produce a distinctive politico-military strategy – guerrilla war – making local resistance much more difficult to defeat, despite *tauche d'huile* methods. Revolutionary guerrilla warfare did not emerge completely new with communist victory on China's mainland. But Mao's doctrine for fighting peasant-based campaigns changed understanding of how successful war could be waged.

Despite $2.6 billion of aid from the United States, France could not sustain its efforts against the People's Army of Vietnam, extricating itself via the face-saving Geneva Accords of 1954. The United States opposed any negotiated settlement with People's Army representatives for it would lead to a relatively popular communist takeover of the entire country. The solution was to turn the anti-colonial war against France into a civil war among Vietnamese. The Geneva Accords allowed for a temporary division of the country, with reunification following general elections in 1956. In fact, two ostensibly independent nations were created, communist North Vietnam with its capital in Hanoi and the authoritarian South in Saigon under the pro-American leadership of Ngo Dinh Diem. With full United States backing, Diem refused to hold national elections. American support for South Vietnam was much more than assistance to an ally in civil war. It was the foundation, the necessary basis for such an ally to exist. After World War II, the United States much preferred to establish 'counterinsurgency-client-states', primarily through training and arming indigenous police and security forces, to direct and open military occupation. This form of decentralised household despotism was United States policy towards Vietnam from 1953. From taking office that year, the Eisenhower administration had nonetheless committed itself to defend the territorial integrity of South Vietnam, to creating and then sustaining the despotic House of Ngo.

The United States would be far more active than Britain and France in their policies of indirect colonial rule, in their attempts to rule through decentralised household despotism in Vietnam. By 1955, the 'paramilitary professors began moving in' (McCarthy, 1967: 63). The CIA-sponsored Michigan State University Group, led by political scientist Wesley R. Fishel, was tasked with creating a police force in South Vietnam, overseeing 'refugee' resettlement, conducting 'cultural studies' of local populations, teaching public administration, and offering other forms of 'technical assistance' to the House of Ngo, including a national identity card programme (Ernst, 1998; Kuzmarov, 2012). The extent of US resources devoted to creating and sustaining the multiple departments of Diem's government was part of a concerted internationalisation of public administration after World War II, and was heavily influenced by structural functionalist social theories.[14] The Carnegie, Ford and Rockefeller Foundations all invested in international training programmes. The Ford Foundation spent $54 million on international programmes between 1951 and 1954, giving scholars of public administration a new role providing technical advice to 'new nations' (Berman, 1983; Guilhot, 2011) Enormous amounts of federal funding were allocated for defence-related research and training of so-called 'foreign area specialists', further integrating university campuses into United States grand strategy. In 1956, the International Cooperation Administration was established to manage foreign aid, including a programme for public administration experts to join

[14] As Brick (2000: 508) notes, during World War II, Talcott Parsons 'lectured on the social structures of China and Japan at the School for Overseas Administration, set up at Harvard to train military officers for work in occupied territories'.

diplomatic missions in Asia and Latin America (Oren, 2003: 127; Simpson, 1998; Solovey and Cravens, 2012).

The level of financial assistance to South Vietnam, more than $1 billion in economic and military aid between 1955 and 1961 alone, tied the United States to the fate of the corrupt and unpopular House of Ngo. In 1955, an import-subsidisation programme was introduced and by 1959 more than $1 billion in US goods had entered South Vietnam. Cities were flooded with 'thousands upon thousands of cars, motorcycles, televisions, stereos, refrigerators, and other modern consumer goods' (Gibson, 1986: 226). In a language that evoked Galliéni's 'oil spot' method of pacification, Walt Rostow explained that a country is ready for take-off 'when the old blocks and resistances to steady growth are finally overcome. The forces making for economic progress, which yielded limited bursts and enclaves of modern activity, expand and come to dominate the society' (1960: 7; see also Pearce, 2001). The homology between counterinsurgency and logics of *oikonomia* would not be lost on US military strategists. Just as counterinsurgents would argue that the first task of pacification was to create an enclave of security, hold it and then build on it, a modern economy would grow from 'limited bursts and enclaves' into self-sustaining economic growth, supported by functionally related social, political and cultural sectors. In fact, by 1960 almost 80 per cent of the total US aid for South Vietnam was for military ends, a proportion easily justified in modernisation theory terms (Carter, 2008: 75–76; Latham, 2000: 162).

In *The Passing of Traditional Society*, Daniel Lerner (1958) claimed that 'a new functional elite' was created in the process of modernisation (see also Apter, 1965). In accord with elite theories of democracy, ideally the select few would be accountable through elections. A degree of democratic participation in leader selection in the 'political' sphere helped legitimise 'the economy' and its inequalities. However, in the difficult transitional period from one social system to another it may be necessary to harness the military's well-known capacity to provide stability and order. In the words of Talcott Parsons' student Marion J. Levy, the military is 'the most efficient type of organisation for combining maximum rates of modernization with maximum levels of stability and control' (1996: 603). Put differently, the military possessed enormous non-military 'governmental potential' (Pye, 1962a: 9, 29–34; 1962b; Klare et al., 1981). As the political scientist and advisor Lucian Pye stated, 'armies in underdeveloped countries can perform many essentially civilian functions more effectively than the existing civilian institutions', including public safety, civil administration and communications (1962a: 8). Seen this way, the army was the modern institution *par excellence* since it was able to act in the interests of 'society as a whole', the modern national household. The military was especially effective at breaking down tribal and class identities. Above all, since they understood the need for authority and hierarchy, military leaders were best placed to build ideological consensus within their societies on the rational form of economic growth. Accordingly, United States military aid for counterinsurgency states across Asia, Africa and Latin America was tightly linked to 'stabilising' economic and technical reforms. 'Stable political systems,' Pye wrote in memorandum to USAID, 'are ... more developed than unstable ones' (1963: 7; see also Janowitz, 1964). With the help of American political scientists, Diem created a powerful secret police that was used to kill tens of thousands of Viet Minh sympathisers and imprison and torture thousands more. The United States practice of building police and military capacities to maintain 'stability' through 'foreign internal defence', building and sustaining counterinsurgency states overseas, was simply the latest system of decentralised despotic household rule, different only in form and ambition from the methods employed by imperial Britain and France.

North Vietnamese Army and National Liberation Front forces continued to successfully infiltrate and disrupt the House of Ngo in the South. The number of US advisors sent to train Diem's army rose to 900 in 1960, but they were not yet engaging in large-scale combat missions themselves. Given the prevailing social theory concerning Vietnam's dysfunction, direct combat operations by US forces were viewed as counterproductive. As Lucian Pye explained, all 'developing' and 'transitional societies' were prone to a 'penetration' and 'legitimacy' crisis. 'At the heart of the penetration crisis,' he claimed, was 'the issue of how to get government to the people' (1963: 27).[15] Financial

[15] The American social science version of Britain's Mau Mau 'psycho-docs' was Lucian W. Pye, who was also fascinated by what he considered to be the psychological ambivalences for individuals and societies of postcolonial national development. In societies transitioning from tradition to modern, individuals lose their sense of identity and thus become attracted to dysfunctional belief systems like communism. Drawing on interviews with

support and technical advice would help Diem build a relationship with his people. As in British Malaya, where Pye had conducted major studies, the penetration crisis was especially acute in rural Vietnam where most people existed almost entirely isolated from central government. As leading strategist, Roger Hilsman put it, United States policy was

> based on the assumption that villages in Southeast Asia are turned inward on themselves and have little or no sense of identification with either the national government or Communist ideology – that the villages are isolated, physically, politically, and psychologically. In such circumstances it is not difficult to create a guerrilla movement.
>
> (in Elliott, 2003: 209)

But, as many would claim then and now, guerrilla communism was defeated in Malaya because the British successfully penetrated Chinese populations, bringing government to the people and winning over their 'hearts and minds' (Thompson, 1966). Through the House of Ngo, the United States would, as one advisor put it, similarly 'reinstate government processes and services, restore productive life among the inhabitants of the area, and develop national spirit and good government' (Komer, 1966: 18).[16] An Overseas Internal Defence Policy document put it thus: 'the *ultimate and decisive target is the people*. Society itself is at war and the resources, motives and targets of the struggle are found almost wholly within the local population' (United States, 1962: 7–8 III D, emphasis in original).[17] This element of counterinsurgency doctrine was disseminated through a succession of State Department-run five-week seminars attended by AID, CIA and State Department officials, which included instruction from Walt Rostow and Lucian Pye. 'Young West Pointers,' comments Mary McCarthy, 'were turned into political strategists on the spot by crash courses in

former communist guerrillas in Malaya, Pye argued that young Chinese people were 'members of a generation in transition' (1956: 8; see also Pye, 1962c).

16 Komer (1972) wrote a 'lessons learned' report on the Malaya emergency.

17 Attention to the population has long been central to small wars doctrine. Since the beginning of the 1960s, the various iterations of 'counterinsurgency' have consistently stressed the significance of the population and appropriate civil-military relations. In the 1920s, 1930s and 1940s, US armed forces serially intervened in Latin America, and civilian agencies usually the State Department, were almost always involved (see Long, 2008: 4).

Communism and native psychology' (1967: 65). The creed of winning hearts and minds would be vastly subsidised and radicalised.

No such hearts and minds or nation-building victory was achieved in Malaya. The British army took 12 years to defeat a disorganised guerrilla movement in that country not through 'winning over' the population, but through depopulation and re-concentration. Nonetheless, modernisation theory gave an American facelift to the much older social language that was used to reconceive depopulation and concentration as one of protection, development and improvement. In a speech to the American Hospital Association, Roger Hilsman reported how 'President Roosevelt once said that "Dr. New Deal" had been succeeded by "Dr. Win the War", but in guerrilla wars in underdeveloped nations both "doctors" are needed. Military action and a social new deal have to proceed together' (in Preston, 2006: 106; see also Hirschman, 1989). In other words, the ideals of technocracy used to control labour relations in industrial societies could be applied in the 'new nations' (Kerr, 1964). Social security, Rostow claimed, served to 'soften the harshness of a society' (1960: 74). Armed social work served to soften the harshness of war on 'society'. 'Presented that way,' as Latham (2000: 196) rightly notes, 'understanding the situation in Vietnam did not demand a thorough knowledge of that country's history or culture. It merely required a familiarity with America's own heroic narrative.' In a less heroic language, but nonetheless drawing on well-worn answers to the Social Question, and more fundamentally the practical task of household management, Ithiel de Sola Pool explained that 'it is clear that order depends on somehow compelling newly mobilised strata to return to a measure of passivity and defeatism from which they have recently been aroused by the process of modernization. At least temporarily, the maintenance of order requires a lowering of newly acquired aspirations and levels of political activity' (1998: 266; see also Ferguson, 1994). To describe and implement the attempt to produce passivity and defeatism in Vietnam, the new and enduring lexicon of 'counterinsurgency' was introduced (Gentile, 2012: 388). The Kennedy administration, taking office in 1961, wanted a more progressive-sounding term than 'pacification' or 'counter-revolutionary'. Like 'sociocracy', 'counter-revolutionary' sounded un-American. Unlike sociocracy, the language of counterinsurgency would endure.

'Those aren't houses. They're just huts'

Rural communities in North Vietnam were clearly providing cover and support for Viet Cong fighters. American political strategists faced a similar dilemma to the British in Kenya. How could support for the Viet Cong be acknowledged and addressed without assigning *political* consciousness and agency to villagers, which implied United States actions lacked legitimacy? The tension was resolved with the abandonment of Sir Henry Sumner Maine's (1876: 110–111) romantic image of the traditional village as a place of simple and paternalistic governance in which 'Authority, Custom, or Chance are ... the great sources of law' and replacing it with next generation sociology. Heavily evoking Durkheim's socio-biological language, Pool explained that rural villages in Vietnam were not pervaded by age-old customary laws, but by 'normless violence' (1968: 14). The village societies in Vietnam were 'anomic' and 'ridden by fear' (1968: 19). Strong traces of political realism are also evident in Pool's claim that the Viet Cong had simply 'used Communist ideology to channel and control violence that already was in part endemic in the situation' (1968: 10). Communist guerrillas were finding support in village households not because they promised and delivered national independence and collectivist land reform, but because they offered 'protection from urban predators' (Pool, 1968: 15). The land reform pursued by the Viet Cong was not the basis of a new or legitimate *oikonomia*, but simply an extension of older networks of patronage. In such a context, peasants could have no meaningful politics other than survival and communists were taking full advantage. Communists were simply the latest in a long line of external predators, offering 'protection' in exchange for material support and intelligence. To be sure, the village provided a strong base of support for guerrilla fighters, but this could not be an expression of peasant *politics*; it was a product of deeper 'sociological' conditions (cf. Wolf, 1969; Scott, 1976).

This denial of peasant agency through sociological generalisation would underpin a classic trope of counterinsurgency writing first articulated as a general social science law during the war in Vietnam and would be frequently evoked thereafter, most recently in Afghanistan and Iraq. 'In any circumstances, whatever the cause,' French officer David Galula advised policymakers in Vietnam, 'the population is split among three groups: (1) an active minority for the cause, (2) a neutral majority, (3) an active minority against the cause' (1963/2006: 70). The 1963 Department of the Army Field Manual, *Counterguerrilla Operations* (FM 31–16), similarly claimed that 'a great part of the population has no concern about the struggle and is sympathetic to neither combatant' (United States, 1963: 7). In turn, Galula's writings developed theories drawn from an idealisation of late nineteenth- and early twentieth-century French pacification wars in North Africa, an idealisation primarily created for domestic consumption in France (Porch, 1986: 376–407). First resident general of French Morocco, Hubert Lyautey, claimed that 'the great mass of the Moorish people were more or less indifferent to political problems' (in Maurois, 1931/1932: 253). Transposed to Vietnam, the majority of people were conceived as essentially neutral regarding the *oikonomia* in which they lived. The masses are 'naturally indifferent to political matters', even in the middle of a war-zone, in the age of de-colonisation, in any circumstances, whatever the cause.[18] The underlying assumptions of such claims are more thoroughly examined in the next chapter. Suffice it to say here, in the Vietnamese context, credibility was given to them by evoking, again, the pervasiveness and anomic character of village violence. Ithiel de Sola Pool circulated old proverbs in which 'the Vietnamese peasant, faced with civil disorder, bends with the wind to whichever side is there with force' (1968: 11). If Vietnamese peasants had no meaningful political agency or even consciousness, then what kind of subjects were they?

United States population policy imagined peasants as entirely *social* beings; that is, as objects of household administration. They were malleable and, above all, primarily concerned with the processes of life, or at least they could be made so. The loyalty, even the entire way of life, of people in rural Vietnam was perceived as truly plastic, perfectly molten and ready to be shaped by military and social intervention.[19] It was as if the only thing required was for Vietnamese villagers to let go and become absorbed by the molten mass of their social existence. In other words, the United States could win in Vietnam if the social

[18] These words are from the July 1959 NSC 51, 'US Policy towards Southeast Asia' (quoted in Shafer, 1988: 84).

[19] Cf. Britain's Liberal Party Prime Minister, David Lloyd George's words from 1917, 'The whole state of society is more or less molten and you can stamp upon that molten mass almost anything so long as you do it with firmness and determination' (quoted in Rodgers, 1998: 291).

milieu were radically transformed, if, as the *Handbook for Military Support of Pacification* put it, 'the political, economic, and sociological imbalances which are the root causes ... of insurgency' were rectified (United States, 1968: 1). Overseas Internal Defense Policy similarly stated, 'Social patterns and institutions in most under-developed nations ... are often a legacy of shapeless, frequently illogical political units which are derived, in part, from a colonial past' (United States, 1962: 3, II B-3). Hence, alongside a major escalation of the use of American airpower, aggressively pushed by now Kennedy advisor Walt Rostow, millions of Vietnamese villagers were forcibly removed from their homes and regrouped into more militarily defensible, more logical and functional social units. Observers involved in the process marvelled at the mobility of village households. As one Air Force sergeant put it, 'everybody just picked up their stuff and went somewhere else. Those aren't houses. They're just huts' (in Cullather, 2006: 35). Entire villages were levelled with ploughs and bulldozers; homesteads were burned down to signal to people that they would never be able to return. From 1959, Diem had already created Agglomeration Camps and Agrovilles for population resettlement. These programmes (and names) were dropped in 1960 (Zasloff, 1962/1963). Revised by the economist Eugene Staley, the new Strategic Hamlet programme was to be far larger in scale, more efficient and compensation more munificent. Because both military and social knowledge is cumulative, lessons would be learned from several sources, including French colonial experience, British practices in Malaya and Kenya, and the House of Ngo itself.

The sequence of depopulation and concentration proceeded in the conventional way, beginning with military operations using heavy firepower to 'clear' a territory of Viet Cong forces. Villagers were then marched at gunpoint to this now 'secure' space where they were forced to dig moats and create a defensible perimeter with barbed-wire fencing and bamboo stakes. The territory in the new villages was divided into plots on which families were mandated to build their accommodation and start work on their new farms; legal titles were issued for individual farm units.[20] 'To get a new house free,' an American

[20] Interestingly in this context of belief in the social malleability of peasants is the etymology of the term 'accommodation'. According to the Oxford English Dictionary, in classical Latin, *accommodātin* referred to the 'action of fitting

official explained, 'even though that would seem only fair in the abstract, would be unfair to them as human beings...: investing their own labor and their own money would make them feel that the house was really *theirs*' (in McCarthy, 1967: 20, emphasis in original). Rural Reconstruction Teams took a census of all families, distributed identity cards and created a photographic map that included information on all inhabitants and recorded past connections with organised communism. As in Malaya, male villagers were drafted into hamlet militia and tasked to perform 'self-defence patrols', protecting the hamlet from inevitable guerrilla infiltration, whether military, political or psychological. Curfews and checkpoints were used to control resources and food. From 1962, defoliants cleared the jungles of Viet Cong, as well as denied food through crop destruction and wetland drainage (Komer, 1970b; Popkin, 1970; Nighswonger, 1967). The military purpose was the physical isolation of insurgents, their separation from food, intelligence, and recruits. Re-concentration made it easier for US and South Vietnamese forces to coerce the population into ending material or political support for the Viet Cong; that is, 'to fabricate a "front" in a frontless war' (Cullather, 2006: 41).

Drawing directly on Britain's public diplomacy campaign in Malaya, US policies in Vietnam were re-described as attempts to win over hearts and minds. Like all forms of household despotism, Strategic Hamlets combined discipline with limited and selective welfare provision. As Robert Thompson, head of the British Advisory Mission to Vietnam, explained, clearly drawing on personal experience, 'the regrouping of houses, which at first sight might have seemed a hardship, has compensating advantages' (1966: 125). In any case, he continued, socially inferior versions of Strategic Hamlets were indigenous to Asia. 'In many rural areas particularly frontier and mountain regions,' Thompson wrote, 'the defended village has existed for centuries as a means of protection against border raiders, local bandits and even man-eating tigers' (1966: 123; see also Tanham, 1966; Fisher, 1996). On the 'upside', social programmes, teachers and health workers revealed to peasants the benefits of living in the House of Ngo. As R.W. Komer (1966) wrote in a progress report on the 'Other War', the

or adapting, willingness to oblige' and entered early modern English as such in the sixteenth century. The use of the term 'accommodation' to refer to lodgings enters later in the seventeenth century.

name given to the population strategy, this was 'not just a war of blood, bombs and bullets' (see also Ahern, 2001; Cooper et al., 1972). Passive peasants were now on a journey to social empowerment and healthier social relations. If only the villagers would more actively join in something so inspirational to its administrators. As Edward G. Lansdale put it in a 1962 speech to the Green Berets, 'adding to the material things in a community, improving the water supply with a new well or pump, drainage for the streets, a generator for village power the community finds itself becoming linked up closely to the nation, a real part of something bigger' (in Cullather, 2006: 35). Or in the words of a minister for Revolutionary Development, the House of Ngo was 'determined to realise a social revolution in the rural area, aiming at destroying the present gloomy, *old life* and replacing it with a *brighter and nicer new life*' (in Gibson, 1986: 290, emphasis in original).

As in Malaya, a long line of commentators reeled off lists of social services that were now – or could be – available to the displaced. Compensation took the form of new 'schools, clinics, markets, improved agricultural methods, water supplies, electricity, radio programmes, newspapers and improved communications' (Thompson, 1966: 125). The emergency programme included 'temporary housing, supplies of clothes and household goods for those forced to abandon their belongings, a temporary subsistence allowance for emergency feeding, medical and healthcare, primary schooling for children, vocational training in new skills, resettlement, and reintegration into the Vietnamese economy' (Komer, 1966: 30; Hunt, 1995: 31–44). Armed social workers were involved in the building of schools, roads, bridges, irrigation dams and canals, breakwaters and dikes, the establishment of teacher and agricultural training, seed distribution and animal husbandry programmes (to distribute thousands of chickens, pigs and ducks). New revolutionary development cadres created medical dispensaries and marketplaces, performed surgical operations and immunisations, and distributed sewing kits. No wonder counterinsurgency could so readily seem to be domestic politics by other means (Kurac, 2011). If the essential problem in Vietnam was village isolation and *anomie*, then the eminently good housekeeping task of 'Quiet Warriors' was 'to help knit the country together' (United States, 1966: 20; Marquis, 2000; Petersen, 1989). From the perspective of the progressive social engineers, many of them social workers from the United States, cruel actions and harsh conditions could be converted into something more benign. Carpet-bombing, environmental destruction and territorial cleansing were unfortunate, even cruel. But the good housekeeping tasks that accompanied these practices in Vietnam seemed worthy of international support.

The other 'Free World' military forces that participated in civic action included the Republic of Korea, Australia, New Zealand, Thailand and the Philippines. The Federal Republic of Germany was especially active with refugees. By 1966, 32 offered non-military support, up from nine in 1963, including Britain, France, Germany, Canada, Malaysia, Israel and Iran.[21] Apart from the material aid from a number of Asian nations, the United States hoped that the appearance of 'Asians in the provinces, especially Filipinos, would also help' (Latham, 2000: 188). A number of US-based voluntary agencies led social programmes in the villages, including the American Red Cross and the Vietnam Christian Service. Ordinary American citizens participated in the Food for Peace programme by donating clothing, medical supplies, school equipment and food (Komer, 1966: 30). In Operation Concern, more than 100 pregnant sows were airlifted from Kansas (McCarthy, 1967: 23). Highlighting the expanding and much discussed ability of the United States to convene a vast array of governmental organisations to achieve its ends, specialist agencies of the United Nations participated in 'non-military' activities, including the UN Development Program, UN Children's Fund, World Health Organization, International Labour Organization and International Atomic Energy Agency. An additional way in which the 'footprints of America' would be imprinted on Vietnam was the proposed Mekong Delta project of dams and dikes modelled on the Tennessee Valley Authority, the largest regional planning agency of the US federal government. The project drew on expertise from 20 other nation-states and 11 United Nations agencies (Carter, 2008: 170).[22] One of the defining features of US-led international social regulation, including

[21] The full list is Argentina, Australia, Belgium, Brazil, Canada, China, Denmark, Ecuador, France, Germany, Great Britain, Greece, Guatemala, Iran, Ireland, Israel, Italy, Japan, Korea, Laos, Luxembourg, Malaysia, Netherlands, New Zealand, Norway, Pakistan, Philippines, Spain, Switzerland, Thailand, Turkey and Venezuela (Komer, 1966: 49).

[22] 'I want to leave the footprints of America in Vietnam ... We're going to turn the Mekong into a Tennessee Valley' (President Johnson quoted in Ekbladh, 2010: 190; see also Adas, 2006: 281–338).

during counterinsurgency, has been its ability to proliferate and coordinate a variety of 'public' and 'private' regulatory institutions, one of the defining features of state-led social policy within and from liberal capitalist states.

After Diem's CIA-backed assassination in 1963, the new military regime under Duong Van Minh withdrew all materials that referenced Diem and Strategic Hamlets.[23] The name was dropped, but the basic principles of the successor programmes remained largely the same. Operation Sunrise and New Life hamlets were also defined by depopulation, re-concentration and coerced collaboration in exchange for minimal supplies of food and shelter. President Johnson had already approved a major escalation of covert action and made a secret decision to launch an unprecedented air offensive and commit US ground forces to independent search and destroy missions. National Security Advisor Walt Rostow the 'development theorist gave way to the bombing advocate as South Vietnam proved immune to modernization on the Western model' (Milne, 2008: 109). From March 1965, Operation Rolling Thunder continued with breaks for the remainder of the war. Six million tonnes of explosives were dropped in the then largest aerial bombardment in history. By the end of 1965, 184,300 American troops were in Vietnam. Within four years the total had reached 536,000. Despite its cruelty and failures, forced resettlement and concentration remained at the heart of population strategy, supported by teams of paramilitary professors. The economists and statisticians importing social systems analysis to Vietnam believed that the basic issues were technical and social. The quantitative revolution for modelling weapons development and procurement pioneered at RAND and MIT – developed to prepare for nuclear war – was transferred to American counterinsurgency in Vietnam.

Social scientists used the latest statistical methods to measure indices of success (more popular than indices of failure) in the pacification war. New model pacification in Vietnam involved far greater

[23] As Gibson (1986: 293) has noted, 'name changes in the pacification war occurred at least every two years starting from the French effort: Reconstruction, Civic Action, Land Development Centers, Agglomeration Camps, Agrovilles, Strategic Hamlets, New Life Hamlets, Hoc Tap (Cooperation), Chien Thang (Victory), Rural Reconstruction, Revolutionary Reconstruction, Revolutionary Development'.

resources and greater mobilisation of information technologies to understand the 'socio-economic' and demographic dimensions of the target population. Secretary of Defence Robert McNamara had established the Office of Systems Analysis, based on the assumption that the national security system needed to be understood as an organic whole. Although Parsons sought to excise Herbert Spencer from American sociology textbooks, Parsons helped create the most scientifically advanced heirs to Spencer. Society was a self-regulating organism, a complex social system and living organism. The science of systems, cybernetics, appended the notion that machines too were systems of communication and control that could interact; through computer simulation, all problems could be understood through and potentially managed by systems analysis. Mathematical formulae, game theory and econometrics simulated social processes, made predictions and ultimately framed advice to state managers. The Simulmatics Corporation (1967), headed by Ithiel de Sola Pool, pioneered large-scale population surveys for South Vietnam, using computers and mathematical game theory for the 'simulation of human behavior' (Pool and Abelson, 1961). Hamlet Evaluation Worksheets generated security and development scores, which were then entered into computers to yield maps and charts measuring pacified territory (Brighton, 1968). Advisors scored individual hamlets across 18 separate indicators related to Viet Cong military and political activities; friendly security and administrative/political activities; and health, education, welfare and economic development. After analysis of these scores and the confidence with which they were made, specific hamlets were placed in one of five alphabetical categories (A–E). 'Psychocultural cold warriors' also engaged in smaller scale 'psychological research on Viet Cong defectors, government soldiers, and Vietnamese villagers' (Rohde, 2009, 2011).

Planners persisted with the view that policy failures in Vietnam were the result of corruption in the South Vietnamese government, coordination and administrative problems, or the imbalance between the size of the population to be administered and the allocated resources. Properly funded and implemented, depopulation and concentration *must* eventually defeat the Viet Cong. Given the available resources, there was always hope that more funding, more advisors, new collaborators, new despots, could overcome the essentially social-technical problem of pacification. As Komer put it,

> we pragmatically sought to build the new model pacification on existing assets, as a concerted series of admittedly inefficient country-wide programs, which nonetheless seemed capable of gradual improvement to the point where they cumulatively offered hope of saturating the enemy and enabling us to build faster than he could destroy.
>
> (Komer, 1970b: 4)

This optimistic faith in the power of managerial prowess was distinctly American, but it was also born of logic fundamental to the initial rise of social regulation and its management of life processes, the tendency to growth and expansion. No matter how ineffective at first, additional social engineering could lead to victory in the end. 'It is difficult', Komer continued,

> to translate into meaningful impact all the AID-type statistics on hamlet or other schools built, teachers trained, fertilizer distributed, rural dispensaries and province hospitals constructed, refugees cared for, wells dug, roads and waterways opened and repaired, tractors imported, markets built, self-help projects completed, or piasters and dollars spent. But there is little question that the range of services and assistance provided the rural population in GVN-controlled areas, mostly through the pacification program, has increased dramatically by 1969–1970 over 1965–1967.
>
> (Komer, 1970b: 15; see also Osborne, 1965)

When the latest round of reforms or resources did not achieve the desired effect, the routine explanation was the failure of local patriarchs to implement the reforms quickly, efficiently and honestly. The United States was working with venal and corrupt despots (Hunt, 1995: 250). But as the authors of one 1962 report on the Strategic Hamlets put it, 'nothing [we] say about weaknesses of implementation should be interpreted as a criticism of the program as a military device or of its over-all potential value' (Donnell and Hickey, 1962: iv; Hickey, 1964).

The depopulation of the Vietnamese countryside had begun as early as 1954, with the deliberate creation of internally displaced populations in the North intended to change the demographic balance in favour of the House of Ngo and against the communists. By the 1968 Tet Offensive, it was clear that the United States was not going to defeat the Viet Cong. It could not win in a war of national liberation by fighting over control of the population in the countryside. But if the population were driven into the government-controlled cities, the underlying, deeper 'social basis' of communism would also be destroyed. Hence, under President Nixon, military strategy evolved from congregating peasants in camps to the systematic depopulation of the entire countryside through massive carpet-bombing and intensified use of chemical weapons. The result was the indiscriminate killing of hundreds of thousands of people, including thousands in neighbouring Laos and Cambodia. At the time, Samuel P. Huntington described the new strategy as a process of 'forced-draft urbanization and modernization', which 'rapidly brings the country in question out of the phase in which a rural revolutionary movement can hope to generate sufficient strength to come to power' (1968: 652). Echoing Walt Rostow's claim that societies were susceptible to socialist revolution only at a specific stage of their development, the solution in Vietnam was not, claimed Huntington, 'the esoteric doctrines and gimmicks of counterinsurgency warfare'. The remedy was the elimination of the rural conditions in which such a revolution could occur. He went on, 'if the "direct application of mechanical and conventional power" takes place on such a massive scale as to produce a massive migration from countryside to city, the basic assumptions underlying the Maoist doctrine of revolutionary war no longer operate. The Maoist-inspired rural revolution is undercut by the American-sponsored urban revolution' (1968: 650). Not forced-draft villagisation but forced-draft urbanisation would decisively end all contacts between insurgents and their base of support. Echoing Robert Thompson's point about the compensatory advantages of the New Villages, another positive aspect of forced-draft urbanisation was that the displaced would eventually benefit from all the social services and material goods available in the modern city.

Conclusion

The United States took social regulation in – and the social science of – small wars to an entirely new level in its war on Vietnam. While there are enormous continuities between US counterinsurgency and the colonial emergencies/small wars conducted by Britain and France, the United States was able to employ far greater financial and technical resources and to convene far greater numbers of allies to the pacification cause. The US Air Force dropped some 100 million pounds of Agent Orange over the forests to deprive the Viet Cong of cover. Large tracts of land were made uninhabitable by napalm, landmines and defoliants. Yet, heavy bombing did not destroy the ability of guerrilla fighters to move through the countryside. The hit-and-run tactics of the mobile guerrillas, with greater understanding of the terrain, proved too challenging for the mostly working-class conscripts who bore most of the fighting burden. The United States simply could not create and maintain political legitimacy for the House of Ngo, nor could it defeat Vietnam's revolutionary forces with industrial scale airpower. Two million American servicemen eventually fought in Vietnam and 47,000 of them died. Eight million Vietnamese were forcibly removed and re-concentrated. Almost one million Viet Cong and North Vietnamese soldiers were killed. Another one million civilians died, not including those who suffered long-term effects from chemical weapons and napalm. Approximately, 6.5 million people fled South Vietnam, many of whom were forced to survive in concentration camps.[24]

Numerous explanations have been offered to account for the scale of United States crimes in Vietnam, with many pointing to the ideological role of modernisation theory; the pseudo-science of systems analysis and quantitative 'metrics of success'; of computer-generated statistics; of economists and business managers in prosecuting techno-war on peasants on the other side of the world. However, the United States' over-reliance on 'massive quantitative' techniques in the 'highly sensitive' task of population pacification was also, of course, an in-house critique, made by those who helped to implement the pacification campaign (Komer, 1970b: 3). The limitations of quantitative methods became part of internal revaluations of United States conduct in Vietnam and its relevance in terms of 'lessons learned' for the most recent counterinsurgencies in Afghanistan and Iraq. More is at stake in – and more is revealed by – the role of social systems theories in prosecuting and justifying the Vietnam War. Modernisation theory was not responsible for the Strategic Hamlets programme. There are too many other precedents. Nor does modernisation theory account for even the

[24] By 1975 and in South Vietnam alone, 'there were 83,000 amputees, 8,000 paraplegics, 30,000 blind, 10,000 deafened, and 50,000 other disabled persons … 800,000 orphans' (Tyner, 2009: 50).

scale of the programme, which dwarfed those pursued by Britain and France. Rather the military and economic power of the United States took the social theory of modernisation to its logical extreme, unleashing what is latent in distinctly social forms of thought: a notion of humans as malleable if the right 'social milieu' is created; a dependence on biological metaphors, leading to claims regarding what is healthy and unhealthy development, as well as diagnosis for a cure; a faith in sociocratic administration to 'improve' dysfunctional behaviour; and an aggressively hegemonic view of 'functionally' interrelated social sub-fields that calls for total social revolution. Social modernisation rationalised an 'invisible mass murder ... carried out on the orders of freely elected officials, during normal times, in keeping with consensually developed and frequently reaffirmed policy' (Aronson, 1983: 142).

It is the *social* in the social science of violent 'modernisation' that provided the intellectual rationale for the scale of social engineering undertaken in Vietnam. The social in social science is aggressively universal in its claims. Integral to social, rather than scientific thought *per se*, is dependence on biological metaphors. The social regulation of dangerous populations is aided by scientific analysis. But it is social theory and social policy that underpins the total administration of the life processes of the population during counterinsurgency. As Mary McCarthy reported from Vietnam, 'you wonder whether this branch of knowledge could ever have been designed for anything but war' (1967: 63). Put differently, the assumptions and practical applications of social theories in counterinsurgency are homologous with the fundamental ontology of the social as a form of despotic household governance, governance that has always been violent. The 'social' in social science is the modern variation on household governance, the domain in which life processes, life itself, is managed and in which populations are to be domesticated. In their different ways, the policy documents such as *Quiet Warriors* and *Pacification in Algeria*, and social science tracts such as *The Social System*, were variations on the old practice of *oikonomikos*, the art of household management. The household of counterinsurgency, like the ancient *oikos*, is a place of violent necessity. The violence of counterinsurgency involves not only military operations against insurgents. Through their violence, counterinsurgents seek to drive populations into an existence governed purely by life necessity and they place themselves in the position to administer, deliver and withhold the necessities of life. Counterinsurgency works through inflicting pain on bodies and making people fear extreme pain to themselves and their families. Through this violence populations are forced to collaborate as if it were a dictate of biological necessity, the essence of household rule and the origins of its un-freedoms.

7 Oikonomia *by other means: counterinsurgency in Afghanistan and Iraq*

Covet your enemy's wife...

David Kilcullen (2006)[1]

Who is neutral in a war zone? In the laws of war, the concept of neutrality has a very specific meaning related to the rights and duties of non-belligerent states as defined by the Hague Convention. Refusing to 'take sides' in a conflict, humanitarian organisations such as the International Red Cross and Red Crescent movements also invoke neutrality to maximise their ability to alleviate suffering. Based on the political judgement of state leaders and the mandate of the oldest humanitarian organisations, these two positions are the most widely understood forms of neutrality in war, even though the true extent of neutrality in specific contexts is usually contested and the very possibility of neutrality is subject to dispute. In recent years, these more or less principled standpoints have been joined by another far more surprising claim regarding who is neutral in war: the majority of the civilian population living through the fighting. One of the most startling but common claims in counterinsurgency texts is that most of the population surviving in the war zone are effectively *neutral* regarding who wins. 'In *any situation, whatever the cause*', claims the United States *Counterinsurgency Field Manual*, 'there will be an active minority for the cause, a neutral or passive majority, [and] an active minority against the cause' (FM 3–24: 1–20, Fig 1–2, emphasis added). In the

[1] This dictum appears as part of Article 19 in Kilcullen's 'The Twenty-Eight Articles', originally written in 2006 on the invitation of a group of US Marine Corps and Army officers. They appear in Annex C of *Small-Unit Leaders' Guide to Counterinsurgency*, United States Marine Corps (Kilcullen, 2006: 121) and were subsequently republished in *Military Review*, *Small Wars Journal* and circulated very widely on the Internet and reprinted and expanded in Kilcullen (2010). For some reason, Article 19 is revised to 'Engage the women, beware the children' in the later versions.

middle of a violent rebellion against a constituted authority or foreign occupation there is a 'passive population'; there is an undecided and neutral middle, literally in the middle, waiting.

The precise wording of the *Field Manual* regarding the political commitments of the population, or lack thereof – like much of the *Manual* – comes from French military officer David Galula's *Pacification in Algeria*, written in 1963 under the auspices of RAND to assist with the US war in Vietnam.[2] As discussed in the previous chapter, Galula was generalising from claims made about French colonial experience by its most effective propagandists (Porch, 1986: 376–407). In the 1920s, French Army General Hubert Lyautey claimed that 'the great mass of the Moorish people were more or less indifferent to political problems' (in Maurois, 1931/1932: 253). According to the 1963 US Army Field Manual for *Counterguerrilla Operations*: 'It is often erroneously believed that the civilian population ... can be broken down into ... those friendly to the resistance movement and those friendly to the local government or occupying group. Often, in fact, a great part of the population has no concern about the struggle and is sympathetic to neither combatant' (United States, 1963: 7). The claim reappears in the influential work of David Kilcullen, adviser to US commanders in Afghanistan and Iraq. Writing of Afghanistan, he stated that 'a minority of the population will support the government come what may, and another minority will back the Taliban under any circumstances, but the majority of the Afghans simply want security, peace, and prosperity and will swing to support the side that appears most likely to prevail and to meet these needs' (2009: 66). In her introduction to the revised *Field Manual*, written in response to the failed occupation of Iraq, Sarah Sewall similarly claimed that there is a passive and neutral mass of people who 'waits to be convinced ... Who will help them more, hurt them less, stay the longest, earn their trust?' (2007: xxv).[3]

[2] 'In any circumstances, whatever the cause, the population is split among three groups: (1) an active minority for the cause, (2) a neutral majority, (3) an active minority against the cause' (Galula, 1963/2006: 70; Kuehl, 2009).

[3] Thomas Rid has similarly equated civilians with neutrality. 'In any popular uprising,' he writes, 'it will be essential to distinguish between combatants and non-combatants, between the neutral civilians and those who chose violent resistance' (2009: 632). Galula's claim also has its counterpart in the corporate field of 'change management'. 'In change management literature a distinction is often made between (1) a group of employees who initiate the change – the

Resist – just for a moment – enquiring into the origins, accuracy and legitimacy of these oft-repeated claims regarding the opinions and beliefs of those living in the middle of a war zone, whether in a high-colonial, late-colonial or postcolonial context. Instead, consider the strategic imperatives for contemporary counterinsurgents that are said to follow from the existence of this 'uncommitted public'. For it has been claimed that this distinction between insurgents and the neutral population has radical implications for the conduct of counterinsurgency, underpinning much that was purportedly new and even progressive about the military and civilian surge of forces in Iraq from 2007 and Afghanistan from 2009 (Kaldor, 2010).[4] The horrors of US actions in Fallujah and Haditha, including deliberate massacres of Iraqi civilians, become the sad but inevitable outcome of 'enemy-centric' approaches, exemplified by the free-fire zones, carpet-bombing and chemical weapons used in Vietnam. However, in the new counterinsurgency, the counterproductive obsession with insurgent body counts was to be replaced by more constructive forms of population protection. Under the stress of military defeat, civil war and incessant critique, a seemingly new 'kinder and gentler counterinsurgency' strategy embodied a 'holistic form of human security' in which the needs and wants of the neutral population are met through armed social work (Sewall, 2007: xxxiv, xxx). In this vision, 'emotionally intelligent' warriors should reduce civilian casualties through calibrated force, while also dramatically increasing funds for development and reconstruction (Sewall, 2007: xxiv).[5] 'Population-centric'

initial guiding coalition, (2) a group of employees that is passive regarding the process of change, and (3) a group that actively tries to undermine the process of change. Statistically the passive employees are always a majority … The challenge for members of the international community is thus to build a guiding coalition of change that shares the same vision with a group of people that wants to initiate and drive change in their own country' (de Lange, 2010).

4 'It may sound counterintuitive', wrote Rachel Kleinfeld (2009), 'but for progressives, Petraeus's victory [sic] is our victory … Petraeus incorporated insights, such as the importance of legitimacy and privileging civilian life in order to gain hearts and minds, that progressives have been promoting for years. However progressives feel about the decision to enter the Iraq War, we should own its success'.

5 In other words, 'the No. 1 fix for the future of America's armed forces is to foster a new vision of leadership, a perspective less wedded to gender-biased models and more focused on creating an emotionally intelligent warrior' (Fraher, 2011).

counterinsurgency was billed as the only way to convince the neutral masses in both Afghanistan and Iraq that the United States – not insurgents – 'will help them more, hurt them less, stay the longest, earn their trust' (Sewall, 2007: xxv). In the context of mounting civilian and coalition casualties, the obvious lack of post-invasion planning, torture scandals and the costs and the chaos of the Iraq campaign, military strategists returned to this older vocabulary regarding the neutral population, the silent majority to be co-opted through armed social work.

The large technical 'lessons learned' literature, much of it written by counterinsurgency advisors, suggests that greater emphasis on 'protecting' the neutral population was real and the result of understanding the mistakes (and successes) of past campaigns (Nagl, 2002; Davidson, 2010). Such claims were widely disseminated by embedded journalists with tales of the 'COIN-dinistas' and 'soldier-scholars' said to have pioneered the new approach (Ricks, 2010; Kaplan, 2013). The 'planning school' of rational choice economists claimed that successful reconstruction is indeed possible with enough resources and other incentives to 'make people prefer ... a liberal democratic order as compared with any available alternatives' (Dobbins et al., 2007; Coyne, 2008: 9). Many military historians and realists doubted the United States' real commitment to population-centric warfare, not to mention its viability even if practised in good faith. 'Social work with guns' leads to 'counter-insurgencies without end'; sectarian power struggles do not disappear with the building of new schools and roads (Luttwak, 2007; Bacevich, 2009; Gentile, 2013; Porch, 2013). Many critical theorists presented reconstruction as an exercise in social engineering guided by liberal and neoliberal ideology, a new imperialism (Dodge, 2009; Tyner, 2006). Feminists rightly maintained that counterinsurgency, like all war, is a field of gender contestation in which systems of patriarchy are reinforced rather than undermined, including when humanitarian aid is targeted at 'an undifferentiated "womenandchildren"' (Khalili, 2011: 1479; McBride and Wibben, 2012). In reality, 'protection' means shelter from the violence of others in exchange for submission to the violence of the 'protector'.[6] Others, drawing on Michel Foucault, conceived the merging of security and development in counterinsurgency as a form of biopolitics in which 'life itself' becomes subject to

[6] On the pervasiveness of the 'protection myth' see Tickner (1992).

ever-greater intervention, regulation and dangerous control (Gregory, 2008; Kienscherf, 2011; B. Anderson, 2011).

In fact, the ironies, paradoxes and clichés surrounding the most recent iteration of armed social work are best understood in terms of the distinctive type of rationality and governance embodied in this form of work. The formulaic character and the public staging of the discourse of population protection, the ritualised spectacle of General David Petraeus testifying before Congress; the repetitious invocation of the centrality of 'politics' from new COIN experts; the same clichés, to borrow Mary McCarthy's words from Vietnam, 'tirelessly inserted into dinner-table conversations, briefings, newspaper and magazine articles' (1967: 61). These are not merely a question of propaganda and an accommodating media. We need a better understanding of how and why counterinsurgency has historically been so amenable to the notion of armed social work. It is in the nature of counterinsurgencies to make the local population a central focus of the campaign given the difficulty of inflicting military defeat on well-armed and well-organised insurgents. 'In counterinsurgency the population is the prize,' writes one enthusiast, 'and protecting and controlling it is the key activity. The war, therefore, is where the people are' (Kilcullen, 2009: 73). But this observation does not tell us very much about the nature and character of population control, or the nature of the government offered under counterinsurgency rule. In fact, the direct 'targeting' and neutralisation of the people in this form of war is homologous with much broader and longer practices of distinctly social governance, a form of household rule. Once again, in the face of military defeat, counterinsurgents innovated methods of household governance to create units of rule in which populations were to be domesticated and insurgencies defeated.

To illustrate, the chapter proceeds in three parts, examining different forms and levels of household governance during the counterinsurgencies in Afghanistan and Iraq. The first section pays particular attention to the distinctly neoliberal forms of social regulation that so catastrophically failed in the early occupation of Iraq, a neoliberalism mistakenly viewed as heralding the very 'end of the social', and examines the re-articulation of military doctrine across a series of contemporary counterinsurgency texts, the quite familiar forms of distinctly social *oikonomia* that have traditionally accompanied this form of war. The second and third sections examine how the counterinsurgencies were actually fought. Perhaps the most effective form of household despotism to emerge in both Afghanistan and Iraq related to the manipulation of sectarian distinctions and the elevation of tribal households as methods of indirect, decentralised despotism. With the support of social anthropological *oikonomikos*, counterinsurgents co-opted native *paterfamiliās* to govern populations defined in terms of sectarian and ethnic affiliation. In Iraq, they armed sectarian militia and death squads to 'cleanse' entire cities and towns. The final section analyses the space of the small-scale family home, the houses demolished or raided for the ends of locating insurgents and intimidating civilians. In both campaigns, and in a highly gendered and sexualised manner, domestic family homes became the 'physical piece of real estate' against which both insurgents and populations could be fixed, and then pacified or killed (Kilcullen, 2010: 9). Counterinsurgency strategy is not predicated on the real existence of a neutral population, but on the assumption that the majority of the population can be domesticated through techniques of despotic household rule. Counterinsurgents wager that civilians can be neutralised; that is, forced into acquiescence through violence, including violent control of their homes and their movement. Populations can be so neutralised because they are conceived as fundamentally social, malleable beings. This assumed malleability informs the counterinsurgency strategy of de-politicisation through domestication.

The end of the social? Military occupation in a neoliberal age

There is no direct correlation between the conduct of counterinsurgency and the prevailing government ideology of the counterinsurgent state; any suggestion that counterinsurgents consciously seek to apply particular social theories must be heavily qualified. Military necessity is the most important consideration in the degree and kind of social regulation. Nonetheless, the particular character of social regulation, and understandings of how it works, is heavily influenced by the dominant ideology of the counterinsurgent state. For example, the Committee to Enquire into the Sociological Causes and Remedies for Mau Mau combined 1950s structural functionalist theories of socio-psychic deviance with colonial welfarist ideologies rooted in the particular late-colonial context to rationalise mass detention, torture and the forced removal and concentration of hundreds of thousands of Kikuyu. In Vietnam, neither the bombing campaign nor the Strategic Hamlet programme required social modernisation theory's vision of a postwar global New Deal. However, modernisation theory provided the distinctly liberal and progressive rationale for crimes against humanity. Equally, much has been written on the explicitly ideological character of the Bush administration's decision to invade and occupy Iraq in 2003. After the 9/11 attacks, prominent neoconservatives revived the language of good versus evil, embracing unilateral military action in the name of defending universal values (Kaplan and Kristol, 2003; cf. Owens, 2007a; Mearsheimer, 2011). However, while neoconservatism provided the rationale for the initial invasion, the earliest reforms of the Iraqi state and economy embodied the core tenets of neoliberalism.[7] This is important because neoliberalism represents an explicit attack on the 'social liberalism' that first emerged in the late nineteenth century and which influenced the framing of armed social work across each of the counterinsurgencies examined thus far. Indeed, the rise of neoliberalism, for some commentators at least, represents the 'end of the social' itself (Baudrillard, 1978/2007; Rose, 1996).

Neoliberalism's basic precepts, which came to prominence in the United States and Britain after the global economic crises of the 1970s, are well-known: deregulation and liberalisation of international trade and finance; attacks on organised labour; the introduction into the public sector of 'self-regulating markets'; the withdrawal of the state from social and other services; the generalisation of competition; and the privatisation of security. In this model, the older social democratic ideal of government coordinating social policy in the name of social solidarity is dismantled in the name of market freedom and consumer choice. The social security state loses its integrative power. Instead, 'society' is imagined as a web of market-based relations, an enterprise populated by individual entrepreneurs and families.[8] In practice this

[7] On neoliberalism more broadly see Harvey (2007) and Dardot and Laval (2013). The distinction between neoconservatism and neoliberalism should not be overdrawn. American 'neoconservatives themselves often describe neoconservatism as … a cross between the conservative political philosophy of Leo Strauss and neoliberal economics of Friedrich von Hayek and Milton Friedman' (Drolet, 2011: 92; see also Brown, 2006).

[8] In an interview with *Women's Own* magazine on 23 September 1987, Margaret Thatcher famously asked 'who is society? There is no such thing! There are

has meant some of the poorest communities have been stripped of their limited 'social' safety nets, a dismantling of social provisions that has characterised neoliberal policies as applied in almost all parts of the globe. However, the neoliberal transformation of social welfare states does not mean the end of social forms of governance. The social realm first emerged towards the end of the eighteenth century as the intermediary between capitalism and state government; that is, before the rise of distinctly social welfare in the nineteenth century. Social welfarism is only one form of social regulation, not its defining type, just as social regulation is only one among many forms of household governance. Hence, rather than view the rise of neoliberalism as signalling the end of the social as such, neoliberalism is better understood as a further transformation of social administration under a more aggressive form of capitalism. Like all forms of governance, neoliberal governance steers the behaviour of governments and people, producing distinctive forms of subjectivity and labour in a more authoritarian national household. For example, in replace of social welfare, neoliberalism relies more heavily on the disciplinary authority of privately delivered penal authority, especially targeted at those unable or unwilling to adjust to what the market demands.

Hence, neoliberal military occupation as witnessed in Iraq was still a form of 'state-crafting' and neoliberal social regulation (Wacquant, 2009: 103). As soon as major combat operations were erroneously declared over in May 2003, coalition authorities launched radical structural reforms to the Iraqi state and economy along clear neoliberal lines. In addition to disbanding the army and the Ba'ath party, state-owned enterprises and assets were privatised; banks were deregulated and opened to full foreign ownership; trade was liberalised; taxes were reduced; foreign companies were permitted to repatriate all profits; public subsidies for electricity and fuel were scaled back; social security, already reduced during the decade of sanctions, was further decreased; trade unions were dissolved; corporate personhood was legally codified; and capitalism was enshrined in the new Iraqi constitution (Chandrasekaran, 2007: 117). These structural reforms seriously undermined the post-Saddam state, contributing directly to civil war and insurgency (Herring and Rangwala, 2006). Before the

individual men and women and there are families and no government can do anything except through people and people look to themselves first'.

decade of US-led sanctions, Iraq had one of the largest social welfare systems in the region (Enloe, 2010: 67). Already impaired by decades of war and sanctions, the 'de-regulated' post-invasion state was in no position to provide basic services such as water and electricity, or resist the growing insurgency and sectarian civil war. The basic tenets of neoliberalism did not – could not – produce even a semblance of democracy, prosperity and dignity for the people of Iraq. Moreover, as local militia were taking towns across Iraq, neoliberal ideology offered no coherent military strategy. As Wendy Brown has put it: 'How is unified and coordinated [military] effort to be expected among agents produced and governed by a neo-liberal rationality whose ruling principle is lack of regulation, restriction, or control by anything outside the private enterprise?' (2008: 356).[9]

The relatively small US military presence demanded by Secretary of Defense Donald Rumsfeld was unprepared for the scale of the violence the invasion had unleashed. Only in 2006 did the Bush administration finally accept, in the words of Toby Dodge, 'that rebuilding the infrastructural and despotic capacity of the Iraqi state was the only way it could stabilize the situation and extricate US forces from what had become a deepening quagmire' (2010: 1286). The creation of despotic capacity – mastering the house – defines counterinsurgency. However, it is surely an exaggeration to suggest that the revival of counterinsurgency doctrine 'marked the complete jettisoning of the neo-liberal policy prescriptions' (Dodge, 2010: 1285). The explicit turn to counterinsurgency did not involve the re-nationalisation of Iraq's industries, greater restrictions on foreign ownership or the repatriation of profits. Occupation forces came to rely even more heavily on private military and security contractors, a degree of counterinsurgency outsourcing without precedent.[10] Both state and non-state agencies in Iraq constructed markets in 'service provision' and expertise, such as emergency food assistance and temporary shelter. Most strikingly of all, bolstering the despotic capacity of the Iraqi state did not contradict one of neoliberalism's (and neoconservatism's) basic tenets: the need

[9] Hence, the clear existence of neoliberal *intent* in the Bush administration, the issuing of decrees and orders, is not the same as possessing a coherent plan and level of expertise to bring about the desired ends. For a devastating critique of the early post-invasion plans for Iraq's economy see Galbraith (2006).

[10] For an argument that this outsourcing harmed rather than helped counterinsurgency in Iraq see Singer (2007).

for a strong military and police state presence to discipline and coerce recalcitrant populations, including through mass incarceration and torture in Iraq's overflowing prisons (Cole, 2009). Nonetheless, we should not exaggerate the centrality of neoliberal social regulation in the counterinsurgency war in Iraq. From 2006, both military doctrine and practice revived and innovated older forms of despotic household rule that cannot be understood within a neoliberal framework and which revived much earlier forms of counterinsurgency *oikonomikos*.

Evolutionary language of development and medical/biological metaphors continued to underpin twenty-first-century claims about successful counterinsurgency and the nature of the 'society' to be constructed. The use of such metaphors has long been fundamental to both social thought and counterinsurgency given their rootedness in household management, organised around the administration of life processes. Organic and biological metaphors were crucial to the initial effort to constitute 'society' as a distinct object of analysis requiring its own science, and are constantly used in the literature on counterinsurgency (insurgencies as biological systems, national 'bone structures', national 'muscle memory' and 'host nations').[11] For the updated US *Counterinsurgency Field Manual*, the theatre of war was viewed as akin to a hospital operating theatre. An initial stage of military intervention attempts to 'stop the bleeding' where 'operations are characterized by emergency first aid for the patient', the 'host society' or nation. In a middle stage of medical/military intervention, 'in-patient care – recovery' is 'characterized by efforts aimed at assisting the patient through long-term recovery or restoration of health'. During this phase, combatants and their civilian followers must be seen to maintain infrastructure; have positive

[11] Walt Rostow referred to national 'bone structures' in relation to Vietnam (in Gilman, 2003: 155). Insurgency is 'pathology', a disease that follows a cycle of 'infection, contagion, intervention, and rejection' (Kilcullen, 2009: 35). In contrast to Iraq, General Petraeus would later lament that the host nation of Afghanistan lacked the 'muscle memory' of a strong central government (in Miles, 2009). The Oxford English Dictionary reports that the etymology of 'host' is both Latin, then Old French, for an armed company; to describe a person who lodges others in their house; and a victim for sacrifice. From the middle of the nineteenth century, the term was used in the new science of biology to describe an animal or plant with a parasite living in or on it and, from the early twentieth century, an animal or person who receives a transplanted organ. The terminology of 'host country' or 'host government' does not emerge until the 1960s.

'interactions' with the population; support religious and cultural institutions; and provide the conditions in which, after war, a healthy and functioning 'civil society' can thrive. The last stage of operations is analogous to outpatient care and the movement to 'self-sufficiency', the ideal self-regulating social realm (FM 3–24: 5-4-5). Indeed, if society is conceived as a human body, then the social structure is the skeleton and culture provides 'the muscle on the bones'. In the accompanying (and pervasive) language of 'social constructivism', culture and social structure are mutually constitutive, unable to function and survive without each other; 'a change in one results in a change in the other' (FM 3–24: 3–36; see also Kalyvas, 2008).

This social constructivist reading of counterinsurgency is wholly consistent with much earlier social theories of intervention in the social *milieu*, including ones associated with political realism. The key functions of the state, according to the *Field Manual*, are 'to regulate social relationships, extract resources and take actions in the public's name' (FM 3–24: 1–115). This variation on Max Weber's influential understanding of the state's 'absolute end' is clearly not the state as envisioned by neoliberal ideology.[12] The role of national government structures is to penetrate 'society', regulate social relationships, extract resources and apply resources to identified group ends, including the delivery of functionally specific services: roads, basic utilities, housing and social insurance, all the mechanisms that steer and guide 'society'. In the classic military mnemonic of 'clear, hold, build', the 'build' (or construction) phase takes centre-stage. For once insurgents have been 'cleared' it is argued that the central task is not destruction but *social* construction. The urgent task is to 'secure' and 'develop' the basic life processes of those conceived as a threat to prevailing order. Recognition of the scale of the task faced is reflected in the extent to which roughly one quarter of the *Field Manual* discusses not only the practical social policy elements of counterinsurgency, such as integrating civilian and military activities, but also the broader sociological context (the 'social system' or now increasingly the 'social network') within which these activities are believed to occur.[13]

[12] The 'modern state is a compulsory association which organized domination. It has been successful in seeking to monopolize the legitimate use of physical force as a means of domination within a territory' (Weber, 1946: 82–83).

[13] The *Field Manual* contains a lengthy discussion of social network theory, which originates in the evolutionary and formal sociological theories of

Initiated in Vietnam, but with roots in nineteenth-century socio-biological thought, social systems analysis continues to claim that successful nation-building depends on the proper functioning and interaction between the 'separate spheres' of capitalist economy, state and local government, the population, and the organisation and use of coercion. RAND Corporation volumes present diagrams of 'social systems', with lines drawn between the words security, political, social and economic (Davis, 2011a: xvii). Analysts then theorise how these separate domains – each with their distinct logic – functionally 'interact' during and after military occupation. Indeed, one could hardly find a better statement of the core insight of sociological functionalism than the accompanying claim that 'virtuous reinforcing circles' are produced when counterinsurgents successfully combine work on economic, political, social and security issues. 'Over time, "everything is connected to everything"' (Davis, 2011a).[14] In another diagram, arrows are drawn between the words 'security', 'political', 'social' and 'economic', and are then punctuated with tautological claims about the connections between separate spheres: the 'need for monitoring and security' is reduced when there is a rise in 'social capital and trust'; engaged members of society 'contribute to public discourse'; 'security decreases risk and improves law enforcement mechanisms'. There is no direct arrow linking the words 'social' and 'economic', presumably because under neoliberal occupation the economy is conceived as a self-regulating domain without the need for 'community' input. One of the most common clichés of social work is that interventions

Georg Simmel (1858–1918) (FM 3–24: B-14–18). The basic premise of social network analyses 'is that the structure of social relations determines the content of those relations' (Mizruchi, 1994: 330). By the middle of the twentieth century, social network analysis emerged as a formal and structural sociological method for mapping relationships between individuals in any given society, including kinship, friendship, tribal relationships and now within insurgent groups. The counterinsurgency purpose is to reveal the structure of otherwise obscure insurgent networks – individual insurgents are referred to as 'nodes' – and exploit this information to fragment the insurgency (Knoke, 2013).

14 German philosopher Hans Albert's critique of the Frankfurt School is more accurately applied to the sociological functionalism of RAND-style social science. He said, 'there is nothing more behind it than the idea that somehow everything is linked with everything else' (quoted in Gödde, 2000: 165). For a discussion of the 'social systems engineering' approach to war see Buley (2008) and Davis and Cragin (2009).

should always 'empower' individuals, groups and nations to help themselves (Lind, 2007; Sitaraman, 2012: 14).[15] But in the absence of such self-regulating economies – individual subjects able to consent to be ruled – social intervention is designed to produce them. On such a view – the epitome of total household governance – armed social work must take a '"whole-of-government approach", addressing all of the "instruments of power"' (Davis, 2011b: 8). Or in the words of General Stanley McChrystal, the task in Afghanistan was to create 'a government in a box, ready to roll in' (in Filkins, 2010).

Several recent social theories of popular support for insurgency focus on the 'internal dynamics within the Muslim world' including feudal and semi-feudal gender relations and 'a generalized *anomie*, a sense of being victimized by a vaguely-defined "West"' (Kilcullen, 2009: 16). Political motives, history and agency are downplayed or ignored. Once again, and in a kind of tautological argument, the sources of violence are understood in primarily sociological and psychological terms; that is, of a kind of lawlessness and/or an absence of accepted norms. Echoing Durkheim's sociological rendering of working-class unrest as evidence of their maladjustment to industrial life, and the 'psycho-docs' that claimed Mau Mau was a deviant response to the transition to modernity, large swaths of young Muslim men are presented as 'maladjusted' to modern society. According to scholars of 'Islamist radicalisation', 'a crisis of identity is considered a risk factor. Where there are unresolved tensions in one's identity, the likelihood of a "cognitive opening" to activism and vulnerability to radical discourse increased' (Liht et al., 2013: 42). These claims, which build on work by preventive psychiatrists (Caplan, 1964), are bolstered by frequent media representations of angry young men demonstrating over Koran burning and Islamophobic films. 'Geo-strategists' offer Durkheimian accounts of the dangerous space between a 'functioning core' in the industrial world and the world's 'non-integrating gap'. In this vision, US armed forces and local proxies are most likely to be deployed in non-integrating dangerous and 'disconnected' regions (Barnett, 2004).

For Durkheim, the solution to maladjustment was social integration and solidarity; the non-integrating core of workers needed incorporation into 'society' to improve its overall healthy functioning. In

[15] For a critique of how social workers in the West failed to respond to the effects of the sanctions on Iraq see Harding (2004).

Kenya, Malaya and Vietnam, sociological theories rationalised the mass depopulation and concentration of peasants as a form of integration into a functioning 'society'. As the authors of RAND's recent *Beginner's Guide to Nation-Building* put it, 'Resistance can be overcome, but only through a well-considered application of personnel and money over extended periods of time' (Dobbins et al., 2007: xx–xxi). The overall image is of counterinsurgents and associated civilians offering financial incentives and disincentives to a largely neutral population, producing more or less compliance with the norms of a healthy liberal democratic 'social system'. For example, the stated purpose of the $644 million Community Stabilization Program in Iraq (2006–2009), which used the labour of local men of military age for public works programmes, was that job opportunities keep young men away from insurgents and politically radical organisations.[16] The social psychological assumption was that integrating men into 'functioning, stable intergroup relationships' can 'reinforce nonviolent means of interaction' (Wilke et al., 2011: 212). Properly socialised, young men may even become indifferent to political problems, such as military occupation and authoritarian government, part of the neutral and passive majority. The increasing numbers of 'radicalized Muslim women' were also explained in terms of a 'societal dynamic' linking 'gender, socioeconomic inequity, resentment, and alienation' (Byrd and Decker, 2008: 96). These women would need to be turned 'into entrepreneurs' with 'a future instead of a suicide vest' (Van Buren, 2011: 4). The philosophy of social science underlying such claims is social constructivism. Identities are malleable, rather than fixed, or, in the context of counterinsurgency, individuals can be coerced into behaving in ways one would not predict from their political commitments (Kalyvas, 2008: 352). 'Antagonists do not yet know what they will, in the end, find satisfactory' (Davis, 2011a: xlvl).

So-called experts – specialist think tanks, policy-planning groups and NGOs – all emphasise the extent to which social problems, including insurgencies, are the result of objective sociological conditions amenable to reform. Accordingly, social policy documents present a scientific image of economic incentives and disincentives in which the cultural and religious affiliations of the population

[16] As Lyautey had put it, 'a workshop is worth a battalion' (in Maurois, 1931/1932: 253; Hodge, 2011: 171–172).

exist, but are not viewed as fundamental to the success or failure of interventions. In fact, the far more prevalent and better-resourced form of household governance practised in both Afghanistan and Iraq eschewed the universal and individualist assumptions of social systems analysis and expert-led social policy. In both campaigns, military policy eventually centred on tribes and sectarian divisions, presenting the passive population as supporting the side that not only 'helps them more' but 'that most closely aligns with their primary group identity' (Kilcullen, 2009: 66–68). In the language of contemporary political science, collaboration with counterinsurgents is not an individual choice but one determined by leaders of 'primary groups' understood in tribal and/or sectarian terms. Because a 'Muslim's heart belongs to Allah', claimed the author of a 'tribal engagement programme', 'shame and honor *not* "hearts and minds" govern individual/group relationships' (McCallister, 2007). During empire's first 'socio-cultural turn', the earliest international historical sociologist explained native violence in terms of a failure of the prevailing universal and individualist assumptions of imperial policies (Maine, 1876). Like the social systems analysts of today, liberal utilitarians had called for wholesale reform of India's governance, legal and economic structures. Yet in the wake of the Indian Mutiny, utilitarianism was accused of failing to respect the 'customary' forms of rule that were the underlying basis of order in 'traditional society'. In this crisis of imperial governance, Sir Henry Sumner Maine developed a new theory of patriarchal despotism in which some of the supposedly longstanding customs of India's village 'society' would be incorporated into British strategies of imperial governance. Maine's work formed the basis of the first functionalist theories of traditional society, later appearing in the guise of seemingly non-ideological anthropological social science. In Afghanistan and Iraq, native culture would again be used to explain and remedy the failure of liberal occupiers to create a functioning civil society with a special focus on the continuing significance of tribal households and sectarian divisions within Islam. For as one US Army Major put it, 'whether the people are a single monolithic block trapped passively between warring combatants or a shifting mosaic of subcultures and factions ... [the] challenge is ... to piece together a sufficiently stable coalition of factions that isolates the insurgents or cuts them off from their critical bases of support' (Packwood, 2009: 70).

Who's your *paterfamiliās*? The household of tribal patriarchs

Again, what is the meaning of 'neutrality' in counterinsurgency texts, the assumed existence of a passive population in the midst of fighting? Professional counterinsurgents, past and present, appear to believe 1) that a neutral population exists in the middle of a war zone, no matter the cause or context; 2) this population wants protection from violent death; and 3) the population is willing to actively support the side that is 'going to make their life better' (FM 3–24: 5–77). As a 1962 RAND evaluation of Strategic Hamlets put it, 'the Vietnamese peasant is likely to support the side that has control of the area in which he lives, and he is more favourably disposed to the side which offers him the possibility of a better life' (Donnell and Hickey, 1962: 15). When French Army General Hubert Lyautey claimed that North African Muslims 'were more or less indifferent to political problems', his primary concern was that they 'be kept in that spirit of indifference' (in Maurois, 1931/1932: 253). In the nineteenth century, European strategists relied heavily on claims that the mass of uncivilised peoples in faraway feudal lands lacked meaningful political consciousness. Tribal and village elders governed through violence and primitive custom. In the wars of the late-colonial period, military strategists distinguished between highly motivated but maladjusted elites swayed by liberationist or communist ideology and the apolitical rural masses whose loyalty was plastic, hence there for the taking: 'the Vietnamese peasant, faced with civil disorder, bends with the wind to whichever side is there with force' (Pool, 1968: 11). If a semi-feudal or essentially tribal population is already assumed to lack meaningful politics, then *in any given context, no matter the cause*, it is not difficult to imagine people to be essentially neutral regarding who wins, as long as they are offered 'protection'.

Behavioural political science has tended to be more candid than social policy science regarding the origins of any popular compliance with what counterinsurgency demands: '*collaboration is largely endogenous to control* ... In the long run, military resources generally trump prewar political and social support in spawning control' (Kalyvas, 2006: 12, emphasis added). The superior military resources of counterinsurgents translate to territorial domination and the related ability to extract collaboration from civilians. In the words of US Army Major Mark E. Battjes (2011: 250), if the population intends to support the insurgents, but the government's population and resource control measures prevent them from doing so, their behaviour is now neutral. If they do not contest this situation, they have acquiesced to the government's control. Therefore, it is important for the government to both enable neutrality and to enforce it.

Despite the discrediting of modernisation theory after the Vietnam War, Talcott Parsons' (1964) structural functionalist writing was also used to explain how populations 'behave' under military occupation.[17] According to one analyst, the civilian population of Southwest Babaji in Afghanistan switched from supporting insurgents to complying with British and Afghan National Security Forces; 'the population's perception of who was in control of the area ... drove their decision-making calculus' (Evans, 2014: 259). In this reasoning, the question for the population becomes less about which cause to support, but which side is going to win and have the power to 'protect' the population from greater harm; that is, the ability to *inflict* the greatest harm and to moderate its violence.[18] Such coercive strategies are assumed to work since over time; as the war goes on and the destruction mounts, any ideological advantage held by insurgents must decline. The very fact of the war itself and the desire for war to end will increasingly play a role in the decision of civilians to collaborate with the government, even though this goes against their political beliefs (or, in the apolitical language of recent social science, their 'preferences'). In any case, for behavioural political science, popular 'beliefs' are vague, changeable

[17] Parsons' essay on the role of force in the 'social process' appeared in *Internal War: Problems and Approaches*, an edited volume that was a product of a 1961 symposium for social scientists to discuss the problem of 'internal war' held at Princeton University. The editor of the volume seemed less than impressed by the papers. Perhaps with the Parsons contribution in mind, Eckstein noted that when 'confronted with a concrete subject like internal war, even the more illustrious masters of social theory are visibly ill at ease' (Eckstein, 1964: 6; see also Latham, 2011).

[18] For example, in the household of counterinsurgency, when a military is trying to govern a population in the middle of a war zone, moderation of violence is important. As Weizman has written, 'it is in its moderation, rather than in the unrestrained application of power, that state violence becomes effective ... Restraint is also what allows for the possibility of further escalation, an invitation for those people on the receiving end of violence to make their own cost-benefit calculation ... This practical form of military restraint is now often presented as the adherence to the laws of war' (2011: 17, 19, 20).

and virtually impossible to measure (Kalyvas, 2006: 100; Packwood, 2009: 70). It is the *behaviour* of the population not its wants and beliefs that count.

Similar claims accompanied the war in Afghanistan. A physical force like Pool's wind, the 'natural tendency' of the Afghan people is 'to triangulate between the government and the Taliban' (Kilcullen, 2009: 67). The 'intrinsic merits of the contending causes' matter less than who 'offers the most protection?' This, Galula reminded his American readers, 'is the reason why a counterinsurgency is never lost *a priori* because of a supposedly unpopular regime' (1963/2006: 246–247). However, the population of Iraq, a modern secular and largely functioning state prior to a decade of sanctions and foreign occupation, was harder to present as lacking political sentience. The population may well have been unfree under Saddam Hussein's 24-year despotism, but a nationalist consciousness had clearly developed under his rule, not least during the war with Iran that lasted nearly a decade (Tripp, 2000). To apply the notion of a neutral or passive population required an additional set of claims about the nature of Iraqi 'society': the removal of Saddam Hussein's despotism had 'created a power vacuum that was quickly filled by resurgent tribes' (McFate, 2008: 298). With a depth metaphor common to social thought, 'tribal structure' was presented as the '*sub rosa*' of Iraqi society (McFate, 2005a: 45). Iraq's state institutions – the national government, modern army, authoritarian leader, national education, social services and widespread inter-community marriages – had not destroyed the underlying 'tribal ethos', but only curtailed it. Credence was given to the notion of a passive population in Iraq through the elevation and use of tribal-sectarian policies. In other words, counterinsurgents turned to, and constituted, more local forms of despotic rule as a form of decentralised household despotism.

Decentralised household rule has a long history, beginning in our context with the incorporation of India's 'primitive society' into post-Mutiny imperial rule. As part of this strategy, social anthropology identified the aspects of native 'custom' of utmost use for empire, above all the most authoritarian forms of 'customary' native power to be co-opted for putting down popular revolts. Transposed from India to colonial Africa, the delegation of power to tribal chiefs or sheikhs led to a form of mediated (indirect) rule: 'decentralised despotism'. 'At its bare minimum,' writes Mamdani (1999: 872), 'this tradition simply claimed the supremacy of the patriarch in the homestead, the chief in the village, and the supreme chief or king in the larger polity. [In fact] this monarchical, authoritarian and patriarchal notion of the "customary" most accurately mirrored colonial practices.' The colonial elevation of despotic 'customary power' – often where it did not formerly exist – is one of the most pernicious legacies of late nineteenth-century empire. However, since it was one of the most effective forms of indirect despotic control, it has been openly adapted and incorporated into forms of counterinsurgency rule. During the late-colonial 'emergencies' and the war in Vietnam, local despots were co-opted and armed to rule the household of the village, tribe or nation. In Malaya and Kenya, loyalists became part of governing coalitions or were rewarded with land. In Vietnam, France created the entity known as South Vietnam; it was kept alive by the United States and would almost certainly otherwise have died by 1960. In Afghanistan and Iraq, with nationalist ideology either weak or too dangerous, local patriarchs were found or created to domesticate populations, to neutralise the population inside the household of tribal patriarchs.

For the purposes of counterinsurgency, state power in Iraq was only one of several sites of centralised power and was not necessarily the most important to the US exit strategy. After the post-occupation dismantling of the army and Ba'ath Party, state power was weak but it was assumed that centralised patriarchal power remained the privileged form of rule (Todd et al., 2006: section 2–44). The intellectual task became one of understanding the nature of 'tribal societies', often explicitly described as households, where this patriarchal power could be found (Karasik and Schbley, 2008). US soldiers began attending 'Tribal Engagement Workshops', seeking 'cultural knowledge' of tribal social structure, kinship and gender relations. Co-opted anthropologists gave instruction on the nature and character of 'tribes' (McFate, 2005a; Kaplan, 2007; cf. Barkawi and Stanski, 2012). Unsurprisingly, tribes were defined in functionalist terms, serving distinct and universal purposes that could be identified and mobilised for counterinsurgency ends. Court anthropologists most often turned to Faleh Abdul-Jabar's description of the historical role of Iraq's tribal warrior households prior to the overlay of various empires and modern authoritarian states. He wrote:

> Each strong tribe was a miniature mobile state, with its patriarchal headship usually head[ed] by a warrior household; its own military force; its customary law…; its non-literate culture; its territoriality in the form of *dira* (tribal pastures) or, later, arable lands; and its mode of subsistence economy, i.e. pastoralism, commerce, and conquest.
>
> (Abdul-Jabar, 2001: 73)[19]

Because kinship systems, honour codes and warrior households still ruled in Iraq coalition forces were tasked with identifying, negotiating with and bribing the local *paterfamiliās* 'one tribe at a time' (Baram, 2003; Gant, 2009). The Ottomans, the British and then Saddam Hussein all made use of strategies of divide and rule deemed necessary for ruling tribes. The United States would do the same, seeking to become the 'strongest tribe' in a 'tribal revolt' (Allbritton, 2005; West, 2008). Much was made of the decision of Sunni tribes in Anbar to 'switch sides', agreeing a ceasefire with the United States and isolating Al-Qaeda in Iraq. In a self-fulfilling prophesy, local sheikhs were enticed with money and weapons that in turn underwrote their power of patronage over members of 'their tribe'. Since tribes are competitive, and since power and honour are zero-sum, the decision of one tribal leader to collaborate with the United States prevented rival tribes from enjoying the spoils of war. Echoing the rationale for culturally specific torture techniques used in Abu Ghraib and elsewhere, social scientists explained that 'Iraqi Arabs are generally submissive and obedient to their superiors' (Todd et al., 2006: section 2–44; on culturally specific torture see Owens, 2010). This meant that once local patriarchs had been co-opted through leveraging inter-tribal disputes, members of the tribal household could *naturally* be expected to conform. 'Arabs rule,' according to the author of one US Army model for tribal engagement, 'they do not administer' (McCallister, 2007: 15). Hence, in addition to controlling access to humanitarian supplies, 'traditional' forms of

[19] This passage is also quoted in McFate (2008: 300) and appears unattributed in Todd et al. (2006: section 4–22). In an earlier essay, McFate quotes R.L. Sproul, Director of the US Defence Department's Advanced Research Projects Agency from 1965. In his words, 'remote area warfare is controlled in a major way by the environment in which the warfare occurs, by the sociological and anthropological characteristics of the people involved in the war' (in McFate, 2005a: 47).

tribal authority 'can be used to induce men to obey' (McFate and Jackson, 2006: 13; see also Hassan, 2008; Stolzoff, 2009).[20]

In Afghanistan, military and financial support for warlords – often renamed 'local commanders' or 'militia leaders' – was central to US-led operations from the start of the war (Stanski, 2009; Hakimi, 2013). To some extent, arming and empowering sectarian militia in Iraq was a belated response to the failed occupation. And yet the notion of a 'cultural turn' in military strategy implies that the United States somehow belatedly responded to the rise of sectarianism. However, it was Bush administration policy from the start of the occupation to establish a sectarian government and collectively punish Sunnis. Iraq was crudely depicted as essentially a tri-national state comprising Kurds, Sunni and Shia. Under L. Paul Bremer, 'the new sheikh of sheikhs' (McFate, 2008: 299), the Coalition Provisional Authority chose members of the provisional government wholly on sectarian or ethnic grounds, an entirely new development in the history of Iraq. The manipulation of sectarian affiliations had been a central strategy for the establishment of post-occupation order: there would – even should – be conflict between Shiite and Sunni political factions to avoid a unified insurgency. To be sure, Ba'athist authoritarianism had made some use of sectarian distinctions and Saddam Hussein sought to weaken and co-opt various tribal affiliations. However, the greatest political division in the country was the level of support or opposition to the Ba'athist regime, a secular dictatorship. As Nir Rosen (2010: 21) has put it, in reverting to factionalism as a form of protection and/or violent power grab, 'Iraqis were merely adapting to the American view of Iraq as a collection of sects and trying to fit into the political system the Americans were building around that idea.' This even greater emphasis on religious differences meant that the country's destruction could be explained not in terms of violent occupation and specific Bush administration policies but as the inevitable result of the fragmented character of Iraq itself. Hence, when no weapons of mass destruction could be found, the 'cultural turn' served the important additional function of adjusting the justificatory discourse of the occupation: the United States military needed to remain in Iraq to reduce

[20] To that extent, counterinsurgents expect their local collaborators to act like 'society' itself, which 'expects from each of its members a certain kind of behavior ... all intended to "normalize" its members' (Arendt, 1958: 40).

the levels of violence among Iraqis. As in post-Mutiny India, when native violence grew out of control, the very nature of traditional/tribal 'society' became the justification for continued imperial presence. That such arguments about the importance of respecting local culture would reappear in this most recent crisis of imperial legitimacy challenges the idea that attention to local tradition indicates the absence of imperial purpose.

When insurgency violence escalated in Iraq, the United States seized upon its capacity to co-opt and collaborate with local strong men, eventually resulting in the deliberate sponsoring of sectarianism, the empowerment of ethnocentric leaders, collective punishment and territorial cleansing. During the wars in Malaya, Kenya and Vietnam, entire communities – hundreds of thousands and then millions – were forcibly removed into detention camps. Once concentrated, a minimal level of basic food and medical services was distributed. Supplies were withheld from those who did not cooperate. In Iraq, US armed forces innovated tactics of population control. The mass exodus of two million Iraqi refugees to Jordan, Egypt and Syria reduced the likelihood that US forces would need to deliberately displace, concentrate and administer large populations. Rather than displacing Sunni populations into newly created villages, US forces encircled existing villages, towns and cities. The effect, to adapt the words of one observer, was like a sectarian 'reverse "strategic hamlet"' (Loeb, 2003). In 2003, the village of Auja, birthplace of Saddam Hussein and insurgency base, was surrounded by razor wire. 'Ethno-sectarian divisions' were plotted onto maps and used to determine the location of blast walls, concrete barriers and the checkpoints to surround newly homogenised cities.[21] Ethnic enclaves were called 'gated communities' and 'safe neighborhoods' patrolled by 'neighborhood watch organizations' (Kilcullen, 2007a). Billed as an effort to clear Sunni insurgents to prevent them from attacking Shia communities, the United States funded and trained sectarian police commando forces, borrowing expertise from similar US policies in El Salvador in the 1980s

[21] Recall Galliéni's claim that, 'An officer who has successfully drawn an exact ethnographic map of the territory he commands is close to achieving complete pacification, soon to be followed by the form of organization he judges most appropriate' (in Thomas, 2008: 57). For an attempt to save evolutionary theory from the explicitly hierarchical and racist claims of Herbert Spencer, so as to better 'apply' it to cultural conflict see Tyrrell (2014).

(Maass, 2005).[22] These police commandos ran torture centres and death squads, and waged war on Sunnis, torturing young men and forcibly removing civilians. Unable to gain territorial control, Rosen writes, US forces 'allowed militia to take over Iraq and allowed the police, who should have been protecting civilians from the predation of militia, to become involved in the conflict as one of the main sectarian militia' (2010: 68). Even less capable of curbing militia violence, British forces were defeated and retreated in humiliation in Basra, striking a deal with insurgents to enable British forces to withdraw in 2007. The city was effectively handed over to Shia militia who were then re-described as local 'security forces'. The surge of US forces in Iraq did not lead to any US victory (Agnew et al., 2008). Any temporary reduction in levels of violence was produced by dynamics among Iraqis themselves, especially once murderous cleansing of major cities and towns was largely complete.

The application of 'cultural' knowledge in Afghanistan and Iraq was justified by one of its leading proponents in terms of a simple utilitarian calculation; that is, 'whether using anthropological knowledge in counterinsurgency ... engenders the greatest good of the greatest number. Since the greatest number is the non-belligerent population, the people's welfare (not that of insurgents or governments) is what counts' (Kilcullen, 2007b: 20). In this tautological logic, ethnographic knowledge can be used to persuade the population to accept counterinsurgency rule, which reduces counterinsurgency violence. Hence, ethnographic knowledge is ethical. As Lyautey had already claimed, 'to handle each tribe according to its own temper, to depend upon the most intelligent of the chieftains, to win over territory from the tribes successively without fighting ... was an intelligent and humane policy' (in Maurois, 1931/1932: 126–127).[23] The notion of culturally sensitive counterinsurgency, like armed social work, could make war appear to some as 'more, not less humane' (Kilcullen, 2007b: 20). This simple utilitarian calculation has been an enormously effective

[22] See the *Guardian*/BBC Arabic 2013 documentary *Searching for Steele*, on the role of James Steele in advising Iraq policy. Steele was in charge of advising those who trained notorious paramilitary death squads in El Salvador to fight left-wing guerrillas in the mid-1980s.

[23] Such humanity and intelligence seems highly suited for multinational war, as witnessed by the Netherlands' Task Force Uruzgan in Afghanistan, which in the Durkheimian language of one observer, managed to co-opt and collaborate with 'previously marginalized elements of the population' (Kitzen, 2012).

form of 'social' as well as ethical reasoning since it involves grand claims about what is best for large populations, particularly regarding their physical well-being. It is also worth noting that these claims are based on a notion of 'culture' as bounded and internally coherent that most serious scholars reject. In the intense debates among anthropologists regarding their role in the Human Terrain System, the scheme for embedding social scientists, a professional consensus seemed to emerge: the way anthropology was actually used was 'incoherent, simplistic and outmoded – not to mention tedious', undertaken by 'second rate mercenary academics' (Lucas, 2009; Sahlins, 2009: iii; Kely et al., 2010).[24] In addition to noting that 'tribe' has largely been discredited 'as an analytical category, or even as a concept for practical application' (González, 2009: 15), critics condemned rather than celebrated anthropology's earlier colonial history revived under the leadership of the much-maligned Montgomery McFate (2005b).[25]

Inside the house of counterinsurgency: coveting and protecting the women

Americans think they can just throw new paint on the walls and it will win people over.

Anonymous observer in Rosen (2006: 99)

It does not matter if the Government policy is to ensure that everyone has a red front door. An Army's job is to kill or capture anyone who seeks to violently contest the colour of the front door.

William F. Owen (2011: 34)

Below the national and tribal household in counterinsurgency is the small-scale family home. In conformity with modern social categories, this is usually the only entity explicitly referred to as a 'household' by counterinsurgents. The ability to effectively coerce a population in this context requires not only the construction of a Leviathan, but the

[24] The Human Terrain System is an updated version of Project Camelot, the attempt to mobilise anthropological knowledge of peasant 'society' to pre-empt and repress revolutionary movements before they became full-blown insurgencies. The Project was abandoned in 1964 (Horowitz, 1967; Kipp et al., 2006). Again, it was Galula that first claimed that the population is 'the real terrain of the war ... where the real fighting takes place' (1963/2006: 246).

[25] McFate has been subjected to graphic, highly gendered and personal attacks (see work by anthropology professor Maximilian Forte, 2010).

co-optation of local leaders or the encirclement of villages or towns. It requires entry into and control of particular houses and homes. Family homes are incorporated into the wider household of counterinsurgency in a highly gendered and sexualised process. Some recent critics have downplayed the significance of women in the prosecution of counterinsurgency. 'The peculiar idea that women somehow hold the key to victory in counterinsurgency', writes Douglas Porch,

> is more evidence that COIN-dinistas grasp at straws, often found in domestic politics, to concoct victory scenarios in the absence of an open admission that counterinsurgency success often depends on the systematic application of intimidation and divide and rule tactics on a grand scale, of which Human Terrain and Female Engagement Teams are simply another example.
> (Porch, 2013: 324)

This argument is partially correct. Counterinsurgency clearly relies on systematic intimidation and divide and rule. However, in dismissing the focus on women as some sort of feminist political correctness overlooks the extent to which women are the objects of intimidation in these wars, governed through patriarchal logics supposedly absent in liberal 'society' and progressive counterinsurgency (Stiehm, 1982; Young, 2003). A focus on the household character of counterinsurgency rule not only moves past the dissimulation of counterinsurgents, but some of the limitations of existing analysis.

The stated military purpose of forcibly entering and searching every home in a district, town or city ('house-to-house raids') is to kill or capture insurgents, to attack the safe houses that provide material support for anti-government forces. During such raids, which often occurred at night, soldiers broke down doors, rushed in with guns and bright lights, shouted orders to civilians, including children, and pushed them into one room while the house was searched, possessions broken and suspects hooded and removed to undisclosed locations where they were interrogated and often tortured (Conetta, 2005). Some houses were not only raided, they were demolished. In Samara and Tikrit, the houses of suspected Sunni insurgents were demolished as retribution, a display of power and to signal the consequences of resisting occupation.[26] In 2003, in Albu Hishma, north of Baghdad, local commanders

[26] The UN Committee Against Torture 'considers that house demolition amounts, in some instances, to cruel, inhuman or degrading treatment or punishment' (Blakeley, 2009: 136).

went further, choosing to 'bulldoze any house that had pro-Saddam graffiti' (Shadid, 2005; Rosen, 2006: 98). Drawing lessons from Israeli conduct in Palestine, coalition forces innovated techniques for the surveillance of houses and the identification of which homes would be subject to raids throughout the Iraq occupation. In preparation for incursions, thousands of Baghdad homes were mapped using satellite photographs. Older systems of identity cards were updated to include biometric surveys, kinship affiliations, detention history, home and work addresses, and data on fingerprints and iris scans. Operation Close Encounters accumulated and recorded personal, photographic and biometric information on the entire population of Baghdad (Crider, 2009). In the words of its creator: 'Once [we] had photos of everyone in the area, [we] created a comprehensive "facebook" binder and had intelligence sources point out militants. Confident [we] had a complete list of targets, [we] launched a series of raids' (Danly in Dubik, 2012: 15). In preparation for the assaults, spray paint cans were used to give new addresses to individual homes. House raids and demolitions were only the most obvious way in which so-called 'war among the people' becomes 'war in the home' (Smith, 2005; Bailliet, 2007: 174).

For counterinsurgents, civilian homes are a legitimate target, especially in urban warfare, given their persistent use as shelters and weapons-stores for insurgents. On this view, to search and even destroy homes is unavoidable, a legitimate practice despite the material and psychological costs and rules of engagement that govern the practice. Yet, the brutal conduct of house raids became one of the most criticised aspects of both the Afghan and Iraq occupations to the extent that they were subjects of internal criticism. According to the *Iraq Tribal Study*, written under contract to the Pentagon, 'the way the raids of houses were carried out by US forces in the middle of the night, harassing families including women, and embarrassing the men in front of their families and tribes, further inflamed tribal passions' (Todd et al., 2006: section 2–47). Accordingly, where possible – when 'house calls began with knocks, not kicks' – male soldiers were instructed to remove helmets and glasses, not talk to women, accept tea if offered and show all due 'respect' (FM 3–24: section 7-4).[27]

[27] 'When visiting a house, it is customary to take a position next to the door to prevent being able to see inside the home ... It is expected that guests will

Much was made of women marines and social scientists embedded alongside male combat brigades during house-to-house searches, now billed as a way for Iraqis to air grievances and explain their 'needs' to a friendlier and more respectful face. As General Petraeus said/sung, Iraqis 'felt disrespected, dispossessed, and disgusted ... *All they wanted*', singing the Aretha Franklin hit, 'was R-E-S-P-E-C-T' (in Ricks, 2010: 164, emphasis added). In a fraternal show of respect for some men, as well as in accordance with longstanding counterinsurgency practice, 'household heads' were made responsible for the surveillance and control of members of family homes. Again, in the discussion of the relevant 'population control measures', the *Field Manual* borrows directly from Galula. 'Family booklets,' he instructed his American readers, 'should be issued to each household in order to facilitate house-to-house control, and family heads made responsible for reporting any change as it occurs ... This last measure ... makes him participate willy-nilly in the struggle' (Galula, 1964: 82).[28] In both Afghanistan and Iraq, census operations were used to determine who lived in which building and who was the head of the house. Given their function in managing and locating their members, counterinsurgency strengthens patriarchal family units, in spite of talk of empowering women and the large numbers of Iraqi households headed by them: men were in jail, in the insurgency or were never present to begin with. Indeed, 'US policies have forced the majority of women back into their home and have increased their daily burden' (Al-Ali and Pratt, 2009: 80). More broadly, to adapt Mamdani's words again, no matter 'in the homestead, the village', or the individual home, when counterinsurgents have to reckon with native forms of rule and rebellion 'authority [is] considered an attribute of a personal despotism' (Mamdani, 1996: 39). In the cultural reproduction of capitalism and empire, the well-ordered family house is the model for the well-ordered society composed of relations

remove their shoes before entering the home; this shows respect' (Todd et al., 2006: section 4–22).

28 'Each household was provided with a family census booklet in which we noted the name, age and sex of every member; the family head was made responsible for reporting any change. This was designed to help house-to-house investigations in case we ever needed to conduct such searches. Every house in the village was numbered, and on the outside wall we painted a summary of the census in this way: No.54 (house number) Abboud (family name) 8/7 (total no. of persons in family/no. actually in house)' (Galula, 1963/2006: 99–100).

between household heads protected by the masculinised/militarised tribe or state.

The conquered and surveilled family home inside the wider household of counterinsurgency is not a space for negotiation and deals, as with tribal leaders. If all that men want is 'respect', then women inside the domestic home are constituted as wanting 'protection' and social administration. The domestic home, in this construction, is a space for tending to 'social' needs. Recall again the claim that in *any given context, no matter the cause*, there is always a minority for the insurgency, a minority against it and a mass of neutral people in the middle (FM 3–24: 1–20, Fig 1–2). The neutral majority is said to be willing to support any side, no matter the cause or context, as long as it meets two requirements. First, 'passive or neutral people' want physical security, above all, protection from violent death. Yet protection merely reduces dangerous emotions such as 'anger' (Sewall, 2007: xxv). More is needed to persuade the uncommitted neutrals to support counterinsurgents more actively. What could be more important than the nature and character of the political, economic or religious order in which people live? Who are these people for whom social needs trump political commitments *no matter the cause or context*? It is difficult to find an explicit answer in contemporary counterinsurgency writing. However, a psychosocial advisor to the British in 1950s colonial Kenya could be more explicit: '*women in any case and everywhere*, are, by the very nature of their lives, more close to certain biological realities; their lives depend more strictly on stable social organization, and they must be more suspicious of experiment and change' (Carothers, 1954: 9, emphasis added). These assumptions about the nature of 'women's lives', this gendered construction of passive people always and everywhere wholly swayed by social necessity, underpins the pervasive claim of mass civilian neutrality and the powerful effects of armed social work.

Where populations in general can be made to acquiesce to counterinsurgency rule despite their political, religious or ethnic 'identities', women are assumed to acquiesce because they have been gendered. Where some patriarchs may be co-opted through decentralised despotism to rule their warrior households, women are to be administered inside the *domus*. '"Fuck 'em and feed 'em" was the cynical way it was referred to in Vietnam, dropping bombs at night on an area where we dropped food during the day ... In Iraq my predecessors', wrote one leader of an Embedded Provincial Reconstruction Team, 'evolved nicer ways of describing' it (Van Buren, 2011: 5). Above all, as indicated by the pervasive talk of 'gender-focused' interventions, much of armed social work is organised around the provision of specific benefits for those with specific and 'various capabilities, needs, and intentions' (FM 3–24: B-18). In Afghanistan, women were steered towards industries in which labour is (made) cheap; for example, traditional forms of embroidery that can earn $2–3 a day. Such schemes rely on reproductive arrangements in small-scale family households in which women provide unpaid or low-wage labour in what is cast as a pre-contractual, pre-capitalist 'natural' arrangement (O'Brien, 1981). In the ugly but revealing words of NATO commander General Stanley McChrystal, counterinsurgents should 'conduct engagements with Afghan females to support the battle space owners' priorities' (McChrystal, 2010: 2; for analysis see Dyvik, 2014). 'Win the women,' claim contemporary counterinsurgents, 'and you own the family. Own the family and you take a big step forward in mobilizing the population' (Kilcullen, 2006).[29] The mass of 'neutral or friendly women' to be 'targeted' through social programmes, must be reduced to objects of social administration, rather than political subjects with ideas of justice and freedom of their own. This is not a polemical statement. It is one of the most fundamental assumptions of counterinsurgency writing, past and present.

If counterinsurgents wish to destroy the civilian base of insurgency ('win the women') they first have to 'locate the women', the population assumed to be contained inside their homes. Civilian homes are so important to counterinsurgents because, unlike the often undetectable armed enemy, they are the spaces visible to counterinsurgents and through which they may access the 'subsurface' of an insurgency. The fixed space of the family home provides a door into the underlying base of support on which insurgency depends, the realm 'below the surface' that 'engages in no armed activity', hidden inside houses (Kilcullen, 2010: 8). In lieu of forcibly removing hundreds of thousands of civilians into camps, the purpose of encircling and controlling existing

[29] Compare Fanon's account of the significance French colonialists placed on veiled, unseen Algerian women, in which 'there was a pure and simple adoption of the well-known formulae, "Let's win over the women and the rest will follow"'. Fanon presents this claim as resting on 'merely … the "discoveries" of the sociologists' (1965: 37).

family homes was to create an immovable object against which populations were to be 'fixed' and insurgents were drawn in and destroyed. Populations could be controlled through the production of this form of domesticated space – a subsection of the counterinsurgency household – because 'people are tied to their homes, businesses, farms, tribal areas, relatives, traditional landholdings, and so on' (Kilcullen, 2010: 10). As Helen M. Kinsella (2014) has perceptively written of this military strategy:

> Women's position ... within the home is re-inscribed in both counterinsurgency doctrine and in practice. The immobility of women is necessary for the prosecution and identification of the insurgents not only because it provides the boundary of the conflict, localizing the population (read as women) ... but because it literally both clears and holds ... 'the center of conflict'.

House-to-house raids clear territory of insurgents. People tied to their homes hold the centre of the conflict in place. The household of counterinsurgency can now be built ('clear, hold, build') on these domesticated spaces. Here the population is not simply analogous to 'a physical piece of real estate'. The masses of people in their homes become a physical piece of land, fulfilling 'the same purpose as decisive terrain' (Kilcullen, 2010: 9–10). The human terrain, already conceived as domesticated space in the sense of a place for social needs, is to become another form of despotic household in which women are sheltered and 'protected'.

In the gendered process of administering and protecting populations, women are symbolically sheltered and defended inside the household of counterinsurgency. 'Protection' was an early modern English euphemism for maintaining and providing for a mistress, an implication not difficult to discern in counterinsurgency discourse. 'To make war,' wrote Jean Larteguy (1961: 280) of French colonial campaigns, 'you always must put yourself in the other man's place ... eat what they eat, sleep with their women.'[30] Or in Kilcullen's more recent and uncensored directions to US counterinsurgents, 'Covet your enemy's wife'

[30] These lines are quoted in McFate and Jackson (2006: 14). Apparently the feeling, or desire articulated by Larteguy could be mutual. As Franz Fanon wrote: 'The look that the native turns on the settler town is a look of lust, a look of envy; it expresses his dream of possession – all manner of

(2006: 121). Observing similar military strategies and 'sociological' depth metaphors in the French war in Algeria, Franz Fanon noted how Algerian women 'appeared ... to assume a primordial importance' (1965: 37). In a kind of tautological logic, the civilian population, already gendered female, is imagined as the key to victory because its proponents already view counterinsurgency warfare as deeply 'sociological' (Mathias, 2011: 124). Counterinsurgency is 'sociological warfare' to the extent that insurgents are overcome through controlling and administering the life processes of their potential civilian base.[31] This homology accounts for what seems otherwise inexplicable to perceptive critics of different aspects of counterinsurgency myth-making. If war is war, the reciprocal killing and maiming of enemies, and counterinsurgencies are so brutal 'because they place the crosshairs on the people', then talk of 'winning the women' must be 'hugaboo' (Porch, 2013: 327).[32] But to place 'the crosshairs on the people' is to wage war precisely 'over the territoriality' of 'female, domestic space' (McClintock, 1993: 62). For the 'sociological' distinction between 'surface and subsurface' elements of insurgency is literally and figuratively mapped onto the assumed existence of a primordial matriarchy inside the domestic home. 'Behind the visible, manifest patriarchy,' observed Fanon of French colonial strategy, 'the more significant existence of a basic matriarchy was affirmed ... '"If we want to destroy the structure of Algerian society, its capacity for resistance, we must first of all conquer the women; we must go and find them behind the veil where they hide themselves *and in the houses where the men keep them out of sight*"' (Fanon, 1965: 37–38, emphasis added). This is not matriarchy in the sense of a government ruled by women. It is a matriarchal household in which women, being closer 'to certain biological realities', are the foundation of the life of 'society'.

possession: to sit at the settler's table, to sleep in the settler's bed, with his wife if possible. The colonized man is an envious man' (Fanon, 1963: 30).

31 In the context of the French war in Algeria, one critic of Galula suggested that 'sociological warfare' led to an 'odd trilogy of propaganda, torture and candy' (Serge Adour in Mathias, 2011: 124).

32 Cf. 'The population is not the prize. The population are spectators to armed conflict ... The population will obey whoever exercises the power of law over them. Power creates support. Support does not create power' (Owen, 2011: 36).

Covet your enemy's wife. But it is not necessarily women as such who are being protected/coveted. Women can stand in for territory, a tract of land, literally the space that counterinsurgents can hold and on which they may build.[33] This longing/coveting for something presumed to belong to another, the enemy, is another form of holding, a 'form of holding territory in an otherwise mobile war' (Kinsella, 2014), a gendered and domesticated terrain protected in the older euphemistic sense of protecting a mistress. Here woman, wife, mistress, house and home are not simply conjoined; they are synonymous.[34] This is the human terrain: a tract of ground defined by its natural features on which the latest despotic governor can stand and on which the house of counterinsurgency can be built. The production of such a thing as 'human terrain' is the epitome of despotic household governance. The etymon of territory in Latin *territōrium*, an enclosed piece of land, meant, by the fifteenth century, 'the extent of the land belonging to or under the jurisdiction of a ruler'. This enclosed land is household space to the extent that it is a unit of rule made possible through controlling the basic needs of those who are protected/sheltered by the despot, especially those constituted as closer to 'certain biological realities'. In the household of counterinsurgency, women must be constituted as subjects entirely governed by necessity. To hold territory (as women are 'coveted'), humans are imagined as terrain, as material objects belonging to the earth and to nature; that is, defined primarily through their relation to life and the needs of life. Houses are built for shelter; households are built to rule through the control and administration of life in which particular bodies must be made more vulnerable to life necessities. As retired Colonel Ralph Peters (2000) put it, the 'human terrain...the people, armed and dangerous, watching for exploitable

[33] McClintock has also written of how women served as boundary markers for empire, for sailors, cartographers, explorers and philosophers. In her words, 'women served as mediating and threshold figures by means of which men oriented themselves in space, as agents of power and agents of knowledge ... [T]he representation of the land as female is a traumatic trope, occurring almost invariably, ... in the aftermath of male boundary confusion ... a historical ... strategy of containment' (McClintock, 1995: 24; see also Khalili, 2013).

[34] According to Diane King, drawing on ethnographic research in Iraqi Kurdistan from the mid-1990s, a 'husband will likely avoid directly discussing [his wife] with non-kin men, speaking euphemistically about his "house" (*mal*) instead' (King, 2008: 321).

opportunities, or begging to be protected … will determine the success or failure of the intervention'. In a tediously familiar story, women remain the prize to be won; waiting to see who will 'hurt them less'; a neutral mass, there for the taking; women relieved to be saved by the strongest man who is also hopefully noble – the kind of warrior pursuing his 'moral obligation' to protect (Kilcullen, 2009: 67). Whoever takes territorial control wins the prize of the population that is forced into acquiescence, whether they like it or not, although audiences back home surely prefer to believe that they like it.

Conclusion

As a direct result of decentralised household despotism, various warlords and militia now govern much of Iraq, and continue to fight with each other across and within sectarian lines over territory and control of the devastated population. According to one former Member of Parliament, Afghanistan is now a mafia state run by a 'house of warlords' (Joya, 2011). Groups empowered by counterinsurgents during both campaigns have assumed the right to police the behaviour of 'their' population, especially women whose bodies have become the target and object of violent competition, trafficking for profit and 'honour crimes'. The role of aid organisations, some of which are complicit in the sexual exploitation of girls, is to prevent the humanitarian catastrophe from reaching publicly unacceptable levels in the West, which is a very high level indeed.[35] In fact, the highly visible presence of NGOs, humanitarian actors, human rights experts and academics at the height of the counterinsurgencies in Iraq and Afghanistan contributed greatly to the conventional notion of what 'population-centric war' entailed, that it was an extension of the West's more or less benign overseas aid programmes. Yet, social work has historically been undertaken in alliance with otherwise potentially critical agents, experts and policy knowledge, for it involves administering the life processes of some of the most vulnerable and exploited, primarily those most threatening to the interests and identity of the dominant powers.

[35] 'Girls who are refugees are more likely to be lured by civilian assistance staff members and men in security forces in exchanging food and other necessities for sex' (Enloe, 2010: 84–85).

In light of the rise and transformation of social forms of government, it should be no surprise that in the face of military defeat in Iraq and lack of progress in Afghanistan, armed social work could be presented as the absorption of liberal and progressive criticism, managing to convince large swathes of media, government and academia. The notion of population-centric war was intended to appeal to a broad constituency, too much of which assumed that the wars had, indeed, become 'kindler and gentler'. In fact, several elements of population control recalled earlier late-colonial food denial strategies. Water and electricity supplies were cut during the siege of Fallujah in 2004 and the delivery of humanitarian supplies, including food and medicine, were also withheld. The deliberate intention was to weaken the civilian base of insurgency, collectively punishing those potentially aiding resistance.[36] When coalition forces attempted to restore electricity supplies, Sunni neighbourhoods were less likely to have their access increased (Enloe, 2010: 71). By the summer of 2007, encirclement, blockade and control of basic supplies had become the defining military strategy in Iraq, along with airstrikes on insurgent bases. In Afghanistan, the escalation of conventional and special operations forces, private military contractors and drones in kill/capture missions led to thousands of civilian deaths (Hastings, 2012). Obama's exit strategy from Afghanistan amounted to increased drone attacks, night raids on Afghan homes by Special Forces and targeted assassination of suspected enemy fighters. The mass slaughter seen in Malaya, Kenya and Vietnam was replaced by the 'militarism of small massacres', when tens of thousands of civilians were killed by US-led forces, but usually in relatively 'small' and seemingly more acceptable and discrete pockets of dozens (Shaw, 2002).

Several critics have already argued that the most recent notion of population-centric war is propagandistic cover for 'dirty wars' (Hunt, 2010; Scahill, 2013). But to understand properly the ideological appeal of armed social work, and what it actually amounts to in practice, requires a deeper understanding of the history and ontology of the social realm as a form of household and its crisis-driven transformations. Why is the existence of a neutral and passive population

[36] There has been an enormous increase in birth defects and miscarriages in Basra and Fallujah, which both endured exposure to toxic metals, including depleted uranium, during heavy US bombing campaigns (Al-Sabbak et al., 2012).

so readily accepted and repeated over and over again in the scholarly and popular literature on counterinsurgency? Why are liberal counterinsurgents so deeply reliant on the notion that there is always and everywhere populations that can be swayed more by 'social' necessity than political commitment? Distinctly social policy first emerged in the nineteenth century as a quintessentially liberal form of 'self-review and self-renewal' in the face of violent and political resistance (Dean, 2010: 66). The theory and practice of social intervention was *the* location for the incorporation of 'legitimate' – non-revolutionary – dissent to both capitalism and empire. For it did not disrupt their fundamental logic. This is why 'liberals' have been particularly susceptible to the ideological pull of social work – the palliative interventions intended to mitigate the worst excesses of wage labour or empire. It is why liberal counterinsurgents, again and again, return to the discourse of armed social work. In fact, recent doctrine not only wagers that a 'passive or neutral people' can be swayed more by social necessity than political commitment. Counterinsurgents assume that large populations back home can believe such a thing. And they generally do. For that is how they too are governed.

8 *Conclusion: 'it's the* oikos, *stupid'*

The household is a school of power. There, within the door, learn the tragi-comedy of human life.

Ralph Waldo Emerson (1838)[1]

In ancient Greece, probably the best-loved goddess among ordinary people was Hestia, the goddess of hearth and home. Every house had an altar to Hestia in which a fire continually burned, representing domestic warmth and care for the household, the *oikos*. Surprisingly perhaps given the widespread denigration of *oikos* activities, a civic fire continually burned in every major city in Hestia's honour. When a Greek city established a new colony, fire was taken from the public hearth and used to light a flame that would continually burn in the government centre of the latest territory as a symbol of the new relationship (Kajava, 2004). The colony was domesticated with the arrival of Hestia's flame. As recently as the late nineteenth and early twentieth centuries, we can still find a literal association between the founding of new colonies and household activities and symbolism. Contemporaries described the turn-of-the-century US occupation of the Philippines as a form of overseas housekeeping. Filipino republicans were defeated through military operations, mass detentions without trial, and the forcible removal and concentration of civilians, activities followed by reform of labour, sanitation and education. That military occupation was imperial household management, or domestic engineering, was as obvious to Progressive Era Americans as it had been to ancient Greeks. Local government was described as municipal housekeeping and it was common to refer to the 'household of the nation'. The incorporation of the Philippines into the American empire was unmistakably imperial housekeeping.

[1] In Barile and Brandon (2004: 1). The subtitle of the chapter is a play on, 'it's the economy, stupid': the 1992 campaign mantra of presidential candidate Bill Clinton.

The Philippines campaign seems to be the last colonial war by a liberal empire explicitly conceived in these household terms. When and why did colonisers, propagandists and other observers stop thinking this way? Talk of household governance declined with the rise of distinctly social forms of governance and discourse, a transformation that affected all forms of government: local, national and imperial. The campaign in the Philippines occurred while American sociology was in its infancy and so household language persisted alongside emerging talk of 'social engineering'; not so the mid- to late nineteenth-century French campaigns in Tonkin, Morocco and Algeria. By this period, France had become the location of the most developed and sophisticated discourses of *société*. *Économie domestique* could have made perfect sense as a paradigm of French colonial war. Yet, its French practitioners were much more likely to deploy new sociological language to understand and rationalise their activities. Strategists wrote pioneering articles on the 'social role' of the colonial soldier and how to fight war in 'the social *milieu*'. Commentators spoke of the need to 'socialise' the local population, social re-engineering, the functional interrelations between parts of the 'social body' and the deeper sociological causes and remedies of anti-colonial resistance. These are the French origins of claims about the power of armed social work. The inner core of local resistance to pacification would be undone through the destruction and reconstitution of the native 'social' base: exemplary massacres, forced removals and re-concentration, selective distribution of basic supplies, the co-optation of local enforcers and opening new markets. In the Philippines, variations on these activities were called 'policies of attraction'; in French Morocco, the 'policy of the smile'; in Britain's late-colonial wars, 'hearts and minds' and 'rehabilitation'; in America's war on Vietnam they were the 'Other War', or the policy of 'fuck 'em and feed 'em'; in Afghanistan and Iraq they were 'population-centric'. In each case, activities undertaken for reasons of military necessity were reconceived and justified in the latest sociological terms because social theories are the distinctly modern form of *oikonomikos*, the science of household rule. Like Hestia's flame, sociocratic household governance has been mobile and highly portable.

The historical rise of social forms of governance did not destroy and replace household activities and forms of thought; they are the distinctly modern and capitalist variant on the science and practice of household rule. All government based on the hierarchical administration of life processes should be understood in household terms. Households are historically variable, but as a unit of rule they are defined by the nature of the relations between people in a particular spatial arrangement. Household relations are hierarchical. However, this despotism need not be personalised, centralised or direct: anonymous bureaucrats can indirectly administer populations in large-scale national or imperial households. While households are always located in space, this space is not always fixed or bounded, as suggested by both ancient Greek and modern practices of colonisation. Moreover, while despotic rule may be enforced through violence and legal dictate, despotism is never absolute. Inside and between households, people often – and often successfully – resist and subvert domestication. During counterinsurgency, populations are deliberately exposed to the exigencies of life so as to create units of rule in which they can be pacified and domesticated. The inmates of concentration camps, resettlement areas, New Villages, Strategic Hamlets and 'cleansed' cities and towns were subject to administration, precisely in an effort to create this domesticated space. Inmates became *of* the counterinsurgency household, subjected to the more or less openly despotic personal or bureaucratic rule of officials, whether colonial or native officers, newly created community leaders or tribal patriarchs, social workers from the metropole, UN personnel, private contractors and other NGOs. Populations were administered in the name of their own welfare and protection, with specific activities largely arranged in accordance with assumed biological attributes; that is, through social categories and techniques. With liberalism's rejection of personal tutelage, such intense and direct population control was always conceived as a temporary expedient with an emphasis on self-help and eventual self-government for individuals in 'society' and nations allowed to join the 'society of states'. Yet this did not signal the end of despotic household government. It became depersonalised and bureaucratic.

Numerous counterinsurgency texts – field manuals, government reports, practitioner memoirs, think tank publications and related scholarship – conceive of themselves as texts of political theory in their own right. In addition to offering sociological explanations and remedies for revolt, counterinsurgents have explicitly sought what they view as political rather than purely military solutions to insurgency. As Wendy Brown (2008: 354) observed, the United States *Counterinsurgency Field Manual*, requires – from the US military no less – a degree of political intelligence and foresight worthy of Rousseau's Lawgiver, a degree of provision for human needs worthy of the farthest reach of the communist imaginary, a degree of stabilization through governance worthy of Thomas Hobbes ... an ability to 'decipher cultural narratives' ... worthy of a trained ethnographer, and an ability to manipulate these narratives worthy of Plato.

The broader canon of counterinsurgency writing incorporates claims and ambitions touching on much of the tradition of Western political thought and explicitly articulates answers to some of its most fundamental questions. What is the basis of stable order? Is it possible, and if so how, to pacify populations by taking away or providing for basic life needs? How can feelings of passivity and defeatism be created in the target population? If people are administered as social beings then will they renounce dreams of political self-determination? The history and theory of household rule suggests that these so-called political questions are not really political. They are rooted in the mentality and techniques of household rule. Counterinsurgency is not a form of 'applied political science' (Isaac, 2008: 347). It is a form of applied *oikonomikos*. *Oikonomia* is not only the source of the modern language of economics. Household rule is at the origin of much of the tradition of political thought. To that extent, it should not be conceived as properly political at all, but as a branch of *oikonomikos*. For when counterinsurgents speak of 'pacification' they mean domestication; *domus* is Latin for house. When they ask whether it is possible, and if so how, to pacify populations by controlling their most basic needs, activities and relations of dependency, they are asking a variation on the Social Question. When they ask how acquiescence can be secured through the reproduction of gender, class, racial and imperial hierarchies, they are seeking new techniques of sociocratic household rule. And many eager social scientists are willing to advise and justify such techniques for this is the shared paradigm of distinctly social thought.[2]

Both counterinsurgency and much political theory are conceived as the science of government, from 'to steer', to rule, regulate and control. That is, politics has been defined entirely from the perspective of despotic governance and this should come as no surprise. Diverse

[2] The problems with the Marxist exception were discussed in Chapters 1 and 2.

historical literatures and scholarly fields indicate that, until the emergence of liberal thought, large-scale government was usually conceived in household terms. An understanding of households-as-government prevailed due to the rich history and geographical diversity of its forms. Yet, there is no necessary reason to subsume politics as such into the hierarchical household, to treat household rule and politics as fundamentally the same. In fact, there are good reasons to understand them as reflecting profoundly different, even antithetical, kinds of relationships between people. This is one of the advantages of using the term 'sociocratic' to name the government offered under liberal counterinsurgency; it withholds the honorific term 'political' from the theory of counterinsurgency rule. Counterinsurgency is defined by its attempt to pacify and domesticate, to seek to negate political agency through violence and control over life. Yet perhaps an affiliation between counterinsurgency and politics can be stated in negative terms. It may be possible to identify what politics is by examining what the counterinsurgency household seeks to domesticate. In other words, just as we cannot properly comprehend counterinsurgency without knowledge of insurgency, we cannot propose a compelling theory of household despotism without its opposite: a theory of politics as non-domestication, the activity of resisting despotic rule.

Household rule seeks to pacify and domesticate specific groups of people through the violent and hierarchical control and administration of life needs usually organised around presumed and largely essentialist biological attributes. People are so administered due to the consequences of their non-domestication on prevailing hierarchies and relations of power; that is, given their potentially disruptive and dangerous political activity. If politics and household rule are understood as opposites, politics might then refer to the actions of plural equals freely debating and acting on their common affairs in a manner that was essentially non-violent and unpredictable; that is, not subject to the calculations of *oikonomia*. Politics would include the non-hierarchical administration of life processes, but politics *as such* would not be reducible to *oikonomia* affairs. The question would be how to organise life processes in a properly political manner; that is, attentive to – rather than destructive of – human plurality and freedom (Arendt, 1958).[3]

[3] This is also partly a question of whether the administration of life processes is necessarily violent. Hannah Arendt thought so, but not because people are fundamentally violent, but because there was something violent about life

Political action may lead to the creation of new laws, institutions and even government forms, but the basic activity of politics does not require government or rulership to begin. Indeed, rather than exemplify politics, sovereign models of government signal an attempt to end politics.[4] To be sure, just as forms of household rule are mutable, the conditions of possibility for political action are always shaped by historically variable gendered, racialised, class and inter-community hierarchies that constrain human freedom. Nonetheless, the potential for people to act politically is as real as practices of household governance. In other words, these claims about the nature of politics are not normative. They are grounded on historical observation of the fact of political action, that every group of humans is capable of political action. The attempt to prevent particular groups from acting in concert to initiate potentially revolutionary change is the purpose of household rule. Is the ever-present existence of households not the best evidence for the ever-present possibility of politics?

If political action and household rule are fundamentally distinct forms of activity, capturing essentially different sorts of relations between people and dissimilar experiences, then much so-called political theory, which imagines politics in terms of rulers and ruled, should not be viewed as properly political at all. What, then, would be the historical and theoretical methodology most appropriate to capture the distinct phenomena of politics and household governance? We could certainly do worse than retrieve the rich language that already exists to describe and analyse household rule, including the vocabulary of despotism, governance, rulership, sovereignty, administration, life processes, violence, hierarchy, patriarchy, pacification, domestication and domesticity. This language captures a great deal of the history and ontology of household rule, including the social regulation under modern capitalist government. Accordingly, it is a more compelling

necessities as such (they compel, they destroy). Fanon also referred to the 'terrorism of necessity' (1967: 88). However, contra Arendt, this does not mean that politics cannot occur inside households or that political action and maintenance of life processes are necessarily incompatible, although they are certainly in tension.

[4] This is why Carl Schmitt's (1996, 2004b) attempts to theorise politics as non-domestication are inadequate. Although he understood politics and domestication as opposites, Schmitt remains within the tradition of political theory to the extent that he effectively assimilates politics to sovereign power, a variant of household despotism.

and precise grammar for theorising governance than associated with distinctly social forms of thought: socialisation, social evolution, social norms and processes, social system, social structure, structural functionalism, social solidarity and social integration. To be sure, much of the language associated with household rule (despotism, governance, rulership) is already the established lexicon of political theory, but again this should not be considered the proper language of politics. Rather than the principles and techniques of despotism, resistance to domestication would be the object of political theory. As Audre Lorde (2007) has put, 'the master's tools will never dismantle the master's house'. In other words, the focus of analysis would shift from the ideologies and practices of household rule towards the episodic and fragmentary moments of political action. Needless to say, from this perspective, social theory is simply the wrong grammar for describing and analysing politics. The problem is that in assimilating politics to household rule, the tradition of political thought has also left us without a good vocabulary to describe and analyse struggles against household governance; that is, a vocabulary for politics as non-domestication. There is a need for a replacement language for political theory, a task beyond the scope of this book, but which others began to develop.[5]

More pointedly, given our real focus, to refuse to assimilate politics to household rule is to abandon the most influential position on the relation between war and politics and no longer conceive social and political as equivalent and interchangeable categories. Politics as non-domestication is an ever-present human potential to act with plural others. The social realm and related discourses are historically specific forms of household rule and thought associated with capitalist empires/states. To the extent that sociology was forged during crises of the social realm, it is a form of *oikonomikos* seeking to explain politics in terms of 'deeper' social causes and remedy political action through social regulation. To that extent, the social and the political could never be equivalent; they are antagonistic opposites. Similarly, if we take

[5] Despite the abundant problems with aspects of her work, of the major thinkers in the political theory canon, Hannah Arendt did most to offer a rich lexicon to replace the language of the household, writing of action, worldliness, appearance, who-ness, freedom, plurality, power, natality and revolution. On this particular aspect of her work see Arendt (1958, 1963, 1968, 2005). The secondary literature is vast but see Canovan (1992); Honig (1995); Benhabib (1996); Villa (1999); Owens (2007b).

seriously a notion of politics as non-domestication then war, including counterinsurgency, is not the continuation of politics by other means, as if politics and war were simply two ends of a continuum of violence defining all human relations. War is the reciprocal activity of killing and maiming people, of seeking to compel others to submit to ones will through force and violence (Clausewitz, 1832/1976).[6] War is fighting in which the essence of relations between people centres on command and obedience. But there is nothing except adherence to Clausewitz to suggest that war is the continuation of politics, properly understood. This would be to claim that politics and war are essentially the same, with one activity simply more explicitly violent than the other. The confusion over the distinction between politics and war is really a failure to distinguish between politics and household government, a failure characteristic of Clausewitz's statist political realism. If war is on a continuum of degrees of violence with anything, then it is not politics. It is household government, including Clausewitz's Prussian state. The serious neglect of households-as-government explains, in part, the poverty of thinking about the ontology of war, as exemplified in social and political theories of counterinsurgency. To be sure, just as politics can occur inside and between households, exemplary forms of political action occur during wartime, right in the midst of fighting. Yet, politics and war are fundamentally different ways of being with others and of making and remaking the human world.

The amount of scholarship grounded on claims about the nature of the social world, the importance of social relations and the explanatory power of social processes should be no surprise given the hegemony of social forms of thought. At their best, this language is used to indicate the cultural thickness of world affairs in opposition to comparatively ahistorical and parsimonious accounts of behavioural social science and theories of rational choice (Mann, 1993; Teschke, 2003; Barkawi, 2006). From this perspective, the social is a useful concept to name the totality of self-instituted relations between humans. It is about contextualisation, placing world politics in its proper 'social context'. Despite the historical conditions of its emergence, social terminology

[6] Under the influence of Clausewitz and Foucault, Barkawi and Brighton's (2011) 'critical war studies' has, as yet, been unable to properly distinguish between war and politics. For them, politics, like virtually everything else, is a product of war (cf. Owens, 2007b: ch. 2).

would therefore seem to be a harmless – even obvious – abstraction that only the dogmatic could refuse to adopt. Yet if we take the historical rise of the social seriously, and accept its household ontology, then there is little justification for using the social in this way, as an explanatory concept to form the basis of general theories of human history. At its worst, social terminology is used at such a general level of abstraction that it substitutes for analysis of history and power; that is, it serves as an intellectual crutch. The point is not to jettison abstractions in general or claim that scholars should never utter the word 'social'. The appropriateness or inappropriateness of social language depends on the kind of statements being made. The old Latin meaning of 'society' as friendship and 'social' as genial retains integrity in some contexts. Moreover, as shown throughout this book, talk of social regulation is also legitimate if used as the historically specific name for a more fundamental type of household rule. In other words, most social talk makes genuine sense only under certain conditions. There are two constraints. These are an explicit understanding of the history of the social as a form of imperial-state and capitalist governance and comprehension of its ontology; that is, as a scaled-up and transformed household. In other words, we need an historical and ontological account of the social, including social forms of thought, without relying on the conventions of social theory. This task requires a distinction between social theory and *a theory of* the historical rise of the social as a distinctively capitalist and highly mobile form of household rule.

International theorists need to rethink the widely held assumption that they are debating and choosing between different social theories of international relations. The field has been deeply ahistorical in its adoption of social terminology as the basis for general explanations for international affairs. Political realism and liberalism have not been interested in historicising social categories and none of the major traditions, mainstream or critical, have considered the dangers of social reductionism. To the limited extent that theorists have approached social language historically it has been anachronistically read into early modern theories of natural law or Enlightenment mythology about the 'discovery of the social' has been uncritically embraced. These are serious problems. To insist on the historical specificity of the rise of the social is not for the sake of vulgar historicism, retrieving a neglected past for its own sake. It is because the story of where, when and why 'social' and 'society' emerged as concrete historical forms and discourses is of enormous and wide-ranging significance. More obviously, it has consequences for how we interpret the meaning and validity of social theories, including social theories of international relations. The major traditions are fragments of different answers to the nineteenth-century Social Question, embodying assorted paradigms of social regulation, rather than objective theories of international relations. None of them are convincing in light of the history and ontology of households, which subsumes realism's emphasis on force and violence and historicises both sociological liberalism and Marx's claims that 'society' or 'social relations' are the deep underlying causes of government and violence. The problem of the ahistorical social affects both traditional and critical social theory. More work on the implications for the status of existing international theories, and the prospects for an alternative theory of international relations, is required. As a starting point, this theory would centre on relations between units of modern household rule, including – but not limited to – states and empires. More importantly, attention to the historicity of the social realm brings to the fore the significance of transformations and crises in household governance in international and imperial history.

Households are a pervasive feature of life to the extent that humans have failed to establish a non-hierarchical, non-despotic method of managing life processes. This is why, in the end, the history and theory of households should be privileged as the analytic for understanding forms of government and, sooner or later, relations between them. Ultimately, households-as-government should be privileged – as they were before liberal theories of contract – because they are the spaces in which rule is achieved through the control and management of bodies in their extreme and irreducible vulnerability and fragility. Household rule is organised around the material life needs and processes of human beings. This fundamental materiality is why control over the provision or withholding of life necessities has been so effective as the basis of rulership, domination and despotism (Butler, 2004). The founding and maintenance of households is not simply a question of determining a particular vision of community, a form of law, or principles of legislation and morality. It is also more than Thomas Hobbes' (1651/1968: 186) claim that fear of the 'danger of violent death' is the foundation of government or, in a more liberal formulation, that 'restraint on the application of violent power upon individual bodies' is the 'first freedom' (Deudney, 2007: 14). This statement should be turned on its head. The requirement to restrain violence to meet basic life necessities has been the fundamental basis of household rule not political freedom. The history and theory of households, including the household of liberal 'society', suggests that the ability to moderate the use of violent power on bodies is not the first freedom. It is the first despotism, the very origin of the protection and welfare of those domesticated inside households.

References

Abdul-Jabar, Faleh (2001) 'Sheikhs and Ideologues: Deconstruction and Reconstruction of Tribes under Patrimonial Totalitarianism in Iraq, 1968–1998', in Faleh Abdul-Jabar and Hosham Dawod (eds.) *Tribes and Power: Nationalism and Ethnicity in the Middle East* (London: Saqi), pp. 69–109.

Adas, Michael (2006) *Dominance by Design: Technological Imperatives and America's Civilizing Mission* (Cambridge, MA: Harvard University Press).

Addams, Jane (1905) 'Problems of Municipal Administration', *The American Journal of Sociology*, 10(4): 425–444.

Adorno, Theodor W. (2000) *Introduction to Sociology* (ed. Christoph Gödde; trans. Edmund Jephcott) (Stanford, CA: Stanford University Press).

Adorno, Theodor W. and Max Horkheimer (1944/1979) *Dialectic of Enlightenment* (trans. John Cumming) (London: Verso).

Agamben, Giorgio (1998) *Homo Sacer: Sovereign Power and Bare Life* (trans. Daniel Heller-Roazen) (Stanford, CA: Stanford University Press).

(2000) *Means without End: Notes on Politics* (trans. Vincenzo Binetti and Casare Casarino) (Minneapolis, MN: University of Minnesota Press).

(2005) *State of Exception* (trans. Kevin Attell) (Chicago: University of Chicago Press).

(2011) *The Kingdom and the Glory: For a Theological Genealogy of Economy and Government* (trans. Lorenzo Chiesa) (Stanford, CA: Stanford University Press).

Agathangelou, Anna M. and L.H.M. Ling (2004) 'The House of IR: From Family Power Politics to the *Poisies* of Worldism', *International Studies Review*, 6(1): 21–49.

Agnew, John, Thomas W. Gillespie, Jorge Gonzalez and Brian Min (2008) 'Baghdad Nights: Evaluating the U.S. Military "Surge" Using Nighttime Light Signatures', *Environment and Planning A*, 40(10): 2285–2295.

Ahern, Thomas L. (2000) *CIA and the House of Ngo: Covert Action in South Vietnam, 1954–1963* (Washington, DC: Center for the Study of Intelligence).

(2001) *CIA and Rural Pacification in South Vietnam* (Washington, DC: Center for the Study of Intelligence).

Aisenberg, Andrew Robert (1999) *Contagion: Disease, Government, and the 'Social Question' in Nineteenth-Century France* (Stanford, CA: Stanford University Press).

Al-Ali, Nadje and Nicola Pratt (2009) *What Kind of Liberation? Women and the Occupation of Iraq* (foreword by Cynthia Enloe) (Berkeley, CA: University of California Press).

Alam, S.M. Shamsul (2007) *Rethinking Mau Mau in Colonial Kenya* (New York: Palgrave Macmillan).

Albert, Mathias and Barry Buzan (2013) 'International Relations Theory and the "Social Whole": Encounters and Gaps Between IR and Sociology', *International Political Sociology*, 7(2): 117–135.

Albert, Mathias, Barry Buzan and Michael Zürn (2013) *Bringing Sociology to International Relations: World Politics as Differentiation Theory* (Cambridge: Cambridge University Press).

Alcobia-Murphy, Shane (2006) 'Safe House: Authenticity, Nostalgia and the Irish House', in Gerry Smyth and Jo Croft (eds.) *Our House: the Representation of Domestic Space in Modern Culture* (Amsterdam: Rodopi), pp. 103–120.

Alker, Hayward R. (1996) *Rediscoveries and Reformulations: Humanistic Methodologies for International Studies* (Cambridge: Cambridge University Press).

Allbritton, Christopher (2005) 'Making Tribal War Work for the US in Iraq', *Time*, 8 November. Available at http://content.time.com/time/world/article/0,8599,1127376,00.html (accessed 25 June 2015).

Allison, Penelope Mary (ed.) (1999) *The Archaeology of Household Activities* (London: Routledge).

Al-Sabbak, M., S. Sadik Ali, O. Savabi, G. Savabi, S. Dastgiri and M. Savabieasfahani (2012) 'Metal Contamination and the Epidemic of Congenital Birth Defects in Iraqi Cities', *Bulletin of Environmental Contamination and Toxicology*, 89: 937–944.

The American Fabian (1898) 4(7).

American League of Philadelphia (1900) *The Self-Governing Filipino: an Open Letter to Bishop Potter, of New York* (Philadelphia: American League of Philadelphia).

Amoroso, Donna J. (2003) 'Inheriting the "Moro Problem": Muslim Authority and Colonial Rule in British Malaya and the Philippines', in Julian Go and Anne L. Foster (eds.) *The American Colonial State in the Philippines: Global Perspectives* (Durham, NC: Duke University Press), pp. 118–147.

Anderson, Ben (2011) 'Population and Affective Perception: Biopolitics and Anticipatory Action in US Counterinsurgency Doctrine', *Antipode*, 43(2): 205–236.

Anderson, David (2005) *Histories of the Hanged: the Dirty War in Kenya and the End of Empire* (New York: W.W. Norton).

(2006) 'Surrogates of the State: Collaboration and Atrocity in Kenya's Mau Mau War', in George Kassimeris (ed.) *The Barbarisation of Warfare* (London: Hurst), pp. 159–174.

(2011) 'Mau Mau in the High Court and the "Lost" British Empire Archives: Colonial Conspiracy or Bureaucratic Bungle?' *The Journal of Imperial and Commonwealth History*, 39(5): 699–716.

Anderson, Perry (1974) *Passages from Antiquity to Feudalism* (London: New Left Books).

Andradé, Dale (1990) *Ashes to Ashes: The Phoenix Program and the Vietnam War* (Lexington, MA: Lexington Books).

Anievas, Alexander (ed.) (2010) *Marxism and World Politics: Contesting Global Capitalism* (London: Routledge).

Apter, David (1965) *The Politics of Modernization* (Chicago: University of Chicago Press).

Arendt, Hannah (1958) *The Human Condition* (Chicago: University of Chicago Press).

(1963) *On Revolution* (New York: Viking).

(1968) *Between Past and Future: Eight Exercises in Political Thought* (New York: Viking).

(2005) *The Promise of Politics* (New York: Schocken).

Aristotle (1962) *The Politics* (trans. with an intro. by T.A. Sinclair) (London: Penguin Books).

Armstrong, Louise (1983) *The Home Front: Notes from the Family War Zone* (New York: McGraw-Hill).

Aron, Raymond (1968) *Progress and Disillusion: the Dialectics of Modern Society* (Middlesex: Penguin).

Aronson, Ronald (1983) *The Dialectics of Disaster: a Preface to Hope* (London: Verso).

Askwith, Tom (1954) *The Story of Kenya's Progress* (Nairobi: Eagle Press)

(1961) 'Self-help Housing', *Journal of African Administration*, 13(4): 204–210.

(1995) *From Mau Mau to Harambee: Memoirs and Memoranda of Colonial Kenya* (ed. Joanna Lewis) (Cambridge: African Studies Centre).

Bacevich, Andrew (2009) 'Social Work with Guns', *London Review of Books*, 31(24): 7–8.

Bailliet, Cecilia M. (2007) '"War in the Home": An Exposition of Protection Issues Pertaining to the Use of the House Raids in Counterinsurgency Operations', *Journal of Military Ethics*, 6(3): 173–197.

Baker, Kenneth Michael (1994) 'Enlightenment and the Institution of Society: Notes for a Conceptual History', in Willem Melching and Wyger Velema (eds.) *Main Trends in Cultural History: Ten Essays* (Amsterdam: Rodopi), pp. 95–120.

Balibar, Etienne (1991) 'Is There a "Neo-Racism"?', in Etienne Balibar and Immanuel Wallerstein (eds.) *Race, Nation, Class: Ambiguous Identities* (London: Verso), pp. 17–28.

Bankoff, Greg (2005) 'Wants, Wages, and Workers: Laboring in the American Philippines, 1899–1908', *Pacific Historical Review*, 74(1): 59–86.

Baram, Amatzia (2003) 'Victory in Iraq, One Tribe at a Time', *The New York Times*, 28 October http://www.nytimes.com/2003/10/28/opinion/victory-in-iraq-one-tribe-at-a-time.html (accessed 25 June 2015).

Barber, Noel (1971) *The War of the Running Dogs: How Malaya Defeated the Communist Guerrillas, 1948–1960* (London: Collins).

Barberis, Damiela (2003) 'In Search of an Object: Organicist Sociology and the Reality of Society in *Fin-de-siècle* France', *History of the Human Sciences*, 16(3): 51–72.

Barile, Kerri S. and Jamie C. Brandon (2004) 'Introduction', in Kerri S. Barile and Jamie C. Brandon (eds.) *Household Chores and Household Choices: Theorizing the Domestic Sphere in Historical Archaeology* (Tuscaloosa: University of Alabama Press), pp. 1–12.

Barkawi, Tarak (2006) *Globalization and War* (Oxford: Rowman and Littlefield).

Barkawi, Tarak and Shane Brighton (2011) 'Powers of War: Fighting, Knowledge, and Critique' *International Political Sociology*, 5(2): 126–143.

Barkawi, Tarak and Mark Laffey (1999) 'The Imperial Peace: Democracy, Force and Globalization', *European Journal of International Relations*, 5(4): 403–434.

Barkawi, Tarak and Keith Stanski (eds.) (2012) *Orientalism and War* (New York: Columbia University Press).

Barkdull, John (1995) 'Waltz, Durkheim, and International Relations: The International System as an Abnormal Form', *American Political Science Review*, 89(3): 669–680.

Barkin, Samuel J. (2010) *Realist Constructivism: Rethinking International Relations Theory* (Cambridge: Cambridge University Press).

Barnett, Michael (2002) 'Historical Sociology and Constructivism: An Estranged Past, a Federated Future?', in Stephen Hobden and John M. Hobson (eds.) *Historical Sociology of International Relations* (Cambridge: Cambridge University Press), pp. 99–119.

(2011) *Empire of Humanity: A History of Humanitarianism* (Ithaca, NY: Cornell University Press).

Barnett, Michael and Thomas G. Weiss (2011) *Humanitarianism Contested: Where Angels Fear to Tread* (New York: Routledge).

Barnett, Thomas P.M. (2004) *The Pentagon's New Map: War and Peace in the Twenty-First Century* (New York: G.P. Putnam's Sons).

Bartelson, Jens (1995) *A Genealogy of Sovereignty* (Cambridge: Cambridge University Press).

(1996) 'Short Circuits: Society and Tradition in International Relations Theory', *Review of International Studies*, 22(4): 339–360.

Bass, Gary (2008) *Freedom's Battle: The Origins of Humanitarian Intervention* (New York: Knopf).

Bates, David William (2011) *States of War: Enlightenment Origins of the Political* (New York: Columbia University Press).

Battjes, Mark E. (2011) *Protecting, Isolating and Controlling Behavior: Population and Resource Control Measures in Counterinsurgency Campaigns* (Fort Leavenworth, KA: Combat Studies Institute Press).

Baudrillard, Jean (1978/2007) *In Shadow of the Silent Majorities or the End of the Social* (Los Angeles, CA: Semiotext(e)).

Bayly, C.A. (2004) *The Birth of the Modern World, 1780–1914: Global Connections and Comparisons* (Malden, MA: Blackwell).

Beck, Herman (1995) *The Origins of the Authoritarian Welfare State in Prussia: Conservatives, Bureaucracy and the Social Question, 1815–70* (Ann Arbor, MI: University of Michigan Press).

Beck, Ulrich (1992) *Risk Society: Towards a New Modernity* (trans. Mark Ritter) (London: Sage Publications).

(1999) *World Risk Society* (Cambridge: Polity Press).

Beckett, Ian (1997) 'Robert Thompson and the British Advisory Mission to South Vietnam, 1961–1965', *Small Wars and Insurgencies*, 8(3): 41–63.

Bell, Daniel (1960) *The End of Ideology: On the Exhaustion of Political Ideas in the Fifties* (Cambridge, MA: Harvard University Press).

Bell, Duncan (2010) 'John Stuart Mill on Colonies', *Political Theory*, 38(1): 34–64.

Bellamy, Alex J. (2014) *Responsibility to Protect: A Defense* (Oxford: Oxford University Press).

Bellamy, Richard (1992) *Liberalism and Modern Society: An Historical Argument* (Cambridge: Polity Press).

Benhabib, Seyla (1996) *The Reluctant Modernism of Hannah Arendt* (Thousand Oaks, CA: Sage Publications).

Bennett, Huw (2007) 'The Other Side of the COIN: Minimum and Exemplary Force in British Army Counterinsurgency in Kenya', *Small Wars and Insurgencies*, 18(4): 638–664.

(2009) '"A Very Salutatory Effect": The Counter-terror Strategy in the Early Malayan Emergency, June 1948 to December 1949', *Journal of Strategic Studies*, 32(3): 415–444.

(2012) *Fighting the Mau Mau: The British Army and Counter-insurgency in the Kenya Emergency* (Cambridge: Cambridge University Press).

Bentham, Jeremy (1789/1823) *An Introduction to the Principles of Morals and Legislation* (Oxford: Clarendon Press).

Berend, Ivan T. (2005) 'Foucault and the Welfare State', *European Review*, 13(4): 551–556.

Berenson, Edward (2011) *Heroes of Empire: Five Charismatic Men and the Conquest of Africa* (Berkeley, CA: University of California Press).

Berman, Bruce J. (1976) 'Bureaucracy and Incumbent Violence: Colonial Administration and the Origins of the "Mau Mau" Emergency in Kenya', *British Journal of Political Science*, 6(2): 143–175.

(1990) *Control and Crisis in Colonial Kenya: the Dialectic of Domination* (London: James Currey).

Berman, Bruce J. and J.M. Lonsdale (1991) 'Louis Leakey's Mau Mau: A Study in the Politics of Knowledge', *History and Anthropology*, 5(2): 143–204.

Berman, Edward (1983) *The Ideology of Philanthropy: The Influence of the Carnegie, Ford, and Rockefeller Foundations on American Foreign Policy* (Albany, NY: State University of New York Press).

Betz, David and Anthony Cormack (2009) 'Iraq, Afghanistan and British Strategy', *Orbis*, Spring: 319–336.

Bhabha, Homi (1992) 'The World and the Home', *Social Text*, 32: 141–153.

Bhambra, Gurminder K. (2007) *Rethinking Modernity: Postcolonialism and the Sociological Imagination* (New York: Palgrave).

Birtle, Andrew J. (1998/2009) *US Army Counterinsurgency and Contingency Operations Doctrine, 1860–1941* (Washington, DC: United States Army Center of Military History).

Blackstone, William (1765/1979) *Commentaries on the Laws of England: A Facsimile of the First Edition of 1765–1769, 4 vols* (Chicago: University of Chicago Press).

Blakeley, Ruth (2009) *State Terrorism and Neoliberalism: The North in the South* (London: Routledge).

Blundell, Michael (1994) *A Love Affair with the Sun: A Memoir of Seventy Years in Kenya* (Nairobi: Kenway Publications).

Bluntschli, J.K. (1921) *The Theory of the State* (3rd edition) (Oxford, Clarendon Press).

Bobbio, Norberto (1993) *Thomas Hobbes and the Natural Law Tradition* (Chicago: University of Chicago Press).

Booth, William James (1981) 'Politics and the Household: A Commentary on Aristotle's Politics, Book One', *The History of Political Thought*, 2: 203–226.

(1992) 'Households, Markets and Firms', in George E. McCarthy (ed.) *Marx and Aristotle: Nineteenth-Century German Social Theory and Classical Antiquity* (London: Rowman and Littlefield), pp. 243–271.

(1993) *Households: On the Moral Architecture of the Economy* (Ithaca, NY: Cornell University Press).

(1994) 'Household and Market: On the Origins of Moral Economic Philosophy', *Review of Politics*, 56: 207–235.

Bottici, Chiara (2009) *Men and States: Rethinking the Domestic Analogy in a Global Age* (trans. Karen Whittle) (London: Palgrave).

Bottomore, Tom and Robert Nisbet (eds.) (1979) *A History of Sociological Analysis* (Portsmouth, NH: Heinemann).

Boucher, David (1998) *Political Theories of International Relations: from Thucydides to the Present* (Oxford: Oxford University Press).

(2009) *The Limits of Ethics in International Relations: Natural Law, Natural Rights, and Human Rights in Transition* (Oxford: Oxford University Press).

Bourdieu, Pierre (1958) *Sociologie de l'Algérie* (Paris: Presses Universitaires de France).

(1979) *Algeria 1960: Essays by Pierre Bourdieu* (Cambridge: Cambridge University Press).

(1998) *The State Nobility: Elite Schools in the Field of Power* (Stanford, CA: Stanford University Press).

(2005) *The Social Structures of the Economy* (Cambridge: Polity).

(2012) *Picturing Algeria* (ed. Franz Schultheis and Christine Frisinghelli) (New York: Columbia University Press).

(2013) *Algerian Sketches* (Cambridge: Polity Press).

Bourgeois, Léon (1902) *Solidarité* (3rd edition) (Paris: A. Colin).

Bowlby, Rachel (1995) 'Domestication', in Diane Elam and Robyn Wiegman (eds.) *Feminism Beside Itself* (New York: Routledge), pp. 71–91.

Branch, Daniel (2005) 'Imprisonment and Colonialism in Kenya, c. 1930–1952 – Escaping the Carceral Archipelago', *International Journal of African Historical Studies*, 38(2): 239–265.

(2009) *Defeating Mau Mau, Creating Kenya: Counterinsurgency, Civil War, and Decolonization* (Cambridge: Cambridge University Press).

(2010) 'Footprints in the Sand: British Colonial Counterinsurgency and the War in Iraq', *Politics and Society*, 38(1): 15–34.

Brands, H.W. (1995) *The Reckless Decade: America in the 1890s* (New York: St Martin's Press).

Brenner, Robert (1985) 'Agrarian Class Structure and Economic Development in pre-Industrial Europe', in T. H. Aston and C. H. E. Philpin (eds.) *The Brenner Debate: Agrarian Class Structure and Economic Development in Pre-Industrial Europe* (Cambridge: Cambridge University Press), pp. 10–63.

Breslau, Daniel (2007) 'The American Spencerians: Theorizing a New Science', in Craig Calhoun (ed.) *Sociology in America: A History* (Chicago: University of Chicago Press), pp. 39–62.

Brick, Howard (2000) 'Talcott Parsons's "Shift Away from Economics", 1937–1946', *The Journal of American History*, 87(2): 490–514.

Briganti, Chiara and Kathy Mezei (2012) 'Introduction', in Chiara Briganti and Kathy Mezei (eds.) *The Domestic Space Reader* (Toronto: University of Toronto Press), pp. 3–16.

Brighton, Erwin R. (1968) *Pacification Measurement in Vietnam: the Hamlet Evaluation System*, prepared for presentation at the SEATO Internal Security Seminar, Manila, 3–10 June. Available at http://pdf.usaid.gov/pdf_docs/PCAAC044.pdf (accessed 14 June 2013).

Brody, David (2010) *Visualizing American Empire: Orientalism and Imperialism in the Philippines* (Chicago: University of Chicago Press).

Brown, Gillian (1990) *Domestic Individualism: Imagining Self in Nineteenth-Century America* (Berkeley, CA: University of California Press).

Brown, Wendy (2006) 'American Nightmare: Neoliberalism, Neoconservatism, and De-Democratization', *Political Theory*, 34(6): 690–714.

(2008) 'The New US Army/Marine Corps Counterinsurgency Field Manual as Political Science and Political Praxis', *Perspectives on Politics*, 6(2): 354–357.

(2010) *Walled States, Waning Sovereignty* (London: Zone Books).

Bruce, C. E. (1932) 'The Sandeman Policy as Applied to Tribal Problems Today', *Journal of the Royal Central Asian Society*, 19(1): 45–67.

Buley, Ben (2008) 'The Science of Strategy: War as a Political Instrument in the Nuclear Age', in *The New American Way of War: Military Culture and the Political Utility of Force* (London: Routledge), pp. 40–62.

Bull, Hedley (1977) *The Anarchical Society: A Study of Order in World Politics* (London: Macmillan).

(1979) 'Natural Law and International Relations', *British Journal of International Studies*, 5: 171–181.

Bull, Hedley, Benedict Kingsbury and Adam Roberts (1990) *Hugo Grotius and International Relations* (Oxford: Clarendon Press).

Burke, Edmund (1790/1993) *Reflections on the Revolution in France* (ed. with an intro. L.G. Mitchell) (Oxford: Oxford University Press).

Burrow, J.W. (1966) *Evolution and Society: A Study in Victorian Social Theory* (Cambridge: Cambridge University Press).

Butler, Judith (2004) *Precarious Life: The Powers of Mourning and Violence* (London: Verso).

(2009) *Frames of War: When is Life Grievable?* (London: Verso).

Buxton, William (1985) *Talcott Parsons and the Capitalist Nation-State: Political Sociology as a Strategic Vocation* (Toronto: University of Toronto Press).

Buzan, Barry (2004) *From International to World Society? English School Theory and the Social Structure of Globalization* (Cambridge: Cambridge University Press).

Buzan, Barry and Mathias Albert (2010) 'Differentiation: A Sociological Approach to International Relations Theory', *European Journal of International Relations*, 16(3): 315–337.

Buzan, Barry and Richard Little (2000) *International Systems in World History* (Oxford: Oxford University Press).

Byrd, Winn Miemie and Gretchen Decker (2008) 'Why the US Should Gender its Counterterrorism Strategy', *Military Review* (July–August): 96–101.

Cable, Larry E. (1986) *Conflict of Myths: The Development of American Counterinsurgency Doctrine and the Vietnam War* (New York: New York University Press).

Callwell, C.E. (1896) *Small Wars: A Tactical Textbook for Imperial Soldiers* (New York: Presidio).

Canovan, Margaret (1992) *Hannah Arendt: A Reinterpretation of her Political Thought* (Cambridge: Cambridge University Press).

Caplan, Gerald (1964) *Principles of Preventive Psychiatry* (New York: Basic).

Carothers, J.C. (1954) *The Psychology of Mau Mau* (Nairobi: Government Printer).

(1970) *The African Mind in Health and Disease: A Study in Enthopsychiatry* (New York: Negro Universities Press).

Carrithers, David (1995) 'The Enlightenment Science of Society', in Christopher Fox, Roy Porter and Robert Wokler (eds.) *Inventing Human Science: Eighteenth-Century Domains* (Berkeley, CA: University of California Press), pp. 232–270.

Carruthers, Susan L. (1995) *Winning Hearts and Minds: British Governments, the Media, and Colonial Counter-insurgency, 1944–1960* (New York: Leicester University Press).

Carter, James M. (2008) *Inventing Vietnam: The United States and State Building, 1954–1968* (Cambridge: Cambridge University Press).

Castel, Robert (2003) *From Manual Workers to Wage Laborers: Transformation of the Social Question* (New Brunswick, NJ: Transaction Publishers).

Castillo, Greg (2005) 'Domesticating the Cold War: Household Consumption as Propaganda in Marshall Plan Germany', *Journal of Contemporary History*, 40(2): 261–288.

Castro, A.P. and K. Ettenger (1994) 'Counterinsurgency and Socioeconomic Change: The Mau Mau War in Kirinyaga, Kenya', *Research in Economic Anthropology*, 15: 63–101.

Chakravarty, Gautam (2005) *The Indian Mutiny and the British Imagination* (Cambridge: Cambridge University Press).

Chambon, Adrienne S., Allan Irving and Laura Epstein (eds.) (1999) *Reading Foucault for Social Work* (New York: Columbia University Press).

Chandrasekaran, Rajiv (2007) *Imperial Life in the Emerald City* (New York: Knopf).

Chatterjee, Partha (1993) *The Nation and Its Fragments: Colonial and Postcolonial Histories* (Princeton, NJ: Princeton University Press).

Chiu, Yvonne and Robert S. Taylor (2011) 'The Self-Extinguishing Despot: Millian Democratization', *The Journal of Politics*, 73(4): 1239–1250.

Chugerman, Samuel (1939) *Lester F. Ward, the American Aristotle: A Summary and Interpretation of His Sociology* (Durham, NC: Duke University Press).

Cloake, John (1985) *Templer: Tiger of Malaya* (London: Harrap).

Clough, Marshall S. (1998) *Mau Mau Memoirs: History, Memory, and Politics* (Boulder, CO: Lynne Rienner).

Clausewitz, Carl von (1832/1976) *On War* (ed. and trans. Michael Howard and Peter Paret) (Princeton, NJ: Princeton University Press).

Coates, John (1992) *Suppressing Insurgency: An Analysis of the Malayan Emergency, 1948–1954* (Boulder, CO: Westview Press).

Cobain, Ian and Jessica Hatcher (2013) 'Kenyan Mau Mau Victims in Talks with UK Government Over Legal Settlement', *The Guardian*, 5 May.

Cohen, Jean and Andrew Arato (1992) *Civil Society and Political Theory* (Cambridge, MA: MIT Press).

Cole, David (ed.) (2009) *The Torture Memos* (New York: New Press).

Collini, Stefan (1980) 'Political Theory and the "Science of Society" in Victorian Britain', *The Historical Journal*, 23(1): 203–231.

Collins, Randall and Michael Makowsky (1972) *The Discovery of Society* (New York: Random House).

Colomina, Beatriz (2007) *Domesticity at War* (Cambridge, MA: MIT Press).

Colony and Protectorate of Kenya (1959/1960) *The Origins and Growth of Mau Mau: An Historical Survey*, Sessional Paper No.5 (Nairobi: Government Printer).

Comaroff, Jean and John Comaroff (1992) *Ethnography and the Historical Imagination* (Boulder, CO: Westview Press).

Comte, Auguste (1875) *System of Positive Polity* (London: Longmans, Green and co.).

Concentration Camp Commission (1902) *Report on the Concentration Camps in South Africa, by the Committee of Ladies Appointed by the Secretary of State for War; Containing Reports on the Camps in Natal, the Orange River Colony, and the Transvaal* (London: HMSO).

Conetta, Carl (2005) *Vicious Circle: The Dynamics of Occupation and Resistance in Iraq. Part One. Patterns of Popular Discontent Research Monograph #10* (Cambridge, MA: Project on Defense Alternatives).

Conklin, Alice L. (1997) *A Mission to Civilize: The Republican Idea of Empire in France and West Africa, 1895–1930* (Stanford, CA: Stanford University Press).

Cooper, Chester L., Judith E. Corson, Laurence J. Legere, David E. Lockwood and Donald M. Weller (1972) *The American Experience with Pacification in Vietnam*, Volume 1, *An Overview of Pacification* (Alexandria, VA: Institute for Defense Analysis).

Cooper, Frederick (2004) 'Development, Modernization, and the Social Sciences in the Era of Decolonization: the Examples of British and French Africa', *Revue d'Histoire des Sciences Humaines*, 1(10): 9–38.

Cooper, Kate (2007) *The Fall of the Roman Household* (Cambridge: Cambridge University Press).

Corrigan, Philip and Derek Sayer (1985) *The Great Arch: English State Formation As Cultural Revolution* (Oxford: Blackwell).

Coser, Lewis A. (2003) *Masters of Sociological Thought: Ideas in Historical and Social Context* (2nd edition) (Long Grove, IL: Waveland Press).

Coward, Rosalind (1983) *Patriarchal Precedents: Sexuality and Social Relations* (London: Routledge).

Cox, Cheryl Anne (1997) *Household Interests: Property, Marriage Strategies and Family Dynamics in Ancient Athens* (Princeton: Princeton University Press).

Cox, David and Manohar Pawar (2012) *International Social Work: Issues, Strategies and Programs* (London: Sage).

Cox, Robert W. (1987) *Production, Power, and World Order: Social Forces in the Making of History* (New York: Columbia University Press).

Coyne, Christopher J. (2008) *After War: the Political Economy of Exporting Democracy* (Stanford, CA: Stanford University Press).

Crider, Jim (2009) *Inside the Surge: One Commander's Lessons in Counterinsurgency* (foreword by Thomas E. Ricks) Working Paper, Center for a New American Century, June. Available at www.cnas.org/files/documents/publications/CNAS_Working%20Paper_Surge_CriderRicks_June2009_ONLINE.pdf (accessed 27 February 2014).

Cullather, Nick (2006) '"The Target is the People": Representations of the Village in Modernization and US National Security Doctrine', *Cultural Politics*, 2(1): 29–48.

D'Altroy, Terence N. and Christine A. Hastorf (eds.) (2002) *Empire and Domestic Economy* (New York: Kluwer).

Daly, Glyn (2006) 'The Political Economy of (Im)possibility', in Marieke de Goede (ed.) *International Political Economy and Poststructural Politics* (London: Palgrave), pp. 177–194.

Dandeker, Christopher (1990) *Surveillance, Power and Modernity* (London: St Martin's).

Dardot, Pierre and Christian Laval (2013) *The New Way of the World: On Neoliberal Society* (London: Verso).
Davenport, Andrew (2013) 'Marxism in IR: Condemned to a Realist Fate?', *European Journal of International Relations*, 19(1): 27–48.
Davidson, Janine (2010) *Lifting the Fog of Peace: How Americans Learned to Fight Modern War* (Ann Arbor, MI: University of Michigan Press).
Davis, Paul K. (2011a) 'Summary', in Paul K. Davis (ed.) *Dilemmas of Intervention: Social Science for Stabilization and Reconstruction* (Washington: RAND), pp. xv–xlvll.
(2011b) 'Introduction', in Paul K. Davis (ed.) *Dilemmas of Intervention: Social Science for Stabilization and Reconstruction* (Washington: RAND), pp. 1–20.
Davis, Paul K. and Kim Cragin (eds.) (2009) *Social Science for Counter-terrorism: Putting the Pieces Together* (Santa Monica, CA: RAND Corporation).
Dean, Mitchell (1991) *The Constitution of Poverty: Toward a Genealogy of Liberal Governance* (London: Routledge).
(2010) *Governmentality: Power and Rule in Modern Society* (2nd edition) (London: Sage).
DeLanda, Manuel (2006) *A New Philosophy of Society: Assemblage Theory and Social Complexity* (London: Continuum).
de Lange, Jeroen (2010) 'Winning Hearts, Changing Mindsets: Interventions as Change Management', *The Broker* (February 3): 449–463.
Derrida, Jacques (1976) *Of Grammatology* (trans. Gayatri Chakravorty Spivak) (Baltimore, MD: Johns Hopkins University Press).
Deudney, Daniel H. (2007) *Bounding Power: Republican Security Theory from the Polis to the Global Village* (Princeton, NJ: Princeton University Press).
Dewey, Clive (1972) 'Images of the Village Community: A Study in Anglo-Indian Ideology', *Modern Asian Studies*, 6(3): 291–328.
d'Ideville, H. (1884) *Memoirs of Marshal Bugeaud, from His Private Correspondence and Original Documents, 1784–1849* (edited from the French, by Charlotte M. Yonge) (London: Hurst and Blackett).
Dillon, Michael and Julian Reid (2009) *The Liberal Way of War: Killing to Make Life Live* (London: Routledge).
Dirks, Nicholas B. (2001) *Castes of Mind: Colonialism and the Making of Modern India* (Princeton, NJ: Princeton University Press).
Dixon, Paul (ed.) (2012) *The British Approach to Counterinsurgency: From Malaya and Northern Ireland to Iraq and Afghanistan* (London: Palgrave Macmillan).

Dobbins, James, Seth G. Jones, Keith Crane and Beth Cole DeGrasse (2007) *The Beginner's Guide to Nation-Building* (Santa Monica, CA: RAND).
Dobby, E.H.G. (1952/1953) 'Resettlement Transforms Malaya: A Case-history of Relocating the Population of an Asian Plural Society', *Economic Development and Cultural Change*, 1(3): 163–189.
(1953) 'Recent Settlement Changes in South Malaya', *The Malayan Journal of Tropical Geography*, 1: 1–8.
Dodge, Toby (2009) 'Coming Face to Face with Bloody Reality: Liberal Common Sense and the Ideological Failure of the Bush Doctrine in Iraq', *International Politics*, 46(2/3): 253–275.
(2010) 'The Ideological Roots of Failure: the Application of Kinetic Neo-Liberalism in Iraq', *International Affairs*, 86(6): 1269–1286.
Donnell, John C. and Gerald C. Hickey (1962) *The Vietnamese 'Strategic Hamlets': A Preliminary Report, Memorandum RM-3208-ARPA* (Santa Monica, CA: RAND Corporation).
Donzelot, Jacques (1979) *The Policing of Families: Welfare versus the State* (London: Hutchinson).
(1984) *L'invention du Social: Essai sur le déclin des Passions Politiques* (Paris: Fayard).
(1988) 'The Promotion of the Social', *Economy and Society*, 17(3): 394–427.
Dorwart, Reinhold August (1971) *The Prussian Welfare State before 1740* (Cambridge, MA: Harvard University Press).
Doty, Roxanne Lynn (1996) *Imperial Encounters: The Politics of Representation in North–South Relations* (Minneapolis, MN: University of Minnesota Press).
Douglass, Michael (2010) 'Globalizing the Household in East Asia', *The Whitehead Journal of Diplomacy and International Relations*, 11(1): 63–77.
Downing, Brian M. (1992) *The Military Revolution and Political Change: Origins of Democracy and Autocracy in Early Modern Europe* (Princeton, NJ: Princeton University Press).
Doyle, Michael W. (1997) *Ways of War and Peace: Realism, Liberalism, and Socialism* (New York: Norton).
Drayton, Richard (2000) *Nature's Government: Science, Imperial Britain and the 'Improvement' of the World* (New Haven, CT: Yale University Press).
Drezner, Daniel W. (2007) *All Politics is Global: Explaining International Regulatory Regimes* (Princeton, NJ: Princeton University Press).
Drolet, Jean-François (2011) *American Neoconservatism: The Politics and Culture of a Reactionary Idealism* (London: Hurst).

Dubber, Markus Dirk (2005) *The Police Power: Patriarchy and the Foundations of American Government* (New York: Columbia University Press).
Dubik, James M. (2012) *Operational Art in Counterinsurgency: A View from the Inside*, Best Practices in Counterinsurgency, Report 5 (Washington, DC: Institute for the Study of War). Available at www.understandingwar.org/sites/default/files/OperationalArt_in_COIN.pdf (accessed 27 February 2014).
Duffield, Mark (2007) *Development, Security and Unending War* (Cambridge: Polity).
Dumont, Luis (1966) 'The "Village Community" from Munro to Maine', *Contributions to Indian Sociology*, 9: 67–89.
Durkheim, Émile (1893/1984) *The Division of Labour in Society* (trans. W.D. Halls; intro. Lewis A. Coser) (New York: The Free Press).
(1912/1915) *The Elementary Forms of Religious Life* (trans. Joseph Ward Swain) (London: George Allen and Unwin).
(1915) *L'Allemagne au-dessus de tout* (Paris: Colin).
(1982) *The Rules of Sociological Method and Selected Texts on Sociology and its Method* (ed. with an intro. by Steven Lukes; trans. W.D. Halls) (London: Macmillan).
Dutta, Simanti (2002) *Imperial Mappings in Savage Spaces: Baluchistan and British India* (Delhi: B.R. Publishing).
Dyvik, Synne Laastas (2014) 'Women as "Practitioners" and "Targets": Gender and Counterinsurgency in Afghanistan', *International Feminist Journal of Politics*, 16(3): 410–429.
Eckert, Andreas (2004) 'Regulating the Social: Social Security, Social Welfare and the State in Late Colonial Tanzania', *The Journal of African History*, 45(3): 467–489.
Eckstein, Harry (1964) 'Introduction: Toward the Theoretical Study of Internal War', in Harry Eckstein (ed.) *Internal War: Problems and Approaches* (New York: Free Press), pp. 1–31.
Ekbladh, David (2010) *The Great American Mission: Modernization and the Construction of an American World Order* (Princeton, NJ: Princeton University Press).
Elias, Juanita (2013) 'Foreign Policy and the Domestic Worker: The Malaysia-Indonesia Domestic Worker Dispute', *International Feminist Journal of Politics*, 15(3): 391–410.
Elias, Juanita and Samanthi Gunawardana (eds.) (2013) *The Global Political Economy of the Household in Asia* (London: Palgrave).
Elias, Norbert (2000) *The Civilizing Process: Sociogenetic and Psychogenetic Investigations* (Oxford: Blackwell Publishers).
Elkins, Caroline (2000) 'The Struggle for Mau Mau Rehabilitation in Late Colonial Kenya', *The International Journal of African Historical Studies*, 33(1): 25–57.

(2003) 'Detention, Rehabilitation and Destruction of Kikuyu Society', in E.S. Atieno Odhiambo and John Lonsdale (eds.) *Mau Mau and Nationhood: Arms, Authority and Narration* (Athens, OH: Ohio University Press), pp. 191–226.

(2005a) *Imperial Reckoning: The Untold Story of Britain's Gulag in Kenya* (New York: Henry Holt).

(2005b) 'Race, Citizenship, and Governance: Settler Tyranny and the End of Empire', in Caroline Elkins and Susan Pedersen (eds.) *Settler Colonialism in the Twentieth Century: Projects, Practices, Legacies* (New York: Routledge), pp. 203–222.

(2011) 'Alchemy of Evidence: Mau Mau, the British Empire, and the High Court of Justice', *The Journal of Imperial and Commonwealth History*, 39(5): 731–748.

Elliott, Charles (1916) *The Philippines: To the End of the Commission Government, a Study in Tropical Democracy* (Indianapolis: Bobs-Merrill Company).

Elliott, David W. P. (2003) *The Vietnamese War: Revolution and Social Change in the Mekong Delta, 1930–1975* (Armonk, NY: M.E. Sharpe).

Elshtain, Jean Bethke (1981) *Public Man, Private Woman: Women in Social and Political Thought* (Princeton, NJ: Princeton University Press).

(ed.) (1982) *The Family in Political Thought* (Amherst, MA: University of Massachusetts Press).

Endenburg, Gerard (1981) *Sociocratie* (Alphen aan den Rijn: Samsom).

Engels, Friedrich (1872/1970) *The Housing Question* (Moscow: Progress Publishers). Available at www.e-text.org/text/Engles%20-%20 Housing%20Question.pdf (accessed 8 August 2011).

Engerman, David C., Nils Gilman, Mark H. Haefele and Michael E. Latham (eds.) (2003) *Staging Growth: Modernization, Development, and the Global Cold War* (Amherst, MA: University of Massachusetts Press).

Enloe, Cynthia (2010) *Nimo's War, Emma's War: Making Feminist Sense of the Iraq War* (Berkeley, CA: University of California Press).

Ernst, John (1998) 'Tutoring Democracy: Michigan State University and the Politics of Reform in South Vietnam', in Philip West, Steven Levine and Jackie Hiltz (eds.) *America's Wars in Asia: A Cultural Approach to History and Memory* (Armonk, NY: M.E. Sharpe), pp. 233–244.

Escobar, Arturo (1995) *Encountering Development: The Making and Unmaking of the Third World* (Princeton, NJ: Princeton University Press).

Evans, Ryan (2014) '"The Population is the Enemy": Control, Behaviour, and Counter-Insurgency in Central Helmand Province, Afghanistan', in Celeste Ward Gventer, David Martin Jones and M.L.R. Smith (eds.) *The New Counter-insurgency Era in Critical Perspective* (London: Palgrave), pp. 257–277.

Evans, Stephen S. (ed.) (2008) *US Marines and Irregular Warfare, 1898–2007: Anthology and Selected Bibliography* (Quantico, VA: Marine Corps University Press).

Ewald, François (1991) 'Insurance and Risk', in Graham Burchill, Colin Gordon and Peter Miller (eds.) *The Foucault Effect: Studies in Governmentality* (Chicago: University of Chicago Press), pp. 197–210.

Fall, Bernard (1965) 'The Theory and Practice of Insurgency and Counterinsurgency', *Naval War College Review*, April. Available at www.au.af.mil/au/awc/awcgate/navy/art5-w98.htm (accessed 30 November 2012).

Fanon, Franz (1963) *The Wretched of the Earth* (New York: Grove Press).

(1965) *A Dying Colonialism* (trans. Haakon Chevalier) (New York: Grove Press).

(1967) *Toward the African Revolution: Political Essays* (trans. Haakon Chevalier) (New York: Grove Press).

Faroqhi, Suraiya (2010) 'The Ottoman Empire: The Age of "Political Households" (Eleventh–Twelfth/Seventeenth–Eighteenth Centuries)', in *The New Cambridge History of Islam: Volume 2, The Western Islamic World, Eleventh to Eighteenth Centuries* (Cambridge: Cambridge University Press), pp. 366–410.

Fassin, Didier (2011) *Humanitarian Reason: A Moral History of the Present* (trans. Rachel Gomme) (Berkeley, CA: University of California Press).

Fassin, Didier and Mariella Pandolfi (eds.) (2010) *Contemporary States of Emergency: The Politics of Military and Humanitarian Interventions* (New York: Zone Books).

Federation of Kenya (1954) *A Handbook on Anti-Mau Mau Operations* (South Africa: Government Printer).

Fee, Mary H. (1910/1988) *A Woman's Impressions of the Philippines* (Quezon City: GCF Books).

Ferguson, Adam (1767/1995) *An Essay on the History of Civil Society* (Cambridge: Cambridge University Press).

Ferguson, James (1994) *The Anti-Politics Machine: "Development", Depoliticization, and Bureaucratic Power in Lesotho* (Minneapolis, MN: University of Minnesota Press).

Feuchtwang, Stephen (1973) 'The Discipline and its Sponsors: The Colonial Formation of British Anthropology', in Talal Asad (ed.) *Anthropology and the Colonial Encounter* (London: Ithaca Press), pp. 71–100.

Filkins, Dexter (2010) 'Afghan Offensive is New War Model', *The New York Times*, 12 February.

Filmer, Robert (1680/1984) *The Patriarcha and Other Political Works of Sir Robert Filmer* (ed. Peter Laslett) (New York: Transaction).

Finch, Michael P. M. (2013) *A Progressive Occupation? The Galliéni-Lyautey Method and Colonial Pacification in Tonkin and Madagascar, 1885–1900* (Oxford: Oxford University Press).

Finlay, Christopher J. (2007) *Hume's Social Philosophy: Human Nature and Commercial Sociability in* A Treatise of Human Nature (New York: Continuum).

Finnemore, Martha (2003) *The Purpose of Intervention: Changing Beliefs about the Use of Force* (Ithaca, NY: Cornell University Press).

Fisher, Christopher T. (1996) 'The Illusion of Progress: CORDS and the Crisis of Modernization in South Vietnam, 1965–1968', *Pacific Historical Review*, 75(1): 25–51.

Fletcher, Eileen (1956) *Truth about Kenya: An Eye Witness Account* (foreword by Leslie Hale) (London: Peace News).

Folbre, N. (1986) 'Hearts and Spades: Paradigms of Household Economics', *World Development*, 14(2): 245–255.

Forte, Maximilian (2010) 'Counterinsurgency: It's Bloody Horrible', *Zero Anthropology* blog posted on 19 July. Available at http://zeroanthropology.net/2010/07/19/counterinsurgency-its-bloody-horrible (accessed 21 February 2014).

Foucault, Michel (1975/1995) *Discipline and Punish: The Birth of the Prison* (trans. Alan Sheridan) (New York: Vintage).

(1978) *The History of Sexuality: An Introduction, Volume 1* (trans. Robert Hurley) (New York: Vintage).

(1991) *The Foucault Effect: Studies in Governmentality: With Two Lectures by and an Interview with Michel Foucault* (ed. Graham Burchell, Colin Gordon and Peter Miller) (Chicago: University of Chicago Press).

(1997) *Ethics: Subjectivity and Truth* (ed. Paul Rabinow; trans. Robert Hurley) (New York: New Press).

(2003) *Society Must be Defended: Lectures at the Collège de France, 1975–1976* (ed. Mauro Bertani and Alessandro Fontana; trans. David Macey) (New York: Picador).

(2007) *Security, Territory, Population: Lectures at the Collège de France, 1977–1978* (ed. Michel Senellart; trans. Graham Burchell) (London: Palgrave).

(2008) *The Birth of Biopolitics: Lectures at the Collège de France, 1978–1979* (ed. Michel Senellart; trans. Graham Burchell) (London: Palgrave).

Fraher, Amy (2011) 'Creating an Emotionally Intelligent Warrior', *The Washington Post*, 9 November.

French, David (2011) *The British Way in Counter-Insurgency, 1945–1967* (Oxford: Oxford University Press).

(2012) 'Nasty Not Nice: British Counter-insurgency Doctrine and Practice, 1945–1967', *Small Wars & Insurgencies*, 23(4–5): 744–761.

Freyberg-Inan, Annette (2012) *What Moves Man: The Realist Theory of International Relations and Its Judgment of Human Nature* (Albany, NY: State University of New York Press).

Friedan, Betty (1963) *The Feminine Mystique* (New York: Norton).

Frisby, David and Derek Sayer (1986) *Society* (London: Routledge).

Frost, Richard (1978) *Race Against Time: Human Relations and Politics in Kenya before Independence* (London: Rex Collings).

Galbraith, Peter W. (2006) *The End of Iraq: How American Incompetence Created a War without End* (London: Simon & Schuster).

Galliéni, Joseph-Simon (1900) *Rapport d'ensemble sur la pacification, l'organisation et la colonisation de Madagascar (octobre 1896 à mars 1899)* (Paris: H. Charles-Lavauzelle).

(1941) *Galliéni au Tonkin (1892–1896) par lui-même* (Paris: Berger-Levrault).

Galula, David (1963/2006) *Pacification in Algeria, 1956–1958* (foreword by Bruce Hoffman) (Santa Monica, CA: RAND).

(1964) *Counterinsurgency Warfare: Theory and Practice* (New York, Praeger).

Gant, Jim (2009) *One Tribe at a Time: A Strategy for Success in Afghanistan* (Los Angeles: Nine Sisters Imports).

Gates, John (1972) *Schoolbooks and Krags: The United States Army in the Philippines, 1898–1902* (Westport, CT: Greenwood).

(2002) *The US Army and Irregular Warfare*. Available at www3.wooster.edu/history/jgates/pdfs/fullbook.pdf (accessed 25 May 2013).

Gendzier, Irene L. (1985) *Managing Political Change: Social Scientists and the Third World* (Boulder, CO: Westview Press).

Genov, Nikolai (ed.) (1989) *National Traditions in Sociology* (London: Sage Publications).

Gentile, Gian P. (2009) 'A Strategy of Tactics: Population-centric COIN and the Army', *Parameters*, 39: 5–17.

(2012) 'Counterinsurgency and War', in Julian Lindley-French and Yves Boyer (eds.) *The Oxford Handbook of War* (Oxford: Oxford University Press), pp. 387–400.

(2013) *Wrong Turn: America's Deadly Embrace of Counterinsurgency* (New York: The New Press).

George, Rosemary Marangoly (1993/1994) 'Homes in the Empire, Empires in the Home', *Cultural Critique*, 26: 95–127.

(1996) *The Politics of Home: Postcolonial Relocations and Twentieth-century Fiction* (Cambridge: Cambridge University Press).

Gerhardt, Uta (2002) *Talcott Parsons: an Intellectual Biography* (Cambridge: Cambridge University Press).
Gibson, James William (1986) *The Perfect War: Technowar in Vietnam* (New York: Atlantic Monthly Press).
Giddens, Anthony (1973) *Capitalism and Modern Social Theory: an Analysis of the Writings of Marx, Durkheim, and Max Weber* (Cambridge: Cambridge University Press).
(1984) *The Constitution of Society* (Cambridge: Polity).
(1986) 'Introduction', in Émile Durkheim, *Durkheim on Politics and the State* (ed. Anthony Giddens) (Cambridge: Polity Press), pp. 1–31.
Gierke, Otto (1934) *Natural Law and the Theory of Society, 1500–1800, Volume I* (trans. with an intro. by Ernest Barker) (Cambridge: Cambridge University Press).
Gillet, Maxime (2010) *Principes de pacification du maréchal Lyautey* (Paris: Economica).
Gilman, Nils (2003) *Mandarins of the Future: Modernization Theory in Cold War America* (Baltimore, MD: Johns Hopkins University Press).
Gilpin, Robert (1981) *War and Change in International Politics* (Cambridge: Cambridge University Press).
(1986) 'The Richness of the Tradition of Political Realism', in Robert O. Keohane (ed.) *Neorealism and its Critics* (New York: Columbia University Press), pp. 301–345.
Go, Julian (2003) 'The Chains of Empire: State Building and "Political Education" in Puerto Rico and the Philippines', in Julian Go and Anne L. Foster (eds.), *The American Colonial State in the Philippines: Global Perspectives* (Durham, NC: Duke University Press), pp. 182–216.
Go, Julian and Anne L. Foster (eds.) (2003) *The American Colonial State in the Philippines: Global Perspectives* (Durham, NC: Duke University Press).
Goddard, Stacie E. and Daniel H. Nexon (2005) 'Paradigm Lost? Structural Realism and Structural Functionalism', *European Journal of International Relations*, 10(1): 9–61.
Gödde, Christoph (2000) 'Editor's Notes', in Theodor W. Adorno, *Introduction to Sociology* (ed. Christoph Gödde; trans. Edmund Jephcott) (Stanford, CA: Stanford University Press), pp. 155–189.
González, Roberto (2009) 'Going "Tribal": Notes on Pacification in the 21st Century', *Anthropology Today*, 25(2): 15–19.
Goodman, Jane E. and Paul A. Silverstein (eds.) (2009) *Bourdieu in Algeria: Colonial Politics, Ethnographic Practices, Theoretical Developments* (Lincoln: University of Nebraska Press).

Goody, Jack (1977) *The Domestication of the Savage Mind* (Cambridge: Cambridge University Press).

Gordon, Daniel (1994) *Citizens without Sovereignty: Equality and Sociability in French Thought, 1670–1789* (Princeton, NJ: Princeton University Press).

Gottlieb, Agnes Hooper (2001) *Women Journalists and the Municipal Housekeeping Movement, 1868–1914* (Lewiston, NY: E. Mellen Press).

Grafton, Anthony, Glenn W. Most and Salvatore Setti (eds.) (2010) *The Classical Tradition* (Cambridge, MA: Harvard University Press).

Greenwood, John D. (ed.) (1997) *The Mark of the Social: Discovery or Invention?* (Lanham, MD: Rowman & Littlefield Publishers).

Gregg, Heather S. (2009) 'Beyond Population Engagement: Understanding Counterinsurgency', *Parameters*, Autumn: 18–31.

Gregory, Derek (2008) 'The Biopolitics of Baghdad: Counterinsurgency and the Counter-city', *Human Geography*, 1: 6–27.

Grimmer-Solem, Erik (2003a) 'Imperialist Socialism of the Chair: Gustav Schmoller and German Weltpolitik, 1897–1905', in Geoff Eley and James Retallack (eds.) *Wilhelminism and its Legacies: German Modernities, Imperialism, and the Meaning of Reform, 1890–1930* (New York: Berghahn Books), pp. 106–122.

(2003b) *The Rise of Historical Economics and Social Reform in Germany, 1864–1894* (Oxford: Oxford University Press).

(2007) 'The Professors' Africa: Economists, the Elections of 1907, and the Legitimation of German Imperialism', *German History*, 25: 313–347.

Grob-Fitzgibbon, Benjamin (2011) *Imperial Endgame: Britain's Dirty Wars and the End of Empire* (London: Palgrave).

Grotius, Hugo (1625/1925) *On the Law of War and Peace* (three volumes) (trans. Francis W. Keley) (Indianapolis: Bobbs-Merrill).

(1665) *De rebus Belgicis; or, The Annals, and History of the Low-Countrey-Warrs* (trans. Thomas Manley) (London: printed for Henry Twyford in Vine-Court Middle-Temple; and Robert Paulet at the Bible in Chancery Lane).

Guha, Ranajit (1988) 'The Prose of Counter-Insurgency', in Ranajit Guha and Gayatri Chakravorty Spivak (eds.) *Selected Subaltern Studies* (Oxford: Oxford University Press), pp. 45–84.

Guilhot, Nicolas (ed.) (2011) *The Invention of International Relations Theory: Realism, the Rockefeller Foundation, and the 1954 Conference on Theory* (New York: Columbia University Press).

Gurman, Hannah (2013) *Hearts and Minds: A People's History of Counterinsurgency* (New York: The New Press).

Gwynn, Charles W. (1934) *Imperial Policing* (London: Macmillan).

Habermas, Jürgen (1962/1991) *The Structural Transformation of the Public Sphere: An Inquiry into a Category of Bourgeois Society* (Cambridge, MA: MIT Press).

(1985/1987) *Philosophical Discourses of Modernity: Twelve Lectures* (Cambridge, MA: MIT Press).

Hack, Karl (1995) 'Screwing Down the People: The Malayan Emergency, Decolonisation and Ethnicity', in Hans Antlöv and Stein Tonnesson (eds.) *Imperial Policy and Southeast Asian Nationalism* (London: Curzon), pp. 83–109.

(1999) '"Iron Claws on Malaya": The Historiography of the Malayan Emergency', *Journal of Southeast Asian Studies*, 30(1): 99–125.

(2013) 'Between Two Terrors: "People's History" and the Malayan Emergency', in Hannah Gurman (ed.) *Hearts and Minds: A People's History of Counterinsurgency* (New York: The New Press), pp. 17–49.

Hagemann, Karen and Stefanie Schüler-Springorum (eds.) (2002) *Home/Front: The Military, War, and Gender in Twentieth-Century Germany* (Oxford: Berg).

Hakimi, Aziz A. (2013) 'Getting Savages to Fight Barbarians: Counterinsurgency and the remaking of Afghanistan', *Central Asian Survey*, 32(3): 388–405.

Hale, Christopher (2013) *Massacre in Malaya: Exposing Britain's My Lai* (Stroud: The History Press).

Hallberg, Peter and Björn Wittrock (2006) 'From *Koinonìa Politikè* to *Societas Civilis*: Birth, Disappearance and First Renaissance of the Concept', in Peter Wagner (ed.) *The Languages of Civil Society* (Oxford: Berghahn), pp. 28–51.

Halliday, Fred (1994) 'A Necessary Encounter: Historical Materialism and International Relations', in *Rethinking International Relations* (London: Macmillan), pp. 47–73.

Halperin, Sandra (2004) *War and Social Change in Modern Europe: The Great Transformation Revisited* (Cambridge: Cambridge University Press).

Hamzah, Sendut (1961) 'Rasah – a Resettlement Village in Malaya', *Asian Survey*, 1(9): 21–26.

(1962) 'The Resettlement Villages in Malaya', *Geography*, 47: 41–46.

Hansen, Karen Tranberg (ed.) (1992) *African Encounters with Domesticity* (New Brunswick, NJ: Rutgers University Press).

Harding, Scott (2004) 'The Sound of Silence: Social Work, the Academy, and Iraq', *Journal of Sociology and Social Welfare*, 31(2): 179–197.

Harper, T. N. (1999) *The End of Empire and the Making of Malaya* (Cambridge: Cambridge University Press).

Harrod, Jeffrey (1997) 'Social Forces and International Political Economy: Joining the Two IRs', in Stephen Gill and James H. Mittleman (eds.) *Innovation and Transformation in International Studies* (Cambridge: Cambridge University Press), pp. 105–117.

Hartman, Mary S. (2004) *The Household and the Making of History: A Subversive View of the Western Past* (Cambridge: Cambridge University Press).

Hartsock, Nancy C.M. (1983) *Money, Sex and Power: Toward a Feminist Historical Materialism* (New York: Longman).

Hartz, Louis (1955) *The Liberal Tradition in America* (New York: Harcourt, Brace & World).

Harvey, David (2007) *A Brief History of Neoliberalism* (new edition) (Oxford: Oxford University Press).

Hassan, Hussein D. (2008) 'Iraq: Tribal Structure, Social, and Political Activities', *CRS Report for Congress*, Order Code RS22626, 7 April, CRS-2.

Hastings, Michael (2012) *The Operators: The Wild and Terrifying Inside Story of America's War in Afghanistan* (London: Orion).

Hatcher, Patrick Lloyd (1990) *The Suicide of an Elite: American Internationalists and Vietnam* (Stanford, CA: Stanford University Press).

Hawthorn, Geoffrey (1977) *Enlightenment and Despair: A History of Sociology* (Cambridge: Cambridge University Press).

Hayden, Tom (2007) 'The New Counterinsurgency', *The Nation*, 24 September.

Haytock, Jennifer (2003) *At Home, at War: Domesticity and World War I in American Literature* (Columbus: Ohio State University Press).

Heilbron, Johan (1995) *The Rise of Social Theory* (trans. Sheila Gogol) (Minneapolis, MN: University of Minnesota Press).

Heilbron, Johan, Lars Magnusson and Bjorn Wittrock (eds.) (1998) *The Rise of the Social Sciences and the Formation of Modernity: Conceptual Change in Context, 1750–1850* (Dordrecht: Kluwer).

Heller, Dana (1995) 'Housebreaking History: Feminism's Troubled Romance with the Domestic Sphere', in Diane Elam and Robyn Wiegman (eds.) *Feminism Beside Itself* (London: Routledge), pp. 217–233.

Helliwell, Christine and Barry Hindess (2002) 'The Empire of Uniformity and the Government of Subject Peoples', *Journal for Cultural Research*, 6(1–2): 139–152.

Herlihy, David (1985) *Medieval Households* (Cambridge, MA: Harvard University Press).

Herring, Eric and Glen Rangwala (2006) *Iraq in Fragments: The Occupation and its Legacy* (London: Hurst).

Herring, George C. (1979) *America's Longest War: The United States and Vietnam, 1950–1975* (New York: Knopf).

Hewitt, Martin (1983) 'Bio-politics and Social Policy: Foucault's account of Welfare', *Theory, Culture & Society*, 2(1): 67–84.

Hickey, Gerald Cannon (1964) *Village in Vietnam* (New Haven, CT: Yale University Press).

Hill, Patricia R. (1984) *The World their Household: The American Woman's Foreign Mission Movement and Cultural Transformation, 1870–1920* (Ann Arbor, MI: University of Michigan Press).

Hindess, Barry and Paul Hirst (1977) *Mode of Production and Social Formation* (London: Macmillan).

Hintze, Otto (1975) *The Historical Essays of Otto Hintze* (ed. and intro. by Felix Gilbert) (Oxford: Oxford University Press).

Hirschman, Albert O. (1977) *The Passions and the Interests: Political Arguments for Capitalism before its Triumph* (Princeton, NJ: Princeton University Press).

(1989) 'How the Keynesian Revolution was Exported from the United States, and Other Comments' in Peter A. Hall (ed.) *The Political Power of Economic Ideas: Keynesianism Across Nations* (Princeton, NJ: Princeton University Press), pp. 347–359.

Hobbes, Thomas (1651/1968) *Leviathan* (London: Penguin).

Hobden, Stephen and John M. Hobson (eds.) (2002) *Historical Sociology of International Relations* (Cambridge: Cambridge University Press).

Hobsbawm, Eric (1962) *The Age of Revolution: Europe 1789–1848* (London: Weidenfeld and Nicolson).

(1975) *The Age of Capital, 1848–1875* (London: Weidenfeld and Nicolson).

(1990) *Nations and Nationalism since 1780: Programme, Myth, Reality* (Cambridge: Cambridge University Press).

Hobson, John A. (1901) *The Social Problem: Life and Work* (London: James Nisbet).

Hobson, John M. (2012) *The Eurocentric Conception of World Politics: Western International Theory* (Cambridge: Cambridge University Press).

Hodge, Nathan (2011) *Armed Humanitarians: The Rise of the Nation Builders* (New York: Bloomsbury).

Hodge, Peter (1973) 'Social Policy: An Historical Perspective as Seen in Colonial Policy', *Journal of Oriental Studies*, 9(3): 201–219.

Hoffmann, David L. (2011) *Cultivating the Masses: Modern State Practices and Soviet Socialism, 1914–1939* (Ithaca, NY: Cornell University Press).

Hoffmann, Stanley (1977) 'An American Social Science: International Relations', *Daedalus*, 106(3): 41–60.

Hoganson, Kristin L. (1998) *Fighting for American Manhood: How Gender Politics Provoked the Spanish-American and Philippine-American Wars* (New Haven, CT: Yale University Press).

Holland, Robert (1998) *Britain and the Revolt in Cyprus, 1954–1959* (Oxford: Oxford University Press).

Home, Robert (2013) *Of Planting and Planning: the Making of British Colonial Cities* (2nd edition) (New York: Routledge).

Honig, Bonnie (ed.) (1995) *Feminist Interpretations of Hannah Arendt* (Pennsylvania: Pennsylvania State University Press).

Hont, Istvan (2005) 'The Language of Sociability and Commerce: Samuel Pufendorf and the Theoretical Foundations of the "Four Stages" Theory', in *Jealousy of Trade: International Competition and the Nation-state in Historical Perspective* (Cambridge, MA: Harvard University Press), pp. 159–184.

hooks, bell (1990) *Yearning: Race, Gender, and Cultural Politics* (Boston, MA: South End Press).

Horn, David G. (1994) *Social Bodies: Science, Reproduction, and Italian Modernity* (Princeton, NJ: Princeton University Press).

Horowitz, Irving Louis (ed.) (1967) *The Rise and Fall of Project Camelot: Studies in the Relationship between Social Science and Practical Politics* (revised edition) (Cambridge, MA: MIT Press).

House, Floyd Nelson (1925) 'The Concept "Social Forces" in American Sociology', *American Journal of Sociology*, 31: 145–156.

Hu, Aiqun (2012) 'China, Social Insurance and the Welfare State: A Global Historical Perspective', *World History Connected*, 9(1). Available at http://worldhistoryconnected.press.illinois.edu/9.1/hu.html (accessed 13 April 2015).

Hu, Aiqun and Patrick Manning (2010) 'The Global Social Insurance Movement since the 1880s', *Journal of Global History*, 5(1): 125–148.

Hume, David (1738/2007) *A Treatise on Human Nature, Volume 2* (Rockville MD: Wildside Press LLC).

(1994) *Hume: Political Essays* (ed. Knud Haakonssen) (Cambridge: Cambridge University Press).

Hunt, David (2010) 'Dirty Wars: Counterinsurgency in Vietnam and Today', *Politics and Society*, 40(4): 35–66.

Hunt, Nancy (1990) 'Domesticity and Colonialism in Belgian Africa: Usumbura's *Foyer Social*, 1946–1960', *Signs*, 15(3): 447–474.

Hunt, Richard A. (1995) *Pacification: The American struggle for Vietnam's Hearts and Minds* (Boulder, CO: Westview Press).

Hunter, F. Robert (1984) *Egypt Under the Khedives, 1805–1879: From Household Government to Modern Bureaucracy* (Pittsburgh, PA: University of Pittsburgh Press).

Huntington, Samuel P. (1968) 'The Bases of Accommodation', *Foreign Affairs*, 46(4): 642–656.

Hurrell, Andrew (2007) *On Global Order: Power, Values and the Constitution of International Society* (Oxford: Oxford University Press).

Huysmans, Jef (2008) 'The Jargon of Exception – On Schmitt, Agamben and the Absence of Political Society', *International Political Sociology*, 2(2): 165–183.

Hynek, Nik (2012) 'The Domopolitics of Japanese Human Security', *Security Dialogue*, 43(2): 119–137.

Irvine, Robert P. (2009) 'Labor and Commerce in Locke and Early Eighteenth-Century English Georgic', *ELH*, 76(4): 963–988.

Isaac, Jeffrey (2008) 'The New US Army/Marine Corps Counterinsurgency Field Manual as Political Science and Political Praxis', *Perspectives on Politics*, 6(2): 346.

Isaac, Joel (2012) *Working Knowledge: Making the Human Sciences from Parsons to Kuhn* (Cambridge, MA: Harvard University Press).

Jabri, Vivienne (2007) 'Michel Foucault's Analytics of War: The Social, the International, and the Racial', *International Political Sociology*, 1(1): 67–81.

Jacoby, Johann (1870) *The Social Question* (printed for private circulation, available for download at Google Books).

Jahn, Beate (2000) *The Cultural Construction of International Relations: The Invention of the State of Nature* (London: Palgrave).

(2005) 'Barbarian Thoughts: Imperialism in the Philosophy of John Stuart Mill', *Review of International Studies*, 31(3): 599–618.

(2013) *Liberal Internationalism: History, Theory, Practice* (London: Palgrave).

James, C.L.R. (1938/1963) *The Black Jacobins* (London: Penguin).

Janowitz, Morris (1964) *The Military in the Political Development of New Nations: an Essay in Comparative Analysis* (Chicago: University of Chicago Press).

Jessop, Bob (1990) *State Theory: Putting Capitalist States in their Place* (Cambridge: Polity Press).

Joas, Hans and Wolfgang Knobl (2013) *War in Social Thought: Hobbes to the Present* (trans. Alex Skinner) (Princeton, NJ: Princeton University Press).

Jones, Gareth Stedman (2004) *An End to Poverty? A Historical Debate* (London: Profile Books).

Jordan, David Starr (1899) *The Question of the Philippines: An Address Delivered before the Graduate Club of Leland Stanford Junior University, on February 14, 1899* (San Francisco, CA: Hicks-Judd Co.).

Joseph, Jonathan (2012) *The Social in the Global: Social Theory, Governmentality and Global Politics* (Cambridge: Cambridge University Press).

Joya, Malalai (2011) *A Woman Among Warlords: The Extraordinary Story of an Afghan Who Dared to Raise Her Voice* (New York: Simon & Schuster).

Joyce, Patrick (2002) 'Maps, Blood and the City: The Governance of the Social in Nineteenth-century Britain', in Patrick Joyce (ed.) *The Social in Question: New Bearings in History and the Social Sciences* (New York: Routledge), pp. 97–114.

Judt, Tony (1997) 'The Social Question Redivivus', *Foreign Affairs*, 76(5): 95–117.

Kajava, Mika (2004) 'Hestia: Hearth, Goddess, and Cult', *Harvard Studies in Classical Philology*, 102: 1–20.

Kaldor, Mary (2010) 'New Thinking in the Pentagon', *Global Policy*, 1(1): 121–122.

Kalyvas, Stathis (2006) *The Logic of Violence in Civil War* (Cambridge: Cambridge University Press).

(2008) 'The New US Army/Marine Corps Counterinsurgency Field Manual as Political Science and Political Praxis', *Perspectives on Politics*, 6(2): 351–353.

Kaplan, Amy (1998) 'Manifest Domesticity', *American Literature*, 70: 581–606.

Kaplan, Fred (2013) *The Insurgents: David Petraeus and the Plot to Change the American Way of War* (New York: Simon & Schuster).

Kaplan, Lawrence F. and William Kristol (2003) *The War Over Iraq: Saddam's Tyranny and America's Mission* (San Francisco, CA: Encounter Books).

Kaplan, Robert (2007) 'It's the Tribes, Stupid!' *The Atlantic*, 21 November. Available at http://www.theatlantic.com/magazine/archive/2007/11/its-the-tribes-stupid/306496/ (accessed 25 June 2015).

Karabell, Zachary (1999) *Architects of Intervention: the United States, the Third World, and the Cold War, 1946–1962* (Baton Rouge: Louisiana State University Press).

Karasik, Theodore and Ghassan Schbley (2008) 'A House of Tribes for Iraq', *The Washington Post*, 25 April.

Karnow, Stanley (1963) 'The Fall of the House of Ngo Dinh', *The Saturday Evening Post*, 21 December, pp. 75–79.

Kaviraj, Sudipta and Sunil Khilnani (eds.) (2001) *Civil Society: History and Possibilities* (Cambridge: Cambridge University Press).

Keene, Edward (2002) *Beyond the Anarchical Society: Grotius, Colonialism and Order in World Politics* (Cambridge: Cambridge University Press).

(2005) *International Political Thought: An Historical Introduction* (Cambridge: Polity).

(2006) 'Images of Grotius', in Beate Jahn (ed.) *Classical Theory in International Relations* (Cambridge: Cambridge University Press), pp. 233–252.

Kely, John, Beatrice Jauregui, Sean Mitchell and Jeremy Walton (eds.) (2010) *Anthropology and Global Counterinsurgency* (Chicago: University of Chicago Press).

Kennedy, Dane (1992) 'Constructing the Colonial Myth of Mau Mau', *International Journal of African Historical Studies*, 25(2): 241–260.

Kenyatta, Jomo (1938/1953) *Facing Mount Kenya: The Tribal Life of the Gikuyu* (intro. B. Malinowski) (London: Secker and Warburg).

Kerr, Clark (1964) *Industrialism and Industrial Man: the Problems of Labor and Management in Economic Growth* (New York: Oxford University Press).

Keuls, Eva C. (1985) *The Reign of the Phallus: Sexual Politics in Ancient Athens* (Berkeley, CA: University of California Press).

Khalili, Laleh (2011) 'Gendered Practices of Counterinsurgency', *Review of International Studies*, 37(4): 1471–1491.

(2013) *Time in the Shadows: Confinement in Counterinsurgencies* (Stanford, CA: Stanford University Press).

Khoo, Agnes (2004) *Life as the River Flows: Women in the Malayan Anti-colonial Struggle: An Oral History of Women from Thailand, Malaysia and Singapore* (Petaling Jaya, Selangor: Strategic Information Research Development).

Kienscherf, Markus (2011) 'A Programme of Global Pacification: US Counterinsurgency Doctrine and the Biopolitics of Human (In)security', *Security Dialogue*, 42(6): 517–535.

(2012) *US Domestic and International Regimes of Security: Pacifying the Globe, Securing the Homeland* (New York: Routledge).

Kiernan, V.G. (1998) *Colonial Empires and Armies 1815–1960* (Stroud: Sutton).

Kilcullen, David (2006) 'The Twenty-eight Articles: Fundamentals of Company-Level Counterinsurgency' in United States Marine Corps *Small-Unit Leaders' Guide to Counterinsurgency* (June), Annex C, pp. 113–126.

(2007a) 'Anatomy of a Tribal Revolt', *Small Wars Journal Blog*, 29 August. Available from http://smallwarsjournal.com/blog/anatomy-of-a-tribal-revolt (accessed 22 March 2013).

(2007b) 'Ethics, Politics and Non-state Warfare', *Anthropology Today*, 23(3): 20.

(2009) *The Accidental Guerrilla: Fighting Small Wars in the Midst of a Big One* (Oxford: Oxford University Press).

(2010) *Counterinsurgency* (New York: Oxford University Press).
King, Diane E. (2008) 'The Personal is Patrilineal: *Namus* as Sovereignty', *Identities*, 15(3): 317–342.
King, John Jerry (1954) 'Malaya's Resettlement Problem', *Far Eastern Survey*, 23: 33–40.
Kinsella, Helen M. (2014) *Afghan Good Enough* (unpublished manuscript).
Kipp, Jacob, Lester Grau, Karl Prinslow and Don Smith (2006) 'The Human Terrain System: A CORDS for the 21st Century', *Military Review*, 86(5): 8–15.
Kitson, Frank (1971) *Low Intensity Operations: Subversion, Insurgency, Peace–Keeping* (London: Faber & Faber).
Kitzen, Martijn (2012) 'Close Encounters of the Tribal Kind: The Implementation of Co-option as a Tool for De-escalation of Conflict – the Case of the Netherlands in Afghanistan's Uruzgan Province', *Journal of Strategic Studies*, 35(5): 713–734.
Klare, Michael T., Cynthia Arnson with Delia Miller and Daniel Volman (1981) *Supplying Repression: US Support for Authoritarian Regimes Abroad* (foreword by Richard Falk) (Washington, DC: Institute for Policy Studies).
Kleinfeld, Rachel (2009) 'Petraeus the Progressive', *Democracy: A Journal of Ideas*, 11: 108–115.
Klinck, David (1996) *The French Counterrevolutionary Theorist, Louis de Bonald* (New York: P. Lang).
Knoke, David (2013) '"It Takes a Network": The Rise and Fall of Social Network Analysis in US Army Counterinsurgency Doctrine', *Connections*, 33(1): 1–10.
Kolko, Gabriel (1985) *Anatomy of a War: Vietnam, the United States, and the Modern Historical Experience* (New York: Pantheon Books).
(1988) *Confronting the Third World: United States Foreign Policy, 1945–1980* (New York: Pantheon Books).
Komer, R.W. (1966) *The Other War in Vietnam: A Progress Report* (Washington, DC: Agency for International Development).
(1970a) 'Clear, Hold, and Rebuild', *Army*, May: 16–24.
(1970b) *Impact of Pacification on Insurgency in South Vietnam* (Santa Monica, CA: RAND Corporation).
(1972) *The Malayan Emergency in Retrospect: Organization of a Successful Counterinsurgency Effort* (Washington, DC: RAND).
Koskenniemi, Martti (2002) *The Gentle Civilizer of Nations: The Rise and Fall of International Law, 1870–1960* (Cambridge: Cambridge University Press).
Kramer, Paul A. (2006) 'The Darkness that Enters the Home: The Politics of Prostitution During the Philippine-American War', in Ann Laura Stoler

(ed.) *Haunted by Empire: Geographies of Intimacy in North American History* (Durham: Duke University Press), pp. 366–404.

Kratochwil, Friedrich (2006) 'History, Action and Identity: Revisiting the "Second" Great Debate and Assessing its Importance for Social Theory', *European Journal of International Relations*, 12(1): 5–29.

Krebs, Paula M. (1992) '"The Last of the Gentlemen's Wars": Women in the Boer War Concentration Camp Controversy', *History Workshop Journal*, 33(1): 38–56.

(1999) *Gender, Race, and the Writing of Empire: Public Discourse and the Boer War* (Cambridge: Cambridge University Press).

Kristeva, Julia (2001) *Hannah Arendt* (trans. Ross Guberman) (New York: Columbia University Press).

Kuehl, Dale (2009) 'Testing Galula in Ameriyah: The People are the Key', *Military Review*, March–April: 72–80.

Kuper, Adam (2005) *The Reinvention of Primitive Society: Transformations of a Myth* (2nd edition) (London: Routledge).

(1991) 'The Rise and Fall of Maine's Patriarchal Society', in Alan Diamond (ed.) *The Victorian Achievement of Sir Henry Maine: A Centennial Reappraisal* (Cambridge: Cambridge University Press), pp. 99–110.

Kurac, Anton (2011) 'Counterinsurgency: Domestic Politics by Other Means', *Small Wars Journal*, 14 January: 1–13.

Kurer, Oskar (1991) 'John Stuart Mill and the Welfare State', *History of Political Economy*, 23(4): 713–730.

Kuzmarov, Jeremy (2012) *Modernizing Repression: Police Training and Nation Building in the American Century* (Amherst, MA: University of Massachusetts Press).

Lambert, H.E. (1956) *Kikuyu Social and Political Institutions* (Oxford: Oxford University Press).

Landauer, Carl (2002) 'From Status to Treaty: Henry Sumner Maine's International Law', *Canadian Journal of Law and Jurisprudence*, 15(2): 219–254.

Larteguy, Jean (1961) *The Centurions* (New York: E.P. Dutton & Company).

Lasswell, Harold D. (1930) *Psychopathology and Politics* (Chicago: University of Chicago Press).

Latham, Michael E. (2000) *Modernization as Ideology: American Social Science and 'Nation Building' in the Kennedy Era* (Chapel Hill, NC: University of North Carolina Press).

(2011) *The Right Kind of Revolution: Modernization, Development, and US Foreign Policy from the Cold War to the Present* (Ithaca, NY: Cornell University Press).

Latour, Bruno (2005) *Reassembling the Social: An Introduction to Actor-Network-Theory* (Oxford: Oxford University Press).

Lawrence, T.E. (1922/1991) *Seven Pillars of Wisdom: A Triumph* (New York: Anchor Books).

Leakey, Louis (1953) *Mau Mau and the Kikuyu* (London: Methuen).

(1954) *Defeating Mau Mau* (London, Methuen).

Ledwidge, Frank (2011) *Losing Small Wars: British Military Failure in Iraq and Afghanistan* (New Haven, CT: Yale University Press).

Leng, Yuen Yuet (1998) *Operation Ginger* (Kuala Lumpur: Vinpress).

Lerner, Daniel (1958) *The Passing of Traditional Society: Modernizing the Middle East* (New York: Free Press).

Leshem, Dotan (2013) 'Oikonomia in the Age of Empires', *History of the Human Sciences*, 26(1): 29–51.

Levi-Strauss, Claude (1966) *The Savage Mind* (Chicago, IL: University of Chicago Press).

Levine, Donald N. (1995) *Visions of the Sociological Tradition* (Chicago, IL: University of Chicago Press).

Levy, Marion J. (1949/1968) *The Family Revolution in Modern China* (New York: Atheneum).

(1996) *Modernization and the Structure of Societies* (two volumes) (New Brunswick, NJ: Transaction Publishers).

Lewis, J.E. (2001) 'The Ruling Compassions of the Late Colonial State: Welfare versus Force, Kenya, 1945–1952', *Journal of Colonialism and Colonial History*, 2(2). Available at http://muse.jhu.edu/journals/journal_of_colonialism_and_colonial_history/summary/v002/2.2lewis.html (accessed 12 May 2014).

Lewis, Joanna (2000a) *Empire State-Building: War and Welfare in Kenya 1925–1952* (Athens, OH: Ohio University Press).

(2000b) '"Tropical East Ends" and the Second World War: Some Contradictions in Colonial Office Welfare Initiatives', *Journal of Imperial and Commonwealth History*, 28(2): 42–66.

Li, Tania Murray (2007) *The Will to Improve: Governmentality, Development, and the Practice of Politics* (Durham, NC: Duke University Press).

Light, Jennifer S. (2003) *From Warfare to Welfare: Defense Intellectuals and Urban Problems in Cold War America* (Baltimore, MD: Johns Hopkins University Press).

Liht, Jose, Sara Savage and Ryan J. Williams (2013) 'Being Muslim, Being British: A Multimedia Educational Resource for Young Muslims', in George Joffé (ed.) *Islamist Radicalisation in Europe and the Middle East: Reassessing the Causes of Terrorism* (London: I.B. Tauris), pp. 34–57.

Lind, Wencke Aamodt (2007) 'Experience from Capacity-Building Courses for Social Workers in Iraq', *International Social Work*, 50(3): 395–404.

Lindert, Peter H. (2004) *Social Spending and Economic Growth since the Eighteenth Century, Volume 1* (Cambridge: Cambridge University Press).

Linn, Brian McAllister (1989) *The US Army and Counterinsurgency in the Philippine War, 1899–1902* (Chapel Hill, NC: University of North Carolina Press).

(2009) 'The Impact of the Philippine Wars (1898–1913) on the US Army', in Alfred McCoy and Francisco Scarano (eds.) *Colonial Crucible: Empire in the Making of the Modern American State* (Madison, WI: University of Wisconsin Press, 2009), pp. 460–472.

Locke, John (1689/1963) *Two Treaties of Government* (intro. and notes by Peter Laslett) (Cambridge: Cambridge University Press).

Loeb, Vernon (2003) 'US Isolates Hussein's Birthplace', *Washington Post*, 17 November.

Long, Austin (2008) *Doctrine of Eternal Recurrence: The US Military Counterinsurgency Doctrine, 1960–1970 and 2003–2006*, RAND Counterinsurgency Study – Paper 6 (Santa Monica, CA: RAND).

Lonsdale, John (1990) 'Mau Maus of the Mind: Making Mau Mau and Remaking Kenya', *The Journal of African History*, 31(3): 393–421.

López, José (2003) *Society and its Metaphors: Language, Social Theory and Social Structure* (New York: Continuum).

Lord, William A. (2002) *Household Dynamics: Economic Growth and Policy* (New York: Oxford University Press).

Lorde, Audre (2007) 'The Master's Tools Will Never Dismantle the Master's House', in *Sister Outsider: Essays and Speeches* (revised edition; foreword by Cheryl Clarke) (Berkeley, CA: Crossing Press), pp. 110–113.

Louis, W.M. Roger and Ronald Robinson (1994) 'The Imperialism of Decolonization', *Journal of Imperial and Commonwealth History*, 22(3): 462–511.

Loyn, David (2008) *Butcher and Bolt: Two Hundred Years of Foreign Failure in Afghanistan* (London: Hutchinson).

Lucas, George R. (2009) *Anthropologists in Arms: the Ethics of Military Anthropology* (Lanham, MD: Rowman & Littlefield).

Lukes, Steven (1972) *Émile Durkheim: His Life and Work: A Historical and Critical Study* (London: Penguin).

Luttwak, Edward N. (2007) 'Dead End: Counterinsurgency as Military Malpractice', *Harpers*, February: 33–42.

Lyautey, Hubert (1891) 'Du rôle social de l'officier dans le service militaire universal', *Revue des deux mondes*, 15 March: Vol. 104, pp. 443–59.

(1920) *Lettres du Tonkin et de Madagascar, 1894–1899* (Paris: Armand Colin).

Maass, Peter (2005) 'The Way of the Commandos', *The New York Times*, 1 May.

Maifreda, Germano (2012) *From Oikonomia to Political Economy: Constructing Economic Knowledge from the Renaissance to the Scientific Revolution* (London: Ashgate).

Maine, Henry Sumner (1876) *Village-Communities in the East and West* (London: John Murray).

(1878/1908) *Ancient Law: Its Connection with the Early History of Society, and its Relation to Modern Ideas* (London: John Murray).

(1886) 'The Patriarchal Theory', *Quarterly Review*, 162: 181–209.

(1888) *International Law: A Series of Lectures Delivered before the University of Cambridge, 1887* (London: John Murray).

Majeed, J. (1990) 'James Mill's "The History of British India" and Utilitarianism as a Rhetoric of Reform', *Modern Asian Studies*, 24(2): 209–224.

Mamdani, Mahmood (1996) *Citizenship and Subject: Contemporary Africa and the Legacy of Late Colonialism* (Princeton, NJ: Princeton University Press).

(1999) 'Historicizing Power and Responses to Power: Indirect Rule and its Reform', *Social Research*, 66(3): 859–886.

(2012) *Define and Rule: Native as Political Identity* (Cambridge, MA: Harvard University Press).

Mandelbaum, Michael (1996) 'Foreign Policy as Social Work', *Foreign Affairs*, 75(1): 16–32.

Mann, Michael (1993) *Sources of Social Power, Vol. II: The Rise of Classes and Nation-States, 1760–1914* (Cambridge: Cambridge University Press).

Mantena, Karuna (2010) *Alibis of Empire: Henry Maine and the Ends of Liberal Imperialism* (Princeton, NJ: Princeton University Press).

(2012) 'Social Theory in the Age of Empire', in Sankar Muthu (ed.) *Empire and Modern Political Thought* (Cambridge: Cambridge University Press), pp. 324–350.

Markel, M. Wade (2006) 'Draining the Swamp: The British Strategy of Population Control', *Parameters*, Spring, Vol. 36: 35–48.

Marks, Michael P. (2011) *Metaphors within International Relations Theory* (London: Palgrave).

Marquis, Jefferson (2000) 'The Other Warriors: American Social Science and Nation Building in Vietnam', *Diplomatic History*, 24(1): 79–105.

Martin, Biddy and Chandra Mohanty (1986) 'Feminist Politics: What's Home Got to Do With It?', in Teresa de Lauretis (ed.) *Feminist Studies/Critical Studies* (Bloomington, IN: Indiana University Press), pp. 191–212.

Marwick, Arthur (1974) *War and Social Change in the Twentieth Century: A Comparative Study of Britain, France, Germany, Russia and the United States* (London: Macmillan).

Marx, Karl (1972) *The Marx-Engels Reader* (ed. Robert C. Tucker) (New York: W.W. Norton).

(1973) *Grundrisse: Foundations of the Critique of Political Economy* (New York: Vintage Books).

(1975) 'Economic and Philosophical Manuscripts of 1844', *Collected Works, Volume 3* (Moscow: Progress Publishers), pp. 229–346.

(1976) *Capital: Volume 1* (London: Penguin).

(1992) *Early Writings* (London: Penguin).

Marx, Karl and Friedrich Engels (1970) *The German Ideology* (New York: International Publishers).

Massy, Doreen (1992) 'A Place Called Home', *New Formations*, 17: 3–15.

Mathias, Grégor (2011) *Galula in Algeria: Counterinsurgency Practice versus Theory* (Santa Barbara, CA: ABC-CLIO).

Matin, Kamran (2012) 'Redeeming the Universal: Postcolonialism and the Inner Life of Eurocentrism', *European Journal of International Relations*, 19(2): 353–377.

(2013) *Recasting Iranian Modernity: International Relations and Social Change* (London: Routledge).

Matthews, Glenna (1987) *'Just a Housewife': The Rise and Fall of Domesticity in America* (New York: Oxford University Press).

Mattli, Walter and Ngaire Woods (eds.) (2009) *The Politics of Global Regulation* (Princeton, NJ: Princeton University Press).

Maurois, André (1931/1932) *Lyautey* (trans. Hamish Miles) (New York: D. Appleton and Company).

Mauss, Marcel (1922/1990) *The Gift: Forms and Functions of Exchange in Archaic Societies* (London: Routledge).

May, Elaine Tyler (1988) *Homeward Bound: American Families in the Cold War Era* (New York: BasicBooks).

May, Glenn Anthony (1980) *Social Engineering in the Philippines: the Aims, Execution, and Impact of American Colonial Policy 1900–1903* (Westport, CT: Greenwood Press).

Mazlish, Bruce (1989) *A New Science: The Breakdown of Connections and the Birth of Sociology* (University Park, PA: Pennsylvania State University Press).

Mazower, Mark (2008) 'Mandarins, Guns and Money: Academics and the Cold War', *The Nation*, 6 October.

McBride, Keally and Annick T.R. Wibben (2012) 'The Gendering of Counterinsurgency in Afghanistan', *Humanity*, 3(2): 199–215.

McCallister, William S. (2007) 'MNF-W Engagement: Engagement Model' DSN: 3404–833 (20 June), pp. 1–17.

McCarthy, George E. (ed.) (1992) *Marx and Aristotle: Nineteenth-Century German Social Theory and Classical Antiquity* (London: Rowman and Littlefield).

McCarthy, Mary (1967) *Vietnam* (New York: Harcourt, Brace & World).

McChrystal, Stanley A., (2010) ISAF Headquarters, *Engagement with Afghan Females Directive*, 2 May. Available at http://cryptome.org/dodi/100531_EngagementwAFFemales_ISAF-3.pdf (accessed 11 April 2014).

McClintock, Anne (1993) 'Family Feuds: Gender, Nationalism and the Family', *Feminist Review*, 44: 61–80.

(1995) *Imperial Leather: Race, Gender, and Sexuality in the Colonial Contest* (New York: Routledge).

McClymer, John F. (1980) *War and Welfare: Social Engineering in America, 1890–1925* (Westport, CT: Greenwood Press).

McCoy, Alfred W. (2009a) 'Police, Prisons and Law Enforcement: Introduction', in Alfred McCoy and Francisco Scarano (eds.) *Colonial Crucible: Empire in the Making of the Modern American State* (Madison, WI: University of Wisconsin Press), pp. 83–86

(2009b) *Policing America's Empire: The United States, the Philippines, and the Rise of the Surveillance State* (Madison, WI: University of Wisconsin Press).

McCoy, Alfred W. and Francisco Scarano (eds.) (2009) *Colonial Crucible: Empire in the Making of the Modern American State* (Madison, WI: The University of Wisconsin Press).

McCulloch, Jock (1995) *Colonial Psychiatry and 'the African Mind'* (Cambridge: Cambridge University Press).

McDowell, Linda (2002) 'Unsettling Naturalisms', *Signs: Journal of Women in Culture and Society*, 27(3): 815–822.

McFate, Montgomery (2005a) 'The Military Utility of Understanding Adversary Culture', *Joint Force Quarterly*, 38: 42–48.

(2005b) 'Anthropology and Counterinsurgency: The Strange Story of their Curious Relationship', *Military Review*, March/April: 24–38.

(2008) 'The "Memory of War": Tribes and the Legitimate Use of Force in Iraq', in J.H. Norwitz (ed.) *Armed Groups* (Newport: US Naval War College), pp. 291–310.

McFate, Montgomery and Andrea Jackson (2006) 'The Object Beyond War: Counterinsurgency and the Tools of Political Competition', *Military Review*, January/February: 13–26.

McGeer, Michael (2003) *A Fierce Discontent: The Rise and Fall of the Progressive Movement in America, 1870–1920* (New York: Oxford University Press).

McIntosh, J.L. (2009) *From Heads of Household to Heads of State: the Preaccession Households of Mary and Elizabeth Tudor, 1516–1558* (New York: Columbia University Press).

McKeon, Michael (2005) *The Secret History of Domesticity: Public, Private and the Division of Knowledge* (Baltimore, MD: Johns Hopkins University Press).

McKinley, William (1898) 'Benevolent Assimilation Proclamation', Executive Mansion, Washington, 21 December. Available at www.msc.edu.ph/centennial/benevolent.html (accessed 24 May 2013).

McLennan, John (1885) *The Patriarchal Theory* (ed. and completed by Donald McLennan) (London: Macmillan).

Mearsheimer, John (2011) 'Imperial by Design', *The National Interest*, 111: 16–34.

Meek, Ronald (1976) *Social Science and the Ignoble Savage* (Cambridge: Cambridge University Press).

Megay, E.N. (1958) 'Treitschke Reconsidered: The Hegelian Tradition of German Liberalism', *Midwest Journal of Political Science*, 2: 298–317.

Mehta, Uday Singh (1999) *Liberalism and Empire: A Study in Nineteenth-Century British Liberal Thought* (Chicago: University of Chicago Press).

Meinecke, Friedrich (1957) *Machiavellism: The Doctrine of Raison d'État and Its Place in Modern History* (London: Routledge and Kegan Paul).

Merom, Gil (2003) *How Democracies Lose Small Wars: State, Society, and the Failures of France in Algeria, Israel in Lebanon, and the United States in Vietnam* (Cambridge: Cambridge University Press).

Mertes, Kate (1988) *The English Noble Household, 1250–1600: Good Governance and Politic Rule* (Oxford: Blackwell).

Metcalf, Thomas R. (1964) *The Aftermath of Revolt: India, 1857–1870* (Princeton, NJ: Princeton University Press).

(1994) *Ideologies of the Raj* (Cambridge: Cambridge University Press).

Midgley, James (1981) *Professional Imperialism: Social Work in the Third World* (London: Heinemann).

Midgley, James and David Piachaud (eds.) (2011) *Colonialism and Welfare: Social Policy and the British Imperial Legacy* (Cheltenham: Edward Elgar).

Migdal, Joel S. (1988) *Strong Societies and Weak States: State–Society Relations and State Capabilities in the Third World* (Princeton, NJ: Princeton University Press).

Miles, Donna (2009) 'Petraeus Notes Difference between Iraq, Afghanistan Strategies', *American Forces Press Service*, 22 April. Available at www.defense.gov/news/newsarticle.aspx?id=54036 (accessed 5 February 2014).

Mill, John Stuart (1843/1988) *The Logic of the Moral Sciences* (Chicago, IL: Open Court Publishing).

(1861/2010) *Considerations on Representative Government* (Cambridge: University of Cambridge Press).

(1999) *'On Liberty' and Other Writings* (ed. Stefan Collini) (Cambridge: Cambridge University Press).

Millett, Kate (1969/1977) *Sexual Politics* (London: Virago Press).

Milne, David (2007) '"Our Equivalent of Guerrilla Warfare": Walt Rostow and the Bombing of North Vietnam, 1961–1968', *Journal of Military History*, 71: 169–203.

(2008) *America's Rasputin: Walt Rostow and the Vietnam War* (New York: Hill and Wang).

Milner, G.C.B. Viscount (1908) *Constructive Imperialism: Five Speeches Delivered at Tunbridge Wells* (London: The National Review Office).

Mirzoeff, Nicholas (2009) 'War Is Culture: Global Counterinsurgency, Visuality, and the Petraeus Doctrine', *PMLA*, 124(5): 1737–1746.

Mitcham, Carol and David Muñoz (2010) *Humanitarian Engineering* (San Rafael, CA: Morgan & Claypool).

Mitropoulos, Angela (2012) *Contract and Contagion: from Biopolitics to Oikonomia* (New York: Minor Compositions).

Mizruchi, Mark (1994) 'Social Network Analysis: Recent Achievements and Current Controversies', *Acta Sociologica*, 37: 329–343.

Mockaitis, Thomas R. (1990) *British Counterinsurgency, 1919–1960* (London: Macmillan).

Moggach, Douglas and Paul Leduc Browne (eds.) (2000) *The Social Question and the Democratic Revolution: Marx and the Legacy of 1848* (Ottawa: University of Ottawa Press).

Montesquieu, Charles de Secondat (1748/1989) *The Spirit of the Laws* (trans. and ed. Anne M. Cohler, Basia C. Miller and Harold S. Stone) (Cambridge: Cambridge University Press).

Moravcsik, Andrew (1997) 'Taking Preferences Seriously: A Liberal Theory of International Politics', *International Organization*, 51(4): 513–553.

Morgenthau, Hans J. (1946/1974) *Scientific Man vs. Power Politics* (Chicago: University of Chicago Press).

(1948) *Politics Among Nations: The Struggle for Power and Peace* (New York: Alfred A. Knopf).

(1971) *Politics in the Twentieth Century* (abridged edition) (Chicago: University of Chicago Press).

Mumford, Andrew (2010) 'Sir Robert Thompson's Lessons for Iraq: Bringing the "Basic Principles of Counter-insurgency" into the 21st Century', *Defense Studies*, 10(1–2): 177–194.

(2011) *The Counter-insurgency Myth: The British Experience of Irregular Warfare* (London: Routledge).
Mundy, Martha (1995) *Domestic Government: Kinship, Community and Polity in North Yemen* (London: I.B. Tauris).
Mungazi, Dickson A. (1999) *The Last British Liberals in Africa: Michael Blundell and Garfield Todd* (Westport, CT: Praeger).
Musicant, Ivan (1990) *The Banana Wars: A History of United States Military Intervention in Latin America from the Spanish-American War to the Invasion of Panama* (New York: Macmillan).
Myers, Janet C. (2009) *Antipodal England: Emigration and Portable Domesticity in the Victorian Imagination* (Albany: State University of New York Press).
Myrdal, Gunnar (1953) *The Political Element in the Development of Economic Theory* (trans. Paul Streeten) (London: Routledge).
Nagl, John (2002) *Learning to Eat Soup with a Knife: Counterinsurgency Lessons from Malaya and Vietnam* (Chicago: University of Chicago Press).
Nagle, D. Brendan (2006) *The Household as the Foundation of Aristotle's Polis* (Cambridge: Cambridge University Press).
Nemo, Jean (1956) 'La guerre dans le milieu social', *Revue de Défense Nationale*, 12: 605–626.
Neocleous, Mark (1995) 'From Civil Society to the Social', *The British Journal of Sociology*, 46(3): 395–408.
(2013) '"O Effeminacy! Effeminacy!" War, Masculinity and the Myth of Liberal Peace', *European Journal of International Relations*, 19(1): 93–113.
Netting, Robert McC, Richard R. Wilk and Eric J. Arnould (eds.) (1984) *Households: Comparative and Historical Studies of the Domestic Group* (Berkeley, CA: University of California Press).
Newman, Louise Michele (1999) *White Women's Rights: The Racial Origins of Feminism in the United States* (New York: Oxford University Press).
Nexon, Daniel H. (2009) *The Struggle for Power in Early Modern Europe: Religious Conflict, Dynastic Empires, and International Change* (Princeton, NJ: Princeton University Press).
Nicholson, Linda J. (1986) *Gender and History: The Limits of Social Theory in the Age of the Family* (New York: Columbia University Press).
Nighswonger, William A. (1967) *Rural Pacification in Vietnam* (New York: Praeger).
Nightingale, Carl H. (2012) *Segregation: A Global History of Divided Cities* (Chicago: University of Chicago Press).
Nisbet, Robert A. (1966) *The Sociological Tradition* (London: Heinemann).

Novak, William J. (1996) *The People's Welfare: Law and Regulation in Nineteenth-Century America* (Chapel Hill, NC: University of North Carolina Press).

O'Brien, Mary (1981) *The Politics of Reproduction* (London: Routledge).

O'Huiginn, Daniel and Alison Klevnas (2005) 'Denial of Water to Iraqi Cities', in Jeremy Brecher, Jill Cutler and Brendan Smith (eds.) *In the Name of Democracy: American War Crimes in Iraq and Beyond* (New York: Metropolitan Books), pp. 55–58.

O'Malley, Pat (1996) 'Indigenous Governance', *Economy and Society*, 25(3): 310–326.

Odysseos, Louiza and Fabio Petito (eds.) (2007) *The International Political Thought of Carl Schmitt: Terror, Liberal War and the Crisis of Global Order* (London: Routledge).

Oren, Ido (2003) *Our Enemies and US: America's Rivalries and the Making of Political Science* (Ithaca, NY: Cornell University Press).

Osborne, Milton E. (1965) *Strategic Hamlets in South Viet-Nam: A Survey and Comparison* (Ithaca, NY: Cornell University Press).

Outhwaite, William (2006) *The Future of Society* (Oxford: Blackwell).

Owen, William F. (2011) 'Killing Your Way to Control', *The British Army Review*, 151: 34–37.

Owens, Patricia (2003) 'Accidents Don't Just Happen: The Liberal Politics of High-Tech Humanitarian War', *Millennium: Journal of International Studies*, 32(3): 595–616.

(2004) 'Theorising Military Intervention', *International Affairs*, 80(2): 355–365.

(2007a) 'Beyond Strauss, Lies, and the War in Iraq: Hannah Arendt's Critique of Neoconservatism', *Review of International Studies*, 33(2): 265–283.

(2007b) *Between War and Politics: International Relations and the Thought of Hannah Arendt* (Oxford: Oxford University Press).

(2009) 'Reclaiming "Bare Life"? Against Agamben on Refugees', *International Relations*, 23(4): 567–582.

(2010) 'Torture, Sex and Military Orientalism', *Third World Quarterly*, 31(7): 1147–1162.

(2011) 'The Return of Realism? War and Changing Concepts of the Political', in Sibylle Scheipers and Hew Strachan (eds.) *The Changing Character of War* (Oxford: Oxford University Press), pp. 484–502.

(2012) 'Human Security and the Rise of the Social', *Review of International Studies*, 38(3): 547–567.

(2013) 'From Bismarck to Petraeus: The Question of the Social and the Social Question in Counterinsurgency', *European Journal of International Relations*, 19(1): 135–157.

Packenham, R.A. (1973) *Liberal America and the Third World: Political Development Ideas in Foreign Aid and Social Science* (Princeton, NJ: Princeton University Press).

Packwood, Lane V. (2009) 'Popular Support as the Objective in Counterinsurgency: What Are We Really After?', *Military Review*, May–June: 67–77.

Paget, Julian (1967) *Counter-Insurgency Campaigning* (London: Faber & Faber).

Parsons, Talcott (1937) *The Structure of Social Action: A Study in Social Theory with Special Reference to a Group of Recent European Writers* (New York: McGraw-Hill Book Company).

(1951) *The Social System* (Glencoe, IL: Free Press).

(1961) 'Order and Community in the International Social System', in James N. Rosenau (ed.) *International Politics and Foreign Policy: A Reader in Research and Theory* (New York: Free Press), pp. 120–129.

(1964) 'Some Reflections on the Place of Force in Social Process', in Harry Eckstein (ed.) *Internal War: Problems and Approaches* (New York: Free Press), pp. 33–70.

(1966) *Societies: Evolutionary and Comparative Perspectives* (Englewood Cliffs, NJ: Prentice-Hall).

(1967) 'Polarization of the World and International Order', in Talcott Parsons (ed.) *Sociological Theory and Modern Society* (New York: Free Press), pp. 466–489.

Parsons, Talcott and Edward A. Shils (eds.) (1951) *Toward a General Theory of Action* (Cambridge, MA: Harvard University Press).

Parsons, Talcott and Neil Smelser (1956) *Economy and Society: A Study in the Integration of Economic and Social Theory* (Glencoe, Il: Free Press).

Pateman, Carole (1998) *The Sexual Contract* (Cambridge: Polity).

Patterson, Cynthia B. (2001) *The Family in Greek History* (Cambridge, MA: Harvard University Press).

Pattison, Mary (1915) *Principles of Domestic Engineering* (New York: The Trow Press).

Payne, Malcolm (2005) *Modern Social Work Theory* (New York: Palgrave).

Peabody, Francis Greenwood (1909) *The Approach to the Social Question: An Introduction to the Study of Social Ethics* (New York: Macmillan).

Pearce, Kimber Charles (2001) *Rostow, Kennedy, and the Rhetoric of Foreign Aid* (Ann Arbor, MI: University of Michigan Press).

Pecora, Vincent P. (1997) *Households of the Soul* (Baltimore, MD: Johns Hopkins University Press).

Peters, Ralph (2000) 'The Human Terrain of Urban Operations', *Parameters*, Spring, Vol. 30: 4–12.

Petersen, Michael (1989) *The Combined Action Platoons: The Marines' Other War in Vietnam* (Westport, CT: Praeger).
Peterson, V. Spike (2010) 'Global Householding amid Global Crises', *Politics & Gender*, 6(2): 271–281.
Pilbeam, Pamela M. (2000) *French Socialists Before Marx: Workers, Women and the Social Question in France, 1796–1852* (Durham: Acumen Publishing).
Pitkin, Hanna Fenichel (1998) *The Attack of the Blob: Hannah Arendt's Concept of the Social* (Chicago: University of Chicago Press).
Pitts, Jennifer (2005) *A Turn to Empire: The Rise of Imperial Liberalism in Britain and France* (Princeton, NJ: Princeton University Press).
Piven, Francis and Richard A. Cloward (1971) *Regulating the Poor: The Functions of Public Welfare* (New York: Vintage Books).
Polanyi, Karl (1957/2001) *The Great Transformation: The Political and Economic Origins of Our Time* (Boston: Beacon Press).
Pomeroy, Sarah B. (1994) *Xenophon, Oeconomicus: A Social and Historical Commentary* (Oxford: Clarendon Press).
Pool, Ithiel de Sola (1968) *Village Violence and Pacification in Viet Nam* (Urbana, IL: University of Illinois Press).
(1998) 'The Public and the Polity', in *Politics in Wired Nations: Selected Writings of Ithiel de Sola Pool* (ed. with an intro. by Lloyd S. Etheredge) (New Brunswick, NJ: Transaction), pp. 263–290.
Pool, Ithiel de Sola and Robert Abelson (1961) 'The Simulmatics Project', *The Public Opinion Quarterly*, 25(2): 167–183.
Poovey, Mary (1995) *Making a Social Body: British Cultural Formation, 1830–1864* (Chicago: University of Chicago Press).
Pope, Whitney (1975) 'Durkheim as a Functionalist', *The Sociological Quarterly*, 16(3): 361–379.
Popkin, Samuel L. (1970) 'Pacification: Politics and the Village', *Asian Survey*, 10(8): 662–671.
Porch, Douglas (1986) 'Bugeard, Galliéni, Lyautey: The Development of French Colonial Warfare', in Peter Paret (ed.) *Makers of Modern Strategy* (Princeton, NJ: Princeton University Press), pp. 376–407.
(2011) 'The Dangerous Myths and Dubious Promise of COIN', *Small Wars & Insurgencies*, 22(2): 239–257.
(2013) *Counterinsurgency: Exposing the Myths of the New Way of War* (Cambridge: Cambridge University Press).
Prakash, Gyan (2002) 'The Colonial Genealogy of Society: Community and Political Modernity in India', in Patrick Joyce (ed.) *The Social in Question: New Bearings in History and the Social Sciences* (London: Routledge), pp. 81–96.
Presley, Cora Ann (1992) *Kikuyu Women, the Mau Mau Rebellion, and Social Change in Kenya* (Boulder, CO: Westview Press).

Presser, Harriet (1998) 'Decapitating the US Census Bureau's "Head of Household": Feminist Mobilization in the 1970s', *Feminist Economics*, 4(3): 145–158.

Preston, Andrew Malcom (2006) *The War Council: McGeorge Bundy, the NSC, and Vietnam* (Cambridge, MA: Harvard University Press).

Procacci, Giovanna (1995) 'Notes on the Government of the Social', in Barry Smart (ed.) *Michel Foucault: Critical Assessments, Volume 7* (London: Routledge), pp. 139–145.

Pufendorf, Samuel (1682/1991) *On the Duty of Man and Citizen According to Natural Law* (ed. James Tully; trans. Michael Silverthorne) (Cambridge: Cambridge University Press).

Pye, Lucian W. (1956) *Guerrilla Communism in Malaya: Its Social and Political Meaning* (Princeton, NJ: Princeton University Press).

(1962a) *Military Development in the New Countries*, paper prepared for the Smithsonian Institute in December 1961, working paper no. C/62-1 (Cambridge, MA: Center for International Studies, MIT), pp. 1–38.

(1962b) 'Armies in the Process of Political Modernization', in John J. Johnson (ed.) *The Role of the Military in Underdeveloped Countries* (Princeton, NJ: Princeton University Press), pp. 80–89.

(1962c) *Politics, Personality, and Nation Building: Burma's Search for Identity* (New Haven, CT: Yale University Press).

(1963) *Political Development and Foreign Aid* (Washington, DC: AID Development Information Center).

Rabinow, Paul (1989) *French Modern: Norms and Forms of the Social Environment* (Chicago: University of Chicago Press).

Rachamimov, Iris (2012) 'Camp Domesticity: Shifting Gender Boundaries in WWI Internment Camps', in Gilly Carr and Harold Mytum (eds.) *Cultural Heritage and Prisoners of War: Creativity Behind Barbed Wire* (New York: Routledge), pp. 291–305.

Raeff, Marc (1983) *The Well-ordered Police State: Social and Institutional Change through Law in the Germanies and Russia, 1600–1800* (New Haven, CT: Yale University Press).

Rafael, Vicente L. (1995) 'Colonial Domesticity: White Women and United States Rule in the Philippines' *American Literature*, 67(4): 639–666.

Raibmon, Paige (2003) 'Living on Display: Colonial Visions of Aboriginal Domestic Spaces', *BC Studies*, 140: 69–89.

Ramakrishna, Kumar (2002) *Emergency Propaganda: The Winning of Malayan Hearts and Minds, 1948–1958* (Richmond: Curzon).

Ramsay, Allan (2000) 'A French Marshal in Morocco', *Contemporary Review*, 267(1613): 302–308.

Rasch, William (2005) 'Carl Schmitt and the New World Order', *South Atlantic Quarterly*, 104(2): 177–183.

Ray, Rajat K. (1984) *Social Conflict and Political Unrest in Bengal, 1875–1914* (Oxford: Oxford University Press).

Rejali, Darius (2007) *Torture and Democracy* (Princeton, NJ: Princeton University Press).

Renzi, Fred (2006) 'Networks: Terra Incognita and the Case for Ethnographic Intelligence', *Military Review*, September–October: 16–22.

Report to the Secretary of State for the Colonies by the Parliamentary Delegation to Kenya (1954) Presented by the Secretary of State for the Colonies to Parliament by command of Her Majesty, February (London: HMSO).

Reus-Smit, Christian (2002) 'The Idea of History and History with Ideas', in Stephen Hobden and John M. Hobson (eds.) *Historical Sociology of International Relations* (Cambridge: Cambridge University Press), pp. 120–140.

(2008) 'Reading History through Constructivist Eyes', *Millennium: Journal of International Studies*, 37(2): 395–414.

Ricks, Thomas (2009) 'The Minds Behind Counterinsurgency's Rise in US Military Strategy', *Foreign Policy*, December. Available at www.foreignpolicy.com/articles/2009/11/30/the_coindinistas (accessed 15 November 2012).

(2010) *The Gamble: General David Petraeus and the American Military Adventure in Iraq, 2006–2008* (London: Allen Lane).

Rid, Thomas (2009) 'Razzia: A Turning Point in Modern Strategy', *Terrorism and Political Violence*, 21: 617–635.

(2010) 'The Nineteenth Century Origins of Counterinsurgency Doctrine', *The Journal of Strategic Studies*, 33(5): 727–758.

Riesebrodt, Martin (1989) 'From Patriarchalism to Capitalism: The Theoretical Context of Max Weber's Agrarian Studies (1892–93)', in Keith Tribe (ed.) *Reading Weber* (London: Routledge), pp. 131–154.

Riley, Denise (1988) *'Am I That Name?' Feminism and the Category of 'Women' in History* (Minneapolis, MN: University of Minnesota Press).

Rodgers, Daniel T. (1998) *Atlantic Crossings: Social Politics in a Progressive Age* (Cambridge, MA: Harvard University Press).

Rohde, Joy (2009) 'Gray Matters: Social Scientists, Military Patronage, and Democracy in the Cold War', *Journal of American History*, 96(1): 99–122.

(2011) 'The Last Stand of the Psychocultural Cold Warriors: Military Contract Research in Vietnam', *Journal of the History of the Behavioral Sciences*, 47(3): 232–250.

Rojas, Cristina (2005) 'Governing through the Social: Representations of Poverty and Global Governmentality', in Wendy Larner and William

Walters (eds.) *Global Governmentality: Governing International Spaces* (London: Routledge), pp. 97–115.

Rose, Nikolas (1996) 'The Death of the Social? Re-figuring the Territory of Government', *Economy and Society*, 25(3): 327–356.

(1999) *Powers of Freedom: Reframing Political Thought* (Cambridge: Cambridge University Press).

Rosen, Nir (2006) *In the Belly of the Green Bird: The Triumph of Martyrs in Iraq* (New York: Simon and Schuster).

(2010) *Aftermath: Following the Bloodshed of America's Wars in the Muslim World* (New York: Nation Books).

Rosenberg, Justin (1994) *The Empire of Civil Society: A Critique of the Realist Theory of International Relations* (London: Verso).

(2013) 'Kenneth Waltz and Leon Trotsky: Anarchy in the Mirror of "Uneven and Combined Development"', *International Politics*, 50(2): 183–230.

Rostow, Walt (1960) *The Stages of Economic Growth: A Non-Communist Manifesto* (2nd edition) (Cambridge: Cambridge University Press).

Rousseau, Jean-Jacques (1755) 'De l'économie politique', *Grande encylopédie*, 5. Available at www.taieb.net/auteurs/Rousseau/economie.html (accessed 20 July 2013).

Rybczynski, Witold (1986) *Home: A Short History of an Idea* (New York: Viking).

Rynbrandt, Linda J. (1999) *Caroline Bartlett Crane and Progressive Reform: Social Housekeeping as Sociology* (New York: Garland).

Sage, Elizabeth M. (2009) *A Dubious Science: Political Economy and the Social Question in 19th-Century France* (New York: Peter Lang).

Sahlins, Marshall (2009) 'Preface', in Network of Concerned Anthropologists (ed.) *The Counter-Counterinsurgency Manual: or, Notes on Demilitarizing American Society* (Chicago: Prickly Paradigm), pp. i–vii.

Scahill, Jeremy (2013) *Dirty Wars: The World is a Battlefield* (New York: Nation Books).

Schabas, Margaret (2005) *The Natural Origins of Economics* (Chicago: University of Chicago Press).

Scham, Alan (1970) *Lyautey in Morocco: Protectorate Administration, 1912–1925* (Berkeley, CA: University of California Press).

Scheuerman, William E. (2011) *The Realist Case for Global Reform* (Cambridge: Polity Press).

Schinkel, Willem (2010) 'From Zoēpolitics to Biopolitics: Citizenship and the Construction of "Society"', *European Journal of Social Theory*, 13(2): 155–172.

Schlatter, Richard (1951) *Private Property: The History of an Idea* (New Brunswick, NJ: Rutgers University Press).

Schmitt, Carl (1950/2006) *The* nomos *of the Earth: in the International Law of the* jus publicum europaeum (New York: Telos).

(1996) *The Concept of the Political* (Chicago: University of Chicago Press)

(2004a) *Legality and Legitimacy* (trans. and ed. Jeffrey Seitzer; intro. by John P. McCormick) (Durham, NC: Duke University Press).

(2004b) *The Theory of the Partisan: A Commentary/Remark on the Concept of the Political* (trans. A. C. Goodson) (East Lansing: Michigan State University Press).

(2005) *Political Theology: Four Chapters on the Concept of Sovereignty* (trans. and with intro. by George Schwab; foreword by Tracy B. Strong) (Chicago: Chicago University Press).

Schultz, Bart and Georgios Varouxakis (eds.) (2005) *Utilitarianism and Empire* (Lanham, MD: Lexington Books).

Schwartz, Nancy L. (1979) 'Distinction between Public and Private Life: Marx on the *Zōon Politikon*', *Political Theory*, 7(2): 245–266.

Scott, H.M. (ed.) (1990) *Enlightened Absolutism: Reform and Reformers in Later Eighteenth-century Europe* (London: Macmillan).

Scott, James C. (1976) *The Moral Economy of the Peasant: Rebellion and Subsistence in Southeast Asia* (New Haven, CT: Yale University Press).

(1998) *Seeing Like a State: How Certain Schemes to Improve the Human Condition have Failed* (New Haven, CT: Yale University Press).

Searle, Geoffrey Russell (1971) *The Quest for National Efficiency: A Study in British Politics and Political Thought, 1899–1914* (Berkeley, CA: University of California Press).

Semmel, Bernard (1960) *Imperialism and Social Reform: English Social-Imperial Thought, 1895–1914* (London: George Allen and Unwin).

Senn, P.R. (2006) 'Economists and the Social Question: A Study of the Periodical Literature in English', *Journal of Economic Studies*, 33(4): 240–268.

Sepp, Kalev I. (2005) 'Best Practices in Counterinsurgency', *Military Review*, May–June: 8–12.

Sewall, Sarah (2007) 'A Radical Field Manual', in *The US Army/Marine Corps Counterinsurgency Field Manual: US Army Field Manual no. 3–24* (Chicago: University of Chicago Press) pp. xxi–xliii.

Shadid, Anthony (2005) *Night Draws Near: Iraq's People in the Shadow of America's War* (New York: Henry Holt).

Shafer, D. Michael (1988) *Deadly Paradigms: The Failure of US Counterinsurgency Policy* (Princeton, NJ: Princeton University Press).

Shammas, Carole (2002) *A History of Household Government in America* (Charlottesville, VA: University of Virginia Press).

Shaw, Albert (1894) 'What German Cities Do for their Citizens, a Study of Municipal House-keeping', *Century Magazine*, 48(3): 380–388.

Shaw, Martin (2002) 'Risk-transfer Militarism, Small Massacres and the Historic Legitimacy of War', *International Relations*, 16(3): 343–359.

Shilliam, Robbie (2009) *German Thought and International Relations: the Rise and Fall of a Liberal Project* (London: Palgrave).

Shils, Edward (1991) 'Henry Sumner Maine in the Tradition of the Analysis of Society', in Alan Diamond (ed.) *The Victorian Achievement of Sir Henry Maine: A Centennial Reappraisal* (Cambridge: Cambridge University Press), pp. 143–178.

Silberman, Charles (1964) *The Crisis in Black and White* (New York: Random House).

Simpson, Bradley R. (2008) *Economists with Guns: Authoritarian Development and US–Indonesian Relations, 1960–1968* (Stanford, CA: Stanford University Press).

Simpson, Christopher (ed.) (1998) *Universities and Empire: Money and Politics in the Social Sciences during the Cold War* (New York: New Press).

Simulmatics Corporation (1967) *A Population Survey in Vietnam: Final Report* (sponsored by Advanced Research Projects Agency).

Singer, Barnett and John Langdon (2004) *Cultured Force: Makers and Defenders of the French Colonial Empire* (Madison, WI: University of Wisconsin Press).

Singer, Brian C.J. (1986) *Society, Theory and the French Revolution: Studies in the Revolutionary Imagination* (London: Macmillan).

Singer, P.W. (2007) *Private Military Contractors and Counterinsurgency*, Brookings Institution Policy Paper No.4, September.

Sinha, Mrinalini (1995) *Colonial Masculinity: The 'Manly Englishman' and the 'Effeminate Bengali' in the Late Nineteenth Century* (Manchester: Manchester University Press).

Sitaraman, Ganesh (2012) *The Counterinsurgent's Constitution: Law in the Age of Small Wars* (New York: Oxford University Press).

Skocpol, Theda (1992) *Protecting Soldiers and Mothers: The Political Origins of Social Policy in the United States* (Cambridge, MA: Harvard University Press).

Slack, Paul (1988) *Poverty and Policy in Tudor and Stuart England* (London: Longman).

Small, Albion W. (1909) *The Cameralists: the Pioneers of German Social Polity* (Chicago: University of Chicago Press).

Smart, Barry (1990) 'On the Disorder of Things: Sociology, Postmodernity and the "End of the Social"', *Sociology*, 24(3): 397–416.

Smith, Adam (1776/1793) *An Inquiry into the Nature and Causes of the Wealth of Nations* (London: W. Strahan; and T. Cadell).

(1869) *Essays On, I. Moral Sentiments* (London: Alex Murray & Son).

(1896) *Lectures on Justice, Peace, Revenue and Arms: Delivered at the University of Glasgow* (Oxford: Clarendon Press).

Smith, D. Vance (2003) *Arts of Possession: The Middle English Household Imaginary* (Minneapolis, MN: University of Minnesota Press).

Smith, Joan, Immanuel Wallerstein and Hans-Dieter Evers (eds.) (1984) *Households and the World-Economy* (Beverly Hills, CA: Sage Publications).

Smith, Joan and Immanuel Wallerstein with Maria Del Carmen Baerga, Mark Beittel, Kathie Friedman Kasaba, Randall H. McGuire, William G. Martin, Kathleen Stanley, Lanny Thompson and Cynthia Woodsong (eds.) (1992) *Creating and Transforming Households: the Constraints of the World-Economy* (Cambridge: Cambridge University Press).

Smith, Rupert (2005) *The Utility of Force: the Art of Warfare in the Modern World* (London: Allen Lane).

Smuts, Jan (1926) *Holism and Evolution* (New York: Macmillan).

(1994) *Memoirs of the Boer War* (ed. Gail Nattrass and S.B. Spies) (Johannesburg: J. Ball).

Solovey, Mark and Hamilton Cravens (eds.) (2012) *Cold War Social Science: Knowledge Production, Liberal Democracy, and Human Nature* (New York: Palgrave Macmillan).

Spencer, Herbert (1867) *First Principles* (2nd edition) (London: Williams and Norgate).

(1877) *The Principles of Sociology* (London: Williams and Norgate).

Spencer-Wood, Suzanne M. (1999) 'The World Their Household: Changing Meanings of the Domestic Sphere in the Nineteenth Century', in Penelope Mary Allison (ed.) *The Archaeology of Household Activities* (London: Routledge), pp. 162–189.

Staley, Eugene (1961) *The Future of Underdeveloped Countries: Political Implications of Economic Development* (2nd edition) (New York: Council on Foreign Relations).

Stanski, Keith (2009) '"So These Folks are Aggressive": An Orientialist Reading of "Afghan Warlords"', *Security Dialogue*, 40(1): 73–94.

Starr, June (1985) 'The "Invention" of Early Legal Ideas: Sir Henry Maine and the Perpetual Tutelage of Women', in June Starr and Jane F. Collier (eds.) *History and Power in the Study of Law: New Directions in Legal Anthropology* (Ithaca, NY: Cornell University Press), pp. 345–368.

Steinmetz, George (1993) *Regulating the Social: The Welfare State and Local Politics in Imperial Germany* (Princeton, NJ: Princeton University Press).

(ed.) (2013) *Sociology and Empire: The Imperial Entanglements of a Discipline* (Durham, NC: Duke University Press).

Stevens, Richard (2008) *Erik H. Erikson: Explorer of Identity and the Life Cycle* (New York: Palgrave Macmillan).

Stiehm, Judith (1982) 'The Protected, the Protector, the Defender', *Women's Studies International Forum*, 5(3–4): 367–376.

Stjernø, Steinar (2005) *Solidarity in Europe: The History of an Idea* (Cambridge: Cambridge University Press).

Stocking, George W. (ed.) (1984) *Functionalism Historicized: Essays on British Social Anthropology* (Madison, WI: University of Wisconsin Press).

(1995) *After Tylor: British Social Anthropology, 1888–1951* (Madison, WI: University of Wisconsin Press).

Stokes, Eric (1959) *The English Utilitarians and India* (Oxford: Oxford University Press).

Stoler, Ann Laura (2010) *Carnal Knowledge and Imperial Power: Race and the Intimate in Colonial Rule* (2nd edition) (Berkeley, CA: University of California Press).

Stolzoff, Sam G. (2009) *The Iraqi Tribal System: A Reference for Social Scientists, Analysts, and Tribal Engagement* (Minneapolis, MN: Two Harbors Press).

Stone, Judith F. (1985) *The Search for Social Peace: Reform Legislation in France, 1890–1914* (Albany, NY: State University of New York Press).

Strachan, Hew (2007) 'British Counter-Insurgency from Malaya to Iraq', *RUSI Journal*, 125(6): 8–11.

Streets, Heather (2010) *Martial Races: The Military, Race and Masculinity in British Imperial Culture, 1857–1914* (Manchester: Manchester University Press).

Stubbs, Richard (1989) *Hearts and Minds in Guerrilla Warfare: The Malayan Emergency, 1948–1960* (Oxford: Oxford University Press).

Suganami, Hidemi (1978) 'A Note on the Origin of the Word International', *British Journal of International Studies*, 4(3): 226–232.

(1989) *The Domestic Analogy and World Order Proposals* (Cambridge: Cambridge University Press).

Sullivan, Antony Thrall (1983) *Thomas-Robert Bugeaud: France and Algeria, 1784–1849: Politics, Power, and the Good Society* (Hamden, CT: Archon Books).

Swingewood, Allen (2000) *A Short History of Sociological Thought* (3rd edition) (London: Palgrave).

Swynnerton, R.J.M. (1954) *A Plan to Intensify the Development of African Agriculture in Kenya* (Nairobi: Government Printer).

Szacki, Jerzy (1979) *History of Sociological Thought* (London: Aldwych).

Tang, Kwong-Leung (1998) *Colonial State and Social Welfare Policy: Social Welfare Development in Hong Kong, 1842–1997* (Lanham, MD: University Press of America).

Tanham, George K. (1966) *War without Guns: American Civilians in Rural Vietnam* (New York: Praeger).

Taylor, T.K. (2007) *Sunset of the Empire in Malaya: A New Zealander's Life in the Colonial Education Service* (London: Radcliffe Press).

Terrier, Jean (2011) *Visions of the Social: Society as a Political Project in France, 1750–1950* (Boston: Brill).

Teschke, Benno (2003) *The Myth of 1648: Class, Geopolitics, and the Making of Modern International Relations* (London: Verso).

(2011) 'Fatal Attraction: A Critique of Carl Schmitt's International Political and Legal Theory', *International Theory*, 3(2): 179–227.

(2014) 'IR Theory, Historical Materialism and the False Promise of International Historical Sociology', *Spectrum: Journal of Global Studies*, 6(1): 1–66.

Thomas, Martin (2008) *Empires of Intelligence: Security Services and Colonial Disorder after 1914* (Berkeley, CA: University of California Press).

Thompson, E.P. (1963) *The Making of the English Working Class* (London: V. Gollancz).

Thompson, Robert G.K. (1966) *Defeating Communist Insurgency: Experiences from Malaya and Vietnam* (London: Chatto and Windus).

Thornton, Thomas Henry (1977) *Colonel Sir Robert Sandeman* (Quetta: Gosha-e-Adab).

Throup, David (1987) *Economic and Social Origins of Mau Mau, 1945–1953* (London: James Currey).

Thucydides (431 BC/2000) *The History of the Peloponnesian War* (London: Penguin).

Tickner, J. Ann (1992) *Gender in International Relations: Feminist Perspectives on Achieving Global Security* (New York: Columbia University Press).

Tilly, Charles (1992) *Coercion, Capital, and European States, AD 990–1992* (Cambridge: Blackwell).

Tocqueville, Alexis de (2003) *Democracy in America: And Two Essays on America* (London: Penguin).

Todd, Lin, Patrick Lang, R. Alan King, Andrea V. Jackson, Montgomery McFate, Ahmed S. Hashim and Jeremy S. Harrington (2006) *Iraq Tribal Study: Al Anbar Governorate: the Albu Fahd Tribe, the Albu Mahal Tribe and the Albu Issa Tribe* (Washington, DC: Department of Defense).

Tone, Andrea (1997) *The Business of Benevolence: Industrial Paternalism in Progressive America* (Ithaca, NY: Cornell University Press).

Tönnies, Ferdinand (1887/1955) *Community and Association* (London: Routledge and Kegan Paul).
Townsend, Joseph (1786/1971) *A Dissertation on the Poor Laws by a Well-Wisher to Mankind* (foreword by Ashley Montagu; afterword by Mark Neuman) (Berkeley, CA: University of California Press).
Treitschke, Heinrich von (1916) *Politics: Vol. I* (trans. Blanche Dugdale and Torben de Bille) (New York: Macmillan).
Trigg, Heather B. (2005) *From Household to Empire: Society and Economy in Early Colonial New Mexico* (Tucson, AZ: University of Arizona Press).
Tripp, Charles (2000) *A History of Iraq* (Cambridge: Cambridge University Press).
Tucker, A.L.P. (1979) *Sir Robert G. Sandeman, K.C.S.I., Peaceful Conqueror of Baluchistan* (Lahore: Tariq Publishing House).
Tyner, James (2006) *The Business of War: Workers, Warriors and Hostages in Occupied Iraq* (London: Ashgate).
(2009) *War, Violence, and Population: Making the Body Count* (foreword by Chris Philo) (New York: Guilford Press).
Tyrrell, Marc W.D. (2014) 'The Use of Evolutionary Theory in Modeling Culture and Cultural Conflict', in Thomas H. Johnson and Barry Scott Zellen (eds.) *Culture, Conflict and Counterinsurgency* (Stanford, CA: Stanford University Press), pp. 46–76.
United States (1962) Overseas Internal Defense Policy, 3, II B-3. Approved as policy by National Security Action Memorandum 182 of 24 August 1962. Available at www.watsoninstitute.org/wiki/images/7/7e/OIDP.doc (accessed 15 June 2013).
United States (1963) Department of the Army Field Manual, 31–16, *Counterguerrilla Operations*. Available at www.survivalebooks.com/free%20manuals/1963%20US%20Army%20Vietnam%20War%20Counterguerrilla%20Operations%20counterinsurgency%20126p.pdf (accessed 25 November 2012).
United States (1966) Department of State, *Quiet Warriors: Supporting Social Revolution in Viet-Nam* (Washington, DC: Department of State Far Eastern Series, Vol. 140).
United States (1968) US Military Assistance Command Vietnam, *Handbook for Military Support of Pacification*, Saigon, February. Available at http://smallwarsjournal.com/documents/militarysupporthandbook.pdf (accessed 21 November 2012).
United States (2007) Army/Marine Corps, *The US Army/Marine Corps Counterinsurgency Field Manual: US Army Field Manual no. 3–24* (Chicago: University of Chicago Press).
Valverde, Mariana (1996) '"Despotism" and Ethical Liberal Governance', *Economy and Society*, 25(3): 357–372.

Van Buren, Peter (2011) *We Meant Well: How I Helped Lose the Battle for the Hearts and Minds of the Iraqi People* (New York: Metropolitan Books).

Vandervort, Bruce (1998) *Wars of Imperial Conquest in Africa, 1830–1914* (Bloomington, IN: Indiana University Press).

van Meerhaeghe, Marcel (2006) 'Bismarck and the Social Question', *Journal of Economic Studies*, 33: 284–301.

Vaughan, Megan (1991) *Curing their Ills: Colonial Power and African Illness* (Cambridge: Polity).

Villa, Dana (1999) *Politics, Philosophy, Terror: Essays on the Thought of Hannah Arendt* (Princeton, NJ: Princeton University Press).

Vincent, R.J. (1974) *Nonintervention and International Order* (Princeton, NJ: Princeton University Press).

Vincent, Susan (2003) 'Preserving Domesticity: Reading Tupperware in Women's Social, Domestic, and Economic Roles', *Canadian Review of Sociology and Anthropology*, 40(2): 171–196.

Viroli, Maurizio (1992) *From Politics to Reason of State: The Acquisition and Transformation of the Language of Politics 1250–1600* (Cambridge: Cambridge University Press).

Wacquant, Loïc (2009) *Punishing the Poor: the Neoliberal Government of Social Insecurity* (Durham, NC: Duke University Press).

Wagner, Peter (1994) *A Sociology of Modernity: Liberty and Discipline* (London: Routledge).

(2000) '"An Entirely New Object of Consciousness, of Volition, of Thought": The Coming into Being and (Almost) Passing Away of "Society" as a Scientific Object', in Lorraine Daston (ed.) *Biographies of Scientific Objects* (Chicago: University of Chicago Press), pp. 132–157.

(2001) *A History and Theory of the Social Sciences: Not All that is Solid Melts into Air* (London: Sage Publications).

Walker, R.B.J. (1993) *Inside/Outside: International Relations as Political Theory* (Cambridge: Cambridge University Press).

Wallerstein, Immanuel (1991a) *Unthinking Social Science: the Limits of Nineteenth Century Paradigms* (Cambridge: Polity Press).

(1991b) 'Household Structures and Labour-Force Formation in the Capitalist World Economy', in Étienne Balibar and Immanuel Wallerstein (eds.) *Race, Nation, Class: Ambiguous Identities* (London: Verso), pp. 107–114.

Walters, William (2000) *Unemployment and Government: Genealogies of the Social* (Cambridge: Cambridge University Press).

(2004) 'Secure Border, Safe Haven, Domopolitics', *Citizenship Studies*, 8(3): 237–260.

Waltz, Kenneth N. (1979) *Theory of International Politics* (New York: Random House).

Ward, Lester F. (1893) *Psychologic Basis of Social Economics* (Philadelphia: American Academy of Political and Social Science).
(1893/1906) *The Psychic Factors of Civilization* (Boston: Ginn & Co.).
(1903) *Pure Sociology: A Treatise on the Origin and Spontaneous Development of Society* (London: Macmillan).
(1906) *Applied Sociology: A Treatise on the Conscious Improvement of Society by Society* (Boston: Ginn & Company).
Warehouse and Drapers' Trade Journal (1883) *A Guide to Window-Dressing* (London).
Watson, Adam (1992) *The Evolution of International Society* (London: Routledge).
Wayne, Martin I. (2012) 'China's Society-Centric Counterterrorism Approach in Xinjiang', in Paul B. Rich and Isabelle Duyvesteyn (eds.) *The Routledge Handbook of Insurgency and Counterinsurgency* (London: Routledge), pp. 335–346.
Weber, Max (1946) *From Max Weber: Essays in Sociology* (trans., ed. and intro. by H.H. Gerth and C. Wright Mills) (Oxford: Oxford University Press).
(1958) *The Protestant Ethic and the Spirit of Capitalism* (trans. Talcott Parsons; intro. by Anthony Giddens) (New York: Charles Scribner's Son).
(1978) *Economy and Society: An Outline of Interpretative Sociology, Vol.1* (ed. Guenther Roth and Claus Wittich) (Berkeley, CA: University of California Press).
Wehler, Hans-Ulrich (1972) 'Industrial Growth and Early German Imperialism', in Roger Owen and Bob Sutcliffe (eds.) *Studies in the Theory of Imperialism* (London: Longman), pp. 71–90.
(1985) *The German Empire, 1871–1918* (Oxford: Berg Books).
Weizman, Eyal (2011) *The Least of All Possible Evils: Humanitarian Violence from Arendt to Gaza* (London: Verso).
Welsh, Jennifer (2003) '"I" is for Ideology: Conservatism in International Affairs', *Global Society*, 17(2): 165–185.
Wendt, Alexander (1999) *Social Theory of International Politics* (Cambridge: Cambridge University Press).
(2004) 'The State as Person in International Theory', *Review of International Studies*, 30(2): 289–316.
Wesling, Meg (2011) *Empire's Proxy: American Literature and US Imperialism in the Philippines* (New York: New York University Press).
West, Bing (2008) *The Strongest Tribe: War, Politics, and the Endgame in Iraq* (New York: Random House).
Wexler, Laura (2000) *Tender Violence: Domestic Visions in an Age of US Imperialism* (Chapel Hill, NC: University of North Carolina Press).

Wheeler, Nicholas J. (2000) *Saving Strangers: Humanitarian Intervention in International Society* (Oxford: Oxford University Press).

Wickham, Chris (1984) 'The Other Transition: From the Ancient World to Feudalism', *Past and Present*, 103(1): 3–36.

Wickham, Gary (2007) 'Expanding the Classical in Classical Sociology', *Journal of Classical Sociology*, 7(3): 243–265.

Wight, Colin (2006) *Agents, Structures and International Relations: Politics as Ontology* (Cambridge: Cambridge University Press).

Wight, Martin (1991) *International Theory: The Three Traditions* (Leicester: Leicester University Press).

Wildenthal, Lora (1996) '"She is the Victor": Bourgeois Women, Nationalist Identities, and the Ideal of the Independent Woman Farmer in German Southwest Africa', in Geoff Eley (ed.) *Society, Culture, and the State in Germany, 1870–1930* (Ann Arbor, MI: University of Michigan Press), pp. 371–395.

(2001) *German Women for Empire, 1884–1945* (Durham, NC: Duke University Press).

Wilke, Elizabeth, Paul K. Davis and Christopher S. Chivvis (2011) 'Establishing Social Conditions of Trust and Cooperation', in Paul K. Davis (ed.) *Dilemmas of Intervention: Social Science for Stabilization and Reconstruction* (Washington, DC: RAND), pp. 187–238.

Williams, Raymond (1961) *The Long Revolution* (London: Chatto and Windus).

Williams, Tony (1996) *Hearths of Darkness: The Family in the American Horror Film* (Madison, NJ: Fairleigh Dickinson University Press).

Wilson, Eric (2008) *Savage Republic: De Indis of Hugo Grotius, Republicanism and Dutch Hegemony within the Early Modern World-System (c. 1600–1619)* (Leiden: Martinus Nijhoff).

Withington, Phil (2010) *Society in Early Modern England: The Vernacular Origins of Some Powerful Ideas* (Cambridge: Polity).

Wolf, Eric R. (1969) *Peasant Wars of the Twentieth Century* (New York, Harper & Row).

(1988) 'Inventing Society', *American Ethnologist*, 15(4): 752–761.

Wolin, Sheldon (1960) *Politics and Vision: Continuity and Innovation in Western Political Thought* (Boston: Little, Brown).

(1987) 'Democracy and the Welfare State: The Political and Theoretical Connections Between *Staatsräson* and *Wohlfahrtsstaatsräson*', *Political Theory*, 15(4): 467–500.

Wong, Bin (1997) *China Transformed: Historical Change and the Limits of European Experience* (Ithaca: Cornell University Press).

Wood, Neal (1994) *Foundations of Political Economy: Some Early Tudor Views of State and Society* (Berkeley, CA: University of California Press).

Xenophon (1923) *Memorabilia, Oeconomicus, Symposium and Apology* (Cambridge, MA: Harvard University Press).

Yette, Samuel (1971) *The Choice: The Issue of Black Survival in America* (New York: Putnam).

Young, Iris Marion (1997) 'House and Home: Feminist Variations on a Theme', in *Intersecting Voices: Dilemmas of Gender, Political Philosophy and Policy* (Princeton, NJ: Princeton University Press), pp. 134–163.

(2003) 'The Logic of Masculinist Protection: Reflections on the Current Security State', *Signs*, 29(1): 1–25.

Zasloff, Joseph J. (1962/1963) 'Rural Resettlement in South Viet Nam: The Agroville Program', *Pacific Affairs*, 35(4): 327–340.

Zimmerman, Andrew (2006) 'Decolonizing Weber', *Postcolonial Studies*, 9(1): 53–79.

(2010) *Alabama in Africa: Booker T. Washington, the German Empire, and the Globalization of the New South* (Princeton, NJ: Princeton University Press).

(2013) 'German Sociology and Empire: From Internal Colonization to Overseas Colonization and Back Again', in George Steinmetz (ed.) *Sociology and Empire: The Imperial Entanglements of a Discipline* (Durham, NC: Duke University Press), pp. 166–187.

Index

Cambridge Studies in International Relations

127 Jordan Branch
The cartographic state
Maps, territory, and the origins of sovereignty

126 Thomas Risse, Stephen C. Ropp and Kathryn Sikkink (eds.)
The persistent power of human rights
From commitment to compliance

125 K. M. Fierke
Political self-sacrifice
Agency, body and emotion in international relations

124 Stefano Guzzini
The return of geopolitics in Europe?
Social mechanisms and foreign policy identity crises

123 Bear F. Braumoeller
The great powers and the international system
Systemic theory in empirical perspective

122 Jonathan Joseph
The social in the global
Social theory, governmentality and global politics

121 Brian C. Rathbun
Trust in international cooperation
International security institutions, domestic politics and American multilateralism

120 A. Maurits van der Veen
Ideas, interests and foreign aid

119 Emanuel Adler and Vincent Pouliot
International practices

118 Ayşe Zarakol
After defeat
How the East learned to live with the West

117 Andrew Phillips
War, religion and empire
The transformation of international orders

116 Joshua Busby
Moral movements and foreign policy

115 Séverine Autesserre
The trouble with the Congo
Local violence and the failure of international peacebuilding

114 Deborah D. Avant, Martha Finnemore and Susan K. Sell
Who governs the globe?

113 Vincent Pouliot
International security in practice
The politics of NATO-Russia diplomacy

112 Columba Peoples
Justifying ballistic missile defence
Technology, security and culture

111 Paul Sharp
Diplomatic theory of international relations

110 John A. Vasquez
The war puzzle revisited

109 Rodney Bruce Hall
Central banking as global governance
Constructing financial credibility

108 Milja Kurki
Causation in international relations
Reclaiming causal analysis

107 Richard M. Price
Moral limit and possibility in world politics

106 Emma Haddad
The refugee in international society
Between sovereigns

105 Ken Booth
Theory of world security

104 Benjamin Miller
States, nations and the great powers
The sources of regional war and peace

103 Beate Jahn (ed.)
Classical theory in international relations

102 Andrew Linklater and Hidemi Suganami
The English School of international relations
A contemporary reassessment

101 Colin Wight
Agents, structures and international relations
Politics as ontology

100 Michael C. Williams
The realist tradition and the limits of international relations

99 Ivan Arreguín-Toft
How the weak win wars
A theory of asymmetric conflict

98 Michael Barnett and Raymond Duvall (eds.)
Power in global governance

97 Yale H. Ferguson and Richard W. Mansbach
Remapping global politics
History's revenge and future shock

96 Christian Reus-Smit
The politics of international law

95 Barry Buzan
From international to world society?
English School theory and the social structure of globalisation

94 K. J. Holsti
Taming the sovereigns
Institutional change in international politics

93 Bruce Cronin
Institutions for the common good
International protection regimes in international security

92 Paul Keal
European conquest and the rights of indigenous peoples
The moral backwardness of international society

91 Barry Buzan and Ole Wæver
Regions and powers
The structure of international security

90 A. Claire Cutler
Private power and global authority
Transnational merchant law in the global political economy

89 Patrick M. Morgan
Deterrence now

88 Susan Sell
Private power, public law
The globalization of intellectual property rights

87 Nina Tannenwald
The nuclear taboo
The United States and the non-use of nuclear weapons since 1945

86 Linda Weiss
States in the global economy
Bringing domestic institutions back in

85 Rodney Bruce Hall and Thomas J. Biersteker (eds.)
The emergence of private authority in global governance

84 Heather Rae
State identities and the homogenisation of peoples

83 Maja Zehfuss
Constructivism in international relations
The politics of reality

82 Paul K. Ruth and Todd Allee
The democratic peace and territorial conflict in the twentieth century

81 Neta C. Crawford
Argument and change in world politics
Ethics, decolonization and humanitarian intervention

80 Douglas Lemke
Regions of war and peace

79 Richard Shapcott
Justice, community and dialogue in international relations

78 Phil Steinberg
The social construction of the ocean

77 Christine Sylvester
Feminist international relations
An unfinished journey

76 Kenneth A. Schultz
Democracy and coercive diplomacy

75 David Houghton
US foreign policy and the Iran hostage crisis

74 Cecilia Albin
Justice and fairness in international negotiation

73 Martin Shaw
Theory of the global state
Globality as an unfinished revolution

72 Frank C. Zagare and D. Marc Kilgour
Perfect deterrence

71 Robert O'Brien, Anne Marie Goetz, Jan Aart Scholte and Marc Williams
Contesting global governance
Multilateral economic institutions and global social movements

70 Roland Bleiker
Popular dissent, human agency and global politics

69 Bill McSweeney
Security, identity and interests
A sociology of international relations

68 Molly Cochran
Normative theory in international relations
A pragmatic approach

67 Alexander Wendt
Social theory of international politics

66 Thomas Risse, Stephen C. Ropp and Kathryn Sikkink (eds.)
The power of human rights
International norms and domestic change

65 Daniel W. Drezner
The sanctions paradox
Economic statecraft and international relations

64 Viva Ona Bartkus
The dynamic of secession

63 John A. Vasquez
The power of power politics
From classical realism to neotraditionalism

62 Emanuel Adler and Michael Barnett (eds.)
Security communities

61 Charles Jones
E. H. Carr and international relations
A duty to lie

60 Jeffrey W. Knopf
Domestic society and international cooperation
The impact of protest on US arms control policy

59 Nicholas Greenwood Onuf
The republican legacy in international thought

58 Daniel S. Geller and J. David Singer
Nations at war
A scientific study of international conflict

57 Randall D. Germain
The international organization of credit
States and global finance in the world economy

56 N. Piers Ludlow
Dealing with Britain
The Six and the first UK application to the EEC

55 Andreas Hasenclever, Peter Mayer and Volker Rittberger
Theories of international regimes

54 Miranda A. Schreurs and Elizabeth C. Economy (eds.)
The internationalization of environmental protection

53 James N. Rosenau
Along the domestic-foreign frontier
Exploring governance in a turbulent world

52 John M. Hobson
The wealth of states
A comparative sociology of international economic and political change

51 Kalevi J. Holsti
The state, war, and the state of war

50 Christopher Clapham
Africa and the international system
The politics of state survival

49 Susan Strange
The retreat of the state
The diffusion of power in the world economy

48 William I. Robinson
Promoting polyarchy
Globalization, US intervention, and hegemony

47 Roger Spegele
Political realism in international theory

46 Thomas J. Biersteker and Cynthia Weber (eds.)
State sovereignty as social construct

45 Mervyn Frost
Ethics in international relations
A constitutive theory

44 Mark W. Zacher with Brent A. Sutton
Governing global networks
International regimes for transportation and communications

43 Mark Neufeld
The restructuring of international relations theory

42 Thomas Risse-Kappen (ed.)
Bringing transnational relations back in
Non-state actors, domestic structures and international institutions

41 Hayward R. Alker
Rediscoveries and reformulations
Humanistic methodologies for international studies

40 Robert W. Cox with Timothy J. Sinclair
Approaches to world order

39 Jens Bartelson
A genealogy of sovereignty

38 Mark Rupert
Producing hegemony
The politics of mass production and American global power

37 Cynthia Weber
Simulating sovereignty
Intervention, the state and symbolic exchange

36 Gary Goertz
Contexts of international politics

35 James L. Richardson
Crisis diplomacy
The Great Powers since the mid-nineteenth century

34 Bradley S. Klein
Strategic studies and world order
The global politics of deterrence

33 T. V. Paul
Asymmetric conflicts
War initiation by weaker powers

32 Christine Sylvester
Feminist theory and international relations in a postmodern era

31 Peter J. Schraeder
US foreign policy toward Africa
Incrementalism, crisis and change

30 Graham Spinardi
From Polaris to Trident
The development of US Fleet Ballistic Missile technology

29 David A. Welch
Justice and the genesis of war

28 Russell J. Leng
Interstate crisis behavior, 1816–1980
Realism versus reciprocity

27 John A. Vasquez
The war puzzle

26 Stephen Gill (ed.)
Gramsci, historical materialism and international relations

25 Mike Bowker and Robin Brown (eds.)
From cold war to collapse
Theory and world politics in the 1980s

24 R. B. J. Walker
Inside/outside
International relations as political theory

23 Edward Reiss
The strategic defense initiative

22 Keith Krause
Arms and the state
Patterns of military production and trade

21 Roger Buckley
US-Japan alliance diplomacy 1945–1990

20 James N. Rosenau and Ernst-Otto Czempiel (eds.)
Governance without government
Order and change in world politics

19 Michael Nicholson
Rationality and the analysis of international conflict

18 John Stopford and Susan Strange
Rival states, rival firms
Competition for world market shares

17 Terry Nardin and David R. Mapel (eds.)
Traditions of international ethics

16 Charles F. Doran
Systems in crisis
New imperatives of high politics at century's end

15 Deon Geldenhuys
Isolated states
A comparative analysis

14 Kalevi J. Holsti
Peace and war
Armed conflicts and international order 1648–1989

13 Saki Dockrill
Britain's policy for West German rearmament 1950–1955

12 Robert H. Jackson
Quasi-states
Sovereignty, international relations and the third world

11 James Barber and John Barratt
South Africa's foreign policy
The search for status and security 1945–1988

10 James Mayall
Nationalism and international society

9 William Bloom
Personal identity, national identity and international relations

8 Zeev Maoz
National choices and international processes

7 Ian Clark
The hierarchy of states
Reform and resistance in the international order

6 Hidemi Suganami
The domestic analogy and world order proposals

5 Stephen Gill
American hegemony and the Trilateral Commission

4 Michael C. Pugh
The ANZUS crisis, nuclear visiting and deterrence

3 Michael Nicholson
Formal theories in international relations

2 Friedrich V. Kratochwil
Rules, norms, and decisions
On the conditions of practical and legal reasoning in international relations and domestic affairs

1 Myles L. C. Robertson
Soviet policy towards Japan
An analysis of trends in the 1970s and 1980s

CPSIA information can be obtained
at www.ICGtesting.com
Printed in the USA
LVOW13s2150290517
536190LV00041B/1542/P